[A TRAGEDY OF DEMOCRACY]

A TRAGEDY OF DEMOCRACY

JAPANESE CONFINEMENT IN NORTH AMERICA

GREG ROBINSON

COLUMBIA UNIVERSITY PRESS *New York*

COLUMBIA UNIVERSITY PRESS

PUBLISHERS SINCE 1893

NEW YORK   CHICHESTER, WEST SUSSEX

Library of Congress Cataloging-in-Publication Data

Robinson, Greg, 1966–

A tragedy of democracy : Japanese confinement in North America / Greg Robinson.

p.   cm.

Includes bibliographical references and index.

ISBN 978-0-231-12922-0 (cloth : alk. paper)

ISBN 978-0-231-52012-6 (e-book)

1.   Japanese Americans—Evacuation and relocation, 1942–1945.   2.   Japanese Americans—Pacific States—Social conditions—20th century.   3.   Japanese Americans—Government policy—History—20th century.   4.   Pacific States—Race relations—History—20th century.   5.   United States—Race relations—History—20th century.   6.   World War, 1939–1945—social aspects—United States.   7.   Japanese—Government policy—Canada—History—20th century.
8.   Canada—Race relations—History—20th century.   9.   World War, 1939–1945—Social aspects—Canada.   I. Title.

D796.8.A6R64 2009

940.53'1773—dc22

2008049150

Columbia University Press books are printed on permanent and durable acid-free paper.

This book is printed on paper with recycled content.

Printed in the United States of America

c 10 9 8 7 6 5 4 3 2 1

[CONTENTS]

[A NOTE ON TERMINOLOGY]

ALTHOUGH THE MOST COMMONLY USED TERM FOR THE WARTIME experience of Japanese Americans is "internment," I have chosen not to use that term. "Internment" properly refers to the detention of enemy nationals by a government during wartime. The United States government, as noted in this book, did intern enemy aliens during the war, in camps run by the Justice Department. In contrast, the vast majority of those of Japanese ancestry who were summarily uprooted, moved, and held by the U.S. government during World War II were American citizens. The fact that there is no commonly understood term to describe such an action with precision hints at how unprecedented the government's policy was. The official language used was of "evacuation" and "relocation." However, the government officials who evolved those terms were clearly less concerned with finding exact language than with inventing euphemisms to make their policy seem more acceptable. Perhaps the most precise equivalent, in legal terms, would be "commitment," in the sense of being held involuntarily in an institution, but this definition hardly explains the treatment of Japanese Americans. Instead, I use the phrase "removal," as in the expulsion of the Cherokee and other Native Americans from the American South during the 1830s, to describe the internal exile of ethnic Japanese, and "confinement" for their experience once removed. Various historians and activists have called the policy "incarceration." Yet "incarceration" is a fancier synonym for "imprisonment": these institutions were not penitentiaries. I thus make use of the more inclusive word "confinement." I do use internment at times when speaking of Canada, where the legal status of aliens and citizens was more fluid.

An even more vexed question, and one that has stirred up considerable controversy in the decades since the war, is what to call the camps in which the Japanese Americans were confined, and those who were placed there. President Roosevelt publicly referred to the camps as "concentration camps" on two occasions, as did other government officials. Nevertheless, the official term developed by the army and the War Relocation Authority was "relocation centers" or "reception centers." The holding areas on the West Coast became "assembly centers" in officialese. Many Japanese Americans and other activists and scholars insist on the phrase "concentration camp," in keeping with the pre-Holocaust definition of the phrase as a settlement where masses of people are concentrated. I have no quarrel with such a practice, but because of the inextricable association of the words "concentration camp" with the Nazi death camps, I have chosen to avoid it and simply use the word "camp," which I think suffices to describe the areas where the Japanese Americans were confined. Rather then the official word "resident," I choose to use the word "inmate" as the most precise description of the status of Japanese Americans involuntarily placed in confinement.

[A TRAGEDY OF DEMOCRACY]

INTRODUCTION

IN THE SPRING OF 1942, A FEW MONTHS AFTER THE JAPANESE attack on Pearl Harbor launched World War II in the Pacific, the United States Army, acting under authority granted by President Franklin D. Roosevelt and confirmed by Congress, summarily rounded up the entire ethnic Japanese population living on the nation's Pacific Coast. These American citizens and longtime residents—some 112,000 men, women, and children—were packed into military holding centers for several weeks or months and then transported under armed guard to the interior of the country. There they were confined in a network of hastily built camps constructed and operated by a new federal agency, the War Relocation Authority (WRA). Although some of these inmates were able after a time to leave the camps and resettle outside the West Coast, most remained in captivity for the duration of the war.

This official action, commonly called the internment of Japanese Americans but more accurately termed their confinement, has often been referred to as the worst civil rights violation by the federal government during the twentieth century. While the government's actions did bring significant pain and hardship to those affected, there was no mass torture or starvation, and sympathetic officials and outside workers worked to ease the situation. In that sense, the suffering of the inmates in the WRA camps was not comparable with that of the masses caught in the agony of total war or targeted by tyrannical regimes—the prisoners in the Nazi death camps, for instance, or the Chinese people under the Japanese occupation—or with the historic degradation of African Americans, although such comparisons are inherently troublesome. Rather, what is particularly noteworthy about the confinement of the Issei and Nisei is its fundamentally ironic character:[1] it was an arbitrary and antidemocratic measure put into effect by a government devoted to humanitarian aims, which occurred as a part of a war the nation was waging for the survival of world freedom. Through its official actions, undertaken in the name of national security, the United States not only brought suffering to its own people but handicapped its war effort. The federal government diverted massive resources to building and maintaining an extensive network of camps to confine an entire population of citizens and permanent residents, people whose loyalty was shaken by official actions premised on their group disloyalty.[2] The WRA's total budget through 1945 was $162 million. In addition, the army spent an estimated $75 million to round up and remove Japanese Americans. In vivid contrast, the Japanese community in Hawaii, whose members were not singled out for wholesale confinement, made exemplary contributions in the form of volunteer soldiers and war workers. Finally, army officers and Justice Department officials, who sought to assure the orderly release of inmates from the camps and their scattering into communities outside, resorted to manipulating evidence and covering up information about the initial removal policy to defend it from judicial review.

The wartime confinement of Japanese Americans remains not only a critical event in the Asian American experience, but a resonant point of reference and touchstone of commemoration for diverse groups of Americans. Dozens of works have appeared describing the signing of Executive Order 9066, the presidential decree that undergirded the action, as well as the court challenges to the government's actions. An equally large literature has sprung up on the camp experience of the inmates—their family relations, their schooling, their resistance, and even their artistic creations. These works have rightly focused on Japanese Americans as important actors in shaping the nature of government policy and camp life, despite the numerous limitations on their freedom and the economic and psychological burdens they faced as a result of confinement. The inmates helped staff and operate schools, churches, hospitals, and cooperative stores. In conjunction with camp administrators, and sometimes in defiance of them, they organized social groups, sports competitions, musical bands, literary magazines, and crafts classes. They also struggled to preserve autonomy from invasive camp administrations. Using their limited channels of self-government, they called for redress of grievances, and on several occasions they expressed their resistance through organized strikes or even rioting. More negatively, hard-line factions of inmates organized harassment and sometimes violence against suspected informers, or those considered too friendly to camp administrators.

Finally, a growing literature has emerged on the later movement by former inmates and their children for compensation for their confinement and for reconsideration of the Supreme Court decisions upholding it. The so-called redress movement triumphed in 1988, when Congress passed the Civil Rights Restoration Act, granting all those affected by Executive Order 9066 an official apology and a $20,000 redress payment. Meanwhile, citing official misconduct and manipulation of evidence at trial, federal courts vacated or overturned the convictions of three Nisei who had challenged their removal.

Given all the attention that these aspects of the wartime experience of Japanese Americans have received—the books, plays, poetry, days of remembrance, museum exhibitions, documentaries, feature films, etc.—it might be wondered what need there is for another historical book on the subject. Indeed, some ten years ago, when I began research on President Roosevelt and the story behind the signing of Executive Order 9066, I was obliged to reject the advice of a distinguished historian who urged me to choose another field of study. How, he asked me, could there possibly be anything new to say on the confinement of Japanese Americans, a matter about which so much had already been published?

The reasons for putting out a new book nevertheless seemed compelling then and are even more so in the case of this volume. First, the camps remain oddly obscure in popular American memory: most ordinary people I have spoken to have never even heard of them. Among those who are informed about the wartime events, there remain serious conflicts over how to interpret their legacy. Were the camps an isolated result of wartime hysteria? How do they fit into the larger history of American racism? What impact did they have on Japanese communities outside the camps? Into the void of public knowledge has stepped a small but tenacious circle of assorted right-wingers and war buffs who continue to deny or rationalize the removal of Japanese Americans from the West Coast and the institution of the camps. Their campaign gained new strength in the post-9/11 crisis, amid the deep national anxiety over immigrants and potential threats to national security. Clearly, the entire subject of Japanese American confinement taps into some deep sources of anxiety, and this makes it call out for clear-minded historical study.

What is more, the existing literature on Japanese Americans does not take account of the profusion of new information (and in a few cases misinformation) that has come to light in recent times. Vast numbers of newly declassified or digitized documents have become available, and family and oral history archivists have put together innumerable testimonies by Japanese Americans that shed light on particulars of their experience. In the course of my ongoing historical research, I have come across collections of previously unseen or unknown material that deepen our understanding in fundamental ways. Meanwhile, the work of a new generation of scholars has left our understanding of supposedly familiar events altered and enriched.

Therefore, a first purpose of this book is to set down a record of Executive Order 9066 and the wartime Japanese American experience in a clear and digestible fashion. In the process, I will join together elements of the generally accepted narrative with significant new information, so as to form a much-needed synthesis. My goal is naturally to help those readers who are new to this history, but also to deepen the understanding of those who have some experience of it.

As important as that initial goal is, this book has a greater purpose: to expand the contours of discussion on Japanese American confinement beyond the overly narrow framework of time and space in which the subject has been placed. First, my history goes beyond the limits of the wartime period in its discussion of events. The main story of confinement properly begins in the prewar years, with the buildup of suspicion against Japanese Americans and "enemy aliens" generally. One element especially worth exploring is the U.S. government's construction, in the months before war broke out, of what it called concentration camps to hold enemy aliens. This book investigates for the first time how these actions created a climate and momentum for mass arbitrary action against perceived "enemies" after Pearl Harbor.

Conversely, much remains to be said on the long after-history of Japanese American confinement. The postwar era is all but forgotten in conventional narratives, which tend to stop with the end of the fighting and the closing of the camps. Yet it is impossible to understand these events fully without also studying the rapid turnabout of official policy and attitudes toward Japanese Americans in the first years after the war, and the attempts by officials in Congress and the White House to make gestures at restitution. In the same way, the eclipse of the wartime events in public discussion during the 1950s and their gradual reappearance in later years, a matter largely uncovered by existing works, merit discussion. Finally, while a number of writings exist on movements among Japanese Americans for reparations and the granting of redress in the 1980s, the story of the camps does not end with the official apology and payment. In a final section, I will look at the period since redress was granted, and how recent events and polemics over historical memory and representation contribute to our overall understanding of the wartime actions and reflect their continuing impact upon American national consciousness.

An even more troubling problem with the conventional narrative is that it discusses Executive Order 9066 and the treatment of Japanese Americans only within fixed spatial and national boundaries, as part of internal (and mainland) American history. Yet the confinement policy fits into a wider international—indeed continental—pattern of official treatment of people of Japanese ancestry, and it is imperative to study other areas in order to understand in-depth the experience of West Coast Japanese Americans.[3] The first of these areas is wartime Hawaii, where "local Japanese" constituted the largest single ethnic population and provided the backbone of the labor force. In the wake of the attack on Pearl Harbor, army commanders pushed through a declaration of martial law and did not restore the territory to full civilian control until late 1944. Military rule in Hawaii—a unique status in modern American history—was shaped in fundamental ways by the fears of the "local Japanese," on the basis of which army commanders justified and built public support for such steps as abolition of civilian courts and their replacement by military tribunals. Conversely, Japanese residents were the focus of an epic conflict between national leaders who urged their mass confinement and local rulers who resisted these orders. The resulting struggle not only had different results from those on the West Coast but helped shape government policy on Japanese Americans elsewhere.

A similarly gaping hole in standard portraits of Japanese American confinement exists with regard to events in Canada. Like their American counterparts, twenty two thousand Japanese Canadians from the West Coast of British Columbia were rounded up during the spring of 1942. They were then dispersed to a variety of destinations: road labor camps, sugar beet farms, or settlements in isolated mining villages. Their property was confiscated and sold by official decree, and they were forced to use the funds to pay for their own expenses. The Canadian government ultimately required the Japanese Canadians to choose between resettling outside the West and being deported to Japan, and it undertook the mass deportation of thousands of inmates as soon as the war was over. Astoundingly, no work has ever been published that looks at the history of Executive Order 9066 and the camps in the United States alongside that of the Canadian government's wartime removal and confinement of Japanese Canadians, a series of events that remains all but unknown south of the border.[4] Yet not only is the Canadian experience compelling within itself, but a study of the similarities and differences across the border provides a greater and more balanced perspective on any number of overall questions relating to the Japanese Americans: What drove confinement? What choices existed in administering it? How important were Nisei soldiers in shifting public opinion about the loyalty of the Japanese?

Finally, there is the experience of the Latin American Japanese in North America to consider. Following agreements between the U.S. State Department and the governments of Peru and other Latin American nations, U.S. forces carried off some 2,300 ethnic Japanese (plus larger numbers of ethnic Germans) from their home countries, brought them to the United States, and imprisoned them in an internment camp operated by the Justice Department at Crystal City, Texas. The Mexican government (though it refused to surrender any of its residents to the United States) decreed mass removal of ethnic Japanese from its Pacific coast in 1942 and confiscated their property. As a result, a refugee trail of thousands of people formed to Mexico City and Guadalajara.

This book offers the first extended analysis of confinement in a North American context. In making this claim, I do not wish to mislead the reader—my presentation of events in Canada and of the removal of Latin American Japanese, though based in part on original research, is meant to serve primarily as a counterpoint to and comparison with those in the United States and is thus more summary, notably where the postwar years are concerned. Also, while the history of the Canadian camps has been well documented by scholars, there are few published archival collections, at least in comparison with the print and microfilm resources compiled on Japanese Americans. I therefore rely mostly on secondary sources, and on published primary materials and memoirs where available, rather than repeating research by others in scattered archives.

[1] BACKGROUND TO CONFINEMENT

JAPANESE IMMIGRATION AND SETTLEMENT

Although the confinement of Japanese Americans was clearly a war measure, its roots reach as far back as the beginnings of Japanese immigration to North America and to the growth of prejudice against these settlers, the so-called Issei (first generation).

Japan had remained almost completely closed off to the world for more than two centuries when a United States Navy fleet commanded by Commodore Matthew C. Perry was sent to the island empire in 1853. Under the threat of destruction from Perry's gunboats, the Japanese agreed to open their ports to American trade and friendship. The "opening up" of their country and the entry of Americans and other Westerners prompted the Japanese leaders to implement a large-scale strategy of "catching up" with Western technology and ideas in order to protect Japan from foreign domination. In 1868 a group favoring modernization deposed Japan's shogun (military governor) and took power under the aegis of the emperor, whom they restored as official head of the government. In the generation following the so-called Meiji Restoration, Japan developed into a modern industrial state. The leaders of the new government at Tokyo built a powerful military machine, and Japan soon displayed its new prowess in two victories over China in wars during the last decades of the nineteenth century.

Under the impetus of the modernizers, the Japanese government began sending students and government observers abroad to study Western societies, and laborers soon followed. In 1868, the very same year as the Meiji Restoration, the then-independent kingdom of Hawaii recruited a pioneer group of some 150 Japanese artisans (who were dubbed the Gannen-mono, or "first-year men") to come work on the sugar plantations of Oahu. Resentful over their treatment by plantation overseers, the Japanese soon left the plantations and settled in Honolulu, whereupon the experiment was abandoned.[1] A year later, a group of Japanese sailed to California and established a short-lived agricultural settlement, the Wakamatsu colony.[2] A few years after, in 1877, a Japanese sailor named Manzo Nagano left his ship to settle in British Columbia and is thereby credited as the first Japanese immigrant to Canada.[3] Emigration nonetheless remained formally illegal in Japan, and few Japanese workers settled in other countries in the immediately succeeding years.

The situation was drastically altered in 1882 by events in the United States, namely, the passage by Congress of the first of the Chinese Exclusion Acts. These acts, born of anti-Chinese racism and pressure by labor unions, journalists, and politicians to end labor competition by Chinese immigrants, barred all laborers of Chinese ancestry from entering the country. For the next sixty years, only a few protected categories of Chinese, such as accredited merchants, students, and ministers, could enter the country legally, and all Chinese were forced to carry passes as proof of legal residence.[4] In 1885, following the completion of the transcontinental Canadian Pacific Railroad upon which masses of Chinese workers had labored, the Canadian government followed suit by imposing the notorious special Head Tax on each Chinese immigrant who wished to enter the country. The amount of this tax rose by 1903 to $500, a vast sum by the standards of the day, and severely limited the number of individuals, especially working-class, who were able to move east to Canada.[5]

The cutoff of Chinese immigration meant that landowners in Pacific Coast areas such as California, where Chinese made up one-half of agricultural laborers by 1884, began to search desperately for other newcomers to take up the arduous and low-paid farm labor work that brought prosperity to the region. Meanwhile, in Hawaii, whose economy depended on production of sugar, planters sought to attract a reliable surplus labor force. Japanese laborers, they concluded, would counterbalance the islands' largely Chinese worker population. Planters would profit from national-based hostility between the two groups, which would work to keep laborers from organizing too closely. With close supervision by the Japanese government, which regarded itself as the protector of its overseas nationals, thousands of young Japanese were recruited by labor contractors for work in Hawaii after 1885. They soon became the dominant group in the islands' plantation labor force.[6] To better assure a stable and controlled worker group, plantation owners ordered recruiters to bring over a significant percentage of women among laborers and encouraged development of family groups. Plantation owners also (for a time) subsidized the implantation of Buddhist temples in Hawaii, as they were thought to encourage morality and docility in workers.

By the early 1890s, numerous individual Japanese began arriving in the United States. Since contract labor was illegal, they came as independent immigrants, often borrowing the price of their tickets. Many more transmigrated from Hawaii after finishing their contracts there, a movement that expanded once the islands were annexed by the United States in 1898. (Ironically, the white officials and businessmen who favored annexation conjured up the menace of Japanese domination of the islands as the main pretext for supporting a takeover by the U.S. government.)[7] By 1900 there were 24,326 people of Japanese ancestry in the United States, and an estimated 127,000 more Japanese arrived to join them in the seven years that followed.

The emigrants who went to Hawaii and the United States were a fraction of a larger international movement of migrants who left Japan in the early twentieth century. Many of them came from a cluster of prefectures in the southwest of the Japanese island of Honshu that had been hard hit by industrialization.[8] Other Japanese emigrated to escape conscription for military service, especially during Japan's wars. In addition, Okinawans, a disdained minority group whose home islands had been annexed by the Japanese Empire in 1879 and settled by "mainland" Japanese, emigrated in large numbers after the turn of the century, first throughout Asia and the Pacific, then to Hawaii and the North American mainland. Beyond those who went to the United States, a few thousand Japanese immigrant farmworkers and fishermen (many of them having previously settled in Hawaii) entered Canada during the first years of the twentieth century and took up residence on Vancouver Island and the West Coast of British Columbia. Other Japanese immigrated to South America—from 1899 to 1924, some 17,000 immigrants arrived in Peru—or to Australia, New Zealand, the Philippines, or the South Pacific. For example, several thousand Japanese were recruited as migrant labor on the French South Pacific island colony of New Caledonia, where they worked as miners. The largest number embarked within Asia and settled in Japan's annexed colonies of Korea and Formosa, and later in Japanese-occupied Manchuria.[9]

The newcomers to the West Coast of North America took up jobs at first as farm laborers in rural districts or as domestics and laborers in urban areas. Large groups worked on fishing boats or in fish canneries, and they formed Japanese-style villages in cannery districts such as Steveston near Vancouver and Terminal Island near Los Angeles. As time went on, significant numbers of Japanese were recruited for seasonal labor in lumber mills or in salmon canning factories in Alaska. Once they had toiled for a number of years in North America, where they could learn new skills and draw much higher wages than in rural Japan, many immigrant laborers were able to save money from their wages in order to buy or lease agricultural land. Through drainage and fertilization techniques inherited from their ancestral homeland, and through intense physical labor, Issei farmers succeeded in transforming marginal land into thriving farms. With help from their growing families, they were successful in growing crops such as strawberries that required too much onerous stoop labor for white farmers to produce. Issei who settled in U.S. West Coast cities such as San Francisco, Los Angeles, and Seattle, or the Canadian cities of Victoria and Vancouver, established themselves in business as fishermen or opened hotels, boarding houses, restaurants, and curio shops.[10] A number worked in gardening and domestic labor (including many students who supported their studies by working as houseboys for elite whites). Although they were barred from liberal professions such as medicine and law, a small fraction of the immigrants did establish themselves as professionals—teachers, newspaper editors, or ministers—within ethnic communities. A tiny handful of the West Coast immigrants, such as actor Sessue Hayakawa, playwright Ken Nakazawa, and political scientist Yamato Ichihashi, found professional employment in the larger community.

The Japanese laborers, even those who did not sign fixed-term contracts, generally came over as *dekasegi* (sojourners), intending to remain for a limited period, and many did go back to Japan. (For example, Yosuke Matsuoka, Japan's foreign minister in the period before Pearl Harbor, lived several years in Oregon as a young man). However, most of those who established themselves on the West Coast gradually abandoned their plans to return home. Their desire to remain was reflected in the powerful body of ethnic institutions they developed, including branches of the Japanese Association (Nihonjinkai) and the Canadian Japanese Association, in Japanese-language (and a few English-language) newspapers, and in religious congregations. They retained a strong sentimental attachment to their Japanese homeland, sent money to bank accounts or relatives in Japan, and kept close ties with the network of consulates maintained by the Japanese government that served to organize and protect overseas communities. Nevertheless, the immigrants demonstrated an ardent desire to adapt themselves to the customs and life of their new home. For example, a significant minority of Issei adopted Christianity—a faith that barely existed in Japan—and even the majority who remained faithful to various strains of Buddhism evolved a hybrid form unknown in Asia, including Western-style elements such as congregational services, Sunday schools, and ministers.

Issei joined in patriotic demonstrations and proclaimed their love for their adopted lands, although they were limited in their claims to belonging. In the United States, the 1790 Immigration Act limited naturalization to white (and, after 1870, African) immigrants and barred Japanese and other Asian aliens from becoming citizens. A few Japanese did succeed in taking out citizenship papers on the grounds that they counted as "white," before the question was definitively decided. Since Issei were unable to naturalize, they could not vote or be licensed for certain professions. By contrast, all native-born children were automatically granted citizenship regardless of their parents' status, a constitutional provision affirmed by the U.S. Supreme Court in the 1898 case of *Wong Kim Ark.* In Canada, where naturalization remained open, some 16 percent of the total Japan-born population adopted British nationality in the period before World War II, which gave them (at least nominal) citizenship in Canada. However, in part because at that time Canada had no written constitution or bill of rights, Japanese Canadians in British Columbia, like black Americans in the Jim Crow South, faced legal discrimination notwithstanding their status as British subjects.[11]

BEGINNINGS OF ANTI-JAPANESE MOVEMENTS

For the balance of the nineteenth century, most elite whites on the Pacific Coast welcomed the Japanese, who seemed willing to work hard for modest wages, and who were eager to learn. Still, there was from the beginning a certain amount of nativist hostility in the Anglo-American world to the overseas Japanese because of their racial and cultural difference from the majority—their "heathen" religion, their poor English, and their tendency to congregate in separate communities (often out of necessity). Australia, whose states had restricted Chinese immigration beginning in the 1850s, was the first nation to legislate Japanese exclusion, and its policy served as a precedent and model for other nations. In 1896, one year after Japan's defeat of China in the second Sino-Japanese War demonstrated Tokyo's growing military progress, various Australian states enacted Japanese exclusion laws. Japanese officials responded by protesting to Australia's imperial masters in Great Britain, who were engaged in forming military and naval alliances with the new power and were anxious not to alienate Japan. The British Parliament disallowed the discriminatory laws, whereupon in 1901 the new Australian Commonwealth government voted an Immigration Restriction Act requiring all immigrants to pass a dictation test in a European language—a version of the "Natal Law," developed by the British for use in South Africa, which restricted Asian immigrants unable to speak European languages. Under further British pressure, the Australians ultimately altered their law to accept the dictation test in any language. In return for this change, and for the Australians' pledge not to pass further discriminatory immigration legislation, the Japanese agreed to an informal "Gentleman's Agreement" (modeled on a deal they had made with the Australian state of Queensland in 1896) through which Tokyo agreed to restrict future visas to a few special categories of workers.[12] The result was a virtual cutoff of Japanese immigration to Australia for the next half-century.[13]

Another British possession, Canada, went through similar wrangling over immigration with the mother country. In 1897, following pressure from a newly formed "Anti-Mongolian Association," British Columbia's legislature passed a law barring Chinese and Japanese aliens from public employment. Two years later, the legislature voted the first of a series of race-based laws that used various stratagems to restrict Japanese immigration. The Dominion government of Prime Minster Wilfrid Laurier disallowed all these laws in order not to disturb British imperial foreign policy toward Britain's Japanese ally.[14] Although officially Japanese subjects had the right of free entry into Canada as a result of Japan's treaty with Great Britain (to which Canada became a signatory in 1906, albeit with expressed reserves on the immigration question), Tokyo agreed to use administrative measures to limit Japanese immigration to Canada in order to calm the situation. As a result of the agreement, and the Russo-Japanese War, Japanese immigration to Canada fell to almost nothing from 1901 to 1905.[15]

In stark contrast to the immigration question, where Japanese and British imperial interests were involved, Laurier did not intervene on purely domestic matters. Most notably, he brought no challenge to British Columbia's 1895 law barring all Chinese and Japanese, regardless of place of birth or citizenship, from voting rights and entry into certain professions. In 1900 Tomeichi Homma, a naturalized Canadian citizen, successfully challenged the law in a British Columbia court. However, two years later the British Privy Council overturned the court's ruling on appeal and upheld the ban, which remained in effect until 1949.[16]

There was pressure for similar restrictive action against Japanese immigration to the United States. Labor unionists and elected officials—many of whom owed the development of their organizations and their political influence to the earlier movement to stigmatize and exclude Chinese immigrants—seized the opportunity to take a position against the Japanese, employing the same racial stereotyping that had worked so well in the case of the Chinese. By 1900 the American Federation of Labor issued a resolution formally opposing immigration of all Asians. Labor leaders asserted that Japanese were a racially inferior horde that threatened the standard of living of white workers (who nevertheless refused to admit Japanese workers to their unions or assure higher pay for all). Soon after, a coalition of groups in San Francisco staged a mass meeting advocating exclusion of Japanese immigrants, on the grounds that they were racially "unassimilable" and thus incapable of citizenship in a democratic society. In May 1905 labor groups combined to found a joint lobbying and propaganda group, the Japanese Exclusion League.[17] Still, public opinion, especially outside the West Coast, was generally favorable toward Japan as a modern country, while Japanese immigrants were considered cleaner and more intelligent than the despised Chinese. Since the American West Coast was more heavily populated, popular fears of Japanese takeover were less plausible than on the Canadian and Australian frontiers.

After 1905, however, elite opinion about Japanese began to shift, in large part because of the interplay between two factors. One was the self-interest of white farmers and businessmen, who tolerated Japanese immigrants as laborers but were threatened by the growth of Japanese enterprise. The Issei who established farms and businesses on the West Coast shrank the pool of available labor and offered economic competition to elite whites. In addition, their success challenged widespread and accepted notions of white supremacy—their failure to "keep to their place" infuriated whites of all classes. The other catalyst of the anti-Japanese movement was Japan's military strength. In 1904–1905, Japan decisively beat Russia in the Russo-Japanese War and thereby became the dominant naval power in the western Pacific. Japan's military might gave rise to widespread fears among Americans of a "yellow peril" of encroaching Asian world mastery. Homer Lea's *The Valor of Ignorance* (1909), a popular book, warned of an imminent Japanese military invasion of the Pacific Coast and presented a detailed plan of such an invasion. White agitators, panicked over a potential Japanese invasion, insisted that the immigrants represented the first wave of penetration of the coming conquest.

In the fall of 1906, barely a year after the Treaty of Portsmouth ended the Russo-Japanese War, San Francisco's school board established a new regulation segregating Japanese schoolchildren into separate "oriental" schools. The action, avowedly designed to stigmatize Japanese Americans as undesirables and protest their presence, set off an international crisis. The Japanese government and Japanese public opinion were extremely sensitive to racial discrimination against Japanese abroad. Not only was unequal treatment an affront to their national honor that evoked painful memories of unequal treaties and foreign domination of Japan, but it also encouraged discriminatory treatment elsewhere. President Theodore Roosevelt feared that the school board's action would affront the Japanese enough to plunge the two nations into a useless war. In his annual message to Congress a few weeks after the crisis arose, he denounced the policy as "a wicked absurdity" and, as a conciliatory gesture, proposed that Congress pass legislation explicitly allowing Japanese immigrants to become naturalized citizens (a measure that was rejected, as Roosevelt must have anticipated). Meanwhile, Roosevelt's Justice Department teamed up with Masuji Miyakawa, the only ethnic Japanese attorney admitted to practice before the American bar, in bringing a court challenge to the pupil placement orders.

After several months of effort, Roosevelt finally persuaded the school board to abandon its segregation policy and dropped the lawsuit. In return, the president promised concrete steps to halt Japanese immigration. He signed an immediate executive order barring Japanese aliens in Hawaii from transmigrating to the mainland, and he promised to negotiate an informal "Gentleman's Agreement," as the Australians had done, with the Japanese government to limit further immigration from Japan. Negotiations lasted over a year, during which a series of diplomatic notes were exchanged. These formed together the "Gentlemen's Agreements" of 1907–1908. Under this informal understanding, the United States promised not to enact immigration curbs or discriminatory legislation against Japanese subjects. In return, the Japanese government pledged to refuse passports to manual laborers wishing to travel to the United States. As a result of the agreement, the only Japanese permitted to enter the country were merchants, ministers, leisure travelers, and students. However, un-

like the Chinese admitted as members of "protected classes" under the
Chinese Exclusion Act, who were examined at great length by U.S. immigration inspectors, Japan was responsible for controlling the entry of
its own nationals, and those Japanese immigrants already admitted to the
United States were permitted to bring over their spouses, children, and
parents to join them.[18]

As Japanese immigration to the United States subsided, Japanese immigrants (notably "transmigrants" from Hawaii) began arriving in Canada in force. During 1906–1907 some five thousand Japanese, more than
double the existing Issei population, entered British Columbia, catalyzing
mass protest by local whites and the circulating of a petition to Parliament that drew thousands of names. With help from a circle of American
nativist agitators, an Asiatic Exclusion League formed in Vancouver. On
September 7, 1907, the league sponsored a mass demonstration against
Asian immigration. It quickly broke into a race riot. White thugs attacked
the city's Chinese and Japanese neighborhoods, damaging property and
looting shops until driven away by armed Japanese residents.[19] In the aftermath of the riot, federal opposition leader Robert Borden joined local
leaders in defending the agitation. Borden asserted that British Columbia
was and must remain "a White Man's province."

The riot and its aftermath forced the government of Prime Minister
Wilfred Laurier to move. To placate Japan (as well as Great Britain), Laurier appointed a team headed by Deputy Minister of Labor—and future
prime minister—W. L. Mackenzie King to tour the riot area and report
on the amount of damages caused by the riot, which the federal government then awarded. (In a sign of the government's priorities, most of the
funds were directed to fixing the Japanese consulate rather than to repairing damaged shops or houses). Meanwhile, hoping to calm the anger
of the restrictionists without violating Japan's treaty rights, in December
1907 Laurier dispatched his labor minister, Rodolphe Lemieux, to Tokyo
to negotiate a new agreement with Japan: the Lemieux mission represented the first-ever occasion on which Canadians bypassed London and
undertook an independent foreign mission. The Japanese government
refused to make any binding commitment, but Prime Minister Count
Hayashi confidentially undertook to limit exit visa certificates to four
hundred laborers (including domestics) per year: as in the United States,
entry of merchants and ministers, as well as families of established immigrants, remained unrestricted. Although Lemieux was unable to make
public any figures upon his return to Canada, he and Laurier assured his

colleagues in Parliament that the Japanese had agreed to limit immigration. The Hayashi-Lemieux "Gentleman's Agreement" was greeted with approval by the Liberal majority in Parliament. Hoping to create a united front against Japanese penetration, U.S. President Theodore Roosevelt offered to send the American Pacific fleet to Victoria and Vancouver in early 1908. Laurier and his British colleagues were suspicious of this initiative, however, and politely declined.

THE ALIEN LAND ACTS

The Gentlemen's Agreements had a similar impact in both countries. In the years after they came into effect, many Japanese immigrants returned to Japan. Many of the Issei who remained decided to marry and raise families, since wives of established residents were permitted unrestricted entry under the agreements' provisions. As a result, tens of thousands of young women came from Japan to the United States and Canada in the following years as "picture brides," often joining husbands they knew only from photos and proxy marriages. Because of universal primary education in Japan, these women were generally quite literate—much more so than their white counterparts—and many of them had trained as teachers, virtually the only profession open to women in Japan. However, they were relegated by racial discrimination and dominant ideas about gender to working alongside their husbands as farmers and shopkeepers, as well as running households and caring for children. Since most of the Issei immigrants of both sexes were young adults of childbearing age, sons and daughters were born from their marriages at a rate that exceeded the average birthrate for the overall white population. As the new generation made its appearance, the ethnic Japanese population on the Pacific Coast became composed increasingly of young native-born citizens.

The anti-Japanese militants on the West Coast were not satisfied with the Gentlemen's Agreements and the cutoff of labor immigration. Rather, these policies only encouraged them to seek other curbs on the Issei. In Canada, the provincial assemblies of Saskatchewan and British Columbia passed laws forbidding the employment of white women in establishments owned by Asian men as a gesture against interracial relationships or indecency (parallel fears of "white slavery"—the abduction and prostitution of white women by Asians—in the United States led to the passage of the Mann Act, a pioneer federal criminal statute, in 1911). There also was low-level agitation by white farmers to bar Asians from landownership or leaseholds. Local politicians in British Columbia and their representatives in Ottawa exerted pressure on the Conservative government of Robert Borden, elected in 1911, to halt all Japanese immigration, though without success. Still, the Canadian climate of hostility to Japanese or Chinese was soon overshadowed by the more powerful exclusionist campaign against East Indians. In 1908 immigrants from the subcontinent were effectively barred entry into Canada by a discriminatory regulation reserving entry only for those who made a "continuous voyage" directly from Asia. In accordance with this rule, in 1914 Gurdit Singh, a rich Sikh based in Hong Kong, chartered a Japanese ship, the *Komagata Maru*, to bring some 350 of his fellow Sikhs directly to Canada. When the ship reached Vancouver, however, local whites denied the crew permission to unload the passengers. They remained stranded aboard ship in the harbor for a month, before the crew was finally forced to weigh anchor and return with the passengers to Hong Kong.

In contrast, anti-Japanese sentiment remained a powerful political force in California, where agitation focused on landownership. In early 1909 the state legislature passed an Alien Land Act, which barred all "aliens ineligible to citizenship" (a transparent euphemism for Japanese and other Asians, who were barred from naturalization) from owning agricultural land. Although Japanese immigrant farmers owned only a tiny fraction of the state's acreage, economic competition from Japanese was a handy cause for political organizers and demagogues to take up. President Theodore Roosevelt feared a negative response from Tokyo since the measure would violate the spirit of the Gentleman's Agreement, and he thus prevailed successfully on Republican governor Hiram Johnson to veto the bill as a matter of national security. Two years later, the California legislature passed a similar bill, but President William Howard Taft again persuaded Johnson to veto it in the national interest.

In 1913 California's legislature once again took up a proposed Alien Land Act. The new president, Woodrow Wilson—a leader not celebrated for his attachment to equal rights for racial minorities—was sympathetic to the passage of such a law, provided it did not explicitly single out Japanese for discrimination. Wilson was unfamiliar with the diplomatic aspects of the situation, but when Japan registered strong protest, the president and his secretary of state, William Jennings Bryan, belatedly and ineffectually changed course. Bryan traveled to California in hopes of persuading Governor Johnson once more to veto the legislation.

However, Johnson was unwilling to take such an unpopular action at the behest of a Democratic administration, and he signed the bill into law in May 1913. Tokyo issued numerous diplomatic protests, raising fears of war, though it ultimately decided not to take more aggressive action.

The Alien Land Act forbade "aliens ineligible to citizenship" or corporations in which they held a majority interest from buying or owning agricultural land. As a result, Issei farmers were forced to put title to their holdings in the names of white friends or representatives, or to hold it in trust for their Nisei children, who were citizens. Some form of alien land legislation would be adopted in a dozen states over the decade that followed. Although the Alien Land Acts were unevenly enforced (there were numerous cases prosecuted under the act in Washington State, while in California only fourteen cases were bought under it in the thirty years after its enactment) and generally ineffective in their stated purpose of reducing control of land by Issei farmers, they sent a powerful message to Japanese Americans that they were unwanted.

THE POSTWAR ANTI-JAPANESE MOVEMENT

The anti-Japanese movement in the United States and Canada slowed during the era of World War I, when Japan was allied with Great Britain and its possessions (and, after 1917, with the United States) against Germany, and there was powerful pressure for national unity on the home front. (Ironically, in view of future events, the same nationalistic fervor that reduced hostility toward Japanese Canadians led the Canadian government to intern as "enemy aliens" some 8,500 Ukrainian immigrants and their children as potential security risks).[20] By 1916, two years after Canada entered the war alongside Great Britain, the supply of Canadian volunteers had grown low. In British Columbia, some 200 Issei men formed a "Japanese Volunteer Corps," hoping to be absorbed into the Canadian Army as an all-Japanese unit. With financial support from local Japanese communities, they began military training. The government of British Columbia declined to support its Japanese recruits, while the army ruled they were too few to be enlisted as a separate unit and ordered them disbanded. However, a recruiter from Alberta invited the Canadian Japanese Association to send the volunteers to help fill his province's quota. By war's end, 202 ethnic Japanese had joined the Canadian Army and gone overseas for duty, of whom approximately three-fourths were killed or wounded.[21] Once the United States entered the war, in April 1917, over a hundred soldiers and sailors of Japanese ancestry, many of whom were Nisei from Hawaii such as Joseph Kurihara and Ernest Wakayama, joined the U.S. Army and Navy. They served during the brief time that American troops were active in combat, before war ended with the armistice in November 1918.[22]

In the years after the armistice, when the prosperity that the war had brought farmers and businessmen sharply declined, anti-Japanese agitation resumed on the Pacific Coast with increased force and bitterness. California, as before, was a center of agitation. In 1920, following a voter initiative, California strengthened its alien land law and passed another measure (later overturned in court) preventing Japanese aliens from serving as guardians for land in the name of underage citizens. In 1921 the California legislature authorized local school districts to send Nisei children to segregated public schools, and Jim Crow education was established in communities such as Florin and Walnut Grove.

In parallel with the trend of discrimination, nativist groups such as the California Joint Immigration Committee (descendant of the Japanese Exclusion League) and the Native Sons and Daughters of the Golden West spearheaded propaganda campaigns for complete exclusion of Japanese immigrants. They charged that the Japanese had violated the Gentleman's Agreement by continuing to bring in picture brides, and they asserted (dubiously) that ethnic Japanese families were breeding at such an accelerated rate that the region would soon have a Japanese majority unless immigration was completely halted. Among the leading agitators were newspapermen such as William Randolph Hearst and Sacramento editor V. S. McClatchy. In countless speeches and writings, McClatchy alleged that all Japanese were primarily loyal to Japan. To obscure the birthright citizenship of the Nisei, McClatchy dismissed them as "dual citizens" who were considered Japanese subjects by the Japanese government. He added that the Japanese schools and community institutions were seats of subversion. These anti-Japanese campaigns continued into the World War II years and helped determine popular images of Issei and Nisei.

Fears of Japanese encroachment spread to Hawaii, where ethnic Japanese comprised some 40 percent of the population. Although the territory enjoyed a real (if exaggerated) reputation for intergroup harmony, racial lines hardened in the 1920s. In the wake of a mass strike by sugar plantation workers in 1920, the haole (white) portrayed the Japanese as scheming to dominate the islands through their control of labor and succeeded in breaking the strike by dividing the Issei strikers from their Filipino allies. In the wake of the strike, the ruling "Big Five" plantation oligarchy took a more confrontational attitude toward Asian militancy and "subversion."[23] Encouraged by McClatchy, who visited Hawaii in 1922, the territorial government of Hawaii targeted Japanese schools with a set of laws, including licensing provisions and discriminatory taxes, designed to put the schools out of business. Conversely, in 1924 the territorial government segregated public schools by establishing "English standard" schools open only to children who passed an English proficiency test—a nearly impossible feat for children of plantation workers brought up speaking the creole dialect of Hawaiian pidgin.[24] Mixing economic self-interest with fear of foreign ways, the Hawaiian Sugar Planters Association ceased its support of Buddhist churches. The association covertly funded an Issei Congregational minister, Takie Okumura, who undertook an "Americanization" campaign, through which he encouraged Japanese Americans to Christianize, speak English, and assimilate to white American culture. Beginning in 1927, Okumura established a series of "new Americans conferences" designed, as he privately admitted, to recruit Nisei to take up plantation labor rather than seeking entry into professions.[25]

Issei activists on the West Coast also took steps to calm the fears of their opponents through an Americanization campaign. They staged patriotic festivals, pushed the use of English, and reformed Japanese school curricula and textbooks. Meanwhile, with help from a small circle of white allies, they struggled vainly to oppose the anti-Japanese canards by issuing their own positive propaganda. They pointed out that the reproduction rate of ethnic Japanese on the West Coast was similar to that of whites in their age group, and they noted that more Japanese immigrants left the country than arrived during those years. Hoping to combat the bugaboo of dual citizenship for the Nisei, Japanese American representatives and their allies pointed out that the Nisei's status as Japanese citizens was purely nominal and had no more significance than that of any other Americans who held foreign citizenship. Overseas Japanese communities also enlisted the aid of the Japanese government. In 1920 they successfully prevailed upon Tokyo to cease providing visas for picture brides. Four years later, in response to Issei lobbying, the Japanese government enacted a new nationality law, according to which Nisei children of overseas Japanese who failed to register their birth with the local consulate were not recognized as Japanese subjects, and the Nisei could renounce their

Japanese citizenship at any time (i.e., without having to first complete military service). As part of their plan for Americanization, Issei leaders urged the Nisei to take steps to "expatriate." However, the rate of renunciation of Japanese citizenship remained fairly low, partly because some Nisei identified with Japan or wished to enjoy the potential benefits of Japanese citizenship, but mostly because the renunciation process was too cumbersome, expensive, or time-consuming to be worth the trouble.[26]

The Issei also fought in court to preserve their rights. With support from Japanese associations, in 1915 Takeo Ozawa, a longtime U.S. resident who had been educated in California and was thoroughly Americanized, attempted to take out citizenship papers. Following a lengthy legal process, in 1922 the U.S. Supreme Court ruled on Ozawa's petition for citizenship. The Court unanimously held that, as a member of the Japanese race, Ozawa was not Caucasian and thus could not be considered eligible for citizenship under the law. By upholding the existing barriers to naturalization against Japanese Americans, the Court's decision solidified laws against land ownership for all categories of Asians. (The Court formally upheld the constitutionality of alien land laws the following year, in *Terrace v. Thompson*). Although they were unsuccessful in securing their right to naturalization or fighting the Alien Land Acts, Issei activists did prevail against anti-Japanese school laws. Following a campaign led by Fred Markino, editor of the *Hawaii Hochi* newspaper, Japanese Americans in Hawaii challenged the registration and tax provisions, which were unanimously struck down by the U.S. Supreme Court in 1927.[27]

Although the Gentlemen's Agreements had all but eliminated Japanese immigration, during the early 1920s West Coast interests campaigned for total exclusion of Japanese immigrants. It was carried along by a larger national campaign for immigration restriction. During those years, there was an enormous surge throughout the country of reactionary nativist and white supremacist thought, whose advocates defined Americanism to exclude many different ethnic and racial minorities. The Ku Klux Klan, a mythic southern white supremacy group of Reconstruction times, was reinvented in 1915 as a force against African Americans, foreigners, Jews, and Catholics, and by the early 1920s it claimed five million members nationwide. Anti-Semitism became more visible nationwide during these years, as elite universities instituted quotas on Jewish students. A wave of antiblack riots swept the country during the "Red Summer" of 1919. During this period there was a strong current of anxiety about immigrants, whom old-stock white Americans connected to radicalism, foreign values, and moral breakdown. Two bestselling books by elite scholars, Madison Grant's *The Passing of the Great Race* (1916) and Lothrop Stoddard's *The Rising Tide of Color against White World-Supremacy* (1920), provided intellectual justification for popular fears that mass immigration was overwhelming the nation's superior Nordic stock and weakening the national character. In response to nativist pressure, in 1921 Congress passed a law drastically limiting immigration and establishing a "national origins" quota that limited future entry by foreign nationals to 3 percent of the population of such nationals residing in the United States in 1910. The quota blatantly discriminated against immigrants from southern and eastern Europe, who were predominantly recent arrivals.[28]

Japanese immigrants were not directly affected by the new law, as their immigration was already restricted by the Gentleman's Agreement. Nevertheless, in the postwar climate of xenophobia and uncertainty, Americans of many different backgrounds and political orientations throughout the United States became convinced that Japanese immigrants were not assimilable into the larger (white) population and that they posed a threat on that basis. Even such a liberal internationalist as Franklin D. Roosevelt wrote that the exclusion of Japanese immigrants and the laws that prevented them from owning property or becoming citizens were justified as a means of preventing intermarriage and protecting white racial purity.[29] In 1924 Congress passed a new Immigration Act. It further reduced immigration quotas from each nation, to 2 percent of the population of those nationals in the United States in 1890, before mass immigration began. Under the leadership of Massachusetts senator Henry Cabot Lodge, a provision excluding all "aliens ineligible to citizenship" was added to the 1924 law. This provision clearly singled out Japanese immigrants, as previous legislation had already eliminated all other Asian immigration (apart from that from the Philippines, which as an American colony enjoyed unlimited entry for its residents). The strong protests of Japanese ambassador Masanao Hanihara over the dangerous consequences of the proposed legislation, rather than working against it, were actually twisted into threats by the bill's proponents and used to help secure passage. Since Japanese immigration would in any case have been minimal under a national origins quota, the legislation served no actual purpose other than to express hostility toward Japanese Americans. Its passage caused considerable outrage in Japan and helped discredit liberal internationalism and catalyze aggressive nationalism in that country.

THE ANTI-JAPANESE MOVEMENT IN CANADA

Canada witnessed a parallel wave of anti-Japanese sentiment in the 1920s. Although the British Columbia government, as a result of various international factors, did not bar Japanese aliens from landownership, various other discriminatory practices were legion. Aside from the continuing denial of voting rights to citizens of Asian ancestry in British Columbia, the arena in which racial discrimination became most visible was that of fishing, where Japanese were more numerous than either whites or First Nations (native) peoples by the end of World War I. In 1919 the Department of Fisheries in British Columbia responded to protests by white fishermen over Japanese competition by freezing the number of licenses issued to Japanese for gill-net fishing. Three years later the department appointed the Duff Commission to investigate industry conditions. White fishermen took the opportunity of committee hearings to complain at length about illegal and unfair practices by their Japanese counterparts, which they alleged (with considerable exaggeration) were driving them out of the business. As a result, the commission recommended that the number of licenses awarded Issei fishermen be cut. In the end, the number of licensed Issei fishermen fell by 1923 by 40 percent, to 1,200, and further reductions followed. Capitalizing on their victory, white fishermen launched a campaign to lobby Parliament for further limits. In 1926 the House of Commons' Standing Commission on Fisheries (a committee dominated by British Columbia MPs representing an all-white electorate) ordered a ban on new licenses to ethnic Japanese fishermen and proposed that the number of existing licenses for ethnic Japanese be cut by 10 percent each year until 1937, when the Issei were to be completely excluded. The Amalgamated Association of Japanese Fishermen challenged this policy in court, and in 1928 the Supreme Court of Canada overturned the exclusion policy. However, the federal government immediately issued orders-in-council that maintained the freeze on licenses and left some 1,300 Issei fishermen unemployed.[30]

Similarly, West Coast lobbyists, headed by the Vancouver Asiatic Exclusion League, exerted considerable pressure for exclusion of Japanese immigrants from Canada. A popular novel, Hilda Glynn-Ward's *The Writing on the Wall* (1921), painted a lurid picture of Chinese and Japanese economic penetration of British Columbia and the impoverishment of the white population. The novel ended by describing a Chinese economic takeover of the province, followed by a Japanese military invasion.

While the work was extreme in its views, and it is unclear how directly influential it was, it was not without echoes in popular attitudes about the "unassimilable" nature of Asian immigrants and the menace of intermarriage.[31] (A Japanese government ban in 1925 on visas for picture brides to Canada, mirroring that for the United States five years earlier, did nothing to halt hateful propaganda over the high "Japanese" birth rate in British Columbia).

British Columbia politicians such as H. H. Stevens and W. G. McQuarrie led the campaign in Parliament for a nationwide ban on Asian immigration. In 1923 Canada passed a Chinese immigration act that barred virtually all Chinese immigration. Shortly thereafter, an Independent MP from British Columbia, A.W. Neill, introduced a bill to extend the exclusion to Japanese. Prime Minister William Lyon Mackenzie King, who declared himself in favor of a culturally homogenous, "White" Canada, preferred to avoid unilateral action. Instead, he held a series of negotiations with the Japanese consul general, using the threat of legislation as a lever to tighten immigration. Under the pressure, the Japanese government agreed in August 1923 to cut the annual number of immigrant laborers admitted under the Gentleman's Agreement.[32]

Encouraged by the American exclusion law of 1924, members of Parliament from British Columbia continued to push for a total federal ban on Japanese immigration, and in 1927 even introduced provisions for repatriation of existing immigrants. However, Japan had become Canada's third largest trading partner, and fears of Japanese retaliation and damage to economic relations blunted pressure for harsher measures. After considerable diplomatic wrangling off and on over several years, in 1929 Japan reluctantly agreed to reduce its total immigration quota under the Gentleman's Agreement to 150 persons per year. To ease Canadian anxiety over the Japanese birthrate, Tokyo further pledged that not more than half of those immigrants permitted would be women. In return, Canada (which shortly before had won from Great Britain the right to its own diplomatic representatives) agreed to establish official ties with Japan.[33]

THE NISEI GENERATION

The end of immigration to North America brought about a significant change in policy by the Japanese government. In response largely to domestic protests within Japan, Tokyo exerted a low-level campaign to influence the Americans to alter the Japanese Exclusion Act and grant Japan an immigration quota, a movement strenuously opposed by V. S. McClatchy and other nativists.[34] However, government officials preferred to shift their attention to encouraging immigration elsewhere. Throughout the early twentieth century, waves of laborers had migrated to Mexico and to South America (often as contract laborers) and provided the workforce for plantations in countries such as Peru and Bolivia. Ultimately, many laborers left the plantations after their contracts expired and migrated to urban areas. After the United States and Canada closed their doors, emigration agents focused their efforts on encouraging workers to settle in Brazil, and over 100,000 Japanese emigrated there in the ten years that followed. However, during the 1930s, in a time of worldwide economic depression, nationalist pressures developed in Brazil and in other countries, to which governments responded by limiting or banning Japanese immigration and reducing the liberties of existing residents.[35]

Meanwhile, Japanese communities in North America shifted their orientation from struggling for the rights of the immigrants to focusing on building for their Nisei children. As citizens by birth in the United States and Canada, the Nisei could not be subjected to legal discrimination as aliens, and the older generation hoped that they would serve as a bridge between their ancestral homeland and their native country. Japanese newspapers in the United States, beginning with the *San Francisco Nichi Bei* and the *Rafu Shimpo* in Los Angeles, began featuring English sections edited by Nisei. Churches and temples planned activities for young people, social clubs and sports leagues grew up, and communities established festivals—in Los Angeles's Little Tokyo, the traditional ceremony of O-Bon was transformed into "Nisei Day."[36] In Canada, where Nisei long remained a minority of the Japanese community and were restricted in their legal rights, Issei leaders followed the same strategy on a smaller scale.[37] A particular focus of community pride in Vancouver's Powell Street, the largest Canadian Japantown, during the interwar years was a Nisei baseball team, the Asahis, who won the Pacific Northwest baseball championship for five straight years from 1937 to 1941.[38]

Yet community leaders acted ambivalently in planning their and their children's future. Many Issei leaders continued to believe in the promise of their adopted nations and urged the Nisei to be good citizens. Others, noting the pervasive discrimination that ethnic Japanese faced in the United States and Canada, sought closer ties with Japan and looked ahead to an eventual return. Parents sought to assure that their Americanized children would be familiar with Japanese language and customs. That way, they could not only adapt in case the families should choose to repatriate but could find jobs with Japanese companies where their advancement would not be blocked by racial prejudice. To teach the second-generation children Japanese and to allow them to communicate more easily with parents who spoke poor English, the Issei communities expended significant community funds on maintaining Japanese schools for their children to attend. The curricula of these schools included Japanese history and moral education.[39] However, between the poor instruction they offered, the often authoritarian Japanese teachers they featured, and the fact that classes were held in the afternoon after regular school, thereby preempting play time, the Japanese schools were widely detested among the young Nisei, many of whom failed to attain fluency in Japanese. In contrast, a large fraction of (predominantly male) Nisei—as much as one-fourth of the entire population—were sent back to Japan for some or all of their schooling during the prewar years. Many of these Nisei, known as "Kibei"(and among Canadians as "Kika"), had great difficulty, at least at first, fitting in with their Japanese classmates, who were suspicious of and hostile to the "Americans" as foreigners.[40] While many Issei, perhaps most, felt an emotional attachment to their birthplace, the attitude of the Nisei toward Japan was more fluid and diverse, and harder to determine. Most Nisei were shaped to a degree by their Japanese background and absorbed a certain outlook from their parents. They regularly ate Japanese food, learned Japanese folk songs and dances, performed translations of Japanese plays, and cheered Japanese athletes in international competitions. A small but indeterminate number—particularly those Kibei who had remained for long periods in Japan and were somewhat isolated within Nisei circles by lack of English fluency—identified themselves fully as Japanese. Nevertheless, the vast majority of Nisei acculturated to American norms and identified themselves entirely as Americans.

In addition to legal inequality, Nisei on the Pacific Coast of both countries faced widespread exclusion in daily life. Minoru Yamasaki, a Seattle youth who would become a distinguished architect, later stated his opinion that the prejudice he experienced growing up on the West Coast was as powerful as that facing blacks in the South.[41] Although the Nisei were outstanding in their educational achievement—West Coast Japanese Americans attended college in disproportionate numbers during the prewar years—they faced restrictive quotas in many local colleges and professional schools. Furthermore, they were largely excluded by custom from white-collar jobs and denied entry into the civil service.[42] In British Columbia (where bars on suffrage rights for Nisei also meant they were formally excluded from practicing law and some fields of engineering), only a single Nisei teacher was hired to teach in the province's public schools, and that in a virtually all-Japanese school. Another university graduate in Victoria was unable to find employment except as a domestic.[43] As a result, Nisei were relegated to working for family stores and businesses or for local Issei merchants. Trained engineers and teachers were forced to take jobs farming or selling fruit. A number of outstanding Nisei, discouraged by limited career prospects, took jobs working for branches of Japanese firms. Sociologist T. Scott Miyakawa worked for the Manchurian Railway, while attorney Minoru Yasui was hired by the Japanese consulate in Chicago, and journalist Larry Tajiri was employed as a correspondent by the Tokyo *Asahi* in New York. A fraction of Nisei left North America entirely and settled in Japan, where they found jobs in business or in the entertainment industry—an article written in 1939 estimated that five thousand Nisei lived in Tokyo. Another set of Nisei, which included journalists Bill Hosokawa and John Fujii of the *Japanese American Courier* and Shinobu Higashi, first editor of the *New Canadian*, accepted jobs under the Japanese occupation in Asian territories such as Manchuria and Shanghai.

In Hawaii, with its Asian majority population, overt racial prejudice was rare, but class and dialect barriers limited advancement for Nisei outside of a small elite group: despite their academic success in public schools, Nisei remained underrepresented at the University of Hawaii. There were also episodes of prejudice. In 1939 Tatsue Fujita, a Nisei woman graduate of Hawaii Teacher's College, was arbitrarily denied a teaching license on the grounds of her allegedly "undemocratic" and "pro-Japanese" attitudes.[44]

Although the majority of the native-born were under eighteen throughout the prewar years, a group of young adult Nisei established a set of fledgling organizations to defend the interests of the new generation, notably the Japanese American Citizens League (JACL), founded in 1930, and its northern counterpart the Japanese Canadian Citizens League (JCCL), created in 1936. In addition, a handful of U.S. Nisei established their own journals, beginning with James Sakamoto's *Japanese American Courier* in 1928, while a circle of activists in British Columbia banded together in 1938 to found the *New Canadian*, which became the voice of Canadian Nisei. These journalists and community leaders stressed love of country, and pushed participation in patriotic festivals such as "I Am an American" Day. At the same time, they lobbied for equal citizenship rights. The JACL lobbied successfully to repeal the Cable Act, which stripped American-born women of citizenship if they married Asian aliens, and to eliminate school segregation.[45] Still, in part because of the relatively small proportion of Nisei who were of voting age, political participation was not extremely marked in West Coast communities. The Nisei leadership was largely Republican and probusiness, although the Nisei Young Democrat clubs that formed in Los Angeles, San Francisco, and Oakland in 1938–1939 proved to be centers of activism.[46] There was little or no Nisei electoral activity apart from the campaign of Clarence Arai, an attorney and JACL founder who ran unsuccessfully for the Washington State Legislature on the Republican ticket in 1933.[47] In Hawaii, by contrast, where the average age of Nisei was higher and patterns of political participation were more established, local Japanese became politically active in both parties. By 1936 there were nine Nisei representatives in the territorial legislature, plus Japanese American political appointees and civil servants. There was a Nisei delegate from Hawaii at that year's Democratic National Convention. In November 1940 Sanji Abe, a World War I veteran, became the first Nisei member of the territorial Senate. As was demonstrated in a series of congressional hearings on statehood beginning in 1935, the voting power of Japanese Americans in Hawaii, and their potential as candidates for public office, weighed powerfully against statehood for the territory during the prewar era, especially among the southern Democratic representatives and senators who dominated congressional committees during those years.

The Canadian Nisei who came of age in the 1930s focused their attention on winning voting rights in British Columbia, where the vast majority of the Japanese population lived. With aid from the Camp and Mill Workers Union, a labor organization staffed by progressive Issei (and also from a few white allies, such as liberal professor Henry F. Angus), the Canadian Nisei lobbied for suffrage. Although in 1931 the British Columbia legislature finally approved, by a single-vote margin, voting rights for Great War veterans of Asian ancestry, neither major party's leaders were prepared to consider enfranchising ordinary citizens in the face of widespread popular opposition: white nativists charged that granting suffrage would lead to demands for further immigration and to Asian rule of the province.[48] Not even the legislators from the provincial wing of the Cooperative Commonwealth Federation (CCF), a Social Democratic Party founded in 1933, dared support Asian suffrage. The Liberal Party nonetheless issued a blatant racist attack on the CCF during the 1935 federal elections, informing voters that a vote for the CCF would give "the Chinaman and the Japanese the same voting right as you have."[49]

Hoping to go over the heads of the British Columbians, in 1936 the JCCL sent a delegation of Nisei, led by the distinguished Canadian-born semanticist Dr. S. I. Hayakawa, to Ottawa for testimony before a parliamentary committee on behalf of a national law granting suffrage to citizens of Japanese ancestry.[50] The national CCF announced its support, and various Liberals outside of British Columbia favored passage. However, Prime Minister William Lyon Mackenzie King, who disingenuously claimed that he had not been aware that the Japanese Canadians wished suffrage rights, opposed the measure out of political expediency. Thomas Reid, a British Columbia MP, publicly asserted that the entire bid for suffrage was part of an attempt by Japan to place its spies in British Columbia.[51] In the end, Parliament decided not to grant suffrage to Asian Canadians until British Columbia did so—already an unlikely event in 1936, and less so as conflict loomed with Japan.

THE CRISIS OF U.S.-JAPANESE RELATIONS

During the 1930s, events in Asia led to increasing strains between Japan and the United States, breeding suspicion over Japanese motives that rebounded against Japanese Americans. Diplomatic relations between Japan and the United States had remained fairly placid during the 1920s. The two countries, along with Great Britain, were major signatories of the Washington Naval Treaty in 1922. The treaty reaffirmed the "open door" policy in China, dissolved the Anglo-Japanese naval alliance, and reduced the number of capital ships in each country's navy to a fixed ratio (Japan, because it theoretically only had one ocean to patrol, accepted a ratio of three ships to five ships for the British or American navies). In exchange, the United States agreed not to further fortify its Pacific possessions of Guam and the Philippines. However, following the onset of the Great Depression, economic and demographic pressure within Japan, mixed with nationalist anger over slights such as the 1924 Immigration Act, had catalyzed a shift toward militarism and imperialism in Tokyo's policy. When Prime Minister Osachi Hamaguchi agreed to extend the limitations of the Washington Naval Treaty, denounced by Japanese nationalists as unfair, he was assassinated in 1931. Soon after, the Japanese Army staged an incident in Chinese province of Manchuria, which it used as a pretext for launching an invasion and occupation of the province. The Japanese government, which lacked the power to countermand the military's popular action, instead absorbed Manchuria, establishing the puppet state of Manchukuo.

The United States, which considered itself the unofficial patron of China, reacted with hostility to the Japanese action in Manchuria. However, President Herbert Hoover, embroiled in facing the Great Depression, was unwilling to oppose the occupation by means of economic sanctions or military action that might lead to war. Instead, Secretary of State Henry Stimson outlined a policy of nonrecognition of Manchukuo, a legalistic solution that alienated the Japanese without applying effective pressure against them. In the fall of 1932, a new president, Franklin D. Roosevelt, was elected. Roosevelt chose to continue the "Stimson doctrine." During the balance of the 1930s, FDR experimented with various means of subtle pressure, including moral suasion, opening diplomatic relations with the Soviet Union, and naval rearmament, to prod Tokyo to abandon its aggressive policy in Asia without either risking war or harming America's lucrative trade with Japan. The pressure failed to accomplish its objective. In 1936 Japan rejected existing naval arms limitations as unequal and signed the Anti-Comintern Pact, associating itself with Nazi Germany against the Soviet Union.

Canada, with a proportionately higher trade with Japan, was even more circumspect in facing off against Tokyo. As noted, Japan was one of the first areas of the Dominion's diplomacy, and Canadians were loath to surrender their position. Although Canada's right to an independent foreign policy was formally recognized by Great Britain under the Statute of Westminster in 1931, Ottawa had little interest in diplomatic initiatives in Asia, especially in the absence of British or American leadership. Further, unlike the mandarins of the U.S. State Department, many Canadian diplomats in the early 1930s disdained China and sympathized with Japanese claims in Manchuria, which they saw as stemming anarchy. In December 1932 C. H. Cahan, Canada's representative at the League of Nations, made a speech in Geneva against sanctions that was so extreme in its pro-Japanese view as to stir fears of a Chinese boycott of Canada. Although the Conservative government of Prime Minister R. B. Bennett nominally disclaimed Cahan and supported the report of the Lytton Commission deploring the Japanese invasion, Canada opposed collective action for sanctions against Tokyo.[52] When the Liberals returned to power in 1935, Prime Minister Mackenzie King promised to pursue an international policy that would satisfy Canadians throughout the country and promote national unity. In practice, this meant appealing to isolationists and French Canadians by distancing Canada from Great Britain and the League of Nations and pursuing a policy of isolationism, except in those few areas where Canada had a direct interest. King neglected the Canadian Army and was embarrassed when President Roosevelt, on a trip to British Columbia in mid-1937, expressed shocked dismay over the poor state of Canada's Pacific defenses.[53]

THE JAPANESE INVASION OF CHINA

In 1937 the Japanese military launched a full-scale invasion of China and within months succeeded in pushing the weak Nationalist government away from the densely populated Pacific coast. News of Japanese atrocities stunned the world—notably the bombing of Shanghai and the "Rape of Nanking," in which the Japanese soldiers taking China's capital slaughtered at least 100,000 civilians and possibly many times that figure. American public opinion, already largely sympathetic to China, was further aroused in December 1937 when Japanese airplanes bombed and sank an American gunboat, the *Panay*, anchored in China, although the Japanese government quickly offered an official apology and compensation. Private groups campaigned for a boycott of Japanese goods, and Chinese American groups and their white allies raised large sums for Chinese war relief.

The Roosevelt administration was limited in the scope of its possible actions on the international front by a set of neutrality laws enacted by Congress during the mid-1930s in response to events in Europe, but the White House refused to invoke neutrality in the Far East and offered limited economic aid to the Chinese government in its struggle against the Japanese occupation. In October 1937 the president, with Japan in mind, publicly proposed international action to "quarantine the aggressors," though he denied that economic sanctions were the goal of the policy. However, Roosevelt and his advisors did not wish to become entangled in any military conflict, even as war drew near in Europe, and the United States continued to sell strategic materials such as gasoline and steel to Japan. Roosevelt chose not to take more provocative action over the two years that followed, until the outbreak of war in Europe inspired a reexamination of American policy. Canada, similarly, offered verbal condemnation of the Japanese occupation of China, as Canadian public opinion swung decisively toward the Chinese—Norman Bethune did much to popularize their cause through a humanitarian medical mission to China, while his subsequent death made him a national martyr. A popular movement arose for the boycott of Japanese goods. However, Ottawa saw no cause for decisive steps such as sanctions or boycotts, especially in the absence of clear action by the United States.[54]

OFFICIAL SURVEILLANCE OF JAPANESE AMERICANS IN HAWAII

As relations with Japan worsened during the 1930s, U.S. government and army officials grew increasingly anxious about potential disloyalty by both Issei and Nisei, especially in the territory of Hawaii, where residents of Japanese ancestry represented the largest single population group. Throughout the 1920s and 1930s, military planners drew up plans for defending Hawaii against a potential Japanese invasion. They assumed that in case of war, Japanese Americans irrespective of background or citizenship would side with the enemy. As early as the 1920s, the army's War Plans Division organized a defense plan for Hawaii (assembled by Col. John DeWitt, who would later order mass removal of Japanese Americans as Western Defense commander) containing provisions for martial law in the territory, registration of Japanese aliens, and selective internment of those thought dangerous. Similarly, in 1933 the Hawaiian branch of G-2 (Army Intelligence) issued a report on the "Japanese problem" in the islands. It characterized both first- and second-generation Japanese Americans as marked by traits of "fanaticism" and racial and "moral inferiority." It also stated that, according to local whites, the increase in the local Japanese population represented a danger to the safety of the islands since the vast majority of Japanese Americans, whether citizen or alien, could be expected to side with Japan in the event of an invasion and to commit sabotage in order to prevent effective response.[55]

In 1935 Hawaii's commanding general Hugh Drum (who as wartime Eastern Defense commander would later push unsuccessfully for mass action against German and Italian aliens) publicly called for martial law in the territory if war broke out. When a subcommittee of the House Military Affairs Committee visited Hawaii, Drum justified his position to committee members by reference to the peril of racial diversity: "It is the experience of all nations, including the United States, that mixtures of widely dissimilar racial elements constitute a serious problem in time of emergency. History . . . shows that during an emergency armed forces are often necessary to protect loyal citizens as against disaffected and rebellious ones."[56]

In May 1936 Secretary of War George Dern submitted to President Roosevelt a report by a military Joint Planning Committee that detailed some problems in the defense of Hawaii. The report noted that Japanese naval personnel traveling on Japanese commercial ships routinely stopped in Hawaii, where they delivered mail to the locals from their relatives in Japan and otherwise mixed with local Japanese in restaurants, temples, and teahouses to spread Japanese propaganda and encourage subversion. The president responded on August 10, 1936, that the committee should make contingency plans to deal with the local Japanese population throughout Hawaii in case of conflict with Japan: "One obvious thought occurs to me—that every Japanese citizen or non-citizen on the Island of Oahu who meets these ships or has any connection with their officers or men should be secretly but definitely identified and his or her name placed on special list of those who would be the first to be placed in a concentration camp in the event of trouble."[57]

Although Roosevelt was clearly thinking in terms of controlling dangerous individuals in a military emergency, his use of the term "concentration camp" and his failure to distinguish between Japanese aliens and American citizens shows that he shared the race-based assumptions that other government officials were making about Japanese Americans and their loyalty. In the months that followed, FDR called for the formation of an interagency committee to develop strategies for curbing Japanese espionage in Hawaii, and he approved measures limiting employment on naval bases in the territory to Caucasians.[58] When Honolulu industrialist Walter Dillingham, a reserve officer, visited the White House in early 1938, Roosevelt asked him "numerous pointed questions" that underlined his doubts regarding the loyalties and sympathies of Japanese Americans.[59]

THE SALICH TRIAL

The government's fears of disloyalty and efforts to control Japanese Americans were not confined to Hawaii. A drumbeat of sensational accusations from both official and unofficial sources raised suspicions about the loyalty of West Coast communities. In 1934 a U.S. State Department memorandum warned that, in case of war between the United States and Japan, "the entire Japanese population" on the West Coast would rise in support of Tokyo.[60] The same year, Lail T. Kane, an officer of the American Legion, aired what would become a familiar canard when he told a House committee that Issei fishing boats could be easily transformed, once in international waters outside the three-mile limit, into torpedo boats for the Japanese Navy. Meanwhile, U.S. Representative John Dockweiler made the absurd announcement that one–fourth of Japanese Americans in California were Japanese Army reserve officers ready to take up arms at a moment's notice.[61] In 1937 the War Department submitted a report on "Japanese activities" in "lower California and Mexico" that claimed (with dubious accuracy) that there had been visits by Japanese naval forces. Popular hysteria went even further. In 1935–36, widespread stories spread about a Japanese fishing fleet of 120 boats operating out of California harbors using ships constructed in Japan, which could be transformed immediately into mine layers, manned by 2,000 trained Japanese naval officers disguised as fishermen. Journalist Carey McWilliams investigated the charges and found that of all the active fishing boats over 115 feet, only two were Japanese-owned, and only ten more were in the 85–110 foot range. There were only 680 licensed Japanese fishermen in California out of a total of 5,399.[62]

In conjunction with the increased government concern over security, the Office of Naval Intelligence was assigned to keep tabs on West Coast Japanese Americans during the late 1930s. The extent of ONI surveillance was publicly revealed by the case of Hafis Salich. Salich, a Russian-born former Berkeley, California, police officer, was hired in August 1936 by the U.S. Naval Intelligence Bureau for the 11th District (Southern California, Arizona, and New Mexico) as a civilian employee. Sent to spy on Japanese activities in Los Angeles, he arrived in Little Tokyo and posed as a friend of the Nisei. According to later testimony, his tasks included "detailing the coming and going on the west coast of Japanese military and civil officials as well as private citizens whose actions were deemed of possible interest to the Intelligence Office."[63] Salich took notes on movements of Nisei-owned fishing boats at Terminal Island and their actions in Mexican waters.[64] Salich was approached by a Soviet agent, Mikhail Gorin, who offered him money in exchange for information. Gorin persuaded him that Japan was the common enemy of the United States and the Soviet Union, so it would be of mutual benefit to share intelligence. Salich ultimately provided a set of over fifty reports that he and others had compiled for the San Pedro branch of ONI.

Arrested by the FBI, Salich and Gorin were brought to trial in January 1939 and ultimately convicted under the Espionage Act. (Gorin's wife, Natasha, was also indicted but was acquitted by the jury).[65] At trial, selections from the reports were introduced into evidence. The information they contained described not only the movements and activities of suspected agents sent by Japan, but the activities and attitudes of Issei and Nisei community members. One report cited a *Rafu Shimpo* columnist as writing articles in "pro-Japanese and anti-American" fashion.[66] Another reported the interrogation of a Nisei woman who had a "suspicious" meeting with a white American sailor.[67] A third listed names and reported activities of several ethnic Japanese whom it described without elaboration as "suspected of being interested in intelligence work."[68] One dispatch, with unintentional irony, recounted keeping tabs on the loyalty of a Nisei dentist who was an officer in the U.S. Naval Reserve (USNR), in case his race-based exclusion caused him to be discontented. "After completion of his sea duty, he was attached to aviation unit of USNR, but because of his Japanese descent, it is evident, he is not being encouraged to consider his career with USNR."[69] A few reports discussed activities of the local JACL and an allied Nisei organization, the Far East Research Institute. The JACL was described, in somewhat melodramatic fashion, as rent by conflict between those who thought it should be primarily a social organization and those who favored civic action.

Taken together, the documents and the testimony surrounding them revealed massive official distrust of Issei and Nisei, even those engaged in harmless activities. The names of many ordinary Japanese Americans appeared on surveillance lists, although Salich himself insisted at trial that he had no idea whether any of the people he reported on were actually espionage agents. Their names were lumped together indiscriminately alongside those of imperial navy officers as "Japanese." The JACL was likewise infiltrated, despite the lack of evidence of disloyal activity.

Furthermore, while Salich described himself as believing in the loyalty of the Nisei, he characterized the Issei as "intensely patriotic to their emperor."[70] Gorin, by contrast, was quoted as saying that, like his Russian superiors, he trusted neither group: "He thought that the Japanese that were born here or in Japan were all pro-Japanese and that Americans were laboring under a delusion [in thinking] that the Japanese could be trusted . . . second generation or not."[71] Reports by other agents suggested that the more extreme view was widely held. One dispatch asserted that the Issei were ardently pro-Japan and were successful in influencing the Nisei to support Tokyo. "The Nisei, during grammar school and high school seem to like their surroundings and are contented to be with the Americans in this country. However, on entering college there is a gradual shift towards the issei ideas and quite a few definitely shift to a strong allegiance towards Japan."[72] A Nisei reporter observing the trial summarized the attitude of government officials uncovered by the trial: "Through cross-examination and detailed testimony it was revealed that the official Russian and American opinion is that Nisei are Japanese and, consequently, potentially dangerous."[73]

AMBIVALENCE AND SUPPORT FOR JAPAN

How much were these reports and estimates guided by reality, and how much by prejudice? On the one hand, there was certainly evidence supporting the case for concern over espionage by Japan. Japanese naval officials regularly visited Little Tokyo communities, which became havens for Japanese agents who were smuggled into the United States as language students. In 1936 an Imperial Navy commander, Toshio Miyazaki, was set up as an exchange student at Stanford University. Miyazaki recruited a white navy yeoman, Harry Thompson, who provided him with naval plans and documents. Thompson and John Farnsworth, a former naval officer, were subsequently convicted of espionage.[74] In the mid-1930s Itaru Tachibana, a Japanese Navy lieutenant commander, came to the United States as a language student. Tachibana constructed an espionage network in Southern California that was exposed in early 1941, with Tachibana being expelled from the country. One of those arrested was Toraichi Kono, a former valet to actor Charlie Chaplin, although he was not charged and was subsequently released.

Government officials and Naval Intelligence officers were also well aware that Tokyo engaged in infiltration of spies through its consulates. Takeo Yoshikawa, a Japanese agent who later confessed to providing the Japanese government with key photographs and information on the defenses at Pearl Harbor, was brought to Hawaii in 1937 as a consular official.[75] Richard Kotoshirodo, a Kibei who was employed by the Japanese consulate in Hawaii, later confessed to being duped by Japanese employees into assisting in gathering of information on American bases during 1941, activities that he was assured were not illegal. (It was clear to government investigators that Kotshirodo had no treasonable intent and was unaware of the seriousness of his actions, and they thus declined, even amid wartime conditions, to prosecute him.)[76]

Fears of Japanese espionage were lent additional plausibility by the close ties that the overseas Japanese communities, both in Hawaii and on the West Coast, maintained with Japan and its government during the 1930s. Japanese consulates remained important centers of community activity and economic life. Japanese-language newspapers featured news from Tokyo, of which a significant proportion came from official news agencies and the censored Japanese press. Visits by members of the imperial family attracted enthusiastic crowds, as did semiofficial publicity tours by Japanese movie stars and athletes. Businessmen and government leaders in Japan made particular efforts to build connections to the Issei and Nisei. Tokyo awarded medals to outstanding Issei, such as the Sacramento agriculturist and "Potato King" George Shima, and provided numerous scholarships and offered propaganda tours of Japan for Japanese Americans (as well as others). Also, beginning in the 1910s if not earlier, Tokyo employed Issei literati as propagandists, and their careers flourished under Japan's continued patronage.[77] Stanford professor Yamato Ichihashi, one of the first Asian American professors on the West Coast, occupied a chair that was secretly funded by the Japanese government. During the 1930s Ichihashi, who had previously served as a representative of Japan in international meetings, undertook a vigorous speech and letter campaign justifying the military's actions in China.[78] Similarly, writer/journalist Kiyoshi Karl Kawakami, who was employed by the official Domei news agency, was commissioned by the Foreign Ministry during the 1930s to lecture and draft newspaper articles in support of Japanese policy. Presumably with imperial government assistance, Kawakami published a set of books in English and in French lauding Japan's control of Manchuria and China. Japanese officials also used newspapers to spread their message. The New York-based *Japanese American Review*, an English-language newspaper founded in January 1939, regularly celebrated the glories of Japanese foreign policy and the achievements of Manchukuo. In any case, Japanese-owned businesses and their American subsidiaries took much of the advertising that financed the vernacular press.

Japanese efforts to woo the overseas communities reaped important dividends. For the balance of the 1930s, North American Japanese either supported Japan's military regime or remained silent. Masses of Japanese Americans cheered the invasion of China in 1937. In Los Angeles, local leaders raised a subscription to donate an airplane to the Japanese military for its fight.[79] Language-school students in Hawaii put together food packages to send to Japanese soldiers in Manchuria.[80] More frequently, West Coast Japanese American communities raised funds for Japanese war relief, a less controversial and more equivocal means of support. For example, a group of Nisei in Salt Lake City, led by Mike Masaoka, formed a Nisei Sincerity Society, which set as a goal the raising of a dollar from each Nisei of high school age or older to be sent to the Japanese Red Cross.[81] Antifascist writer/activist Ayako Ishigaki (Haru Matsui), a columnist for the *Rafu Shimpo*, deplored the widespread enthusiasm in Little Tokyo for Japan's war machine, which she attributed to the wounded pride of Japanese Americans isolated by prejudice.[82] (She might have also added the impact of endemic anti-Chinese prejudice among the Issei, some of which the Nisei absorbed.) There were some who had more pragmatic reasons for supporting the Japanese position. The calls for embargoes of Japanese goods by Chinese groups and their allies targeted overseas Japanese merchants and included boycotts of locally produced goods. The Issei merchant organizations, such as the Vancouver Jinkyoku Iinkai (Emergency Committee), that sprung up to combat the boycotts were thus fighting for their livelihoods, and not just over matters of international policy.[83]

Whether out of principle or opportunism, many West Coast Issei and Nisei journalists and community figures publicly defended the Japanese cause. In 1937 Editor Sei Fujii of *Kashu Mainichi*, an Issei, categorically denied stories of Japanese atrocities in Nanking and praised the "kindly . . . and friendly manner" in which all Japanese soldiers treated the Chinese.[84] At the same time, Togo Tanaka, Nisei editor of the *Rafu Shimpo*'s English section, called on the United States to recognize Manchukuo and blamed the Sino-Japanese War on Chinese provocation of a peace-loving Japan. A number of young Japanese Americans, notably Professor Kazuo Kawai of UCLA (who was born in Japan but was raised from boyhood in the United States and considered himself a Nisei) took the Japanese side in public debates with Chinese Americans and others. Reporter Kazumaro "Buddy" Uno, who traveled to China in 1937 and 1938 to cover the war, offered a series of pro-Japan lectures, sponsored by local chapters of the JACL, upon his return. As late as February 1940, Nisei columnist Tad Uyeno blamed the war on aggression by a pro-Communist Chinese government and praised Japan's "policy of peace in the Orient."[85] Seattle Nisei lawyer Kenji Ito, whose practice depended on business he obtained through the local Japanese consulate, was so vociferous in his speeches defending Japan at the end of the 1930s that after Pearl Harbor the U.S. government would prosecute him unsuccessfully as a suspected Japanese agent.[86] Indeed, so powerful was the trend of support and the community sanctions against dissent that antifascist intellectuals such as Larry Tajiri, English editor of the San Francisco *Nichi Bei*, rather than openly opposing Japan's policy in the vernacular press, counseled the Nisei to remain neutral and distance themselves from the Far East question.

The public position taken by Japanese American and Canadian communities on Japanese militarism must have encouraged intelligence agencies and government officials in North America to suspect their loyalty and to investigate their actions.[87] All this said, it is essential not to lose sight of the fact that these expressions occurred against a background of continuing and unstinting community fidelity to the United States and Canada. In particular, it was perfectly legal for Americans of all sorts to favor Japan over China during the 1930s, a time of peace between Japan and the United States, and many did so without compromising their allegiance to America, a notable example being African American activist W.E.B. DuBois. (Ironically, many of those who supported China against Japan during that period were later termed "premature antifascists" and investigated for Communist sympathies.) The support offered by Japanese North American communities for the Imperial Army's occupation of China during 1937–1940 certainly did not mean that they would assist the Japanese military against their own countries. In contrast, the vast majority, particularly Nisei, fiercely proclaimed their Americanism. As we shall see, they would grow increasingly vociferous as war loomed between the United States and Japan.

WAR IN EUROPE AND THE JAPANESE CANADIANS

Although Canada did not intervene officially against the Japanese occupation of China, public opposition to Tokyo and growing fears of global conflict became prominent parts of the Canadian political landscape. These served as a boon to racist groups such as the Native Sons and Daughters of British Columbia, who drew a parallel between Japanese militarism and the domestic threat, and to the opportunistic politicians who sought their support. Thomas Reid, MP for New Westminster, argued in the magazine *Saturday Night* in July 1937 that the twenty-two thousand Japanese Canadians were a menace to national security. Because of their high birthrate, Japanese Canadians were encroaching on the economic and political centers of power, but their racial inassimilability and their attachment to the Japanese emperor made them incapable of supporting Canada. Liberal Premier T. D. "Duff" Pattullo of British Columbia, responding to Conservative charges that illegal immigration of Japanese was causing a rise in the Japanese population of the province, wrote to Prime Minster King to propose that a commission be appointed to study the question and offered his personal recommendation that Japanese immigration be completely banned.[88] An investigatory committee soon found the charges of illicit entry to be baseless and blamed nativist forces for spreading stories of smuggling rings: "Unfortunately the situation in British Columbia is complicated by the circulation of rumours which have little proven substance but which are disseminated assiduously as records of fact."[89] On the basis of the report, King held firm against abolishing the remnant of the Gentleman's Agreement, but agitation continued. An outstanding demagogue, Vancouver City Council alderman Halford Wilson, called for the abolition of Japanese schools as a menace to state security and campaigned unsuccessfully to block commercial licenses for Japanese-owned shops in the city.

In September 1939 Germany invaded Poland and World War II began in Europe. As a sign of its independence, Canada waited one week after Great Britain and France declared war on Germany before following suit with its own declaration of war on September 10. The inevitability of Canadian involvement, however, was demonstrated by the declaration by Parliament on September 1 that the War Measures Act was in effect, and two days later that the Defense of Canada Regulations were in force. Under these provisions, the government claimed the power to ban political parties deemed subversive, censor the press, and intern any person deemed dangerous to public security. In the weeks that followed, 325 Canadian citizens and residents of German ancestry would be taken into custody. Once Italy declared war on the allies in June 1940, some 800 Italian Canadians would be rounded up en masse and interned.[90]

At the same time, hoping to appease opposition to the war (especially in Quebec, where French Canadians opposed intervention to support England), Prime Minister King pledged to limit Canada's direct involvement in combat and restricted Canada's military participation in Europe to a single division. King promised not to impose conscription for overseas duty—a promise whose withdrawal after 1942 would set off angry debates inside Canada. However, in August 1940 the government adopted the National Resources Mobilization Act, which provided for universal manhood conscription for home duty. (Despite the ban on overseas service, there was vocal opposition to the act, especially among French Canadians. Montreal mayor Camillien Houde, who publicly called for resistance to conscription, was arrested and interned at a camp in Petawawa, Ontario, thereby becoming a popular martyr of draft resistance.)

The onset of war and the issue of military service revived the controversy over voting rights for Nisei. Defenders of Japanese Canadians argued that if the Nisei were called upon to fight for their country, they should be allowed suffrage rights. The Vancouver City Council responded by asking the federal government for assurances that no soldiers of Asian ancestry would be granted suffrage rights. Premier Duff Pattullo wrote Ottawa demanding a ban on conscription of Japanese Canadians. In addition to fearing the effect on public opinion in British Columbia (and the Liberals' electoral chances) of arming Japanese Canadians, King himself felt it was illogical to offer military training to Japanese Canadians. After all, he told his cabinet, Canada might soon go to war against Japan, and their loyalty was suspect.[91] In the end, a new parliamentary advisory group, the Special (later Standing) Committee on Orientals in British Columbia, was formed. Its membership was all white, and prominently included local politicians. Their mission was to investigate whether the hostility toward the Japanese (and Chinese) population in British Columbia represented a danger to national security, to recommend ways to either reduce hostility or take precautionary measures against activities "prejudicial to civil security or national defense," and most importantly to advise on permitting Nisei military service.[92] The committee strongly opposed extending the draft to Nisei.

On January 8, 1941, following the committee's report, Ottawa officially announced the exemption of Japanese Canadians (including veterans), although not Chinese, from conscription. King was careful to state publicly that the decision to exclude Nisei did not reflect "mistrust of their patriotism" but the possibility of hostile reaction and anti-Japanese race riots in British Columbia.[93] Still, the official discrimination eloquently testified to the importance of West Coast public opinion in driving official policy in Canada. Even the liberal *Vancouver News-Herald* praised the military exemption and called for a ban on all Japanese immigration, although it deplored (with unconscious irony) scapegoating of Japanese residents: "We cannot send 20,000 people packing just because we do not like the color of their skins or their business methods or what their fellow Japanese do in China."[94] Nisei communities, despite strong expressions of resentment over the exclusion, turned to other methods to support the nation, including buying $42,000 worth of Victory bonds.[95] These proofs of loyalty failed to dent official mistrust. Rather, in March 1941, based on another recommendation of the Special Committee on Orientals, Ottawa imposed (or rather renewed) a registration requirement for all Japanese Canadians irrespective of citizenship (to avoid legal obstacles, registration by citizens was theoretically "voluntary"). The committee used the registration process to inquire into the loyalty of the ethnic Japanese community.[96] Following the process, each registrant was allotted special "Japanese" alien registration numbers.[97] Japanese nationals were required to report in monthly.

ROOSEVELT AND THE LEAD-UP TO WAR

In contrast to Canada's somewhat nominal participation among the Allies, the United States remained officially neutral on the war between 1939 and 1941, during most of which time public opinion remained sharply divided between the advocates of intervention and the different currents of the population who opposed it. Still, President Roosevelt and his advisors were actively concerned about the threat to world democracy and national security from both Germany and Japan. In the fall of 1939 Roosevelt pushed through Congress an amended Neutrality Act that permitted the United States to sell arms to nations at war on a "cash and carry" basis. Using a loophole in the law, the Americans sent airplanes to Canada and used the Dominion as a conduit to ship goods to Great Britain. In mid-1940, following the Nazi Blitzkrieg through Europe and the fall of France, the president reorganized his cabinet to include two internationalist Republicans, Secretary of War Henry Stimson and Secretary of the Navy Frank Knox. With Stimson's backing, Roosevelt arranged a special executive accord with Great Britain, then besieged by the threat of Nazi invasion, under which the Americans swapped fifty overage destroyers in exchange for leases on British bases in Newfoundland (then a separate British colony) and the Caribbean. Meanwhile, FDR proposed military conscription for service in the Western Hemisphere. Following the vote in Congress, in September 1940 Roosevelt signed the Selective Service Act—the first peacetime draft in American history. Unlike the Canadian government, the U.S. War Department opened conscription to Japanese Americans—a point that will be discussed further in chapter 5. After the November presidential election, in which Franklin Roosevelt won an unprecedented third term, the White House announced a plan of military and economic aid, dubbed Lend-Lease, to allow a bankrupt Great Britain (and, following the Nazi invasion on June 22, 1941, the Soviet Union) to carry on the burden of war. Following significant debate, Lend-Lease, too, was enacted by Congress in March 1941.

A secondary element of Roosevelt's wartime partnership with Great Britain was to strengthen Canadian-American military cooperation, which had been minimal throughout the interwar period.[98] FDR had already declared in a speech in Kingston, Ontario, in August 1938 that the United States "would not stand idly by" if Canada were ever invaded. In August 1940 he and Prime Minister Mackenzie King met officially at the Canadian-American border. The two released a joint statement, the Ogdensburg Agreement, in which they announced the creation of a Permanent Joint Board on Defense. Eight months later, following the enactment of Lend-Lease, the leaders of the two countries signed the Hyde Park Agreement, which cut Canada in on the Lend-Lease credits granted Great Britain and instituted a large-scale North American partnership in war production. Following these agreements, waves of Americans migrated to Canada to work on large-scale defense installations, notably the Alcan Highway linking the Alaska and the Canadian Northwest, where work would commence in the spring of 1942. Conversely, despite the pledges of cooperation there was little if any high-level coordination of policy, certainly where planning maneuvers was concerned.[99]

After the beginning of 1940, the United States took an increasingly hard line against Tokyo. In January the United States refused to renew the expiring 1911 Japanese-American Commercial Treaty, and in midyear the State Department instituted an embargo on export of strategic goods such as high-quality iron and steel in hopes of using economic pressure to squeeze Japan into renouncing its conquests. To demonstrate the power of American naval force, FDR ordered the Pacific fleet massed at Pearl Harbor, America's main forward base. Japan responded to the pressure by signing the Tripartite Pact with Germany and Italy in September 1940, allying itself definitively with the Axis and heightening American suspicions of the Japanese menace. Further American initiatives were hindered during the latter half of 1940 by the November election.

In February 1941 a new cabinet led by Prince Konoye, the emperor's brother, was formed. Konoye sent Admiral Kichisaburo Nomura to Washington in hopes of relaxing tensions. Although Roosevelt and his advisors placed scant trust in diplomacy to contain Japan, over the next several months Nomura and his associate Saburo Kurusu negotiated fruitlessly with U.S Secretary of State Cordell Hull in an atmosphere of growing mutual suspicion. In July, after Japan occupied French Indochina and threatened the rest of Southeast Asia, the United States cut off sales of high-octane gasoline for aviation, and through bureaucratic means soon halted all petroleum exports to Japan. Their goal was to use economic pressure to deter further Japanese aggression. It soon became clear that neither side was prepared to give up its position, and both prepared for the possibility of armed conflict. In November the Japanese presented the Roosevelt administration with their final proposal for a modus vivendi to avoid war. The Americans responded with an ultimatum of their own. Roosevelt and his military advisors, like many Americans, clearly understood that war was looming. The president had already polled his cabinet as to whether the American people would support the sending of an American fleet into Asia for a naval war with Japan, and Stimson had discussed the possibility of luring Japan into firing the first shot in such a conflict so as to justify American intervention. Nevertheless, fearing that an overt move would divide the country, the Roosevelt administration did not take definitive action, and it was Japan that set off open warfare with a devastating attack on Pearl Harbor on December 7, 1941.

THE MAGIC INTERCEPTS AND JAPANESE AMERICANS

As the United States drifted toward war with Japan, American concerns over Japanese espionage and counterintelligence efforts increased, especially since American military and civilian intelligence officials were aware of Japanese spying. An element of some (if indeterminate) importance in the American response to the Japanese threat was Operation MAGIC. In early 1941 American intelligence officers succeeded in breaking the secret diplomatic code used by Japan to communicate with its overseas officials. MAGIC was the code name given to the secret intercepts of those messages, which were made available to a small list of recipients, notably Secretary of War Henry Stimson and Army Chief of Staff General George Marshall. (President Roosevelt was on the list of recipients for a period but then was removed for several months after a copy of the intercepts was found in his oval office wastebasket.)[100]

Assertions about the value and interpretation of the MAGIC cables, and their impact on decision making, are difficult to assess, especially as against other sources of intelligence. The decrypts were raw data and not easily comprehensible—indeed, the army finally ceased distribution of MAGIC in early 1942 for that very reason—and it is not immediately clear which officials actually looked at them. What the cables did reveal were the assiduous efforts of the Japanese government, acting through consular officials and other agents, to recruit spies. To the extent that American political leaders and military officials automatically conflated Japanese Americans with agents of Tokyo, MAGIC and other counterintelligence products could have contributed to increasing hostility and mistrust toward Issei and Nisei among those who did have access to the information they contained.

That said, it would strain credulity to attribute further importance to MAGIC in regard to Japanese Americans. In recent years, several rightwing authors have claimed that the MAGIC intercepts demonstrate massive pro-Japanese espionage by Issei and Nisei in the prewar period and have relied on them to offer an ex post facto defense of the wartime confinement.[101] Still, even leaving aside the essential point that the West Coast military officers who would be chiefly responsible for the decision to remove Japanese Americans (as will be discussed in chapter 2) had no access to the MAGIC intercepts or the information contained within, an examination of the contents of the cables does not provide any serious case for implicating masses of Japanese Americans in espionage activities. Only a handful of the thousands of messages decrypted discuss overseas Japanese at all, and a portion of those come from Tokyo or Mexico City and refer to areas outside the United States. Those few cables that speak at all of the United States mention various efforts by agents from Japan to build espionage networks, but they project hopes or intentions rather than list concrete actions or results.[102] On January 30, 1941, a message from Japanese foreign minister Yosuke Matsuoka ordered Japanese consulates to increase their espionage efforts in the United States and authorized them to recruit "second generations." However, he advised against such recruitment, since Japanese Americans would be subjected to "considerable persecution" if their activities were discovered. He therefore suggested that "utilization of U.S. citizens of foreign extraction (other than Japanese), aliens (other than Japanese), communists, Negroes, labor union members, and anti-Semites, in carrying out the investigations . . . would undoubtedly bear the best results."[103] The most serious indication of activity among Issei and Nisei was a memo from the Los Angeles consulate to Tokyo from May 1941, detailing the various actions of the consulate. Within the accounting, the cable stated, "We shall maintain connection with our second generations who are at present in the U.S. Army." From the language, the cable appears to speak of continuing efforts to recruit agents. (In the words of one analyst, the main phrase sounds like a bureaucrat's report justifying inactivity rather than a picture of success).[104] Similarly, the Los Angeles consulate reported some months later that it was doing all it could to recruit agents; that it would "maintain connections" with the Japanese associations and with Nisei in the army; and that it had made connections with Nisei in aircraft plants. Again, the cable did not state that any individuals had actually *been* recruited as agents, still less that they were actively giving information. On the contrary, the consulate made clear, once again, that it was concentrating on white people and Negroes and admitted that it could not "trust completely" the Japanese Americans.[105] There was indeed some cause for suspicion of Japanese Americans by Tokyo. As was revealed in postwar years, Ichiro Ted Miwa, a California Nisei, and his wife Edna traveled to Japan in mid-1941 in an unsuccessful effort to meet up with underground resistance agents and work against the militarist government.[106]

In sum, not only do the MAGIC intercepts not provide any specific information about any Japanese American spying, they tend to discredit the possibility. The essential fact is that all nineteen people who were arrested during World War II for being agents of Japan (of whom eleven were convicted) were white Americans. The same pattern of generalized propositions against specific refutations operates on the larger level of Japanese American loyalty. As historian John Stephan has demonstrated, Imperial Army staffers, with assistance from a few Japanese Americans, planned the invasion and occupation of Hawaii, sincerely believing that they would be actively welcomed by the local Japanese population.[107] However, the basis for this belief is unknown, and its reliability is not susceptible to evaluation. Conversely, Takeo Yoshikawa, the chief Japanese intelligence agent in Hawaii, who was in a position to observe directly, stated flatly that local Japanese Americans were not involved in any pro-

Japanese activity. "They had done nothing. . . . You see, I couldn't trust them in Hawaii to help me. They were loyal to the United States."[108]

PREWAR FEARS FOR SECURITY AND PREPARATIONS FOR CONCENTRATION CAMPS

Despite the lack of documented threat, during the eighteen months before Pearl Harbor the administration stepped up contingency planning for war with Japan, including curbs on Japanese Americans considered dangerous. After the outbreak of World War II in Europe, the U.S. government enormously increased its efforts to coordinate counterintelligence. In September 1939 Roosevelt ordered the Army G-2 division and the Office of Naval Intelligence (ONI) to coordinate efforts with the Federal Bureau of Investigation to keep tabs on Japanese Americans, especially on the Pacific Coast. The ONI was given responsibility for collecting information on Japanese American communities, while the FBI followed individual subversives.[109] In 1940 FDR transferred the Immigration and Naturalization Service from the Labor Department to the Justice Department to increase security and signed the Smith Act, which required registration by all aliens. In early 1941 the army's existing list of enemy alien "suspects" to be arrested and confined in case of war was united with lists compiled by the ONI and the FBI. The result was a master list of suspects maintained by the Justice Department, known as the "ABC list" (because individuals were assigned grades of A for "immediately dangerous," B for "potentially dangerous," or C for "possible Japan sympathizer"). Although the lists were confined to Issei (plus German and Italian aliens), their presence was primarily based on their positions—community leader, Buddhist or Shinto priest, etc.—rather than any notion of their individual sentiments or actions. The government took other action to target the Issei. Following persistent (if unfounded) reports of espionage by agents in fishing boats around military areas in Hawaii, in May 1941 officials of the Customs Service arrested eighty fishermen (mostly Issei, with a few Nisei) on charges of false registration and seized their boats.[110] In October 1941 the FBI launched a midnight raid on the Central Japanese Association, an Issei group linked with the Japanese consulate.

Authorities in Hawaii also tightened their grip. Army policy makers formulated detailed plans for martial law and total civilian control in case of war.[111] One widespread topic of discussion among both military and civilian officials was preparing the forced evacuation and detention of the entire local Japanese population on an outlying island, such as the famous "leper island" of Molokai.[112] Meanwhile, naval commander Admiral Husband Kimmel ordered the airplanes based near Pearl Harbor to be bunched close together on the ground in order to guard them more easily against sabotage by Issei and Nisei. Despite the lack of evidence that such sabotage was likely, and the fact that bunching the planes made them easy targets for aerial bombardment, Kimmel considered the "local Japanese" the chief danger to security. With the support of the army and navy, the Hawaii Defense Act, a bill to grant broad powers to the governor in case of war, consistent with minimum safeguards for constitutional rights, was introduced into the territorial assembly during the spring of 1941. It grew entangled in partisan conflict and was killed.[113] Hoping to avert martial law, on September 15, 1941, Governor John Poindexter called the Hawaii legislature into special session in order to enact legislation for operations in case of war. General Short told legislators that such legislation would limit or prevent the need for martial law. As a result, the Hawaii Defense Act was passed into law in October.[114] Nevertheless, on November 4 Secretary of War Henry Stimson asked Congress to grant President Roosevelt emergency powers to declare martial law in Hawaii and Puerto Rico to prevent subversive activities. He pointed primarily to the threat posed by the forty thousand enemy aliens, mostly Japanese, residing in Hawaii.[115]

In tandem with its war plans, the executive branch prepared a network of camps designed for mass confinement of aliens. As early as October 1940, the Navy Department submitted to the president a list of potential steps to be taken to demonstrate the seriousness of American preparations for war, including plans for concentration camps.[116] Although the president told the navy not to proceed further without his approval, rumors of the existence of such facilities were soon widespread.[117] In October 1941 Brigadier General Irving J. Phillipson, commander of the Second Corps Area, publicly announced the completion at Camp Upton, New York, of a concentration camp for the "safeguarding of such aliens as the war department may deem it necessary to hold." The camp, built over the training area where the first draftees had been housed a year earlier, was designed to house seven hundred people. It consisted of a stockade and enclosure surrounded by barbed wire and guard posts with searchlights.

In his interview, Phillipson strongly implied that commanders of other corps areas were building their own camps.[118] In fact, the Immigration

and Naturalization Service (INS) had already built detention centers at
Fort Lincoln, North Dakota, and Fort Stanton, New Mexico, where some
seven hundred German sailors who could not be deported were interned.
Another thousand aliens, mostly Italian, were confined in Fort Missoula,
Montana.[119] The Justice Department publicly affirmed in November that
it was holding several hundred people accused of sabotage.[120] A few days
later, Attorney General Francis Biddle acknowledged that the department
had over two thousand German and Italian nationals in custody and was
tripling the number of spaces in internment camps as war dangers became more serious.[121]

At the same time, the *Los Angeles Times* reported, Attorney General
Biddle officially confirmed that the government had plans to intern "dangerous" Japanese aliens promptly if the U.S. and Japan should sever relations, and he added that what he referred to as concentration camps had
been built to hold Japanese aliens. The article continued: "The government has plans for segregation of Nipponese alien groups for a 'temporary period' if relations between the United States and Japan are broken
off. It was indicated that this might include government protection of
the Japanese area here, numbering about 150,000 Japanese, by the Army
and Navy."[122] It is not clear what this "protection" might consist of, nor
whether the Justice Department or the *Times* was responsible for conflating Issei and Nisei (who together made up barely 110,000 people on the
West Coast) as "Japanese."

Certainly, the attorney general, despite his proud reputation as a civil
libertarian, sought to extend government control over aliens. In late
November Biddle testified on behalf of H.R. 3, popularly known as the
"Hobbs Concentration Camp Bill," a measure introduced earlier that
year to provide for summary confinement for up to six months in a concentration camp or detention center of any alien who was deemed deportable by an immigration inspector or a three-person panel but who
could not be deported, and for unlimited detention of "criminal aliens."
The bill was extremely broad and severe. It provided for unlimited detention without hearing or due process of any alien who "at any time . . .
shall act, or have acted, in the United States . . . on behalf of any foreign government or foreign political party or group," among which it explicitly named the Communist Party of the USA, the German American
Bund, and the Kyffhaeuser Bund.[123] Biddle (following the policy set by
his predecessor, Robert Jackson) supported the bill, despite protests by
labor unions and civil liberties groups, insisting he simply wished to hold

deportable aliens who could not be expelled in the war emergency. Yet Representative Sam Hobbs of Alabama, the bill's sponsor, warned that aliens "pollute, degrade, and poison our body politic."[124] In any case, Opponents, such as Representative Thomas Eliot of Massachusetts, responded that the bill targeted aliens based only on their political or economic views, and would lead to creation of concentration camps similar to those of the Nazis. It was narrowly defeated in Congress a few weeks before Pearl Harbor, though as much through opposition by conservative Republicans who decried the expanded bureaucracy the bill would have created as from liberals concerned over civil liberties.[125] Its high-level sponsorship and broad support strongly suggested a strong official presumption of disloyalty among aliens.

JAPANESE AMERICANS ON THE SPOT

So far from supporting Japan, as war grew closer the Nisei rushed to demonstrate their American patriotism. After the beginning of 1940, the Nisei press and the JACL rapidly abandoned their support for Tokyo's occupation of China and adopted a neutral or hostile attitude toward Japan.[126] The Los Angeles Nisei Week festival, formerly a showcase of Japanese-American biculturalism, now became an American patriotic festival.[127] Groups such as the JACL pushed ever harder for renunciation of Japanese citizenship by Nisei and raised funds for the American Red Cross. Officers of the JACL, notably Fred Tayama, Ken Matsumoto, and Tokie Slocum, became (not very) confidential informants for the ONI. After Selective Service was instituted in mid-1940, several thousand Nisei men on Hawaii and the West Coast were inducted into the army and served honorably. Their dedicated service helped persuade liberals of the loyalty of Japanese Americans.[128]

Some Japanese Americans did seek the protection of influential allies. In March 1941 Gongoro Nakamura, an Issei legal counselor and president of the Central California Japanese Association, wrote the Department of Justice to ask whether Issei would be sent to concentration camps in case of war. Lemuel Schofield, special assistant to the attorney general, replied that law-abiding Japanese citizens would be treated as residents and not enemy aliens in case of war, and that no arbitrary confinement of any person could be upheld under the Fourteenth Amendment.[129] Sufficient

doubt remained over the future, however, that in October 1941 Nakamura, along with Nisei journalist Togo Tanaka, traveled to Washington
to request an official statement on the Issei from the Justice Department.
Attorney General Biddle affirmed that law-abiding Issei would not be
harmed (the Nisei, being citizens, presumed they had ample constitutional protections and did not ask seriously about government attitudes
toward *themselves* in case of war). Tanaka and Nakamura tried unsuccessfully to see the president as well. However, they did secure a meeting
with Eleanor Roosevelt, the activist First Lady, who made an immediate
public statement praising the loyalty of both Issei and Nisei.

In Hawaii, local Japanese leaders likewise pushed for demonstrations
of loyalty, such as expatriation, and reached out to allies. As a spur to
denationalization, Fred Makino proposed in the *Hawaii Hochi* that dual
citizens be prohibited from public employment in the territory.[130] Some
fifty thousand local Nisei, proclaiming their sole allegiance to the United
States and seeking to facilitate the elimination of dual citizenship, signed
a petition asking the U.S. State Department to use its influence to sim-
plify the expatriation process.

The local Japanese also joined with prominent non-Japanese allies
to protect the community in case of war. Hawaii's congressional delegate, Samuel Wilder King, was an influential champion of the Nisei in
Washington. "Frankly, my sympathies are with these young Americans.
Their record in this Territory is as high, or higher, than that of any of
the recent immigrant groups of the mainland. . . . They take their citizenship seriously, and they accept their obligations and duties as citizens
conscientiously."[131] In April 1941 King carried the denationalization petition to Washington and presented it to Secretary of the Interior Harold
Ickes, whose department was responsible for overseeing the territory.[132]
Charles E. Hemenway, a liberal businessman and University of Hawaii
trustee and a scion of the plantation oligarchy, convened a race relations
advisory group that brought together members of various racial groups
with local FBI chief Robert Shivers and military intelligence officers to
maximize morale and security.[133] Nisei school administrator Shigeo Yoshida (who had gained public notice during testimony at the 1937 congressional hearings on statehood by alleging that he would find it easier
to face the Japanese enemy in war than to stand up under the endless
suspicion and criticism the Nisei faced) became a central member of the
group.[134]

Both in Hawaii and the mainland, the dominant tone among Nisei writers and newspaper columnists (as well as some Issei) was a sense that Japanese Americans were "on the spot." In mid-1941 editor James Omura of the San Francisco–based Nisei monthly *Current Life* stated, "WE ARE AT WAR." Reminding readers of the "inhuman persecution" of German Americans during the First World War, he added that the same "can and will happen to us Nisei Americans unless we take cognizance of the future now." Omura recommended Nisei political and social organization into such bodies as the Japanese American Citizens League, strenuous efforts to gain the goodwill of the surrounding community, and lying low to avoid potential violence: "We are all under suspicion. We are all being observed, whether by our neighbors or by federal agents. We should act accordingly. We know we have nothing to conceal, but this does not preclude the fact that people living around us may not know it. And we cannot produce convincing enough evidence to acquit ourselves of suspicion. Our course, then, is to remain inconspicuous."[135]

A sympathetic observer, sociologist Forrest La Violette, argued in similar terms, asserting that the growing war climate between Japan and the United States was forcing Japanese Americans to choose sides more clearly, a process that could have positive results for clarifying the marginal position the Nisei held in both American and Japanese communities. "This means that individuals are now more fully committed to being Americans. It means a more definite incorporation into the American social system. American national sentiments are for the time being superior to family sentiments which may have their roots in Japan." However, La Violette was prophetic on the dangers that still loomed in case of war: "Rumors have it that the *Nisei* would be the first to be sent to the front; others say they will be sent to concentration camps. One *nisei* told the writer that he was fattening himself up for the 'long lean days behind barb [*sic*] wire.'"[136]

As if to confirm La Violette's words, the war crisis also heightened popular xenophobia and rumor-mongering. Throughout the 1930s, West Coast tabloids and popular magazines had spread improbable tales of Japanese American spies and saboteurs, especially in connection with Japanese activities in Mexico and Latin America. In 1938–39, *Ken* magazine (apparently using material obtained through naval intelligence files) published a series of articles by John Spivak accusing fishermen in Little Tokyo of massive spying at the Panama Canal.[137] Syndicated columnist Sutherland Denlinger stated, "No informed person would deny that Japanese espionage constitutes a real problem in Hawaii." While many of the spies disguised as fishermen were "Japanese," he insisted that some were Nisei: "This second generation Japanese of American birth is not always . . . the indoctrinated citizen of the United States of happy fancy."[138] *Liberty* magazine (repeating past charges that had already been discredited) ran a series of articles that purported to cite naval intelligence officers as affirming that 250 Japanese torpedo boats had been camouflaged as fishing boats. In a 1940 article, author Jerry D. Lewis claimed that once war broke out between Japan and the United States, these boats would emerge, cripple all American warships, destroy portside gasoline supplies, and burn harbors.[139]

In the tense atmosphere during 1940 and 1941, nativists and headline hunters circulated further unfounded stories of Japanese American disloyalty, whipping up hysteria against Japanese communities. Lail Kane of the California American Legion, which sponsored bills to bar Issei from being granted fishing licenses, told Nisei, "If we ever have war with Japan and I have anything to do with it, the first thing I'll do will be to intern every one of you."[140] The celebrated evangelist Sister Aimee Semple McPherson called for the government to get rid of all Issei truck farmers because "they could poison crops in time of a war."[141] A former FBI agent, Blayney F. Matthews, charged that Issei truck farmers sprayed their crops with arsenic to poison them, and the story spread even after FBI inquiries demonstrated that the charges were fabricated.[142] Another story spread that a Kibei soldier in San Diego had bragged that he would fight for Japan if war broke out and that all Nisei soldiers were then rounded up. The story spread widely despite immediate and authoritative denials.[143] Perhaps the most fertile developer of anti-Japanese propaganda was a Korean nationalist, Kilsoo Haan of the Sino-Korean People's League, who accused Japanese Americans of organizing subversion and aid for Tokyo through the Black Dragon Society.[144]

Various officials joined the anti-Japanese American wave. In October 1940 California Republican Richard J. Welch recommended that all "Japanese fishermen and their families" be relocated away from Terminal Island and other army and navy facilities because they were "nonassimilable."[145] In January 1941, using information in part provided by Kilsoo Haan, Iowa Senator Guy Gillette repeatedly alleged, despite indignant denials by Tokyo, that Japan was conscripting Japanese American dual citizens, including fifty thousand military-age Nisei in Hawaii.[146] In the summer of 1941 Representative Martin Dies of Texas, chair of the

House Un-American Activities Committee, seized the national spotlight by announcing that he would convene a set of hearings on espionage and subversive activities of Japanese on the West Coast. On July 31 Dies publicly stated that he had acquired massive evidence of subversion by Japanese naval officers, who he alleged were meeting with Japanese American fishermen at Terminal Island. Fishing craft, he charged, were being transformed into torpedo boats, which sailed out into international waters for drill practice. Dies threatened to hold public hearings unless the Justice Department promptly arrested all concerned, adding that he favored a preventive roundup of all "Japanese seamen" in the United States to protect against subversion.[147] After FBI chief J. Edgar Hoover noted that Dies's public statements did not match his private ones and cast doubt on his information, the Justice Department refused to take any action.[148] His bluff called, Dies announced in September that he had turned over his information to the White House and had suspended his hearings at the request of the president and of Secretary of State Cordell Hull.[149] In August 1941, after Tokyo refused to permit 100 U.S. nationals to leave Japan, Representative John Dingell, Democrat of Michigan, urged that 10,000 Japanese aliens in Hawaii be confined as hostages until Japan released the Americans. Conflating Issei and Nisei populations, Dingell added that the government could then use the territory's remaining 150,000 Japanese aliens as a reserve hostage force pending Japan's next move.[150]

The unjust targeting of Japanese Americans as disloyal by white nativists was clear to a number of outside observers. Magner White of *The Saturday Evening Post*, who conducted interviews with over 100 Nisei over two months in mid-1939, concluded that they were loyal Americans.[151] In October 1940 *Life* deplored discrimination against the Nisei, who wore their citizenship with pride. "Their U.S. citizenship and patriotic loyalties mean little to race conscious Americans. Their color imposes a barrier which few of them ever manage to transcend."[152] Independent journalists Jim Marshall and Ernest Hauser reached similar conclusions.[153]

KENNETH RINGLE AND THE MUNSON REPORT

In response to their justified concern over Japanese espionage, fortified by the rumors of Japanese American disloyalty, government and army officials continued to investigate Japanese Americans, despite a mountain of reliable evidence that the actual threat they represented, particularly the Nisei, was greatly exaggerated. In November 1940 the FBI's Honolulu branch (which had been closed in 1931 and only reactivated shortly before) reported that, outside of a small "esoteric" (and easily identifiable) group of consular officials and Japanese schoolteachers, most of whom had been in Hawaii for only a short time, the long-resident local Japanese community was Americanized in culture and ideas and largely loyal to the United States.[154]

In March 1941 ONI intelligence officer Kenneth Ringle led a daring midnight raid on the Japanese consulate in Los Angeles and discovered detailed information on Japanese spy networks. His findings allowed the American government to break up the Tachibana spy ring. Drawing on the information he recovered and on his close familiarity with the status of Japanese espionage efforts, Ringle would repeatedly advise his superiors over the following months that Japanese American communities were loyal—that, indeed, Japanese agents were suspicious of Nisei as "cultural traitors" not to be trusted—and did not pose a security threat as a whole.[155]

Perhaps the most significant government project to investigate the loyalty of West Coast Issei and Nisei came in the shape of the Munson report. In early 1941 President Roosevelt, dissatisfied with the intelligence he was receiving from all official agencies, commissioned the writer/journalist John Franklin Carter to organize an unofficial political intelligence unit, which was paid through undisclosed White House funds. In the fall of 1941 Roosevelt commissioned Carter to investigate secretly the Japanese American communities on the West Coast and Hawaii and assess their loyalty. Carter selected Curtis B. Munson, who had previously impressed Roosevelt by his investigative report on the political situation in Martinique, to pursue an undercover investigation. (Carter simultaneously dispatched other agents to report on Japanese activities in Texas and Mexico). Munson visited the West Coast, adopting the guise of a State Department official. Although he was not a professional investigator, his inquiry was lent credibility by the assistance and records he received from the FBI and ONI, and the testimony of the numerous Japanese Americans he interviewed.

Munson rapidly reached the conclusion, as he put it, that "there is no Japanese Problem." While there might be the odd fanatic who might commit sabotage, he told Roosevelt, the majority of Issei were actively or passively loyal to the United States and would eagerly take U.S. citizenship if it were permitted them. The Nisei (apart from the Kibei) he estimated at 90–98 percent loyal, and he added, "They are pathetically eager to show this loyalty." Munson concluded that the greatest danger to security lay in violence against Japanese Americans rather than in disloyal action by them. He and his assistant Warren Irwin urged that the government take immediate steps to enlist the loyalty of the Nisei through supportive public statements by political leaders, and by assuring Issei and Nisei that they would not be put into concentration camps in the event of war.[156] Munson visited Honolulu immediately after leaving the West Coast, and during the first week of December he reported in a summary memorandum that the attitude of the Japanese Americans there was substantially identical to that on the West Coast. Although FDR was willing to consider provisions for protecting "loyal Japanese" from attacks in case of war, he dismissed Munson's conclusions about their loyalty as "nothing much new" and did not order the surveillance relaxed.

CONCLUSION

In sum, the fears of Japanese American disloyalty before December 7, 1941, while not entirely without foundation, were based overwhelmingly on bias. Government and military officials were legitimately concerned about Tokyo's direction of espionage activities. It is difficult not to sympathize with the frustration of those entrusted with national defense over the limits of their sources in regard to Japanese activities, and the task of determining the authenticity and reliability of information amid the myriad invented tales of subversion launched by race-baiting journalists, agitators, and unscrupulous government officials. Nevertheless, political leaders and intelligence officials acted on the basis of unexamined race-based assumptions about Japanese Americans. They failed to make any real distinction between agents infiltrated from Japan, who were clearly loyal to Tokyo, and the mass of American citizens and long-term residents of Japanese ancestry who were expending considerable effort to demonstrate their loyalty to the United States. Instead, officials in Washington approved extensive surveillance of Issei and Nisei and prepared mass actions against them, including concentration camps and protective custody. The government considered Japanese Americans inherently dangerous and did not relax these control efforts even in the face of evidence regarding their lack of involvement in subversion. Ethnic Japanese communities did, in fact, have a record of attachment to Japan and support for Japanese policy in Asia, particularly in its aggression in China. However, there were not and have never been any documented cases of sabotage or spying by any West Coast Japanese Americans (or, with the inconsiderable exception of Kotoshirodo, any in Hawaii). In fact, when the United States occupied Japan after the end of World War II and Americans working in the occupation read through Japanese documents from before the war, they were unable to discover any evidence from such documents that remained that the Japanese Americans helped Japan. Although twenty people were charged and convicted with performing espionage for Japan before the war, none was a Japanese American.

Tetsuden Kashima has argued that in the prewar period the government engaged in such widespread preparations for internment that a bureaucratic momentum was created and would have resulted in mass confinement no matter how war eventually came.[157] This may overstate the case somewhat, as neither mass confinement of the entire group nor mass occupation of Japanese neighborhoods, both of which were discussed in the prewar period, actually occurred once war was declared. Still, if the government's and military's well-developed plans for the establishment of concentration camps and internment of Japanese aliens do not add up to their subsequent policy of mass confinement of all Japanese Americans, neither can it be said, based on such evidence, that their actions after Pearl Harbor were simply in reaction to the surprise bombing, without precedent or forethought. On the contrary, the prewar hysteria created a climate of suspicion and hostility that made arbitrary action logical (and politically expedient) afterwards.

Similarly, white Californians and British Columbians, following a long tradition of anti-Japanese racism, contributed to the torrent of negative opinion that overwhelmed Issei and Nisei. Newspaper articles and politicians continued to describe all ethnic Japanese residents, whatever their background and citizenship, as a monolithic whole that could be assumed on racial grounds to offer primary loyalty to Tokyo. Reliable evidence to the contrary offered by objective reporters was effectively ignored. Well before the onset of the Pacific War, nativists and publicity seekers manufactured widespread and demonstrably false stories of Japanese American fifth columnists. These stories left government officials prepared—even overprepared—to believe the worst, and expect the worst, of Issei and

Nisei after Pearl Harbor. If the Japanese bombing in Hawaii lent greater plausibility to stories of subversion spread by West Coast whites, it also rationalized pre-existing and reflexive suspicions born of prejudice, which existed independent of any fact. It was these suspicions that led the Canadian government, even without evidence of subversion, to close its armed forces to Nisei in January 1941. The reactions of West Coast whites would be similarly decisive in settling the fate of the Issei and Nisei in both countries during 1942.

[2] THE DECISION TO REMOVE ETHNIC JAPANESE FROM THE WEST COAST

PEARL HARBOR AND ITS AFTERMATH

On the morning of December 7, 1941, Japanese naval and air forces executed a mass bombing raid on the United States Naval Station at Pearl Harbor, chief base of the navy's Pacific fleet, and on other American military bases on the island of Oahu. The attack, launched without warning, devastated the fleet; Japanese planes sunk or damaged eight battleships and ten lesser ships. The raid was also costly in human life. According to official statistics, 2,390 American soldiers and civilians were killed in the bombing, and 1,178 more were wounded. Japanese bombers subsequently launched a similarly devastating bombardment of the fortifications of the American colony of the Philippines.

A curious, if minor, incident occurred after one Japanese plane crash-landed on the remote (and privately owned) Hawaiian island of Niihau. Although none of the island's residents had been informed of the attack on Pearl Harbor, they took the pilot, Airman 1st Class Shigenori Nishikaichi, into custody. Nishikaichi persuaded a local Nisei, Yoshio Harada, who was new to the island, to help him recover his papers. After terrorizing the island's residents, the two were cornered by local resident Ben Kanahele, even as a relief force headed by a local Nisei, Jack Mizuha, prepared to relieve the beleaguered island. Kanahele shot Nishikaichi, and Harada committed suicide.[1]

The government's pre-existing, exaggerated fears of Japanese Americans played an important role in amplifying the disaster at Pearl Harbor and its aftermath. As mentioned, the airplanes based at Hickam Field had been bunched close together on the ground in order to guard them more easily against the danger of sabotage by local Issei and Nisei. Japanese bombs caught the American planes on the ground during the first wave of attacks and swiftly put over 250 of them out of commission, thereby crippling any American defense of the naval base.[2]

Almost as soon as the Japanese bombing occurred, Governor Poindexter invoked the provisions of the Hawaii Defense Act to put the Islands on a war footing. The same day, General Walter Short visited Poindexter and warned of the urgent menace of sabotage by local Japanese. He insisted that unless the governor granted full powers to the army, he would not be responsible for guaranteeing Hawaii's safety, and then he threatened to take such power unilaterally. Poindexter, unable to reach Interior Secretary Ickes and assured by Short of the president's accord, was pressured to sign a martial law proclamation, prepared by the army, that "during . . . the emergency and until danger of invasion is removed" gave the commander not only all powers of the governor but also those exercised by the judiciary and "employees of the territory." Under its authority, Short declared himself "military governor" and proceeded to assume all legislative, executive, and judicial powers. Roosevelt quickly signaled his consent to the imposition of martial law and the suspension of habeas corpus (but was silent on Short's actions in seizing power).[3]

The Pearl Harbor attack had an immediate impact on Japanese American communities. Dozens of Japanese American civilians in Hawaii were killed or wounded by stray bombs.[4] Nisei soldiers rushed to their posts during the attack to fire at the enemy, while Japanese American Red Cross workers helped care for the wounded. A telephone summons to male Nisei graduates of the University of Hawaii who had gone through required ROTC courses led to the immediate organization of a militia unit, the Hawaii Territorial Guard. Meanwhile, on the mainland, Japanese American organizations and individuals nationwide publicly expressed outrage over the attack and wrote or wired to offer the government their full support. "We in our hearts know we are Americans—loyal to America. We must prove that to all of you," declared the JACL in a telegram to the White House.[5] The organization immediately formed an Anti-Axis Committee to determine ways to support the war effort. Dozens of Nisei rushed to join the United States Army, but the War Department froze enlistments by Japanese Americans, and almost all of the recruits were refused.

Starting just hours after the attack, FBI agents began arresting Japanese (as well as German and Italian) nationals on the West Coast and Hawaii, using the ABC lists the Justice Department had prepared early in 1941. The individuals rounded up were selected on the basis of their status as community leaders or their membership in organizations the government deemed suspect, rather than on the basis of their individual records. Within a few days some 1,300 ethnic Japanese (including a small number of Nisei) were taken into custody. In Hawaii, where most arrestees were concentrated, an internment camp was established by the Department of Justice at Sand Island, a former quarantine station.[6] Issei arrested on the mainland were held in immigration stations on the West Coast, then transferred to the newly built concentration camp at Fort Missoula in Montana. By February 1942 approximately 2,300 Issei had been arrested, of whom 1,291 were West Coast residents. In many cases these Issei were held incommunicado, and weeks passed before their families were allowed to learn anything about their whereabouts or communicate with them.[7] The removal of these leaders paralyzed Japanese American community structures and hindered the formation of a coherent collective response to later events.

ENEMY ALIENS

Although it had been clear to many people both in and out of the government by early December 1941 that the United States and Japan were on the brink of war, the destruction at Pearl Harbor united Americans in shock and anger. It also put an end to the long dispute between isolationists and interventionists over American military action. On December 8, 1941, President Roosevelt asked Congress for a declaration of war against Japan, and a resolution swiftly passed both houses with only a single dissenting vote (by pacifist congresswoman Jeannette Rankin).

Once war was declared, all Issei (minus the handful of World War I veterans naturalized after 1935) throughout the United States immediately became enemy aliens—as did German and Italian nationals, although those countries did not declare war on the United States until a few days afterward. They were subjected to a special curfew, forbidden to travel more than five miles from home without permission, and ordered to turn in short-wave radios, cameras, and other contraband. On the West Coast, Issei fishing boats were ordered grounded, and produce markets were temporarily closed (allegedly to deter sales of poisoned vegetables). Japanese consulates and press agencies closed, and the Japanese-language press was shut down. The three Japanese newspapers outside the West Coast—the *Utah Nippo*, *Colorado Times*, and *Rockii Nippo*—were permitted to resume publishing after the new year, within strict government-imposed limits. They were required to publish government bulletins in their entirety and were not supposed to publish Japanese-language articles without an English translation. The Treasury Department froze the bank accounts of all Japanese aliens, and it was only after the personal intervention of First Lady Eleanor Roosevelt (who flew to the West Coast immediately after Pearl Harbor to inspect conditions and met with Nisei groups to show her trust in them) that the restrictions were eased sufficiently to allow Issei to withdraw one hundred dollars per month for living expenses. Meanwhile, the FBI undertook a series of warrantless (and doubtless illegal) raids on Japanese American households, during which they searched the possessions of both aliens and citizens for contraband. They struck fear into Japanese American families, who rushed to destroy or bury their heirloom Japanese swords, archery bows, dolls, and pottery, out of fear of being incriminated. Frightened Issei and Nisei also destroyed countless books, family letters, private papers, and business records.

Despite the enormous uncertainty that Japanese Americans on the West Coast felt in the days after Pearl Harbor, the immediate public reaction to them was impressively restrained. The predominant attitude among West Coast whites may have been summed up in the editorial that appeared in the *Los Angeles Times* on December 10, "Let's Not Get Rattled." A number of West Coast speakers and editorialists reminded their audience that the Nisei were loyal American citizens and entitled to protection. John Boettiger, the president's son-in-law, wrote in the *Seattle Post-Intelligencer*, "Many of the Japanese in America are as loyal as any white Americans, and it would serve only evil purposes to cause them to suffer. Those few Japanese who will side with the mother-country must be ferreted out so that they can do no harm, and it is our thought that the loyal Japanese-Americans themselves will be the first to help in this connection."[8] Nevertheless, Nisei children were targeted for harassment at school (despite the efforts of sympathetic school principals and others to shield them), and there were a few reported acts of racial violence against individual Japanese Americans. A large mob in Seattle descended on the city's Japantown on December 8, allegedly checking for blackout violations, and broke a number of store windows before being dispersed by local police.[9]

Official attitudes toward Issei and Nisei were also mixed. On December 9 President Roosevelt dispatched Secretary of the Navy Frank Knox to tour Pearl Harbor. Upon his return, Knox, anxious to divert responsibility for the disaster from the navy, stated at a press conference in Los Angeles, "I think the most effective Fifth Column work of the entire war was done in Hawaii with the exception of Norway."[10] Knox's high position and presumed firsthand information lent his public comments authority.[11] In his official report to the president, Knox repeated his accusations of espionage by fifth-columnists and further falsely accused local Japanese of misleading defenders at Pearl Harbor by deliberately broadcasting confusing and contradictory rumors regarding the positions of the attackers.[12] Meanwhile, Secretary of the Treasury Henry Morgenthau proposed to Attorney General Biddle and FBI Director J. Edgar Hoover that large groups of Japanese aliens be removed from strategic coastal areas.[13] The matter came to a head at a cabinet meeting on December 19. Knox repeated his stories of Japanese subversion and advocated removing Japanese aliens from the island of Oahu. His charges were rebutted by reports from Hawaiian commander General Walter Short and FBI director Hoover. No immediate action was taken, but the matter had clearly not been fully resolved.[14]

Meanwhile, FDR's agents John Franklin Carter and Curtis Munson joined forces with Kenneth Ringle to propose to the president a plan for control of Japanese Americans. The plan, reflecting Munson's inquiries on the West Coast and Hawaii, called for taking *investigated* Nisei of confirmed loyalty (Ringle undoubtedly had the JACL in mind) and entrusting them, under close supervision by government handlers, with control of the property and safety of Japanese aliens. Although Roosevelt expressed support for the plan to its authors, he made no effort over the following weeks to push its application, nor did he respond to these advisors' urgent request that he make a public statement on behalf of the loyalty of Japanese Americans. The plan ultimately died of neglect. The silence from the White House about Japanese American loyalty, especially when set against Knox's public statements about sabotage, played a large role in stigmatizing Japanese Americans in the public mind.[15]

CANADA AFTER PEARL HARBOR

The Japanese attack on Pearl Harbor also threw the Canadian government into action. Though Canada was already at war with Germany and the Dominion's own territory had not been touched, there was widespread shock and anger at Japan, and fear of Japanese incursions in the

Pacific. As early as July 1941 officials in Ottawa had scheduled a confidential meeting, during which they had produced various proposals for measures to be taken in the event that war broke out with Japan.[16] On December 8 Canada declared war in Japan, following which the federal government proceeded to implement portions of the plan. An official decree ordered all fishing boats owned by Japanese nationals immobilized and conveyed to an impound yard. The Nisei secretary of a local Japanese fisherman's group later vividly described his meeting with the local naval commander the day after the attack. The commander greeted him with the frank comment, "Mr. Suzuki, we were caught with our pants down,' and then proceeded to outline procedures for the seizure of fishing boats, adding, "We expect your full cooperation."[17] Meanwhile, the Canadian government decreed that all Japanese nationals, plus those Issei naturalized after 1922, were "on parole" and proceeded to issue them special parole cards and numbers.[18] Although there was no Canadian equivalent of the mass arrests and raids on Issei homes by the FBI in Hawaii and on the U.S. Pacific Coast, thirty-eight Japanese aliens considered dangerous, including judo instructors, language school teachers, a school principal, a banker, and a barber, were rounded up by the authorities and later sent to Camp Petawawa, a prisoner-of-war camp in Ontario.[19] The Royal Canadian Mounted Police used the threat of further arrests to pressure all Japanese-language newspapers and Japanese schools on the West Coast to "voluntarily" close their doors.

As in the United States, authorities declared cameras and shortwave radios contraband over the following days and established a dusk-to-dawn curfew for enemy aliens. Like their American counterparts, Issei in British Columbia began destroying Japanese books and paraphernalia that might appear compromising. (These similarities, it is important to note, were almost exclusively the product of coincidence rather than of planned bilateral action).[20] On December 16 a new order-in-council made registration of all people of Japanese ancestry compulsory. While the measure had little practical effect, since the vast majority of Nisei had "voluntarily" registered eleven months before, it was the first occasion in which Ottawa officially placed all people of Japanese ancestry, on racial grounds, in the category of enemy aliens.

With the United States now in the war, Canada's military and civilian leaders spoke about the need to coordinate their policies with those of the Americans (as well as those of Great Britain). However, while the previously established joint boards continued to meet, and representatives of both countries expressed the hope that they could maintain unity of action, it was clear from the beginning that the United States had no serious intention of tying its hands by offering its neighbor more than a minimum of consultation, still less relying on Canada to design policies in defense matters for the Americans to follow. Conversely, in its policy on ethnic Japanese (as elsewhere), while Canadians did make an effort to take note of American policies, Canadian leaders from Prime Minister King downward also continued their longstanding habit of making use of American policies and the need to keep in lockstep with them, less as a guide to action than as an expedient justification for it (or sometimes for inaction) when it suited them.

As in the United States, the situation remained generally calm for West Coast Japanese Canadians in the days following the outbreak of war, although there was scattered vandalism of shops in Vancouver's Powell Street Japantown, and Nisei children faced some harassment at school. The *Vancouver Sun* urged calm and reminded its readers that Japanese Canadians were loyal and had nothing to do with the attack.[21] However, following Frank Knox's allegations of Japanese American fifth-column activities in Hawaii, the paper adopted a harsher line, and on December 16 it ran an editorial, "Should British Columbia's Japanese People Be Interned?" Its answer was that the fate of Japanese Canadians rested with their own conduct: the *Sun* recommended mass internment at the least sign of sabotage or fifth-column activity. It might be noted that *Vancouver Sun* journalist Bruce Hutchison warned Jack Pickersgill, Prime Minister Mackenzie King's assistant, of the calls for mass internment within ten days after Pearl Harbor: "We are under extraordinary pressure from our readers to advocate a pogrom of Japs."[22] In fact, numerous British Columbia whites sent letters to local newspapers urging internment of all ethnic Japanese, irrespective of citizenship.[23]

MILITARY GOVERNMENT IN HAWAII AND JAPANESE AMERICANS

On December 17, ten days after the outbreak of war, a new commander, General Delos Emmons, arrived in Hawaii and assumed the post of military governor. Under Emmons, martial law continued in force, and the U.S. Constitution was considered suspended. Military authorities issued a series of 181 general orders, which overturned existing territorial law and regulated all aspects of civilian life, including curfews, setting of wages and of prices for vegetables and other consumer goods, rationing of gasoline and other scarce commodities, and censorship of mail. Military authorities forbade any speech or action critical of the government. The regulations were generally applied in a race-neutral fashion. Nevertheless, it was widely understood that they existed in large part to control the local Japanese, and some measures particularly targeted the Japanese population. For instance, Japanese schools were shuttered by official decree, and the buildings seized. The two chief Japanese-language newspapers, the *Hawaii Hochi* and the *Nippu Jiji*, were closed for four weeks. Entry to the West Loch area of Pearl Harbor was limited for those of Japanese ancestry. Farmers who lived in the vicinity were ordered away from their residences and forbidden to retrieve furniture or belongings, although they were permitted to enter the area to work their farms during daylight hours. Fifteen hundred residents were ordered out of Honolulu's Iwilei district overnight.[24]

Local Japanese were soon faced with more stringent official discrimination. In the days following his arrival, General Emmons ordered the Nisei of the newly organized Hawaiian Territorial Guard forces armed, using scarce munitions at hand, and mobilized to maintain public safety and protect military bases. Nisei troops secured the defenses of the Islands with efficiency. However, pressure arose both in Hawaii and the mainland for disarming Japanese Americans. On January 21, 1942, Emmons ordered the 317 Nisei serving in the Territorial Guard discharged without warning. In a further sign of mistrust, Emmons created a Businessman's Military Training Corps made up of haole (whites) and native Hawaiians, who were charged with watching the local Japanese.[25] Even harsher moves would soon be proposed.

THE INTERNATIONAL CAMPAIGN AGAINST JAPANESE

Hawaii and the western shores of the United States and Canada were not the only regions of the Pacific Rim (as it would later be termed) where ethnic Japanese communities were scrutinized and their status debated after Pearl Harbor. The governments of the five Central American republics, anxious to win the favor of Washington, rapidly declared war against Japan following the attack. Costa Rica's president swiftly declared war on Japan on December 7 in order to issue a decree providing for the immediate arrest and confinement of all Japanese in the country. Nicaragua swiftly incarcerated both of its Japanese residents.[26] The first nation to undertake large-scale confinement of Japanese was Australia. Although Australia had declared war on Germany in 1939, the government had followed a selective internment program for aliens, and no more than a few hundred of the thousands of German aliens in Australia were rounded up (in addition, a group of some 2,500 German and Austrian refugees, many of them Jews fleeing persecution, who had previously been confined in Great Britain were transferred to Australia for custody). By contrast, within a short period after Pearl Harbor, police authorities took into custody 1,141 men, women, and children of Japanese ancestry, some 97 percent of Australia's total ethnic Japanese population. These prisoners were housed at a previously constructed center, the Loveday camp, in South Australia.[27] At the same time, in the French colony of New Caledonia, the ethnic Japanese settler population (which then numbered approximately 1,500, down from perhaps 5,000 in the prewar years) was confined by official order in the wake of Pearl Harbor. In the days that followed the outbreak of war in the Pacific, the colonial government gave orders for several hundred ethnic Japanese to be removed from the countryside and concentrated in a prison camp in Nouméa. On December 19, 1941, some 300 men were taken from Nouméa, locked in a wooden cage, transported by boat to Sydney, Australia, and sent on from there to the Hay internment camp in New South Wales. A few weeks later, a second shipment of equivalent size of ethnic Japanese arrived in Sydney, and its residents were also sent to Hay. A third voyage was then prepared after the boat returned to New Caledonia. This shipment included prisoners to be sent to Loveday, as well as family groups, who would be confined in a family camp in Tatura, Victoria.[28] All these civilians would remain confined under guard throughout the war and were then deported to Japan afterward.

THE WESTERN DEFENSE COMMAND

The relative calm that reigned on the West Coast in the immediate aftermath of Pearl Harbor soon wore off. During the weeks that passed, the Japanese military swept through Southeast Asia and the western Pacific, and Japanese troops invaded the Philippines. Although Japan occupied the Aleutian islands of Attu and Kiska in June 1942 and planned an invasion of Hawaii before the Japanese Navy was crushed and turned back at the Battle of Midway, responsible military authorities universally discounted the possibility of a Japanese invasion of the West Coast. Nevertheless, the Japanese victories triggered fears among the leaders of the Western Defense Command, based at the Presidio in San Francisco, that a Japanese invasion might be forthcoming and led them to seek emergency powers to deal with Japanese Americans.

The central figure in the process was Commanding General John L. DeWitt, a career officer with a mediocre record. In the days after Pearl Harbor, DeWitt focused his attention on the specter of a Japanese invasion of the West Coast. In his anxiety over threats to security (and no doubt his eagerness to avoid the fate of Hawaiian commanders General Short and Admiral Kimmel, whose careers had been ruined by the Pearl Harbor attack), DeWitt failed to distinguish between fact and supposition. On December 10 a supposed Treasury official, who proved to be a disgruntled former FBI agent, informed army authorities that twenty thousand Japanese Americans in San Francisco were planning a mass uprising. DeWitt and his staff worked out evacuation plans for the city, even after the fraud was discovered the following day. In mid-December DeWitt reported as truth stories that a squadron of Japanese planes had passed over Los Angeles, and that suspicious fires in Washington State had been set as signals. These reports were rapidly discredited by navy investigators, who discovered that the planes in question were American, and that the suspicious flames were a farmer's brush fires.

From the beginning, DeWitt seems to have harbored suspicions against all Japanese Americans, regardless of citizenship. He refused to meet with Curtis Munson and Kenneth Ringle to implement their plans for Nisei control of Japanese American communities, even after they received President Roosevelt's encouragement to proceed. DeWitt also lent credence to the wild and unfounded rumors that continued to circulate about Japanese Americans. In particular, he informed his superiors that Japanese submarines were receiving radio signals from Japanese American houses ashore, even after the FBI cast doubt on such claims (the Federal Communications Commission examined the charges, and it reported in early January that they were totally unfounded). DeWitt told Justice Department officials in early January 1942 that he did not trust either Issei or Nisei. He was careful nonetheless to confine his recommendations at first to control of Japanese (and German and Italian) aliens. The reason for this may have been that he feared the economic dislocation that mass removal would cause.[29] On December 17, 1941, the general suggested that a hundred-mile strip extending from the Pacific Coast inland be designated a military area, and that the army remove those people inside whom it considered a risk to security. Two days later DeWitt issued an official recommendation requesting his War Department superiors to grant him authority to round up all Japanese aliens over fourteen years old and move them to internment camps inland to keep them from siding with the enemy. However, when a delegation led by the Los Angeles Chamber of Commerce visited him at Christmas 1941 to request the removal of all Japanese Americans in the city, regardless of citizenship, DeWitt demurred. As he explained to army provost marshal General Allen W. Gullion, whom he considered an important ally, he considered mass removal of ninety-three thousand West Coast Nisei to be too large a job for the army to handle, and one that would alienate loyal individuals. In any case, he added, the army had no constitutional right to make such a move: "an American citizen is an American citizen."[30]

Gullion expressed his sympathy with DeWitt's plight. His own main goal was to secure military control over defense areas from interference by civilian authorities. He feared that the army would not be able to defend the coast effectively without a proclamation of martial law, as in Hawaii, or at least unchallenged authority for detention of any civilian suspects. As a result, Gullion suggested that DeWitt work through the provost marshal general's office, and he dispatched his deputy, Captain Karl Robin Bendetsen (aka Bendetson), to San Francisco to meet with him. Bendetsen, a West Coast–born and bred military lawyer, was an ambitious and unscrupulous careerist.[31] Whether out of opportunism or genuine belief, he took the initiative in pushing for mass removal of all Japanese Americans from the West Coast. Bendetsen soon persuaded General DeWitt to demand increased authority over civilians from the attorney general, and he drafted a memo to the president proposing that the Justice Department's Alien Enemy Control Division be turned over to the army.

THE STRUGGLE BETWEEN THE MILITARY AND THE JUSTICE DEPARTMENT

DeWitt's and Bendetsen's desire for control pitted them against Attorney General Francis Biddle. Biddle was proud of his reputation as a civil libertarian and was anxious to avoid a repeat of the harassment that had plagued German Americans during World War I. He had taken steps to protect law-abiding aliens, including making public statements opposing unlimited detention of enemy aliens and denouncing employers who discharged alien workers as "stupid and un-American."[32] Biddle did not believe that mass removal of Japanese aliens was necessary, and he resisted taking arbitrary action against American citizens. However, in hopes of establishing a climate of cooperation and reducing military fears, he agreed to have General DeWitt designate military zones around army bases, defense factories, and other areas from which all enemy aliens would be excluded, and to declare all such areas as off-limits to aliens. Biddle further agreed to have the FBI undertake selected further warrantless raids of alien homes and businesses as an alternative to mass raids. Although these were described as raids on aliens, and the FBI did not visit homes where no alien resided, the searches also clearly involved property of citizens and were thus of dubious constitutionality. Although Biddle subsequently admitted that the government had discovered nothing in the course of those raids that it could not have uncovered by other means, West Coast newspapers stoked public outrage with sensational details of the arrests.

In the first week of January 1942, Biddle sent his assistant James Rowe to California to meet with DeWitt and Bendetsen. DeWitt did not mention the control of Nisei to Rowe, and he deprecated the necessity for wholesale removal of Issei as well. On the contrary, he expressed willingness to work together with the Justice Department and Navy Department on drawing up a list of military areas. Yet DeWitt failed to submit the first list of proposed military areas until January 21, despite his urging that the situation was urgent (part of the trouble was dealing with the navy's demand that American citizens who could not show "actual severance of allegiance with Japan" be excluded as well).[33] When the list of proposed military areas was finally presented to Biddle, the attorney general was astounded. He noted that the proposed area was enormous, including the entire cities of Seattle and Tacoma, and far too broad—most of the enemy aliens who would be removed from them were not Japanese. Biddle concluded that unless a specific military rationale for such wholesale exclusion could be furnished, the Justice Department would not and could not undertake such an operation. If the army insisted on carrying out evacuation, he informed DeWitt, it would have to declare martial law and handle the operation itself. Biddle clearly assumed that the army would be unwilling or unable to undertake such drastic action.

DeWitt refused to attempt to find such a rationale—a task he clearly recognized was impossible. Instead, he regarded Biddle as going back on his word to create whatever defense areas the general selected, and he complained to his War Department superiors about Justice Department delay and uncooperativeness. More legitimately, he expressed concern over the problems that a selective operation would cause, whether in excluding Issei spouses in mixed couples or in dealing with and caring for the children of excluded aliens. Meanwhile, despite the findings of the FCC, the general, egged on by Bendetsen, continued to issue warnings about alleged shoreline signaling of Japanese submarines, which he asserted were responsible for attacks on all American ships leaving coastal ports.[34] These accusations were clearly groundless: while German submarines on the East Coast engaged in large-scale sinking of American ships—during 1942 ships in the Atlantic were sunk faster than they could be built—there were only a handful of attacks by Japanese submarines on shipping anywhere near the West Coast, and the SS *Montebello* on December 23, 1941, was the only sinking.[35] By the time of the army commanders' warnings, no Japanese vessels had been even sighted in the region for a month, as they had reason to know. Indeed, shortly afterward, the *New York Times* publicly cited a Japanese communiqué—a source unlikely to minimize Japanese successes—which claimed that since the outbreak of war the entire Japanese Navy had sunk a total of sixty-five allied ships, including fifteen in the area of Hawaii, and none around the Pacific Coast.[36] Stimson nevertheless passed the charges of submarine attacks on to Biddle with a request for immediate action. Meanwhile, Bendetsen returned to Washington. He and Gullion concentrated on gaining support from Assistant Secretary of War John J. McCloy, an able and well-connected figure who was the right-hand man of aged Secretary of War Henry Stimson.

POPULAR MOVEMENTS AGAINST JAPANESE AMERICANS

Even as the debate went on among military officials over appropriate action, the West Coast remained calm, and there were no episodes of mass hysteria or anti-Japanese incidents of any importance. Nevertheless, the wild rumors and tales of Japanese-American treachery that had been launched over the months before Pearl Harbor were given new life, and greater credibility, by the attack.[37] Numerous Californians expressed genuine, if irrational, anxiety that Japanese raids on the U.S. mainland would be forthcoming.[38] In this climate, an outcry arose among circles of West Coast whites for the expulsion from the West Coast of all Japanese Americans, irrespective of citizenship. The center of agitation was California, which dwarfed its neighbors in size and wealth, and housed the largest interest groups. There nativist and commercial associations, eager to dispose of the long-despised Japanese American population, take over their fertile lands, and eliminate the economic competition they represented, stepped in to encourage and take advantage of popular insecurity. As one official of the Joint Immigration Committee put it, "This is our time to get things done that we have been trying to get done for a quarter of a century."[39] On December 22, 1941, as noted, the Los Angeles Chamber of Commerce petitioned General DeWitt for the "evacuation" of all persons of Japanese ancestry from the city. Soon after, the California American Legion called for the imprisonment of all Japanese "dual citizens" in concentration camps, and the California Joint Immigration Committee and Native Sons and Daughters of the Golden West passed resolutions favoring removal of all Japanese Americans from the state. Another center of agitation was the members of white agricultural groups, who resented the domination of the fresh-produce market by ethnic Japanese growers and middlemen. Groups such as the Western Growers Protective Association, the California Farm Bureau, and the White American Nurserymen of Los Angeles lobbied for expulsion of Japanese farmers and promised that there would be no loss to farm production if the Japanese Americans were expelled.[40] A representative of an allied group, the Grower Shipper Vegetable Association, publicly admitted the roots of the position taken by the white groups: "We're charged with wanting to get rid of the Japs for selfish reasons. We might as well be honest. We do. It's a question of whether the white man lives on the Pacific Coast or the brown man."[41]

Meanwhile, beginning in mid-January 1942, West Coast newspapers and magazines, especially the historically anti-Asian "yellow press" organs of the Hearst and McClatchy chains, began running sensational stories of FBI raids on "Japanese" homes and businesses that turned up dynamite, poisons, and ammunition (the stories did not mention that these were standard equipment for West Coast farmers). The well-known columnist Damon Runyon alleged falsely that Japanese sympathizers with radio transmitters had been uncovered. Popular actor Leo Carillo published an open letter in which he referred to West Coast Japanese Americans a menace and called for their mass removal inland to preserve "the safety of the people."[42] Inspired by the tabloids (whose clippings they sometimes enclosed), letter writers, first on the West Coast and then elsewhere, began sending messages to the White House and War Department urging mass control of the "sneaky" and "treacherous" Japanese in order to avoid a "second Pearl Harbor." Several correspondents also complained of the expensive cars and prosperous farms and shops owned by the Japanese Americans. The racial hatred and economic jealousy that lay behind these letters was reflected in their language and recommendations.[43]

Spurred by their own fears and by the popular hostility toward Japanese Americans, West Coast political leaders began to lobby for action. On January 15 (a week after the California legislature considered and tabled a resolution calling for mass evacuation) Los Angeles Mayor Fletcher Bowron met in Washington, D.C., with Biddle. Bowron proclaimed his readiness to be guided by the FBI but expressed concern over the potential dangers posed by enemy aliens and by Nisei civil servants and called for a coordinated propaganda campaign to maintain the loyalty of the Nisei. In his presentation to the government, Bowron shared with the Justice Department his principal sources, a set of confidential reports by his assistants Alfred Cohn and Orville Caldwell, both of whom drew on undocumented and absurd information provided by House Un-American Activities Committee investigator James Stedman.[44] Cohn (a onetime screenwriter turned Los Angeles police commissioner) described Japanese Americans as racially "unassimilable" and inherently loyal to Japan and repeated wild charges that Japanese American fishing fleets were run by officers of the Japanese Navy. Caldwell echoed the accusations that Nisei were dual citizens and passed on charges that Japanese spies had infiltrated the Central Avenue District by buying up pool halls and restaurants (all of which, he claimed, had been suspiciously closed the night before Pearl Harbor) and were using sales of marijuana as a means of spreading antiwhite propaganda and race hatred among Negroes and Mexicans. The same day, the mayor met with Commander Edward Hayes and Lieutenant Commander Robert Thayer, special assistants to Navy Secretary Knox. Bowron stressed to the officers that the Nisei represented "the most serious problem we have to face" since, although they enjoyed American citizenship, "[t]heir first loyalty may be and in many cases probably is to the Mikado."[45] In a follow-up letter, in which he revealed the private disdain for the FBI that he had concealed from Biddle, Bowron urged the navy to take action against both Issei and Nisei "for the accomplishment of many things" that the Justice Department refused to undertake.[46]

On January 16, 1942, Representative Leland Ford, a Republican in a tough campaign for reelection (which he ultimately lost) in a district that included many white farmers, sent an open letter to FBI Director Hoover,

Secretary of War Henry L. Stimson, and Navy Secretary Knox, urging that all those of Japanese ancestry, whether citizens or not, be removed from the coast and placed in camps. He followed it up with a similar speech in Congress four days later. Ford produced no evidence to support claims of a threat. Instead, he insisted that it was up to Issei and Nisei to prove that they were truly patriotic by agreeing to be confined—if they did not do this, their refusal demonstrated their doubtful loyalty and proved that they should be incarcerated nevertheless. This placed Japanese Americans in a classic no-win situation in terms of resisting arbitrary confinement.[47] Although Biddle replied that the Justice Department had matters under control, and that there was no way of forcibly resettling American citizens except by suspending the writ of habeas corpus, Ford (on the initiative of the Los Angeles Chamber of Commerce) joined with other West Coast congressmen to form a bipartisan ad hoc committee on the "Japanese problem," chaired by Representative Clarence Lea, dean of the California delegation.

THE CRISIS IN CANADA

While in the United States the calls for mass action against ethnic Japanese issued from both the military and interest groups, in British Columbia it was a cabal of elite politicians and lobbyists who took the leading role. Profiting from the terror caused by Japan's victories in Asia and the Pacific (notably the Japanese Army's conquest of Hong Kong during Christmas of 1941, which resulted in the imprisonment of two thousand Canadian soldiers sent to defend the British colony), and widespread insecurity over the inadequate state of Canada's Pacific defenses, they campaigned for removal or confinement of Japanese Canadians from the coastal regions. In late December 1941 British Columbia's new Liberal premier John Hart and his Conservative attorney general R. T. Maitland publicly demanded that the federal government "remove the menace of Fifth Column activity from B.C."[48] The Pacific Coast Security League, formed by Vancouver city alderman and anti-Japanese extremist Halford Wilson, criticized the government's handling of enemy aliens and called for drastic military action to protect the coast. The Canadian Legion, which had a long record of hostility to Japanese in the Canadian West, planned a series of demonstrations to demand internment of Japanese Canadians as protection against subversion. Despite the lack of military necessity, Major General R. O. Alexander, commanding officer of the Pacific Command, who sympathized with anti-Japanese Canadian forces, pointed to the threat of violent demonstrations and to the selected letters in the press urging confinement of all ethnic Japanese as a pretext for imposing mass internment. In a message to the General Staff he stated, "Public feeling is becoming very insistent, especially in Vancouver, that local Japanese should be either interned or removed from the coast."[49]

Meanwhile, the local members of the Standing Committee on Orientals in British Columbia, which had previously advised against military service for Japanese Canadians, took up their own pressure tactics in favor of mass removal. On December 20, 1941, the chair of the committee, F. J. Hume, mayor of the town of New Westminster (and future mayor of Vancouver), warned Prime Minister King that public opinion was inflamed against the local Japanese by the military successes of Tokyo and added that any small incident could catalyze racial conflict. Two weeks later, on January 3, 1942, the majority of the committee publicly advised the Department of External Affairs in Ottawa that they favored the internment of all male Japanese nationals of military age, both to avoid racial conflict and to preserve national security. Meanwhile, several members of Parliament from British Columbia from both major parties warned their federal government colleagues that national security would be endangered if they did not move immediately against Japanese Canadians. At the annual meeting of the British Columbia Conservative Association in early January, Howard Green, a local MP, predicted a Japanese invasion of offshore Canadian islands. A resolution urging removal of Japanese Canadians was voted by acclamation. For the moment, the pressure failed to register elsewhere. The correspondent for *La Presse* referred to "The Japanese, whose loyalty to Canada is not placed in doubt, except in isolated cases." An editorial in the Toronto *Globe and M ail* praised the Dominion government for its mix of vigilance and "civilised tolerance" in not interfering wholesale with Japanese Canadians in British Columbia.[50]

Still, the anti-Japanese pressure from the West Coast was sufficiently strong that the cabinet ordered an inquiry into policy and invited the Standing Committee on Orientals to consult. On January 8–9, 1942, a meeting on Japanese Affairs took place in Ottawa between the Standing Committee and a group of cabinet members, army officials, provincial B.C. police, and RMCP authorities. (No Japanese Canadians, of course, were invited or consulted for their views). The cabinet members hoped to find a resolution to the twin dangers of sabotage and racial conflict. Many of those present were surprised by the Standing Committee's presentation. Hugh Keenleyside, representing the Department of External Affairs, expressed great skepticism. Keenleyside, a veteran diplomat who had served several years in the Canadian legation in Tokyo, argued that there was no good reason to undertake mass internment and that such a policy would contravene the principles of humanity for which the Allies were at war. The military chiefs present agreed. Major General Maurice Pope, vice-chief of the General Staff, stated pointedly, "from the army point of view I cannot see that they [Japanese Canadians] constitute the slightest menace to national security." The navy's representative, a resident of British Columbia, added that he believed that government confiscation of Japanese-owned fishing boats had eliminated any potential menace.[51] Both questioned seriously how a group of unarmed civilians could possibly jeopardize national defense. The RCMP delegate chimed in that those few Japanese Canadians considered potentially subversive had already been interned, and no further action was required. The British Columbia representatives steadfastly refused to accept official assurances that their anxiety was unfounded. Their openly racist attitudes shocked the federal government representatives—General Pope was revolted when a Pacific Coast politician told him privately that his constituents considered war with Japan a heaven-sent excuse to eliminate Japanese Canadian economic competition.[52] The conferees agreed to reinforce coastal defenses, suspend fishing licenses for Japanese Canadians, and establish a work corps to send volunteers away from the coast, but the conference bitterly divided on the matter of forcible removal. The majority opposed the idea and even suggested that Nisei be permitted to enlist in the army to show their loyalty (a proposal rejected by the government), but the British Columbians held fast to it.[53]

It was then that Ian Mackenzie, who had chaired the meetings, was charged with presenting a conference report to the cabinet. It was a fateful turn of events. Mackenzie, a Scotland-born graduate of Edinburgh University and Canadian officer in the First World War, had been elected to Parliament from British Columbia in 1930. Over his years as an MP, he had served in a number of cabinet posts, notably minister of immigration and national defense, and had established a close relationship with his colleagues and Prime Minister King. Although he had been relegated to the minor cabinet position of minister of pensions, as the only B.C. member of the cabinet he enjoyed unchallenged status as an advisor on Pacific

Coast affairs. His deep-seated racial hostility toward Japanese, combined with a keen interest in survival within British Columbia politics, had led him to take an extreme position against the rights of Japanese Canadians during the 1930s. Now he carefully constructed a summary of the meeting and recommendation that misrepresented the positions of both sides, repeated the demands of Alexander and local Canadian legion allies for mass confinement, and presented the removal of Japanese nationals to "work camps" in the interior as a reasonable and humane alternative to internment. General Pope submitted a memorandum repeating his insistence that there was no legitimate security threat. He noted that U.S. FBI director J. Edgar Hoover had expressed confidence that Japanese Americans had not engaged in subversion and were behaving appropriately. Mackenzie responded by validating the security fears of Alexander and his Canadian Legion allies.[54]

Mackenzie's report was submitted to Prime Minister W. L. Mackenzie King. In addition to ever-present military questions, about which he was generally ill-informed, King was beset during the period by anxieties over the political issue of instituting military conscription for overseas service, which his advisors supported as a boost to inadequate enlistments for war postings but which was bitterly opposed by Quebec. He was also occupied with vain attempts to keep informed on the strategy conferences taking place in Washington between Prime Minister Winston Churchill and President Roosevelt. In the face of these greater concerns, King had limited interest in the problem of Japanese Canadians in British Columbia, and no wish to expend political capital defending them. Rather—like many in the government—he seems to have viewed his duty as finding ways to appease West Coast public opinion without provoking Japan to taking reprisals against Canadians in its custody. He was prepared to go along with Mackenzie's recommendations, which appeared to him to represent a moderate middle course.

King had the text of an order crafted over the weekend of January 11–12. Finding it "rather badly prepared and not too well drafted," he then set to work himself to design his provisions and consulted Norman Robertson, chief advisor of the Office of External Affairs, on the best balance to take between internal security and the needs of diplomacy.[55] The measure was approved by the cabinet on January 14, 1942, and made public two days later. Issued under authority of the War Measures Act, its provisions included the long-term grounding of Japanese Canadian fishing boats and a ban on fishing by any person of Japanese ancestry, the imposition of restrictions on purchase of explosives or gasoline by Japanese nationals, and the establishment of a Civilian Corps of Japanese Canadians to provide employment for able-bodied Japanese men. Somewhat hidden in the announcement was a section providing for the creation by the RCMP of "protected zones," with limits to be determined, from which all such Japanese men were to be forcibly removed. Even as it silently decreed the summary expulsion of some 1,500 – 4,000 Canadian residents from their homes, the government rhetorically reaffirmed its interest in just treatment of persons of Japanese ancestry and called on Canadians to adopt a reasonable attitude and not participate in arbitrary action that might trigger reprisals from Tokyo.[56]

Although the moving out of men to the camps did not actually begin until the end of February, the January 14 announcement was hailed in British Columbia. Rather than seeing it as a final measure, many whites considered it a positive intermediate step toward the ultimate goal of total removal of ethnic Japanese. The reaction of Japanese Canadians was shock, mixed with outrage. Seen from the point of view of those affected, the government's policy seemed not moderate, but punitive. Although the government refused to state where those who "volunteered" for the Civilian Corps would be sent or what work they would perform, it was generally accepted that heads of families and their adult Nisei sons would be placed in road labor camps in isolated wilderness, with extreme weather conditions. Families were offered no assurance that they would be able to communicate with, much less see, their husbands and fathers, sons and brothers. Whether as an unintended consequence of the disorder of the hasty announcement, or consciously to ensure that Japanese Canadians unemployed after Pearl Harbor would be forced to accept employment elsewhere, the government failed to offer compensation or welfare assistance to wives and dependents to make up for the loss of family breadwinners. Those who remained were plagued by worry over how they would be able to make ends meet.[57]

The callous policy of breaking up families and the government's failure to consult those affected cost it considerable goodwill among Japanese Canadians, who had little in the way of means and no incentive to assist.[58] The *New Canadian*, the organ of Canadian Nisei, had been initially receptive to the idea of a work corps as a solution for war-related Nisei unemployment, but its leaders were skeptical of what amounted to a forced labor scheme and demanded details of the program, which were not forthcoming, before offering any endorsement.[59] Many Japanese Canadians no doubt sensed the handwriting on the wall. During February 1942, with encouragement from the *New Canadian*, families of agricultural laborers began to leave British Columbia for the sugar beet fields of Alberta and Saskatchewan, or for domestic service jobs in Toronto. Such migration was impossible for most of the region's ethnic Japanese, who had children or family members in ill health or lacked funds for the journey.[60]

THE ROBERTS COMMISSION REPORT AND ITS AFTERMATH

Canada's outright expulsion of adult Japanese males from the Coast went beyond what was being discussed in the United States. Although representatives of the United States and Canada had expressed at various moments the intention (or pious hope) of coordinating policy, there is no evidence that Canadian authorities consulted their southern neighbors on it. Surprisingly, in view of the dramatic change of policy, the announcement received almost no attention in the United States, from either the government or the press.[61] It is not clear why the Canadian government's mass removal of enemy aliens seemed insufficiently noteworthy to attract attention south of the border—beyond the tendency of Americans not to pay great attention to Canadian affairs.

Instead, while Leland Ford's lobbying for mass removal of all Japanese Americans had attracted attention in Washington, the turning point in popular opinion regarding Japanese Americans and security was reached on January 24, 1942, with the public release of the Roberts Commission report. This commission, chaired by Supreme Court Justice Owen Roberts and composed of military offers friendly to the executive branch, had been appointed in December 1941 to inquire into the Pearl Harbor disaster and report on military errors that made it possible (the commission's mandate was carefully drawn to avoid questioning the responsibility of the White House). The final report was devoted chiefly to analyzing failures of communication and coordination within the government. The role of espionage in making the attack possible was not a major concern of the committee members in assembling their report. In one section, the report briefly mentioned the role of Japanese spies in providing information to Tokyo and stated that the consulate in Honolulu was the center of recruitment: "Some [spies] were Japanese consular agents and others were persons having no open relations with the Japanese foreign service."

This reference was exceedingly ambiguous: it could well have referred to Caucasians—the Hawaiian counterparts of Harry Thompson and John Farnsworth, who, as previously noted, were convicted of spying for Japan in 1937—or to the agents sent directly from Japan as "language students." Furthermore, the FBI and military investigators universally agreed that there had been no cases of sabotage by any Japanese American during the Pearl Harbor attack, or any cases of sabotage on the West Coast in the month that followed. Nevertheless, in the overheated and panicked atmosphere of January 1942, anti-Japanese American militants immediately seized on this single vague comment as definitive proof of the untrustworthiness of all Japanese Americans, irrespective of citizenship. Columnist Harry McLemore spoke for many outraged West Coast whites when he commented on January 29, "I am for immediate removal of every Japanese on the West Coast to a point deep in the interior. I don't mean a nice part of the interior, either. Herd 'em up, pack 'em off and give 'em the inside room in the badlands. Let 'em be pinched, hurt, hungry, and up against it. Personally, I hate the Japanese. And that goes for all of them."[62]

Such extreme reactions were not limited to the Pacific Coast: newspaper editorialists nationwide, even those who had at first been supportive of Japanese Americans, fulminated about the Japanese "peril." The tabloid *New York Daily News*, which had the largest circulation of any daily paper in America, cited General DeWitt (and unnamed navy and FBI officials) as authority for the proposition that immediate action was needed because the threat of Japanese American sabotage on the West Coast was real. In one statement—unattributed but clearly taken from DeWitt— the article starkly testified to the extraordinary capacity of the general and his associates to twist reality to suit their fears: "There hasn't been any real sabotage on the Pacific Coast since Pearl Harbor. But to the men in command that very fact is a dangerous sign. It means that the saboteurs are definitely under enemy control. It means that sporadic, individual attempts at bombings or arson have been ruled out, biding the time for launching a highly organized thrust at the plants which are turning out the weapons of war—particularly war in the air."[63]

The paper continued in the same vein by casting doubt on the "suspect loyalty" of the Nisei because of their concern for "enemy alien" parents: "Immediately after Pearl Harbor, Japanese draftees were questioned by their commanding officers in an endeavor to determine their loyalty. Many bitterly denounced the Japanese attack at Hawaii and protested their love for America. But almost without exception, the deep filial love that is inherent in the Japanese came to the surface. In one form or another, the sentiment was voiced, 'What will happen now to my parents? What will happen to my relatives, to other members of my family?'"[64]

Following the Roberts report's release, coordinated campaigns began to pressure thousands of Issei truck farmers to leave their land. Newspapers publicized incidents of West Coast employers firing Japanese American employees.[65] The San Francisco branch of the American Red Cross refused aid or donations by Japanese Americans, until pressure from Mrs. Roosevelt on the national organization led them to reverse the policy.[66] On January 27, three days after the Roberts report was made public, the Los Angeles County Board of Supervisors voted a resolution asking the government to remove all Japanese aliens from the West Coast to "inland points." The board also voted to force all city employees of Japanese extraction (of whom there were approximately three dozen) immediately to take "voluntary" indefinite leaves.[67]

That same day, General DeWitt met with Governor Culbert Olson of California, a liberal Democrat. Olson proclaimed that as a result of the report, Californians no longer felt safe around any Japanese Americans, and he requested military action to displace the entire ethnic population from the West Coast. Two days later, California Attorney General Earl Warren, a moderate Republican, added his public endorsement of mass evacuation. Warren's and Olson's demands prompted DeWitt (who throughout the period showed himself more concerned with satisfying local opinion than examining the actual needs of the military situation) to abandon his last reserves and openly to request authority from his superiors to remove both Issei and Nisei from military areas.[68] On January 31 DeWitt told Bendetsen he wanted to expel all 100,000 West Coast Japanese Americans from the West Coast, then German and Italian aliens, and confine them all in internment camps.[69] Meanwhile, energized by the Roberts report, the Ford-Lea committee began meetings (with a paid lobbyist from the Los Angeles Chamber of Commerce sitting in) to draw up recommendations for removal of West Coast Japanese Americans.[70]

THE CONFLICT OVER JAPANESE AMERICANS

Over the first two weeks of February 1942, the pace of developments increased markedly. The pressure from politicians on the West Coast, mixed with DeWitt's desire for military control, compelled a reluctant War Department leadership to turn its attention to methods of handling removal of Issei and Nisei. On January 26, two days after the Roberts report was released, Secretary of War Stimson responded to Leland Ford's earlier letter advocating mass removal. The message (evidently drafted by Bendetsen) stated that the problem was complex and that the task involved in such an operation would be huge but assured Ford that the army was prepared to carry it out if necessary. This was the first authoritative signal that the army was interested in mass removal. The message was confirmed by Bendetsen personally on January 30 when he, Assistant Attorney General James Rowe, and Justice Department Alien Enemy Coordinator Edward Ennis met with members of the Pacific Coast congressional delegation. To the dismay of the Justice Department representatives, Bendetsen expressed strong support for summary removal of all Japanese Americans from the Pacific Coast, although he presented the recommendation as his personal opinion and insisted that he could not speak officially for the War Department. By these signals, he gave the green light to Ford and committee members to exert political pressure on the White House to overrule Attorney General Biddle. The committee immediately sent President Roosevelt a letter supporting removal of all residents of Japanese ancestry and asking him to grant the army full authority over civilian agencies to carry out the operation.

By this time, Attorney General Biddle, who had been placed on the defensive by the Roberts report, clearly believed large-scale exclusion of Japanese aliens unavoidable. He rushed to present a moderate program to meet the challenge and fend off calls for more extreme action. On January 29 he publicly announced the creation of eighty-eight military zones from DeWitt's list and ordered all enemy aliens (who included a significant percentage of the Issei population) to leave the designated areas within twenty-six days. In hopes of keeping himself informed on the West Coast situation, Biddle sent Assistant Attorney General Tom Clark out to San Francisco as his liaison with the War Department. (So far from advocating for Biddle's program, Clark instead became a firm supporter of mass evacuation, although initially on a "voluntary" basis.) At the same time, the attorney general instituted a program of reregistration of enemy aliens, including the issuance of photo identification cards, in order to watch over Issei more efficiently.

To carry out the "migration" of Japanese aliens and help plan relief and resettlement efforts for those dispossessed, Biddle convened an interagency conference.[71] He then turned for help to the Federal Security Administration (FSA), a New Deal agency that had been founded to aid resettlement of agricultural workers.[72] FSA Director Paul McNutt formed immediate plans to coordinate removal and resettlement of aliens with state social welfare agencies and secured the aid of voluntary organizations. It was clear that McNutt intended substantial moving and employment assistance for the refugees. If speed was of the essence and the restricted area extensive, he proposed, "Farm Security Migratory Labor Camps will be used for temporary reception centers rather than CCC [Civilian Conservation Corps] Camps." However, he quickly added, "Even this is regarded as a last resort."[73] Within days, the White House appropriated $500,000 for relocation and temporary aid. The FSA opened offices in San Francisco and Los Angeles under local director Richard M. Neustadt, though its social workers were uncomfortable offering advice on travel or employment and had difficulty persuading Japanese American families to seek assistance. Only some $3,000 of the appropriation was spent. Still, official interest in taking a case-by-case approach, and in avoiding the confinement of prisoners in camps, would soon cease with FSA involvement.[74]

POLITICAL LEADERS AND THE MOVEMENT FOR REMOVAL

In the first two weeks of February, official hostility toward Japanese Americans became increasingly visible, both on the West Coast and in Washington. Following a round of conferences in Sacramento, California Governor Olson and his advisers (including Assistant Attorney General Tom Clark, whom Biddle had dispatched to the West Coast to coordinate with the army) put together a plan to move all adults of Japanese ancestry inland, if possible by "voluntary" means, and settle them in deserted agricultural areas. On February 4 Olson made a radio speech in which he asserted falsely that "Japanese residents of California" had communicated with the enemy and were preparing fifth-column activities, and that as a result the federal government had agreed to his plan.[75] Olsen summoned JACL and Nisei community leaders to "consult," but rather than asking their views he pressured them to show their loyalty by removing themselves "voluntarily." The Nisei delegates firmly rejected this transparently self-serving advice.[76] On February 6 Los Angeles Mayor Bowron made a public address in which he stated that Japanese Americans were unassimilable on racial grounds and unvaryingly loyal to Japan, and that therefore mass confinement was the only way to avoid "another Pearl Harbor."[77] That same week, a meeting of California law enforcement agents voted to petition Attorney General Earl Warren for the removal of all persons of Japanese ancestry within two hundred miles of the Pacific Coast.[78]

Meanwhile, back in Washington, the Ford-Lea committee expanded into a larger group of senators and representatives from the three Pacific Coast states, under the leadership of senior California senator Hiram Johnson (who as governor had signed the anti-Japanese Alien Land Act twenty-nine years previously) and organized various lobbying efforts for mass removal. The committee drew up a united petition in favor of imme-diate evacuation of "all persons of Japanese lineage" from the West Coast states and Alaska, which was sent to the White House on February 13.[79] The actions of the West Coast representatives were paralleled by postur-ing by members of Congress from other districts, who joined the battle for public opinion. On February 7 Representative Martin Dies, chairman of the Dies Committee, proclaimed that he had irrefutable evidence that Japan and Germany had a joint invasion of the United States in prepara-tion and urged that all Japanese Americans be moved five hundred miles inland. Dies was outdone in extremism by Representative John Rankin of Mississippi, a notorious racist bigot and anti-Semite, who on February 18 called for concentration camps for all Japanese Americans: "This is a race war . . . I say it is of vital importance that we get rid of every Japanese, whether in Hawaii or on the mainland. . . . Damn them! Let's get rid of them now!"[80]

Amid the clamor for action against Japanese Americans, liberal Cali-fornia Democrat John Tolan (allegedly with encouragement by the presi-dent) announced that he would take his House Committee on Defense Migration to the West Coast to investigate and hear testimony on "the Japanese question." His goal was to reduce tension and decide on effec-tive action.

Outside official circles, anti-Japanese American sentiment likewise began to overflow West Coast boundaries and reach a national audi-ence. On February 12, the distinguished syndicated columnist Walter Lippmann, following talks with California Attorney General Earl Warren, repeated Warren's charges that the West Coast was in imminent danger of Japanese attack and charged that Japanese Americans on the West Coast were signaling Japanese ships. Lippmann recommended that all Japanese Americans should be moved inland. Although Lippmann's accusations of signaling were discredited by Assistant Attorney General Tom Clark, who pointed out that there was no evidence of any Japanese ships in the area, the columnist's great prestige furnished authoritative backing for advocates of exclusion.[81] On February 13, cartoonist Dr. Seuss (Theodor Geisel) published a political cartoon in the left-wing New York daily *PM* with the caption "Waiting for the Signal from Home." It depicted a long train of identical-looking bucktoothed Japanese converging on California from Oregon and Washington to pick up "TNT" from a dealer identified as the "Honorable 5th column," while another Japanese looks out to sea, obviously awaiting a signal to commit sabotage.[82] Two days later the *New York Times*, the nation's most influential newspaper, editorialized that West Coast fears of Japanese American fifth columnists were justified and called for strenuous action against both Issei and Nisei. Taking a leaf from the Hearst press, with its sensational accounts of arrests, the *Times* justified its position by reference to reports of an FBI raid launched on Japanese-owned homes and businesses in one area, which uncovered rifles, binoculars, knives, shotguns, maps, and sixty thousand rounds of rifle ammunition. The fact that all this material belonged to a single (and licensed) Issei-owned sporting goods shop was left unmentioned.[83]

REACTION BY JAPANESE AMERICANS

With Issei leaders interned and the rest of the immigrants under suspicion as enemy aliens, the Nisei—who regarded themselves as American citizens and thus without limitations on their freedom to express themselves—took up the burden of defending the entire ethnic Japanese community against the unfair attacks. Japanese American newspapers, the leading voices of the community, strongly proclaimed both the loyalty of the Nisei to their country and their resentment over attacks on their citizenship rights. Working through the JACL and Nisei Democrats and through newly created organizations such as the Nisei Writers and Artists Mobilization for Democracy—as well as the New York-based Issei-Nisei collective Japanese American Committee for Democracy (JACD)—groups of Nisei mobilized to offer their patriotic support for the war effort. Nisei organizations held blood drives, circulated petitions and sponsored letter-writing campaigns to express their support, and provided services for those who had lost their jobs. Community members also assisted government agencies. JACD members offered their services for government-sponsored radio propaganda broadcasts. In a poignant demonstration of the besieged feeling of community leaders, JACL leader Mike Masaoka seriously proposed in February 1942 that the army establish a "suicide battalion" of Japanese American soldiers to fight on battlefields as a token of Nisei patriotism.

Nisei simultaneously sought to demonstrate loyalty by collaborating in the search for spies. Editor James Omura of *Current Life* wrote that the Nisei were "on trial" and that the discovery of a single Nisei saboteur might lead to "race war, vigilantism and witch-hunting." All Nisei thus had a duty to discover and report on all potential fifth columnists, "even if these should be our father, our mother, or even our own brothers."[84] San Francisco left-wing activist Karl Yoneda wrote letters to the FBI and to Attorney General Biddle urging that the Japanese-language press be censored and editors detained as enemy agents.[85] Members of the newly created JACL Anti-Axis Committee informed the FBI about those (mainly Issei) whom they considered potentially disloyal—one leader proudly asserted that the committee had turned in "nearly a dozen Japanese sympathizers and active enemy agents"—and were thereby scorned as government "stooges."[86]

Various Nisei groups and individuals turned to political action and organized against threats of removal. Togo Tanaka editorially advised the Nisei to contact their representatives, and Setsuko Matsunaga sent a wire to the president declaring that the Nisei were loyal and that internment was a violation of their constitutional rights.[87] Sculptor Isamu Noguchi and editor Larry Tajiri of the Nisei Writers and Artists Mobilization, working with progressive minister Rev. Fred Fertig, assembled a series of studies on ways to combat anti-Nisei prejudice and on the occupational and financial difficulties that Los Angeles Japanese Americans were facing. Different groups scheduled strategy sessions. In collaboration with Noguchi, Togo Tanaka organized a public meeting of a united committee to organize strategy.[88]

Nevertheless, the Nisei were unable to shift the hostile climate of opinion. Most Nisei were too young to vote, and they lacked influence with political leaders. Their leaders were too inexperienced in community and political affairs to offer a coherent or timely response to the developing campaign against them. Notably, the united committee meeting, the first large-scale Nisei public forum on the question of removal, did not take place until the evening of February 19, 1942, after Executive Order 9066 had been signed.[89]

Nisei activists found a few allies inside and outside government. Archibald MacLeish, director of the Office of Facts and Figures, sent representatives to the West Coast in early January 1942 to talk to newspaper editors about toning down hysterical and inaccurate stories about Japanese American spies. At MacLeish's suggestion, the president of the Hollywood Writers Group, Ralph Block, joined Nisei colleagues to plan positive newspaper information campaigns. (The project tallied a success when cartoonist Ham Fisher placed an endorsement of Nisei loyalty in his popular comic strip "Joe Palooka.") Radio broadcaster George Knox Roth featured Nisei on his radio program, despite threats to his job.[90] African American lawyer Hugh E. MacBeth, chair of the California Race Relations Commission, charged that internment of Issei was being fomented by white groups seeking to take over Japanese Americans' land. MacBeth sent materials to sympathizers (notably Socialist Party leader Norman Thomas) and lobbied local groups to support the rights of all citizens.[91] Writer Carey McWilliams and singer/activist Paul Robeson agreed to testify before Congress on the loyalty of the Nisei. However, like the efforts of the Nisei themselves, these supportive efforts could attract little attention against the popular anti-Japanese movement.

THE BATTLE WITHIN THE WHITE HOUSE

In the face of the pressure from the War Department, Biddle redoubled his efforts on preserving the rights of American citizens of Japanese ancestry. The attorney general was reinforced by new reports from FBI Director Hoover and ONI investigator Lt. Comm. Kenneth Ringle, who confirmed that there had been no incidence of sabotage or espionage by Japanese Americans in the six weeks since Pearl Harbor and asserted that the overwhelming majority of the population was loyal. On February 1 Biddle and his assistants met with Assistant Secretary of War McCloy, who had become the West Coast officers' chief advocate within official circles, and with Gullion and Bendetsen to work out a joint position. Gullion made it clear that not only DeWitt, but all the West Coast political leaders that the general had consulted, favored removal inland of all Japanese Americans regardless of citizenship and asked whether mass removal could be undertaken as a matter of military necessity. According to Gullion, McCloy agreed that if it was a matter of national security, "The Constitution is just a scrap of paper to me."[92]

To Gullion's outrage, the attorney general countered that he opposed mass evacuation of civilians and that the Justice Department would "be through" if it came to interference with American citizens under any circumstances. If the army was determined to remove them, he insisted, it would have to carry out any such operation itself—Biddle gambled on the assumption that the army lacked the will and ability to carry out such an operation. To calm West Coast opinion, the attorney general proposed the issuing of a joint press communiqué asserting that the military situation made mass evacuation of Americans citizens unnecessary. The War Department staffers objected to the provision, and McCloy insisted that he did not wish to foreclose any options before hearing more from General DeWitt. The meeting broke up without any agreement being reached.

On February 3 McCloy telephoned DeWitt to determine the progress of the situation. The general (withholding from his superiors his strong agreement with Bendetsen and Gullion that forced removal of all Issei and Nisei was necessary) reported that he favored Governor Olson's plan to move all adult Japanese Americans to agricultural areas inland. McCloy made clear his and Secretary Stimson's opposition to mass evacuation, and he told DeWitt to work out instead a system of licensing whereby military areas around selected areas such as essential defense installations could be closed to all, and once those from suspected groups (including all Japanese Americans) had been excluded, all other residents could then be permitted to "return" (i.e., remain). DeWitt was scornful of adopting a selective policy, especially to evade constitutional restrictions on removing citizens based on ancestry, and told McCloy, "Out here, Mr. Secretary, a Jap is a Jap to these people now."[93] However, the general finally agreed to devise a selective removal plan in accordance with McCloy's orders. Bendetsen continued to insist that a large percentage of Nisei were disloyal and that selective evacuation would be too "weak."[94] He and Gullion stepped in on February 6 to push their new plan for wholesale removal of Japanese aliens and American citizens.

In the face of the continuing demands, McCloy's last opposition to mass removal softened, though he was evidently not thinking in large-scale terms. He ordered DeWitt to come up with a new plan (according to a set of notes dated February 8),[95] which included limited evacuation of Issei and Nisei from small military areas (such as those which had been created at the end of January) using a permit system. McCloy asked DeWitt to provide a formal defense rationale for removal by the military and sent Bendetsen back to San Francisco to work with him on it. Stimson seems to have decided by this time that the Nisei were "even more dangerous" than the Issei. However, he told his diary, if a permit system was insufficient, then total military removal of all Japanese Americans on a racial basis might be necessary, but that "it would make a tremendous hole in our constitutional system to apply it."[96]

Even as Stimson agonized over military action, dissension appeared within the ranks of the army. As in Canada, the army's General Staff rejected the counsel of the West Coast officers. At the request of army staff headquarters, General Mark Clark undertook a report on the West Coast situation. On February 10 Clark and Admiral Harold Stark were invited by the Pacific Coast congressional subcommittee to testify on defense matters. Clark told the subcommittee that people in California were unduly excited, since the chances of a Japanese invasion or heavy attack were effectively zero.

Unlike in Canada, however, the navy chiefs remained hostile to Japanese Americans, and the navy soon announced its own evacuation plans for Terminal Island in the Los Angeles harbor area. Before the war, 2,000–3,500 Japanese Americans lived on the island and worked in its canneries or in the Japanese restaurants and stores that operated there. Following Pearl Harbor, all fishing boats operated by ethnic Japanese, including American citizens, were grounded, and local canneries laid off Issei and Nisei workers. On January 27, after release of the Roberts report, the navy privately informed the army and Justice Department of its intention to use eminent domain to buy all the land occupied by Japanese Americans on Terminal Island, so that it could remove both aliens and citizens of Japanese ancestry.[97] On February 2 government agents made mass arrests of some four hundred Issei fishermen on the island. On February 10 the navy announced publicly that all Japanese aliens would have seven days to leave the island. Five days later, Navy Secretary Knox changed his mind and gave all Japanese Americans thirty days to pack their belongings and depart. Then, without warning, on February 25 the navy issued a forty-eight-hour deadline for departure. Residents were forced to flee to the mainland with little more than what they could carry. Although the navy operation did not call for confinement of those expelled, virtually all of those displaced were later included in the mass removal of West Coast Japanese Americans.

Biddle, under fire from West Coast newspapers and members of Congress, sought once more to forestall demands for action by the War

Department. On February 7 he scheduled lunch with the president, during which he told FDR that any such removal would threaten morale.[98] To resolve his uncertainties over whether evacuation of citizens on a racial basis was constitutional, Biddle went outside the Justice Department and solicited the opinion of a trio of New Dealers, Oscar Cox, Benjamin Cohen, and Joseph Rauh. He was disappointed by their response. The three lawyers reported that it was certainly constitutional for the president as commander in chief to authorize the army to undertake evacuation of civilians from military zones, although they refused comment on the advisability of such a policy.

Meanwhile, Biddle and Rowe mobilized allies within the administration, notably Archibald MacLeish. MacLeish forwarded the president a secret government report on public opinion showing that most West Coast residents approved the government's existing policy and suggested that FDR make a speech against wartime hysteria. MacLeish and Biddle likewise attempted to enlist the help of Mrs. Roosevelt, who had endorsed the loyalty of Japanese Americans in a radio address in January. MacLeish and his advisors at the Office of Facts and Figures (including future U.S. senator Alan Cranston, a native Californian) met with the First Lady to propose arguments against mass evacuation that she could take back to the president, and he sent her material for speeches. However, while Mrs. Roosevelt was sympathetic and made a second radio address endorsing the loyalty of aliens, she was unable to intervene effectively within government circles in support of Japanese Americans. She was reluctant to confront the president on military questions, and she was in any case distracted by political attacks on her management of the Office of Civil Defense, the post to which she had been appointed in 1941—her first and last official position during the Roosevelt years, and from which she would resign on February 20.

THE PRESIDENT'S DECISION

In the end, the attorney general's effort to avert mass expulsion of all Japanese Americans from the West Coast was too little, too late. Biddle was unwilling (to his later regret) to confront directly Stimson, his esteemed elder, and dissuade him from pushing removal. Instead, his readiness to exclude Japanese aliens without proof of wrongdoing, and his strategic retreats on removing citizens, only encouraged the War Department to pursue action. In the end, it was the secretary of war who made the decisive approach to the president. On the morning of February 11 Stimson met with McCloy and Mark Clark. Torn between DeWitt's demands (presumably presented by McCloy) for mass removal of all persons of Japanese ancestry—for which the secretary had not yet received the requested specific military rationale—and General Clark's opposition, Stimson decided that he could not resolve the matter himself, and he contacted the White House to ask for a meeting for guidance.[99] President Roosevelt stated that he was too busy for a meeting (implying by his action that he considered the matter fairly unimportant). Later that afternoon Stimson reached the president by telephone. Referring to a memo that McCloy and Clark had drafted, Stimson asked whether the president would approve the moving of citizens as well as aliens from military areas, and if so whether he wished the army to evacuate the entire West Coast, the larger cities, or small areas around military installations.[100] Roosevelt willingly consented to leave the choice of action to Stimson, asking only that the War Department be as "reasonable" as possible in conducting the operation—if citizens were involved, the army could take care of them too. As Stimson told his diary: "I took up with him the west coast matter first and told him the situation and fortunately found that he was very vigorous about it and told me to go ahead on the line that I had myself thought the best."[101] There would doubtless be repercussions, FDR continued, but military security took precedence.

It does not appear that Roosevelt gave much thought to this step, and his full reasons for it can only be surmised. Although he had kept himself informed of developments on the West Coast in the weeks since Pearl Harbor, he had not taken any official action or commented more than in passing over that time. Although FDR had genuine humanitarian instincts, he also had clear racial prejudices against Japanese Americans, whom he had long considered as racially "unassimilable" and innately Japanese on racial grounds. In a pair of articles written in the 1920s, he had justified exclusion of Japanese immigrants and discriminatory legislation against them in the name of defending "racial purity."[102] He was also a supremely practical man, responsive to political pressure in Congress and on the West Coast and to the demands of the War Department, especially his distinguished secretary of war. The military situation in the Pacific was serious—the Japanese Army was besieging the Philippines, which fell on February 15. FDR's essential goal was to win the war. He clearly viewed the rights of a small number of American citizens of Japanese ancestry as a minor abstraction compared to the tasks of preserving domestic unity and keeping up production and shipping on the West Coast, which racial conflict might threaten. Removing Japanese Americans was a much less drastic solution than declaring martial law in the West Coast.[103]

In any case, Roosevelt's telephone conversation was the decisive moment as far as the War Department was concerned. After the call, McCloy immediately contacted Bendetsen and DeWitt to notify them that that the president had granted them "carte blanche," whereupon all the previous debate about licensing small areas disintegrated in favor of a policy of complete removal. On February 14 DeWitt submitted his final recommendation for complete "evacuation" of all aliens and citizens of Japanese ancestry. Pointing to the "undiluted racial strains" of the ethnic Japanese population and to the likelihood that they would commit sabotage in case of a Japanese invasion, DeWitt recommended the relocation of all Japanese Americans to the interior. Although the report contained no new elements or rationale for mass removal, beyond the already discredited charges of signaling of Japanese ships plus the vague fears and suspicions that had already been discussed, it sealed the case for mass removal. Three days later, following Bendetsen's return to Washington, Stimson met with Bendetsen, Clark, Gullion and McCloy to plan further steps. At length they agreed to obtain an executive order to grant DeWitt authority to act.[104] Biddle, who still believed that the question was open, sent a letter to Stimson on February 12, explaining how martial law would work if it had to be declared, but he simultaneously countered it with a memo to the president on February 17 in which he made a final plea that the government not undertake exclusion of American citizens on a racial basis, which he compared to "shouting fire in a crowded theater." Roosevelt evidently told him then that his decision had already been made because when Biddle and his staff held a meeting with the War Department staffers that evening, the attorney general ordered his assistants Rowe and Ennis (over their angry protests) to help work out the text of an executive order. Stimson looked it over the following day and proposed a few minor changes. He told his diary that the order represented "a long step forward" toward solving a difficult problem, but that he underestimated neither the magnitude of the task nor "the wails which will go up in relation to some of the actions which will be taken under it."[105] On February 19,

1942, the text of Executive Order 9066 was presented to the president, who approved it without further consultation or change.

EXECUTIVE ORDER 9066

The text of the order that came down from the White House did not mention Japanese Americans. Instead, it simply granted the secretary of war or his designees the power to create military zones, "from which any or all persons may be excluded" and for which the right of any person to "enter, remain in, or leave" was placed at the discretion of military authorities. It also authorized the army to offer assistance to civilians in the course of such exclusion. Despite the order's neutral language, the government officials involved well understood that the order was designed solely to permit mass removal of Japanese Americans, irrespective of citizenship, from the West Coast. The bland, legalistic language of the text and the vague nature of the action encompassed concealed the order's unprecedented grant of authority. Through its provisions, the president and the secretary of war arrogated to themselves and their assignees the right to round up and expel entire communities from their homes without compensation, and without due process or proof of any wrongdoing.

It is not clear precisely what policy White House and Army officials envisioned would result from the president's order—after a cabinet meeting the following week, Stimson fumed that FDR had given "very little thought" to the practical questions involved.[106] Roosevelt and his advisors may have believed that the order would lead to a process of voluntary evacuation by Japanese Americans, at least in part, or a system for removing Japanese Americans from the immediate area of strategic areas, with eventual resettlement to agricultural settlements further inland. Stimson himself reported to the cabinet that the goal of the order was to allow the army to step in and move Japanese Americans quickly away from the West Coast. Once they had moved, he added, those who were found to be loyal could be moved back.[107] It is also uncertain whether those making the order contemplated that Italian or German aliens would also be subjected to wholesale removal from the coast. What is certain, however, is that DeWitt, Bendetsen, and Gullion, who had pushed hardest for the order, had already foreseen that the likeliest (and most desirable) result would be confinement of those removed in what they called "internment camps."

THE CRISIS IN CANADA

The compromise policy devised by the Canadian government and announced on January 14, 1942, by which military-age male Japanese nationals were to be sent away from coastal areas to labor camps, attracted widespread praise. The *Toronto Globe and Mail*, giving credence—what it called an "open secret"—to the various fantastic rumors that Japanese Canadian fishermen were Japanese naval officers in disguise and that "secret servicemen in the employ of Tokyo" worked as chauffeurs and gardeners for prominent West Cast whites, claimed that the order was a wise precaution and warned Japanese Canadians that they ought to welcome the order since it was intended "for their own protection."[108] Nevertheless, the action failed to dampen agitation against Japanese Canadians in British Columbia. As in the United States, the drumbeat of invasion fears and hostility against Nisei on the West Coast, seasoned by the efforts of racist agitators, built up as January turned to February 1942. As in California, Washington, and Oregon, Canadian nativist groups such as the Canadian Legion and Native Sons organizations pushed the same exclusionary agenda they had been demanding for years. That their bigotry was informed by a strong streak of greed and economic self-interest was obvious from the visible organizational role occupied in public campaigns by chambers of commerce and farmers' organizations. A particular impetus for removing Issei and Nisei lay in the desire of white fishermen's groups to take back the trade, as they had attempted to do throughout the 1920s. "Although arguments for removing the Japanese Canadians in 1941–42 were couched in terms of the need for protection against the enemy, few British Columbians failed to see that removing the Japanese would create economic opportunities for white people, especially in the fisheries."[109] By the same token, native people working in British Columbia's fishing industry strongly supported removal of their Japanese competitors.[110]

Still, the mix of elements that fueled anti-Japanese anxiety and racism among Canadians was somewhat different from that obtaining further south. By proposing a partial evacuation policy, the Canadian government had made clear by implication that Japanese Canadians did indeed pose a threat of sabotage and fifth-column activity—a point that was not settled in the United States for several weeks thereafter. Once this idea was officially endorsed, it only remained to determine the scope of the necessary preventive action. Thus, so far from placating the fears of British Columbians, the announcement of the partial removal policy fed them.

Various newspaper reports, and undoubtedly many West Coast whites, assumed that "evacuation of Japanese" meant not just transportation of enemy aliens but removal of all ethnic Japanese.[111] After all, the Canadian government itself had made no distinction between Japanese nationals and the Canadian-born or naturalized when it conducted its census and registration, or in its blanket exemption of Japanese Canadians from military service. There was therefore legitimate cause for British Columbians to assume that sending Japanese nationals to work camps was the first step in a more complete process of removal.

Similarly, the government's failure to provide prompt enforcement of its removal policy excited widespread anxiety. The original announcement of January 14 left unclear the size of the area from which "Japanese" men would be excluded and the timetable for sending them away. There was delay caused by the considerable confusion within the ranks of the government over how to prepare an evacuation and create road labor camps—in the middle of winter and amid anticipated wartime shortages of supplies—especially when no single ministry was assigned authority over the move. Neither of the two men who would normally have been given the portfolio, Minister of Justice Louis St. Laurent and Minister of Labor Humphrey Mitchell, was able to take charge, due to other pressing matters. As a result, while some details were forthcoming on January 23, it was not until February 4, three weeks after the policy was made public, that the government announced that the boundaries of the military zone had been defined as encompassing a hundred-mile strip from the coast inland, and that the final deadline for expulsion was fixed as April 1.

By making such a schedule, the federal government wished to assure itself time to set up the delicate operation and to assure proper housing and job facilities for the internal refugees. However, none of the other provinces was willing to accept the "Japs."[112] In particular, local groups in northern Ontario, backed by provincial premier Mitchell Hepburn, blocked a proposed plan whereby Issei men would be sent to work in lumber mills.[113] Meanwhile, during early February the Japanese Army swept through much of Asia and marched on Singapore, the last British strongpoint in the western Pacific. To white British Columbians worried over Japan's military strength and afflicted with nagging uncertainties about the possibility of attacks by Tokyo on North America (despite the firm conviction of Canadian defense staff officials that such an invasion was virtually impossible), such a schedule seemed alarmingly lackadaisical and ineffective as a protection against potential fifth columnists and saboteurs.

By the last week of January, civic and veterans' groups in British Columbia, profiting from public insecurity, began forming into groups to press for immediate official action to remove all ethnic Japanese. On January 28, when Parliament reconvened following the Christmas recess, the circle of British Columbia members of the Liberal caucus proposed that all Japanese who refused to join the new Civilian Corps as "volunteer" laborers be placed in internment camps as potentially dangerous. The following day Conservative MP Howard Green asserted on the floor of the House of Commons that Japan might be plotting an invasion of the Prince Rupert or Queen Charlotte Islands on the British Columbian coast. He denounced the "treacherous" Japanese Canadians who stood poised to lead the invaders to strategic locations. "We should be protected from treachery, from a stab in the back. . . . The only complete protection we can have from this danger is to remove the Japanese population from the province." Later the same week, another British Columbia MP, R. P. Mayhew of Victoria, restated the call for evacuation, arguing that Pearl Harbor had proven the essential disloyalty of all ethnic Japanese: "Blood is thicker than water."[114] Local bodies soon picked up the refrain. On February 16 the Vancouver City Council formally voted a resolution "imploring" the federal government to remove all people of Japanese ancestry from the Pacific Coast. Four days later, after a Victory Bond luncheon, a mixed group of influential Vancouverites, including members of the Vancouver Board of Trade, created the Citizens Defense Committee and added their names to a formal resolution asking that Japanese be removed from key strategic points and evacuated from the coast.[115]

THE DECISION IN OTTAWA

The pressure from the West Coast, especially from opposition politicians, carried the "Japanese question" back into the hands of Ottawa. Unlike in Washington, the internal struggle within the federal government was a completely civilian one—the Canadian Staff's opposition to mass removal and internment was ignored. Also, whereas Attorney General Biddle was the chief opponent of mass removal within the Roosevelt administration, Canada's minister of justice (and future prime minister), Louis

St. Laurent, declined to take any visible stand in support of the rights of Canadian citizens. The best that "the King of Quebec" could manage was a single speech reminding the Vancouver City Council that the government was removing Japanese aliens only as a precautionary measure and asking for time to prepare their reception inland.[116] Rather, the only noticeable opposition to removal within the Canadian government came from staffers in the Department of External Affairs. On January 26 J. E. Read, the department's legal advisor, submitted a memorandum warning that interference with Japanese Canadians on a racial basis would add strength to Japan's propaganda efforts. Read's chief, Hugh Keenleyside, forwarded the memo on the following day to Ian Mackenzie, noting in a covering letter that wholesale removal was unjust—Canada was not contemplating similar controls on German or Italian aliens, although those of German or Italian ancestry were also difficult to distinguish and watch over. He warned that any more drastic action could imperil the lives of two thousand Canadian POWs in Japanese hands.[117]

On the other side, once again pushing mass removal as the spokesperson for British Columbia, was Ian Mackenzie. Although Mackenzie had been prepared at first to accept the internment of Japanese males as sufficient and had informed B.C. Premier John Hart that such a policy was "as far as we could possibly go,"[118] in the weeks that followed he received a new stream of letters and messages from British Columbia's attorney general, the province's minister of labor, and others. Provincial officials in Victoria warned that stronger measures were necessary and rightly viewed him as the man who could exercise the strongest influence on the prime minister to enact them. Mackenzie was energized by this anti-Japanese juggernaut, and by the fear that opposition politicians would make political hay at the government's expense by supporting more extreme action. Mackenzie first persuaded the cabinet to abolish the Standing Committee on Orientals as ineffective, and the committee disbanded on February 9. With the way cleared of opposition and the Conservatives outflanked, he organized a caucus of MPs from British Columbia in a united front for mass removal of all ethnic Japanese, to which he added his voice in the cabinet and in correspondence to the Prime Minister Mackenzie King. On February 14, the day before Singapore fell, Mackenzie wrote King that the West Coast was seriously underdefended and advised the sending of two mobile divisions and halting all delivery of soldiers overseas until the coast was protected. Although he did not explicitly mention the

Japanese Canadians, he had cause to know that the prime minister would naturally connect the defense of the Pacific Coast with protection against subversion.[119]

By that time, King was prepared to accede to Mackenzie's arguments in favor of moving the entire Japanese community from the Pacific Coast, in spite of the advice he received from military authorities. On February 17 the cabinet approved an order-in-council to create a Canadian National Service Corps to organize Canadian citizens of Japanese ancestry along paramilitary lines and ship them to areas outside British Columbia to do civilian labor. This effort would soon be withdrawn in the face of public opposition.[120] On February 19 King brought the "Japanese question" up at cabinet and obtained his ministers' consent to set up road labor camps for Nisei. As King remarked to his diary later that day:

> I fear that it is going to be a very great problem to move the Japanese and especially to deal with the ones who are naturalized Canadians or Canadian born. There is every possibility of riots. Once that occurs, there will be repercussions in the Far East against our own prisoners. Public prejudice is so strong in B.C. that it is gong to be difficult to control the situation; also moving men to camps at this time of year very difficult. I did my best to get decisions from the Cabinet and matters sufficiently advanced to be prepared for afternoon questions. Was able to get policy definitely settled to stop purchasing of land by Japanese [in] other parts of British Columbia.[121]

King's comments made clear that he had clearly already made up his own mind on some sort of action and sought a consensus. The announcement that day that President Roosevelt had signed Executive Order 9066 demolished the last hesitation of Canadian leaders about the wisdom of mass removal. Under King's leadership, the War Committee was formed on February 20. It decided that, without ignoring European needs, Canada needed to devote more resources to Pacific defenses, which meant concentrating on meeting the danger of subversion. (Ironically, the prime minister spoke that same day to representatives of the Toronto Civil Liberties League and promised them rapid action to assure trials and appeals to those—mainly German and Italian aliens—already interned.) Following a weekend break, King held a secret session in the House of Commons on Monday, February 23, in which he discussed the "Japanese" situation. Fortified by his consultation, he drew up an order-in-council, P.C.

1486. Dated February 24, 1942, it authorized the minister of justice (rather than the military, as in the United States) to take control over individuals of Japanese origin with respect to certain protected areas and gave him authority to determine whether such people could be moved out an area, "prohibited from entering, leaving, or returning," and restricted in their residence, employment, and other areas. Unlike in the United States, Japanese Canadians were explicitly targeted in the exclusion order. Two days later the government announced that, by authority of the order, all ethnic Japanese would be moved out from the strip encompassing all areas within one hundred miles of the coast of British Columbia.[122]

In appearance, Prime Minister King's participation in the creation of the order was limited to making a final decision—like Franklin Roosevelt, he gave a free hand to a trusted advisor to set policy. Yet King was a far more active figure in bringing forth the issue of mass removal to his advisors and designing the contours of the policy than was his counterpart in the White House, and his motivations seem somewhat different. Scholars have tended to attribute King's actions to political calculation, mixed with anxiety over security. For example, West Coast reporter Bruce Hutchison claimed that King overplayed the Japanese invasion threat for both military and political reasons and "acceded to the demands of a frightened British Columbia government" to remove Japanese Canadians. King did genuinely fear, at least by turns, a Japanese invasion of Canada, though he seems to have believed that it would not come unless the Japanese had first made themselves masters of all of Asia. Yet he did not challenge his military advisors' recommendations or seek alternate views, which suggests that this was a less important factor.[123]

Ann Gomer Sunahara has suggested that King approved Japanese removal as part of an expedient policy to divert Canadian defense forces to the Pacific Coast.[124] Since during February 1942 King was beset by calls for more troops for service on European battlefields, such a concentration would offer him a pretext to refuse, thus avoiding the consequences (especially among French Canadians) of breaking his previous promise not to resort to conscription for overseas service. It is true that the idea of justifying a defense buildup on the coast offered a tempting rationale for moving Japanese Canadians. "The Japanese problem in B.C.," he mused, "might become more difficult to handle, requiring more in the way of troops."[125] At the same time, he decided within a few days after he signed P.C. 1486 to schedule a national referendum on releasing the government from its promise not to impose overseas conscription, at which point he dropped the emphasis on protecting British Columbia. (The referendum led to further splits between the English Canadian provinces, where voters approved conscription by large majorities, and French Quebec, which voted against it by a large margin). Since King did not cancel mass removal in the process, it seems doubtful that the conscription question played that direct a role in the fate of Japanese Canadians.

Another possible motivation, which Patricia Roy and others have embraced as central, was the fear of collective violence.[126] Even more than his counterparts in Washington, King feared the disruptive potential of anti-Japanese riots, especially if they set off reprisals against Canadians held in the Far East. King had lived through the 1907 anti-Asian riots in Vancouver and had visited the city afterward to report on the damage caused. He was sensitive to the danger of vigilantism, and the lack of facilities the federal government had for assuring calm on the Pacific Coast. Clearly, King thought it easier, all things considered, to move Japanese Canadians away—for their own protection. This does not mean that King felt a particular moral responsibility for the security of Issei and Nisei; rather, they represented a problem he was anxious to resolve.

Still, as in the case of Franklin Roosevelt, one factor of importance that has not been explored by historians is King's racial hostility toward Japanese Canadians.[127] He had a nasty background of anti-Asian prejudice, as indicated in numerous prewar comments in his private diary about the undesirability of Asian immigration, and was prepared to believe the worst of Japanese Canadians as innately loyal to Japan. King starkly revealed his attitude in a discussion with Chinese envoy T. V. Soong the same week that he issued P.C. 1486. As King described the conversation in his diary, Soong stated strongly that he did not trust any Japanese "no matter how honourable they might appear to be, or how long they may have been away from Japan, naturalized, or even those who were born in the country. Everyone of them, he thought, would be saboteurs and would help Japan when the moment came." King quickly made clear his own feelings: "I agreed with him."[128] Clearly, in the face of such an undifferentiated threat, King was prepared to take action against the entire community, irrespective of citizenship. He was aware that action against naturalized or birthright Canadians would pose a thornier problem than aliens in propaganda terms. Nevertheless, as his earlier refusals to contemplate Nisei suffrage rights or military service made clear, King was not concerned about citizenship rights of Canadians of Japanese ancestry—in any case, the War Measures Act gave full power to the government to protect national security, so there were no legal or constitutional barriers to any action that the nation's leaders might consider necessary.

CONCLUSION

The bombs dropped on Pearl Harbor by its Japanese attackers set off a series of ripples that ended by engulfing the various communities of overseas Japanese throughout the Pacific Rim. Only those in Hawaii itself—the eye of the storm—were able to retain their liberty, within certain limits. Those in North America and Australasia were less fortunate, as they were singled out on racial grounds for "control," which meant mass removal from their homes, farms, and businesses. In all of these places, evacuation was foreshadowed and informed by bitter prewar prejudice against Asians and economic jealousy of Japanese immigrants, who were barred from citizenship rights. In Australia, New Zealand, and New Caledonia, as in Central America, blanket action against small colonies of Japanese settlers followed immediately on the heels of a declaration of war with Japan. The rapidity of these official actions and the lack of explanation for them suggest not only a pressing fear of Japanese fifth-columnists but an overarching desire by governments for revenge against Japan through mass internment of its nationals and their few descendants.

In contrast, on the West Coast of the United States and Canada, which were farther from Japan and where the resident ethnic Japanese populations were primarily composed of native-born citizens, the decisions to undertake mass removal did not come immediately after the outbreak of war in the Pacific. Instead, each evolved over the weeks that followed, in response to West Coast political and economic pressure—in that sense, as historian Page Smith has argued about the United States, removal was a "decision nobody made."[129]

Although similar in their provisions, the policies designed by the governments of Franklin Roosevelt and Mackenzie King were arrived at independently, with no effective coordination. All the same, the Canadian experience points strongly to certain conclusions regarding events south of the border. First, military necessity was not the governing factor in the removal of Issei and Nisei. The same arguments were made in British Columbia as in California about ethnic Japanese being fifth-columnists, yet Canadian Army and Navy leaders, as well as the RCMP, opposed mass evacuation. General Maurice Pope, vice-chief of the Canadian General

Staff, like General Mark Clark in Washington, considered the threat of Japanese invasion a chimera and deplored the manipulation of invasion fears by West Coast political leaders as a pretext for arbitrary action against Japanese. Nevertheless, the military chiefs were passed over by civilians more interested in political realities than strategic questions.

Conversely, the Canadian experience underscores the primary role of West Coast prejudice and the specter of anti-Japanese violence in forcing reluctant national leaders to take dramatic action. It will be recalled that General R. O. Alexander recommended relocation of Japanese Canadians out of a—partly manufactured—fear of violent demonstrations arising from the campaign against them on the coast. Similarly, Prime Minister Mackenzie King told his cabinet (and his diary) that the escalation of racial prejudice and the threat of rioting made it necessary to remove Japanese Canadians to avert racial violence—although, once again, King's own statement that he could not trust any Japanese Canadians suggests the importance of his own bigoted sentiments in inspiring his action.

It might be noted that there is an interesting piece of evidence for this view on the American side as well: a few months after Executive Order 9066 was issued, Assistant Secretary of War McCloy was asked by his superior, Undersecretary Robert Patterson, about the food being given "Japanese internees." McCloy responded with a brief summary of the expenses for food. In a handwritten postscript, he then added, "These people are not 'internees'—they are under no suspicion for the most part and were moved largely because we felt we could not control our own white citizens in California."[130] This does not mean that either government intended to move ethnic Japanese from the coast solely for their own protection. There is no evidence that protection as such was ever discussed during the period by any of the government officials responsible, and logically the various heavy restrictions placed on those removed would have been needless if such were the case. Nevertheless, the evidence does lend credence to the notion that concerns about racial violence and civil disorders were present in the minds of the deciders.

Finally, both the Canadian experience, like the American one, suggests that the scope and nature of the removal policy were determined primarily by political interests, without regard for framing policies that mixed security with protection of democratic rights. In the United States, the army pushed for military zones encompassing entire cities, and eventually an entire region, even though the ostensible danger of Japanese subversion related only to a coastal invasion. In Canada, West Coast interests demanded arbitrary action against people of Japanese ancestry within a few weeks after Pearl Harbor. A compromise policy was worked out, which initially satisfied West Coast representatives. However, even before the plan could be developed or put into operation, it was scorned by West Coast extremists dedicated to achieving their historic goal of getting rid of the "Japs." This indicates that the "security" sought by the West Coast could not be resolved by ordinary means because it did not depend on meeting and neutralizing actual threats—the only way to placate them was by an official policy of forcible segregation.

[3] REMOVAL FROM THE WEST COAST AND CONTROL OF ETHNIC JAPANESE OUTSIDE

THE LEGAL BASIS OF REMOVAL

In the first days after President Franklin Roosevelt signed Executive Order 9066, the federal government began to organize plans for dealing with the "Japanese problem," and the mass removal of West Coast Japanese Americans was set into motion with a series of decrees. On February 20, 1942, one day after Executive Order 9066 was signed, Secretary of War Stimson delegated to General DeWitt, as Western Defense commander, the authority to create a defense zone and remove civilians from it as he saw fit, offering only some suggestions as to procedure. Ten days later, on March 2, General DeWitt issued a public proclamation announcing the creation of two military areas: Military Area 1, which comprised the western half of the states of Washington, Oregon, and California and the southern half of Arizona; and Military Area 2, which made up the rest of those states. DeWitt announced that Military Area 1 might be cleared of "such persons or classes of persons as the situation may require"—Western Defense Command officials publicly stated that this provision referred to all persons of Japanese ancestry, irrespective of citizenship, plus German and Italian enemy aliens—and added that there were no plans to restrict residence in Military Area 2, except for those zones within that had already been designated by the Justice Department as restricted. Soon after, DeWitt issued a further proclamation imposing a curfew and five-mile limitation on travel on all Japanese Americans.[1]

The military orders were swiftly given enforcement power by Congress. Legislation was hastily drafted making disobedience of military exclusion orders a federal offense. Secretary of War Stimson and General DeWitt endorsed the legislation and asked Congress to approve it as a matter of urgent importance. Senator Robert Reynolds of North Carolina, chair of the Senate Military Affairs Committee, spoke in favor of the bill, adding that it was necessary to curb the rampant fifth-column activity that he claimed existed on the West Coast. Reynolds repeated as fact the false rumor that Japanese pilots shot down during the Pearl Harbor attack wore local Hawaiian school insignia and university rings.[2] Although Senator Robert Taft, a leading Republican, objected that the legislation was "sloppy" and would obviously not be permissible in peacetime, Public Law 503 was approved without dissent and signed into law on March 21, 1942.[3]

Even as Congress approved mass expulsion of Japanese Americans from military areas, a set of senators pressured the administration to define its goals explicitly to encompass mass incarceration. On March 24 and 25, 1942, Democratic senators Tom Stewart of Tennessee and Burnet Maybank of South Carolina and California Republican Hiram Johnson held subcommittee hearings on a punitive bill Stewart had introduced shortly before Executive Order 9066 was issued. It authorized the secretary of war to detain all enemy aliens and any native-born citizen believed to have ties with the enemy—Stewart clearly stated that this meant Nisei. The hearings demonstrated that the senators did not consider evacuation without confinement to be sufficiently stringent, for when Justice Department officials claimed the bill was unconstitutional, the senators asked how they could meet its purposes. Edward Ennis assured the subcommittee during his testimony that the goals of the bill were already being met through Executive Order 9066, since under its provisions Japanese Americans were being encouraged to move with the threat of forcible removal if they did not. Ennis made clear that the government's intentions included confinement, and he added a tortured explanation why this did not violate habeas corpus: "We are not subjecting a citizen of the Japanese race to incarceration under guard. By our proclamation we have removed him from any dangerous areas, and we have required him to go, and so far he has done it entirely on a voluntary basis, to the encampments that we have set up for him where, of course, there will be guards, but the purpose of the guards will be to police the camp for them, without putting any citizen of the Japanese race behind bars. But we will be able to control the entire subject of their evacuation and their re-settlement."[4] Ennis stated explicitly that the government's program would last the duration of the war.

Once Executive Order 9066 was signed, the War Department and the Justice Department quickly agreed, with the president's concurrence, that only the army had the authority to undertake the initial evacuation, but that once that was accomplished, the "relocation" of Japanese Americans was a social welfare task that should be handled by a civilian agency. On the advice of Budget Bureau Director Harold Smith, in mid-March President Roosevelt created a new agency, which was dubbed the War Relocation Authority (WRA). To permit it to coordinate the efforts of other agencies, the WRA began life as an independent body within the Executive Office of the President, rather than under the aegis of an existing cabinet department. Roosevelt likewise adopted Harold Smith's suggestion that Milton S. Eisenhower, brother of General Dwight D. Eisenhower, be transferred from the Agriculture Department to head the agency.[5] The WRA was given official life on March 18, 1942, by Executive Order 9102. The order authorized the director of the WRA to "effectuate a program for the removal, relocation, maintenance and supervision of persons designated under Executive Order No. 9066."[6] Although the agency's name prominently featured "relocation," the presence of the final two terms of its mission, maintenance and supervision, indicated that extended custody of Japanese Americans was already being contemplated.

THE TOLAN COMMITTEE

Even as the government put its plans into motion, the force of West Coast public demands for large-scale removal of Japanese Americans accelerated. Newspaper editors and columnists and letter writers continued to call for strict controls to be placed on Issei and Nisei. The overwhelming pressure for evacuation was further demonstrated by the testimony before Representative John Tolan's House Select Committee on National Defense Migration, which had assumed the task of reporting on the West Coast situation in the days before Executive Order 9066 had been signed. By the time the committee began holding hearings on February 21, 1942, evacuation of Japanese Americans was a fait accompli. The committee decided not to challenge the president's wisdom, but to limit its mandate to reporting on relocation policies and plans.

Still, committee members were anxious to explore the rationale behind mass removal, and West Coast nativist, commercial, and community groups took the opportunity of the committee's hearings to expound on the innate disloyalty of the Japanese race. For example, the California Joint Immigration Committee presented a report in which it deplored the granting of citizenship to American-born children of Asian parents, which it compared to the "grave mistake" of "granting of citizenship to the Negroes after the Civil War."[7] Dozens of official witnesses endorsed wholesale removal. San Francisco Mayor Angelo Rossi, who issued a warm defense of the loyalty of German and Italian aliens, said that all Issei should be removed immediately, and Nisei carefully investigated. Attorney General Earl Warren claimed that there was no way to distinguish a loyal from a disloyal Japanese American and pointed to the many Issei farms located near military camps, airports, and telephone lines as unmistakable proof of the "Japanese" peril—the fact that the farms had been in existence long before the military installations had been built he conveniently ignored. The state attorney general admitted that there had been no reports of fifth-column activity by Japanese Americans—at the committee's request, FBI and Hawaii police authorities had formally confirmed that there had been no sabotage or interference by Japanese Americans during and after the Pearl Harbor attack—but Warren agreed with General DeWitt that this fact demonstrated, not that Issei and Nisei were innocent, but that a concerted attack had been planned.

On February 23, 1942, a Japanese submarine lobbed shells at an oil refinery in the Southern California town of Goleta, causing no casualties and only minor damage. Although it was the only direct attack Japanese forces would make on the mainland, it seemed to confirm the danger and to comfort those favoring evacuation in their opinions. The committee took the testimony under advisement and soon after issued a series of reports. It urged loyalty hearings for German and Italian aliens but stopped short of proposing them for Japanese Americans, although it did urge the government to create an Alien Property Custodian to care for the property of those removed.

OPPOSITION TO MASS REMOVAL

A small number of non-Japanese witnesses appeared before the Tolan Committee and attempted to rebut the wave of anti-Japanese testimony. Local Farm Security Administration director Richard Neustadt, reporting on FSA efforts, bluntly denounced the manufactured agitation to despoil Japanese Americans "and to give to greedy others the fine gardens and farms that have been developed by these people on land that originally the white man did not care to improve."[8] University of Washington professors Jesse Steiner and Robert O'Brien and California CIO secretary Louis Goldblatt denounced the movement for evacuation as racist and harmful. However, they were drowned out by opposing voices and skeptical questioners.[9]

Apart for the hearings, few commentators outside the West Coast paid much attention, positive or negative, to the military orders and the implementation of removal plans on the West Coast. Most Americans no doubt assumed that there was a real danger, and the government knew what it was doing. By and large, liberal and left-wing groups failed to make any significant protest, and there was little organized opposition outside of a small circle of progressive church groups such as the American Friends Service Committee and the Fellowship of Reconciliation.[10] The American Communist Party, which had expelled its Nisei members after Pearl Harbor as part of its strategy of full support for the war effort, expressed strong approval for evacuation. Minority groups were mixed in their reaction. Jewish organizations, many of which were led by Roosevelt supporters, were silent or positive, though various individual Jews protested. Similarly, although African American groups took no official action, individual African Americans proved to be disproportionately visible among supporters of the rights of Japanese Americans. In particular, *Pittsburgh Courier* columnist George Schuyler and the editors of the *Los Angeles Tribune* published numerous articles in opposition to the government's policy. In contrast, Mexican Americans remained largely silent. A few individuals opposed removal. However, the conservative Los Angeles daily *La Opinion*, the largest Mexican American newspaper, endorsed mass removal of Issei and Nisei, whom it termed "actual or potential enemies of the United States," and opening up landownership and economic opportunity for Mexican immigrants.[11]

The American Civil Liberties Union (ACLU), the major organization that defended constitutional rights of Americans, was equivocal and compromised in its support of Japanese Americans. When a set of board members of the ACLU, led by Director Roger Baldwin, sent a letter to the White House asking for the institution of loyalty hearings for Issei and Nisei, a circle of ACLU board members—many of them Jews sympathetic to the New Deal—called a board referendum. The result was that the board, by majority vote, barred the ACLU from directly challenging the constitutionality of Executive Order 9066. ACLU lawyers were authorized to support legal challenges to the order's discriminatory enforcement against Japanese Americans, but the concession of principle involved clearly made for a much weaker case.[12]

The only national political organization to oppose the removal publicly was the Socialist Party, which had been discredited by its leaders' prewar opposition to military intervention. Socialist leader Norman Thomas denounced the government's actions as "totalitarian Justice" in a series of newspaper and magazine articles, in radio talks, and in a pamphlet, "Democracy and Japanese Americans." Other party members organized lobbying and aid efforts and wrote in the party newspaper, the *Call*.[13] Working under the auspices of the Post War World Council in New York City, Norman Thomas circulated a petition calling for the immediate rescission of the president's order. Some two hundred intellectuals and progressives signed, including a number of well-known individuals, such as novelist Pearl S. Buck, writer/activist W.E.B. DuBois, and theologian Reinhold Niebuhr. However, the petition failed to alter official policy. Thomas himself claimed shortly afterward that he had never seen an important issue on which he had experienced more difficulty in arousing the American public, particularly liberals and labor unionists.[14]

JAPANESE AMERICAN REACTIONS

Japanese Americans, who had been largely taken by surprise by Executive Order 9066, were dazed by the onslaught against them. The response of the Issei to mass removal has often been described, in somewhat exaggerated terms, as a passive acceptance based on a sense of *shigata kanai* (a Japanese expression meaning "Go fight City Hall" or "It can't be helped"). Farmwife Fumi Kawaguchi told her diary of feeling relieved that the uncertainty everyone had been facing would soon be over. "[My husband] came home and said it was announced at last that this coastline area 70 to 80 miles around will have to be evacuated in about 60 days. If this is so, at least it's better than not knowing." Nevertheless, Issei from the region actively considered mass migration, despite the logistical and financial obstacles to such a move—the Kawaguchi family ended up organizing a caravan and migrating to central Utah to escape camp.[15]

Although small groups of Nisei, as mentioned, had met with California Governor Olson and with federal officials during February, community leaders had scarcely been consulted regarding their opinions or plans for action, and the Nisei only belatedly realized that their citizenship rights were in danger of being violated. In the days after the president's order was announced, community newspaper commentaries ranged from disbelief and anger to relief that at least decisions about their fate were being taken out of the hands of local (and racist) authorities.[16] Sue Kunitomi Embrey later recalled: "We had all these meetings in Little Tokyo. I went to one of them. There were some people who wanted to protest and others who wanted to wait and see what the government was going to do. There was a big debate over whether we should go quietly and cooperate with the government, or whether everybody should go on their own wherever they could. There was a lot of opposition to that because of all the discrimination out there."[17]

The range of Nisei views was revealed in testimony before the Tolan Committee. San Francisco journalist James Omura, despite his previous support for spying on potentially disloyal Nisei, attacked evacuation forthrightly: "Has the Gestapo come to America? Have we not risen in righteous anger at Hitler's mistreatment of Jews? Then is it not incongruous that citizen Americans of Japanese descent should be mistreated and persecuted?"[18] However, most Nisei questioned by the Tolan Committee tried their best to balance assertions of their citizenship rights with assurances of patriotic loyalty. Michio Kunitani of the Oakland Nisei Democrats asserted that Nisei liked baseball, jazz, and hot dogs just as other Americans did and expressed great skepticism about the racist motives behind the call for evacuation. JACL secretaries Henry Tani and Mike Masaoka asserted their Americanness and protested the involvement of pressure groups in the movement for evacuation. All but Omura, however, agreed that Japanese Americans would support the government's action as an emergency measure. "With any policy of evacuation definitely arising from reasons of military necessity and national safety, we are in complete agreement."[19]

In the end, despite grave misgivings, the executive board of the Japanese American Citizens League, the largest Nisei group, decided the organization had no choice but to support the government. Many other Nisei leaders followed suit, in varying degrees: Togo Tanaka, English editor of *Rafu Shimpo*, urged his readers in a headline, "Let's Cooperate Cheerfully!" Organized opposition by a small and vulnerable group during wartime, the leaders reasoned—no doubt correctly—would be suicidal in triggering wholesale military intervention, and might confirm the taint of disloyalty on which mass evacuation had already been based. Much better to compromise on principle on a temporary wartime step, they decided, and to concentrate on defending their citizenship rights. In hopes of having a voice in the fate of the Nisei, the JACL offered the government its assistance with planning and implementing evacuation. The JACL's policy of collaboration, which presented the odd spectacle of a civil rights organization colluding in mass violations of civil rights, was a fatal step that split the community and ultimately caused lasting bitterness among those who accused the JACL of "selling the Nisei down the river."[20]

Most Issei and Nisei alike were apprehensive and saddened to be removed from their homes to face an uncertain future, and they reacted as best as they could, by continuing to work and by making arrangements for their departure. West Coast newspaper editors devoted themselves to assisting relocation, even as they wound up their own journals. Togo Tanaka (along with the JACL and other groups) recruited volunteers to help establish an Assembly Center at Manzanar in California's Owens Valley, first by building barracks and facilities, later by conducting automobile convoys to the center. Larry Tajiri, longtime editor of the San Francisco *Nichi Bei* (with assistance from Isamu Noguchi) intervened with the Office of War Information in hopes of creating a government-sponsored vernacular newspaper to help keep Japanese Americans informed. Offered a job by the OWI, Tajiri agreed instead to take over the JACL newsletter *The Pacific Citizen*. After following the JACL to its new quarters in Salt Lake City, Tajiri and his wife Guyo transformed the journal into a nationally based biweekly newspaper.[21]

A number of Nisei designed schemes for large-scale voluntary migration and resettlement. For example, Isamu Noguchi presented a comprehensive plan for government-sponsored resettlement by Japanese American farmers and craft workers in pioneer communities on public land so that they could contribute food to the war effort. San Francisco-area nurseryman Hi Korematsu (whose brother Fred would soon after challenge evacuation in court) proposed the establishment of farm cooperatives in desert areas. James Sakamoto, editor of the Seattle-based *Japanese-American Courier*, wrote to the White House to propose colonization of interior agricultural areas by caravans of West Coast farmers. Fred Wada, an Oakland-based produce merchant, organized a caravan of 130 Japanese Americans and moved to Utah, where he founded a successful agricultural cooperative. However, federal officials were unprepared to offer encouragement or large-scale financial or material help to make relocation possible, although a small number of Japanese Americans who submitted a detailed "relocation plan" for official approval received token sums from the army for transportation expenses.[22]

A few brave individuals, with the aid of sympathetic non-Japanese counsel, challenged Executive Order 9066. Gordon Hirabayashi, a student at the University of Washington, and Minoru Yasui, an Oregon-born attorney, deliberately violated the official curfew and registration requirements and sought arrest in order to bring legal challenges.[23] Soon after, Fred Korematsu, who tried to evade removal by passing as non-Japanese before being caught and apprehended, was recruited as a test case by Ernest Besig of the Northern California ACLU. Lincoln Kanai and Mr. and Mrs. Ernest Wakayama also brought suit in federal court challenging incarceration.[24]

Here, once again, the JACL was caught in an unhappy dilemma by its decision to advocate collaboration with the federal government. Believing that legal challenges to government actions would be destructive, the JACL refused to support the test cases and issued public statements denouncing the plaintiffs.[25] Yet JACL leaders did take actions to support the rights of Japanese Americans. For example, the organization officially endorsed Norman Thomas's pamphlet "Democracy and Japanese Americans," which criticized removal and called for immediate reversal and reparations, and the JACL arranged for its widespread distribution to supportive groups. Also, its members held fast in support of the principle of citizenship, in the face of action by militant nativists. During the spring of 1942 the American Legion and the Native Sons of the Golden West, represented by former California attorney general Ulysses S. Webb, brought a lawsuit in federal court, *Regan v. King*, to overturn the citizenship and voting rights of Nisei. With assistance from ACLU attorney A. L. Wirin and support from a set of African American attorneys, Loren Miller, Hugh Macbeth, and Thomas Griffith, the JACL successfully opposed the suit.[26]

The Nisei dilemma of loyalty versus civil rights was ironically dramatized by an incident in New York City on June 18, 1942. JACL Secretary Mike Masaoka accepted Norman Thomas's invitation to join a forum on Japanese Americans, sponsored by the Post War World Council and attended by representatives of a coalition of groups. At the forum, Thomas introduced a resolution opposing "military internment of unaccused persons in concentration camps" and calling for the immediate convening of hearing boards to determine the loyalty of those held. Masaoka expressed his support. Stating that the treatment of the Nisei was a "test of democracy," he warned his listeners "If they can do it to one group, they can do it to other groups."[27] The resolution was swiftly opposed by delegates of the New York-based Japanese American Committee for Democracy (JACD), a circle of progressive Issei and Nisei who were influenced by the Communist Party and its policy of 100 percent support for the war effort. The JACD members introduced a counterresolution approving roundup of potential Axis supporters and affirming that criticism of government policy hampered the war effort.[28] The JACD resolution was defeated, but the intervention prevented the meeting from reaching any consensus on reconsideration of Executive Order 9066.[29]

THE CONDITION OF HAWAII'S JAPANESE AMERICANS

The signing of Executive Order 9066 and its aftermath were mirrored during 1942 by a tug-of-war over the status of Japanese Americans in Hawaii, in which opposing factions expressed differing views and the president and his advisors faced off against the territory's military and civilian rulers. Over the weeks following Pearl Harbor, in the shadow of a potential Japanese invasion, the new military governor's office began a process of reconstruction and conversion of the territory to a wartime footing. While the army operated, as mentioned, on a formally race-neutral basis, it privately and publicly justified its rule over the territory by the "Japanese threat." This meant primarily the threat of invasion from Tokyo, but it was also sometimes defined to include locals.

At the same time, wartime uncertainty and fear of invasion bred a climate of public anxiety that was easily deflected onto local Japanese. Those Issei on the "ABC lists," as well as some Nisei, who were arrested in the hours after Pearl Harbor were confined at the internment camp at Sand Island. They bore the brunt of ambient suspicion and hostility against the entire community. Beyond being confined without charge, they were subjected to continual strip searches, kept busy on mindless labor jobs, and denied contact with families.[30] The Issei and Nisei outside, who were cut off from the rest of the nation and received only censored letters and news bulletins, could not but be aware that their own fragile liberty rested on sufferance and that they would face mass repression at the least sign of any conduct deemed "disloyal." The supportive efforts of Japanese American aid workers after Pearl Harbor, the patriotic activities of Nisei in the 298th and 299th Infantry Units, and their rush to take up service in the Territorial Guard helped push public opinion in Hawaii to an overall supportive, or at least indifferent, posture toward Americans of Japanese ancestry (AJAs).[31] Yet community leaders were taking no chances. They urged local Japanese to disassociate themselves from Japan in any way possible, by ceasing to wear kimonos, listening to Western music and changing their family names. Public Buddhist practice was discouraged (with most of the islands' ministers interned, it was not easy at any rate to organize services), while Christian ministers such as Reverend Okamura supported the closing of temples and agitated for group conversion.

To promote unity and avoid interracial conflict, the territory's Office of Civilian Defense created a Public Morale section. On Charles Hemenway's recommendation, YMCA director Charles Loomis, Chinese-American YMCA secretary Hung Wai Ching, and Nisei official Shigeo Yoshida, who had been leading members of the prewar interracial advisory group Hemenway had put together, were selected to direct the new section. The three served as liaisons between the military and the community. They put together teams of contacts from different Asian ethnic groups and organized public meetings, lectures, and propaganda to promote fair treatment for all, including Issei and Nisei. Meanwhile, they worked to establish a subgroup, the Emergency Service Committee. The committee encouraged Japanese Americans to show their patriotism by buying War Bonds and participating in blood drives and rallies, and meanwhile supervised the liquidation of property and assets of closed prewar community centers, converting them for use by military service organizations. In cooperation with Honolulu Police Chief John Burns and local FBI director Robert Shivers, the committee pushed "Americanization" by offering classes in American history and culture, and members inaugurated a widespread "speak English" campaign.[32]

Nevertheless, throughout 1942 there remained troubling signs of anti-Nisei sentiment. The New Year's issues of the *New York Times* and *Time* magazine, undoubtedly relying on Hawaiian sources, both featured vague and invented tales of sabotage by local Japanese.[33] In February 1942 Atherton Richards, an elite rancher whose parents, ironically, had founded a multiracial colony and created a scholarship fund for Japanese students, submitted a confidential report to William Donovan, the coordinator of information (and future chief of the Office of Strategic Services). The report referred to Japanese Americans in Hawaii as subject to "unpredictable activities and loyalties" and advised mass evacuation of Issei and

Nisei to one of the outlying islands, where they could be watched and could grow food.[34] Local businessman John A. Balch complained about the "mollycoddling" of the Japanese, who were left free to buy up choice real estate and earn large incomes. In a pamphlet, he revealed his plan for wholesale transportation of ethnic Japanese to the mainland, to prevent Hawaii from becoming "a super Japanese-colony." When the Hawaii Chamber of Commerce rejected his plan and neither the army nor navy expressed interest, Balch pursued his goal through the anti-Asian California Joint Immigration Committee.[35] Angus Taylor, who was posted to Hawaii as U.S. attorney some months before the outbreak of war, testified before the Roberts Commission with charges that Japanese Americans were engaged in large-scale subversion, and he subsequently submitted reports to the White House advocating mass incarceration of ethnic Japanese. In April Taylor dispatched former Hawaii Housing Authority chairman Charles Pietsch to Washington to lobby the Justice Department. Pietsch insisted that "most of the responsible people" on Oahu considered a Japanese invasion imminent, and unless action were taken to control those of Japanese ancestry, local whites were ready to engage in wholesale slaughter at the least incident.[36]

Several weeks after Pietsch's memo, Albert Horlings, a former University of Hawaii journalism professor, chimed in publicly with an article in the liberal weekly *Nation* in which he asserted as a universal belief among reputable authorities in Hawaii that Japanese Americans in Hawaii were massively disloyal. Putting a more sophisticated gloss on prewar racial stereotyping about assimilation and "dual citizenship," Horlings insisted that most Japanese Americans had a continuing material interest in Japan's victory. "The majority have nothing to gain by the defeat of Japan. Their prestige as expatriates depends in large part upon the prestige of the Japanese empire. Their economic fortunes are often tied more closely to Japan than to America; they work for Tokyo banks and business houses; they import goods from Japan; they invest in Japanese securities."[37] (Undoubtedly Horlings meant their past actions—just how much investing and economic activity any local Japanese could engage in with an enemy nation against which there was a trade embargo and naval conflict the article did not make clear.) Horlings concluded that mass internment, however desirable, was impractical, since any Japanese invasion would quickly liberate the disloyal. Instead, he advocated mass removal of local Japanese to the mainland.

THE PUSH FOR MASS REMOVAL IN HAWAII

Meanwhile, even as suspicions against Japanese Americans engulfed the Army's Western Defense Command during early 1942 and spread to the upper echelons of the War Department, official policy in Hawaii toward Issei and Nisei began to shift. As noted, in mid-January General Emmons, the military governor, issued orders disbanding the 317 Nisei serving in the Territorial Guard units and organized troops of non-Japanese home guards for close surveillance of Issei and Nisei. Even this, however, was not enough for determined War and Navy Department chiefs and members of Congress. Navy Secretary Frank Knox, who had made sensational accusations of fifth-column activity by local Japanese after Pearl Harbor, continued to repeat them despite the fact that Army Intelligence, G-2, and the FBI had all agreed that there had been no sabotage during or after the Pearl Harbor attack, and the Tolan Committee had subsequently publicized their findings.[38] In any case, the War Department maintained that since Hawaii was under martial law, responsibility for security lay with Emmons, the local commander. As the new year dawned and Japan's military swept through the western Pacific, Knox grew increasingly insistent that all local Japanese in Oahu be transported for internment. Seizing on the proposals offered over the prewar months, he proposed creating camps on Molokai or one of the other outlying islands. Asked his opinion of such an operation, General Emmons responded in politic fashion that it was fine as a long-term goal but that the territory lacked the construction and shipping facilities to make mass confinement practical, and he had need of all available labor resources for reconstruction of territorial defenses and for agriculture. The matter remained in abeyance until the end of January, while the Roberts Commission completed its hearing on Pearl Harbor and issued its report. By that time, Secretary of War Stimson (undoubtedly fortified by Justice Roberts's own private comments over his distrust of Japanese) had likewise become convinced that stringent action was necessary. On February 1, 1942, the War Department informed General Emmons that it favored discharging the remaining Nisei soldiers of the 298th and 299th Infantry Units from active duty. While the soldiers could not lawfully be summarily discharged from their units, they were relieved of their weapons and confined to barracks under armed guard over the next weeks. Emmons sought a compromise by proposing that the units be relegated to the status of a labor battalion (like most African

American units of the era) but insisted he needed manpower. His request was granted as a temporary measure.[39]

Meanwhile, War Department officials asked Emmons for more specific recommendations on a mass internment plan. Emmons responded that those who were considered immediately dangerous were already in custody, and that there was no way to eliminate every conceivable threat short of removing 100,000 local Japanese to the mainland (which he implicitly considered an unrealizable objective). Instead, he insisted, the logical priority would be to evacuate 20,000 white civilians who were dispensable. As a sop to his superiors, on February 20, 1942, Emmons approved the transfer to the mainland of 172 Sand Island internees considered "troublemakers." Still, when Navy Secretary Knox inquired about mass confinement, Emmons responded that he did not favor any "wholesale movement" of the local Japanese.[40]

The military governor's approach failed to satisfy Washington. On February 12 (the day after President Roosevelt granted the War Department his consent for mass removal on the West Coast), General George Marshall, army chief of staff, prepared a draft document for the Joint Chiefs that he called "an appreciation" of Hawaiian defense forces. The document, given the name J.C.S. 11, set forth options regarding defense construction and other matters. In a final section, it proclaimed that Japanese Americans were "inimical" to the defense of the territory and would all "probably" be placed together under close surveillance. The immediate objective, the text continued, was to confine the approximately 20,000 people considered most dangerous, and it proposed two alternatives: "a) Instituting a *concentration camp* on one of the Hawaiian Islands, such as Molokai. b) transferring the Japanese population to a *concentration camp* located on the U.S. mainland" (emphasis in original). There was no mention, even euphemistic, of "resettlement."

By the time J.C.S. 11 was sent to the Joint Chiefs for consideration, Executive Order 9066 had been signed. Its promulgation reminded high administration officials of the more glaring menace to Hawaii. Thus, on February 23 Navy Secretary Knox wrote the president asking permission for mass removal of Japanese Americans in Hawaii, and inquiring whether the provisions of the new Executive Order could be extended to constitutionally justify it. Knox admitted that such a program would be costly, but it was imperative to protect the territory from a population he considered to have "predominantly enemy sympathies." Roosevelt responded the following day with a memo in which he agreed that most Japanese Americans on Oahu should be moved. He added that he was not concerned about any constitutional difficulties, not only because of Executive Order 9066, but also since Hawaii was under martial law. Knox also met with Stimson, who expressed strong agreement that mass confinement was necessary and ordered Marshall to see to it.[41]

Faced with a clear mandate for action from the White House, the War and Navy departments organized a task force with other agencies to arrange mass confinement. Still, the policy was not easy to institute. On February 27 Stimson told FDR that putting Hawaiian Japanese in a "cantonment" on Molokai was not practical because of the great costs involved in guarding and supplying them there, and that he agreed with Marshall that it would likely be necessary to ship all potential internees to the mainland. The president, Stimson reported, was "staggered" by the idea of mass expulsion of local Japanese to the mainland and clearly preferred Knox's idea of placing them under guard on the "leper island."[42] However, on March 13 Stimson and Knox (with support from the Joint Chiefs, who on March 11 had formally approved J.C.S. 11) together won Roosevelt's endorsement for a plan to send 20,000 Japanese Americans from Hawaii to confinement on the mainland, as an initial step. Yet the secretary of war—who had first won fame as a lawyer—almost immediately began to have doubts over the constitutionality of such a move. It might be permissible, he reasoned, to transport Japanese Americans from a military zone and to hold them—in transit, as it were—as part of that move, but it was a completely different matter to confine American citizens indefinitely without charge outside an area where martial law was in force. His doubts increased when the American Civil Liberties Union threatened to bring habeas corpus petitions on behalf of all American citizens transported from Hawaii once they reached the mainland. Meanwhile, Assistant Secretary of War McCloy expressed misgivings about transporting Hawaiian internees to the mainland, which he feared would strain shipping and supplies and further inflame the delicate West Coast situation. In a newspaper interview, McCloy praised that the "keen and enthusiastic" work of the local Japanese and pointedly added that the connection of "the Japanese problem" with labor and defense needs made mass evacuation "at present" impossible."[43]

By mid-April Stimson decided to abandon further thought of bringing over Japanese in custody to the mainland. Roosevelt, prodded by Knox— and by influential Progressive senator Burton Wheeler of Montana, who complained of the administration's dilatory approach to Japanese in Hawaii—responded to Stimson's hesitation over ordering removal to the mainland by ordering him to work with the Navy Department on a new plan for mass removal within the territory of Issei and Nisei from Oahu and the main island of Hawaii.[44] Stimson and Knox met once again on April 28. They once more agreed that supplying a small outer Hawaiian island would be too difficult and resolved again to determine some legally acceptable way to ship dangerous Japanese Americans away from the territory. Attorney General Biddle, when consulted, suggested declaring martial law in enclaves on the mainland, but the president refused. The War Department, he insisted, should set up internment camps in Hawaii itself. Stimson was aware of the opposition of Emmons and the army staff to mass confinement of local Japanese on a smaller Hawaiian island. He nevertheless warned McCloy to focus on getting at least ten to twelve thousand people moved from Oahu. "I think you had better keep steadily on this because the president is very much worried over the situation."[45]

THE VARSITY VICTORY VOLUNTEERS

Although the War Department once again set to work on a plan to satisfy the president, his orders were defeated, not only by the enormous difficulties of the task, but by countervailing forces from Hawaii itself. With support from non-Japanese allies such as FBI chief Robert Shivers, Colonel Kendall Fielder of Army Intelligence, and Hung Wai Ching of the Morale Section, local Japanese organized to claim their place in the war effort. Most notably, in the days following the discharge of Nisei recruits from the Territorial Guard, local Japanese inspired by Ching organized public meetings and circulated petitions to General Emmons requesting alternate service as volunteer laborers. As a result, in late February 1942 Emmons approved the creation of the Corps of Engineers Auxiliary, a work battalion attached to the Thirty-Fourth Combat Engineers. The unit, dubbed the "Varsity Victory Volunteers," quickly attracted 169 enlistees, mostly Nisei college students who had formerly served in the Territorial Guard. The work the unit performed, amid the tropical heat of the islands, was arduous—clearing brush, building roads, quarrying rocks, painting buildings, and fixing fences.

The patriotism and enthusiasm of the volunteers and their supporters encouraged General Emmons to oppose wholesale confinement. In early May Assistant Secretary of War McCloy proposed that the Hawaiian commander draft a compromise plan for removal of twelve to fifteen thousand Japanese Americans to the big island of Hawaii, in order to defuse pressure from the president and the navy. Emmons, who considered the whole idea illogical, countered by proposing to ship five thousand "voluntary internees" to the mainland, to be made up of those considered dangerous and their families, plus children, dependents, and aged people who represented a drain on the islands' resources.[46] Emmons, in turn, secured McCloy's aid in mobilizing Nisei GIs. After visiting Hawaii in early March 1942 and reviewing the volunteers, the assistant secretary became convinced that Japanese Americans would make good soldiers. With McCloy's support, Emmons persuaded army chiefs that it would be better for overall morale not to discharge the Nisei soldiers of the 298th and 299th, although he agreed to move them away from the Pacific Coast. At the urging of Colonel Fielder, Army Chief of Staff George Marshall further intervened to assure that the Nisei units remain designated as combat troops, rather than labor brigades. In June 1942, as the Battle of Midway approached, the War Department decided to make use of the units but to oust them from Hawaii to forestall any danger they might pose. Some 1,432 soldiers, organized into the 100th Infantry Unit, were shipped for training to Camp McCoy in Wisconsin.[47]

Emmons' "voluntary evacuation" gambit was successful in stalling mass incarceration. The Joint Chiefs quickly devised a new plan for incarceration—Hawaiian residents, once on the mainland, would be transported to camps alongside West Coast Japanese Americans. Since they were officially there awaiting "resettlement" by the WRA, according to the official fiction adopted by the government in regard to the mainlanders, the army could keep them in custody indefinitely while avoiding the risk of habeas corpus petitions. On July 17—shortly after the U.S. Navy's crushing victory at Midway removed the major threat of Japanese invasion of Hawaii—President Roosevelt approved the plan for transportation of up to fifteen thousand people, and the WRA began reserving space for them. Emmons obtained a further delay by asking for extra time to make the selection of those to be transported and recruiting "volunteers." This was done primarily through visits by army officers to the families of those already in custody. Family members were offered the opportunity to join their relatives if they would agree to be transported. Although the army officers had reason to know that the Pacific Coast was closed to Japanese Americans and that all those sent to the mainland would be confined there, they pledged (either rashly or deceitfully) to "recommend" that prisoners be freed on arrival. Meanwhile, Emmons and McCloy persuaded Stimson that all those who posed an identifiable danger were already in custody, and that removal of more than a few thousand people would harm Hawaii's economy.

By the time the transport operation began, it was October and the danger of Japanese invasion of Hawaii had long subsided. Emmons restricted transport of Japanese to three hundred per ship, with an upper limit of five thousand. When Roosevelt learned of the plan, through Knox, he was stunned and wrote Stimson to ask for an explanation of why his orders for mass removal had not been obeyed. Stimson assured the president that removal of more than a few thousand people would drain Hawaii's labor force and harm its economy. FDR fired back a message to Stimson and Marshall that "the only consideration is that of the safety of the Islands and that the labor situation is not only not a secondary matter but should not be given any consideration whatsoever."[48] He grumbled to his cabinet that Emmons was guided by pineapple and sugar interests who wanted to keep their Japanese laborers (Interior Secretary Harold Ickes, prompted by McCloy, responded that Issei and Nisei were needed for vital war labor).[49]

Roosevelt's irritation perhaps bespoke his knowledge that he was beaten. Three days after the president sent his memo, Emmons, with the blessing of the War Department, publicly guaranteed that there would be no large-scale evacuation of Japanese Americans in Hawaii. While Knox continued to rumble his dissatisfaction, it was clear that the plan was dead. In the end, only some 1,700 Japanese Americans from Hawaii were sent to confinement on the mainland during 1942, either in Justice Department camps or the WRA camps, in addition to the 1,500 who remained confined in Hawaii. Many of these were innocents who were effectively taken away by General Emmons and the War Department to placate the fears of the president and the secretary of the navy. Their sacrifice—it is hard not to think of it in those terms—averted arbitrary action against some 100,000 other Americans and the destruction of the Hawaiian economy.

VOLUNTARY EVACUATION AND JAPANESE AMERICAN PROPERTY

On the West Coast, General DeWitt's intention, at least initially, was to undertake a gradual, orderly removal, first of all Japanese, then of German and Italian aliens, from the West Coast. He explained to his superiors in early March that he did not believe in giving "preference" to any alien group (except, of course, that he regarded *all* persons of Japanese ancestry on a racial basis as aliens). To manage evacuation and custody of Japanese Americans until they could be taken over by the WRA, the War Department organized the Wartime Civilian Control Agency (WCCA), with Karl Bendetsen (promoted to the rank of colonel for the position) as its director. Bendetsen and his aides immediately began scouting out sites for temporary holding facilities near the coast and for more permanent camps in the interior (a task that was subsequently taken over by the WRA). In selecting potential sites, the government agencies insisted that the installations be located on publicly owned land, have access to sufficient soil and water resources for farming, and have potential employment for the "evacuees." The WCCA also approved designs for camp layout and barracks, which were adapted from standard military combat area base designs.[50]

Once the military areas had been declared, Army and Justice Department officials on the West Coast encouraged Issei and Nisei to relocate "voluntarily" as much as possible outside the excluded zone, on the grounds that this would lead to a more rapid and humane operation and would lessen the army's own financial and logistical burden in removing and confining them. Such a move was no easy task, especially for the Issei, whose bank accounts were restricted. Most Japanese Americans had farms and businesses in coastal areas, assets that could not be disposed of quickly. Few coast residents had friends or job contacts elsewhere. As mentioned, a number of Nisei proposed plans for large-scale voluntary migration and resettlement, but the Western Defense Command did not take these schemes seriously and took no steps to appoint liaison officers to assist in developing migration plans. Nonetheless, in the weeks that followed the declaration of military zones, some 10,000 Issei and Nisei did leave the coast: 4,889 left the region entirely, mostly to settle in the Rocky Mountain states of Utah and Colorado. The majority settled in the agricultural areas of eastern California, relying on General DeWitt's public statements that they would not be subject to exclusion there.[51]

As voluntary evacuation proceeded, the question of caring for Japanese American property grew increasingly pressing. Once Japanese Americans learned that they would be removed, they rapidly began making plans to sell or lease their farms and businesses, generally at a fraction of their actual value. Even before the military orders were announced, the Tolan

Committee sent an urgent request to the White House that a special custodian be appointed to take care of Japanese American property.[52] Military officials, realizing that concern for property was inhibiting Issei and Nisei from leaving the West Coast, also pushed for the appointment of an alien property custodian able to step in. Reports soon spread of large-scale losses by Japanese Americans, and of scavengers and bargain hunters descending on Japanese communities to pressure the residents into disposing of their belongings for absurdly low sums. These stories scandalized even congressional supporters of mass removal such as Clarence Lea and Leland Ford, who asked the White House to intervene.[53]

However, the appointment of such a custodian was blocked, in large part by the efforts of Secretary of the Treasury Henry Morgenthau. Although Morgenthau was eager to seize control over large Axis-owned businesses, he did not wish to undertake the thankless "social welfare" task (as he described it) of operating small shops and farms—especially since he believed removal of Japanese Americans would be a permanent process. When requested by colleagues to step in to hold vacated property, he justified his refusal on the legalistic grounds that no Alien Property Custodian had the power to take over the possessions of American citizens. McCloy soon joined with Harry Hopkins, FDR's right-hand man, to propose drafting legislation so that the government could take over properties of citizens—the Nisei, most of whom were children or young adults, generally had little in the way of possessions anyhow, apart from the agricultural property held under their names by Issei barred from ownership by alien land laws. When pressed to act, Morgenthau took the matter to Roosevelt, who agreed that the government could not protect Japanese Americans against losses. The president told Morgenthau that while he cared for the lives of the people who would be transported, he was not concerned about their property.[54]

Instead, the treasury secretary arranged to dispatch special representatives of the Federal Reserve Bank to the West Coast to provide a voluntary service to aid Japanese Americans in liquidating their possessions. The bank officials were largely ineffective in protecting Japanese Americans from catastrophic losses. They were based in urban areas, inaccessible to the rural areas where most farms were located, and were untrained and often unsympathetic in dealing with Issei and Nisei. Although officially armed with (legally dubious) authority to freeze unjust transactions, bank officials refused to actually make use of it and instead put greater pressure on the Japanese Americans to sell. In any case, the government could not use moral suasion to suspend the laws of supply and demand—the Japanese Americans who were facing impending removal were forced to take the best offer they could get for their immovable property, and bargain sales of farms and household items continued.[55] Car owners had the choice of leasing or selling them or of storing them at their own expense. Those who refused and chose to drive themselves and their belongings to assembly centers were then required to sell their cars either to the military or to civilians, on pain of official seizure and requisitioning.

Meanwhile, despite complaints from the Tolan Committee, the army delayed making storage facilities available to Japanese Americans. The Federal Reserve Bank ultimately contracted out limited warehouse space, at army expense, to store evacuee belongings but did not provide guards or insurance for such facilities, with the result that they were vandalized and pillaged during the war. In the end, the vast majority of Japanese Americans were forced to either entrust their belongings to white friends (many of whom damaged or never returned them) or church groups, throw them out, or sell them off, generally at fire-sale prices. A postwar study, which took lost income as well as lost property into account, estimated the total damage wrought by mass confinement at $347 million. Researchers in later decades, using different methods, ultimately estimated total losses by Japanese Americans during evacuation at between 67 and 116 million dollars (1945 dollars).[56]

THE SHIFT TO INVOLUNTARY EVACUATION

The army soon decided that the process of "voluntary evacuation" was too slow and cumbersome. More important, mountain state authorities complained to DeWitt about the negative public reaction to the Japanese passing through, although there was no actual wave of violence against the migrants. The government's own removal policy was largely responsible for the unfriendly attitude because it placed an enormous stigma on Japanese Americans among Americans nationwide. As Philip Glick, WRA Solicitor, put it, "The agitation for mass evacuation had repeatedly asserted that West Coast residents of Japanese ancestry were of uncertain loyalty. The government's later decision to evacuate was widely interpreted as proof of the truth of that assertion."[57] Residents of these interior areas assumed that if the Japanese Americans were too dangerous to remain on the coast, they should not be "dumped" into the region. Continual (exaggerated or unfounded) newspaper stories about arrests of Japanese Americans for possession of contraband or violation of curfew fueled panic.[58]

Although in theory such matters were unrelated to any issue of military necessity and hence unworthy of consideration, DeWitt bowed to the popular pressure. On March 27, 1942, he ordered all departures by Japanese Americans out of the excluded zone halted within forty-eight hours. (DeWitt ordered residents to await official removal, but his announcement nevertheless set off a final movement of desperate refugees fleeing inland.) The general responded to popular pressure in other ways as well. At the request of white Arizona farmers fearful of losing their Japanese American labor force, DeWitt redrew the borders of the West Coast military area to leave certain districts in central Arizona unrestricted. Similarly, in June 1942, in response to pressure from East Californians fearful of entering Japanese Americans, the general suddenly declared the California section of Military Area 2 an excluded area. The five thousand migrants who had moved to the region, mostly on short notice, relying on the general's promise that they would not be evacuated, were trapped and subsequently rounded up and incarcerated.[59]

Once voluntary migration was halted, the Western Defense Command prepared and executed involuntary mass removal. General DeWitt, at least initially, considered wholesale removal unnecessary and beyond the Army's capacities. Nevertheless, the War Department chiefs—despite their continued insistence, then and later, that their removal policy was based on the judgment of the military commander on the spot—left him no choice in the matter.[60] Shortly thereafter, the War Department also formally overruled DeWitt's unpopular plan to empty the Western Defense Command of German and Italian aliens. As a result, only individual German and Italian aliens considered dangerous were ever arrested, and they had a right to speedy administrative hearings where they could present witnesses and evidence to prove their loyalty. A small fraction of these aliens, who were unable to establish their innocence, were interned. In contrast, the Western Defense Command refused to institute loyalty hearings for *any* Japanese Americans, irrespective of citizenship, or to segregate pro-Japanese and pro-American elements, on the grounds that this would undercut the entire basis for mass removal—that the loyalty of Japanese Americans could not be determined or trusted.[61]

The extreme nature of the removal policy and the racist ideas that underlay it were starkly demonstrated by General DeWitt's insistence that all people of Japanese ancestry be cleared from the West Coast, and that no exceptions be granted. Apart from those Japanese Americans who were incarcerated in prisons and those confined in hospitals who were too ill to be moved (plus one older navy veteran, presumably protected by naval authorities, who was exempted for his meritorious service), Japanese Americans of all ages were carried away. Even the army language school at the Presidio, with its Japanese instructors, was forced to decamp.[62] Colonel Bendetsen carried out the "no exceptions" policy with horrifying literalness. As DeWitt's final report on the evacuation stated, "Included among the evacuees were persons who were only part Japanese, some with as little as one-sixteenth Japanese blood; others who, prior to evacuation, were unaware of their Japanese ancestry; and many who had married Caucasians, Chinese, Filipinos, Negroes, Hawaiians, or Eskimos."[63] Not since the denial of citizenship rights in the Jim Crow South to those with tiny gradations of African American ancestry had a single ancestor been determined to have such an inherent corrupting force. The army quickly drew up a mixed marriage policy, based on a tortured mixture of gender, biological, and sociological stereotypes. According to this policy, ethnic Japanese women who were married to white American men or those from "friendly" countries (generally Filipinos), plus the mixed-race children of these marriages, could be exempted from evacuation on a case-by-case basis, depending on their overall level of "Americanization" (that is, assimilation to white American norms). If these Japanese women divorced their husbands or were widowed, they would then be immediately subject to removal. Conversely, non-Japanese wives and unemancipated mixed-race children of Japanese American men would be spared evacuation—but *not* the Japanese American men themselves. In fact, a number of Caucasian women, including artist Estelle Ishigo and activist Elaine Black Yoneda, and their children accompanied their family members to camp.[64] Bendetsen and his aides stripped Japanese American children from their Caucasian foster families and toured orphanages to make sure that any infant or child who appeared to have Japanese ancestry would be removed. The Shonien orphanage, which housed Japanese American children, organized a "children's village" at the Manzanar camp for the orphans in their charge.

Once mass removal was decreed, Bendetsen and the WCCA assumed full responsibility for carrying out the operation. WCCA staffers divided up Military Area 1 into a set of 99 (later 108) exclusion areas and produced plans for removing the ethnic Japanese populations of each district. The Census Bureau, in an illegal breach of confidentiality, provided an advisor who obtained raw data from 1940 census files, with precise details on the ethnic Japanese population of individual city blocks and tracts. This information enabled the Western Defense Command to divide up districts efficiently and locate Issei and Nisei inside.[65] Meanwhile, in order not to interrupt food production, the army ordered Japanese American farmers to continue with their spring planting on pain of arrest for interference with the war effort, even though they recognized that the farmers would not be permitted to remain long enough to produce the season's harvest. In the end, the overwhelming majority of Nikkei farmers were forced to abandon their farms to white (or in some cases Hispanic) tenants and purchasers and were unable to realize any profit from the expense and arduous labor they devoted to growing their crops during 1942.[66]

Evacuation began in the last week of March 1942, with the most militarily sensitive districts given priority. (Bainbridge Island, near Seattle, Washington, which the navy considered a danger zone, was the first area to be emptied.) The Western Defense Command created "civil control stations" in schools and other public buildings in the designated districts, then posted notices on billboards, schools, and windows. The notices proclaimed the evacuation of all Japanese Americans within the boundaries of the delineated area and gave them seven days to report for evacuation. The notices also required a member of each family to register immediately at the station. There they received identification numbers and directions for evacuation day. Japanese Americans were informed that they would be permitted to bring with them only as many belongings as they could carry and were instructed to use the following days to make final disposition of their belongings. Agents from the Farm Security Administration and other agencies were present to assist with storage and advise on disposition.[67]

Over a period of ninety days in the spring of 1942, 109,427 Japanese Americans were removed from the West Coast to assembly centers under military supervision. (In addition, 641 people—mostly Issei released from Justice Department internment camps and permitted to join their families—were transferred from elsewhere, and 151 people of Japanese ancestry were arrested and expelled from the Territory of Alaska).[68]

The removal process was repeated dozens of times. Japanese American residents of a district would be ordered to assemble at the control station, generally at dawn. Their luggage was tagged with their family number, then placed in large piles loaded for transport. Often non-Japanese friends and neighbors came to see the evacuees off. Sometimes, volunteers from local groups or the Red Cross or the American Friends Service Committee provided refreshments; other times, the evacuees had nothing to eat. As Yuri Tateishi recalled:

> The day of the evacuation was April 26. The day before, we had to sleep on the floor because all the furniture was gone. . . . I recall we had to get up very early in the morning, and I think we all walked to the Japanese school because so one had a car then. And everybody was just all over the place, the whole Japanese community was there, the West L.A. community. The Westwood Methodist Church had some hot coffee and doughnuts for us that morning, which helped a lot, and we were loaded in a bus.[69]

A few Japanese Americans who owned cars drove to assembly centers in auto caravans under armed escort. The rest boarded buses and/or trains to their destinations. They were then sent to an assembly center on the West Coast (a few later departures went directly to a camp inland).[70]

By all accounts, even those written by critics of the government's policy, the army's action was handled with commendable swiftness, courtesy, and lack of deliberate cruelty. There was little or no violence against Japanese Americans by hostile civilians during evacuation (not least because Issei and Nisei were under armed guard), and the army worked well with the associated civilian agencies. Perhaps inevitably, though, there were horrors and humiliations stemming from the removal process. Paul Okimoto, sent to Santa Anita, as a child, recalled an interrupted farewell as Japanese Americans boarded trains:

> A young man embracing his girl friend was having a hard time saying goodbye to her. An MP guard shoved him away from the train as the train tooted its whistle, announcing its imminent departure. The man ran to the other side of the train to kiss her once more. An MP cocked his shotgun and ran after him. When the MP reached the young man, he clubbed him with his rifle butt. The young man was taken away with blood streaming down his face. I was shocked to see the blood, but relieved to see that he wasn't shot.[71]

THE ASSEMBLY CENTERS

Once they were rounded up and moved from their homes, the West Coast Japanese Americans were sent to a network of fifteen temporary facilities controlled by the army's Wartime Civil Control Administration, which the government termed "assembly centers." The assembly centers were Puyallup, Washington (dubbed "Camp Harmony" by the authorities); Portland, Oregon; Mayer, Arizona; and Santa Anita, Tanforan, Tulare, Turlock, Marysville, Merced, Pinedale, Pomona, Sacramento, Salinas, Stockton, and Fresno, California. These assembly centers, formed out of requisitioned racetracks and fairgrounds along the West Coast—such activities having been officially halted for the duration of the war—were designed by the WCCA to provide immediate mass confinement of evacuated Japanese Americans until permanent camps could be created inland. Meanwhile, with help from Nisei volunteer labor, the Army Corps of Engineers began constructing two larger centers, Manzanar and Poston, from the ground up.

Conditions at these centers were crowded and uncomfortable. Army workers hastily cleared and painted racetrack horse stalls and fairground livestock pens to make into barracks for the inmates. One inmate recalled, "The horse stalls had been whitewashed, but they still had straw and horsehair between the planks of the walls, and they maintained the smell of the animals throughout."[72] Another added, "We are infested with tiny fleas that bite like hell. They must be horse fleas or something that come from the old stables. Gods, they certainly make life miserable."[73] Meanwhile, shacks were constructed in infields and parking lots. Entire families were crowded into a single room, while single adults shared with strangers. The only furniture given the inmates upon arrival was a mattress cover, which they were assigned to fill with straw in order to make beds for themselves. As Miné Okubo, who was confined at Tanforan, recalled: "The mattress department was a stable filled with straw. We were given bags of ticking and told to help ourselves to the straw. The few cotton mattresses available were reserved for the sick and the old. When we had finished filling the bags, the openings were sewed roughly together and we carried the bags away."[74]

The army built group showers or used existing horse showers, and dug latrine pits for toilet facilities. The facilities at Santa Anita were located far from living quarters, had long lines of inmates waiting to use them, and were uncomfortable. In the words of one inmate, the toilets were "10 seats lined up; hard, fresh-sawed, unsandpapered wood; automatic flushing every fifteen minutes."[75] While these were (officially) gender-segregated, they had no partitions or coverings for privacy, and shyer inmates would wait until late hours to visit them. Sanitation in all the camps was sufficiently poor, said a United States Health Service report, that epidemics were a constant threat.[76] The heat added to the toll, especially as summer dawned. As one inmate at Portland recalled, "Cool places were nonexistent in the crowded compound, and people were frequently fainting. Adding to the oppressive hot weather, I had vaccination fevers and frequent diarrhea."[77] Medical care was extremely primitive. The handful of Nisei doctors who worked overtime to care for the inmates were unequipped to deal with serious cases. The WCCA was slow to build hospitals, and it was difficult to get permission to take ill inmates to outside facilities in ambulances, especially on an emergency basis—confining the inmates was clearly more crucial in the eyes of administrators than preserving their health.[78] Restricted to a small space, the inmates also suffered from boredom, particularly those too young to take paid employment. Because Japanese Americans were removed from their homes toward the end of the school year, WCCA authorities did not plan schools for the young Nisei, although ultimately a few schools, staffed by Japanese American teachers, were formed. Recreational facilities were likewise limited, at least at first. However, with the help of YMCA and YWCA and other civic groups who donated ping-pong tables, playground equipment, and sporting goods, sports and play activities became more common (at Tanforan there was even fishing and toy sailboat racing on lakes), and inmates organized crafts classes, beauty contests, and music groups and dance bands.[79] Libraries were set up with assistance from outside librarians and Quaker and religious groups.[80] In some centers, limited self-government was established, with election of Relocatee Councils formed of inmates.

In addition to the hurried nature of their confinement, the privations Japanese Americans faced reflected the government's efforts to appease (or appeal to) anti-Japanese opinion and deflect accusations that the inmates were being "coddled."[81] Food supplies were poor in amount and quality. The WCCA ordered that expenditures on food be limited to 50 cents daily per inmate, and the actual food bill ranged from thirty-three to thirty-nine cents per day—a fraction of the amount offered soldiers. The inmates had to line up three times a day for meals, with long waits, and then line up a second time to clean their dishes. Inexperienced cooks working with rationed materials on these tiny budgets produced food, such as Vienna sausages on rice, that ranged from inedible to uninspiring. Similarly, inmate wage scales were deliberately set below the rate of pay of army privates and ranged from eight dollars per month for unskilled jobs to sixteen dollars per month for professionals. Thousands of inmates were put to work on the camouflage-net factory set up at Santa Anita (Issei were later barred from such war production, since it violated the Geneva Convention), and a guayule (synthetic rubber) project was established at Manzanar. The dyes and chemicals from the net works caused numerous inmates to fall ill, and there was therefore accelerated worker turnover.[82]

WCCA center regulations imposed harsh restrictions on basic liberties. To begin with, the Japanese Americans were crowded into small areas surrounded by barbed wire and armed sentries. In Santa Anita, searchlights constantly swept up and down the "streets" (which had been named, in tongue-in-cheek fashion, for famous racehorses such as Man o' War) after dark and shined even on inmates visiting the bathroom.[83] Also, use of the Japanese language—the first language of many inmates, and in some cases their only language—was strictly banned in public meetings without the express consent of the administration. All writing in Japanese was forbidden, and Japanese-language books and other written materials were confiscated, except for dictionaries and Christian Bibles, which had to be officially checked for authenticity and approved. All center spaces, including "private" living areas, were subject to unannounced invasion by inspectors, who searched for contraband. Inmates were required to report for roll call each morning. Incoming mail was subject to opening and censorship. Officially endorsed mimeographed newspapers were founded in assembly centers in order to distribute news. However, all contents other than official bulletins had to be read and approved by the center's Public Relations Representative before publication would be permitted.[84] In sum, as a JACL inspection committee report stated of one center, "The entire atmosphere lends itself to that of a concentration camp or jail."[85]

Inmates struggled against the invasions of their rights. A group at Santa Anita, led by Kay Hirao, produced an illegal underground newsletter, "The Evacuee Speaks." To circumvent restraints on press freedom, Kiyoshi Conrad Hamanaka, editor of the Fresno *Grapevine*, smuggled stories that had been excised from the paper by censors to outside sympathizers for free distribution.[86] When a group at Santa Anita, led by Shuji Fujii (Kibei editor of the prewar left-wing newspaper *Doho*), circulated petitions demanding that bans on Japanese language and on public assembly be lifted, they were arrested by center police.[87] On August 4, 1942, the center's direction at Santa Anita summarily forbade possession of the hot plates, which families had brought in under existing rules and had been using to heat formula for babies and food for sick people. Center police invaded the barracks to seize contraband. Mobs of young Nisei and mothers challenged the guards and drove them away from the living quarters by throwing rocks and bottles. Military police were then called upon to disperse the crowds, although no arrests were made. The riot succeeded in reversing the hot-plate ban and relaxing surveillance.[88]

Because Japanese American inmates were generally confined in the assembly centers for several months at most, there has been a tendency to overlook their role in shaping the Japanese American wartime experience. However, as scholars such as Noriko Shimada and Takeya Mizuno have pointed out, the assembly centers were key in establishing the essential psychology of Japanese Americans.[89] It was in the assembly centers that Japanese Americans first experienced confinement in an enclosed space surrounded by military guards, and the privations of life with poor food and inadequate medical care. There they were struck by the blows to their dignity and self-respect caused by living amid makeshift surroundings without privacy. According to many later testimonies, the fact that the inmates were housed in converted animal pens starkly revealed the government's view of them as subhuman. Similarly, it was in the assembly centers that the inmates first interacted with officialdom. The shifting and arbitrary nature of the regulations under which they were forced to live and the undercurrent of hostility they experienced from white guards and workers quickly led inmates to feel outrage and bitterness.

MASS EXPULSION IN CANADA

Even as Japanese Americans were removed from the West Coast during the spring of 1942, the signing of P.C. 1481 by Canadian Prime Minister Mackenzie King gave rise to a parallel expulsion of 22,000 Japanese Canadians from their homes. To a certain extent, the Canadian government attacked the logistical question of removal with greater dispatch and precision than their American counterparts. Within ten days after the policy was announced, the cabinet created a new agency, the British Columbia Security Commission (BCSC), to direct the emptying out of the coastal districts and supervise the Japanese Canadians. Austin C. Taylor, a West Coast industrialist who had previously lobbied for removal of ethnic Japanese as a member of Vancouver's Citizens' Defense Committee, was named to chair the commission. Assistant Commander Frederick J. Mead of the RCMP and John Shirras of the B.C. provincial police were named as the BCSC's other members. The selection of civilians indicated that the military was not to participate at the highest level. At the same time, the makeup of the commission suggested that the government was primarily concerned with removing Japanese Canadians rather than attending to their needs, even though Taylor pronounced himself personally sympathetic to Issei and Nisei and expressed a wish to treat them as kindly as possible.[90] In a further sign of its distance from Japanese Canadians, the commission appointed as its sole Japanese community interlocutor a three-man liaison committee directed by Etsuji Morii, a rich underworld figure and owner of gambling houses. Although Morii enjoyed wide influence, he was widely despised among respectable members of the community as immoral and corrupt—one Nisei later complained that Morii's selection was akin to appointing Al Capone to represent Italian Americans. The appointment smacked of favoritism, especially when Issei who joined Morii's committee were exempted from immediate transportation to road labor camps. Eventually, the commission also appointed Nisei to balance the choice of Morii, but they were unable to exercise visible influence.[91]

The initial stages of relocation in Canada were carried out in more abrupt and significantly harsher fashion than in the United States, though not nearly as brutally as had been the imprisonment of ethnic Japanese in Australia and the South Pacific. As soon as it was created, the British Columbia Security Commission imposed an immediate curfew on all Japanese Canadians and proceeded to confiscate a list of contraband items, including radios, cameras, and guns. Letters to and from Japanese Canadians were censored, and their telephone conversations monitored. Most galling of all, Japanese Canadians were forbidden to make or buy liquor.[92]

Moving people out, however, posed a dilemma for officials in both Ottawa and Vancouver. The BCSC lacked resources, and the powerful Department of National Defense largely refused their assistance. A related problem was that, just as the mountain states had refused to permit Japanese American migrants to enter, leaders in the Canada's prairie provinces refused to permit Japanese Canadians from B.C. to resettle there except under military supervision. Federal officials therefore decided to create road work camps for Japanese Canadians as the fastest means to get them away from the coast, as well as a way to use their labor to improve the inadequate road system. In accordance with the cabinet's original February 19 decision to open road labor camps where enemy aliens and "volunteer" citizens could work, the government established projects near Hope, Revelstroke, and Yellowhead, B.C, and Schreiber, Ontario, under the authority of the Department of Mines and Natural Resources. On February 23 the first trainloads carried into the wilderness 1,300 of the able-bodied male Japanese nationals who had been ordered excluded under the January 14, 1942, order-in-council. There they were assigned to clear brush or upgrade existing roads once the weather permitted. The BCSC (at Ottawa's direction) then ordered all other Japanese Canadian males between eighteen and forty-five to report as of March 9, so that they could be sent off in shifts to whichever road labor camp they had "volunteered" to staff.

By the end of May more than two thousand men, predominantly Issei but also Nisei, were at work on the road projects. Forcibly separated from their wives and families, they were put to labor for which often they had no experience, or they froze in the deep snow of a Canadian winter, unable to work. Since they had been removed before any facilities could be created for them, the men were housed in flimsy railroad boxcars while tents and shacks were constructed. Their pay averaged around fifty dollars per month, significantly lower than that of non-Japanese elsewhere with similar employment. Approximately half of this inadequate sum was then deducted for their room and board (as well as, for a time, unemployment insurance) and twenty dollars more was removed from the pay of married men for support of the families left behind.[93]

In March the government began implementing the summary expulsion of the remaining Japanese Canadians from the West Coast. Unlike in the United States, there were no community centers established to register people and advise them on what to take, and no pretense of assistance with settling their affairs. Instead, during these first weeks the government implemented plans to transport 2,500 rural Japanese to the city. On March 16 the first Issei and Nisei were taken away from their homes in the countryside. The RCMP invaded rural Japanese communities, sometimes in the early hours of the day, and residents were carted off without warning, carrying only a hastily packed suitcase or pillowcase. Japanese Canadians were forced to leave behind houses and belongings—even food and dirty dishes. Once in custody, they were placed on trains, steamboats, and cars and carried to Vancouver. City residents remained at liberty in their homes, though subject to a strict curfew. Knowing they would soon be sent away, they struggled to sell of or dispose of their belongings. White scavengers and bargain hunters profited from their haste. On April 29 the Vancouverites were ordered to terminate their leases and prepare to move.[94]

To house the Japanese Canadians from outlying areas (and eventually the Vancouverites), the commission took over the Livestock Building and the Women's Building in Hastings Park (now the Pacific National Exhibition grounds) at Vancouver's eastern edge and rapidly reshaped the animal stalls to make holding pens for the Japanese Canadians until they could be shipped away from the coast. As the involuntary migrants arrived, they were placed in the holding pens, officially termed the Hastings Park Manning Pool, while the commission decided how to deploy them. Within a few months, the confined population was near four thousand women, children, and young men, and ultimately eight thousand passed through the cramped confines of the buildings. Conditions in Hastings Park were primitive and humiliating. The inmates were divided by sex, with men and boys housed separately from women and children. Packed in horse paddocks that still smelled of their former inhabitants—one inmate described "the pungent smell of animal urine and feces—some still sitting fresh in the stalls"[95]—they huddled together in the cold on rows of bunk beds covered by army blankets and straw mattresses. One inmate later recalled, "It was awful. Where the horses were, that's where they put us."[96] There were only three feet between each bunk, with no partitions, although inmates hung blankets in an attempt to secure privacy. At first the only toilets were old troughs, and there was no other running water for the inmates to wash or take baths, though ultimately a set of showers was rigged up. Food, provided by an outside firm, was dull and inadequate, reflecting the commission's limited budget, and dysentery and diarrhea were widespread. Menus improved after inmates launched a food strike on April 27. Meanwhile, a canteen and bake shop were set up to sell candy, soda, and bread to supplement the fare. Medical care was primitive, so much so that a system of passes was arranged to take away those with serious troubles to the hospital.[97] Bored inmates, with little in the way of recreational facilities, sat and talked or gambled to pass the time—so much so that one joke circulated that the bunks were separated only by individual crap games.[98]

Soon Japanese Canadians made efforts to improve conditions. Groups of volunteers signed up to help build more housing. One group formed the Hastings Park Japanese Committee to work with white social workers to ease conditions. Committee members visited families, organized gymnasiums and play areas, and arranged supplies of milk and cooking facilities for care of newborns. Until they, too, were taken from their homes, Vancouver-based groups did what they could to help the inmates. The staff of the *New Canadian* newspaper (which would soon move its offices and eventually leave the forbidden zone entirely) and the Japanese Canadian Citizen's Council (JCCC) attempted to intervene with the BCSC, but unlike the JACL they were unable to secure any official status or influence with the commission. Finally, with the aid of volunteer and haphazardly paid Nisei, a school was established in the hockey forum building and eventually attracted several hundred children, though it was difficult to arrange classes for a student population that was constantly arriving and departing.[99]

REACTIONS TO EXPULSION IN CANADA AND THE NISEI MASS EVACUATION GROUP

The first reports of mass removal were widely hailed in British Columbia, where anti-Japanese panic was at its height. While there continued various meetings of local whites pressing for action and urging that Japanese Canadians be removed permanently, the first signs of government round-ups cheered the populace. An editorial in the *Vancouver Sun* expressed impatience to have the Pacific Coast cleared of all ethnic Japanese, and the editors stated their firm hope that it was "Saying goodbye, not au revoir" to the Japanese presence.[100] In response to such pressure, on March 27 further orders-in-council were passed. One granted the BCSC control over all Japanese Canadians removed from the West Coast, whether they migrated "voluntarily" or otherwise, and even after they resettled elsewhere. Another gave the custodian of enemy alien property the power to seize and dispose of any property belonging to an enemy alien. Unlike in the United States, this was quickly interpreted as referring not only to Japanese nationals, but also to naturalized Issei and native-born citizens. While these regulations were presented as a rational system for supervising the Japanese Canadians as they migrated and disposing of their property, their promulgation was designed to placate white racist opinion in

British Columbia by cutting the ties of the ethnic Japanese community to the coast and leaving them less reason to return. They would soon prove to have devastating consequences for the Japanese Canadians.

The Japanese Canadians, like their counterparts in the United States, were paralyzed with shock and outrage by the news of the orders expelling them from the only home they had ever known. "We are bitter," proclaimed the *New Canadian*, "with a bitterness we can never forget, which will mark us for the rest of our lives."[101] Takeo Nakano summed up his feelings in *tanka*:

> Against such a thing as tears
> Resolved
> When taking leave of home.
> Yet at that departure whistle,
> My eyes fill.[102]

Although leaders such as Kunio Shimizu of the JCCC and Thomas Shoyama, editor of the *New Canadian* (which continued publication in censored form), counseled Nisei to follow orders and make the best of a tragic situation, the harsh official actions soon sparked resistance. A particular source of anger was the daily calling up of detachments of naturalized Issei and Nisei men from Vancouver (both from Hastings Park and from the city at large) to be sent to road labor camps around Schreiber, northern Ontario. There was real fear that the men would freeze to death in the icy climate, and the threat of being buried in an avalanche was very real for those working in mountainous areas. Even worse was the prospect of families being divided. The Naturalized Japanese Canadian Association (NJCA), a group of Japanese-born Canadians, devised a plan for mass transportation of all Japanese Canadians, in family groups, to a single settlement on crown lands, where they could build their own loghouse settlements with materials provided by the government. The plan included detailed cost and time estimates. NJCA leaders called a meeting of community organizations on March 29. They unanimously approved the plan and asked that removal to road labor camps be suspended in order that it be considered.[103] However, BCSC Director Taylor refused to accept the proposal and warned that any Japanese Canadian who refused to report for the road labor camps faced a $4,500 fine and one year in prison.[104]

When JCCC leaders again called for cooperation, a group of fourteen Nisei and naturalized Issei, predominantly young husbands, broke off from it and organized the Nisei Mass Evacuation Group. They demanded that family groups be permitted to remain together, as was the case with the Japanese Americans. On March 29, the same day as the NJCA meeting, the group circulated a petition asking Nisei to refuse to report for labor service unless the government offered a written guarantee that they would be transported in family groups and given decent housing (or materials to build it) and means of securing a living. The committee followed with an open letter denouncing the government's policy as a violation of their rights as native-born British subjects: "We have said 'YES' to all your previous orders, however unreasonable they might have seemed. But we are firm in saying 'NO' to your last order which calls for the break-up of our families."[105] Group founders spoke to Nisei in Hastings Park and Vancouver Japantown and sent speakers to outlying areas such as Steveston.[106] Leaders sought a meeting with the BCSC, but, as with the NJCA petition, BCSC leaders refused to meet them. While privately sympathetic, they felt powerless to alter official orders and were designing their own removal plans. The BCSC warned that all those who resisted faced prison or internment. Attempts to intervene by the consul of Spain—as a representative of the "protecting power" responsible for the interests of Japanese nationals under the Geneva Convention—were similarly unavailing.

Within a few weeks, over two hundred men had resisted, failing to report for the buses to take them to road work camps. Some were primarily concerned over families being broken up. Others supported action as a form of protest against the larger removal policy. Their protest attracted hundreds of sympathizers among Japanese Canadians. Some resisters went underground, hiding out in different areas of Vancouver. Others attempted to surrender themselves and demanded that the government intern them, on the theory that internment camps were preferable to prison as a way to dramatize their protest and pressure the government to meet their demands. (To the disgust of more patriotic Nisei, a small group, predominantly Kibei, volunteered for internment after being persuaded by the deposed Japanese consul, Mr. Miura, that Japan would win the war within six months and would reward them for their show of loyalty to the fatherland.)[107]

On April 25 the government, caught short by the movement, began confining resisters under armed guard in the Vancouver Immigration Building, even as RCMP officers conducted house-to-house searches and hunted down the road labor camp evaders. Yet it was not immediately clear how to treat the resisters—both those who demanded to be interned and the labor camp evaders—nor on what basis to confine citizens whom the government described as "troublemakers" without charge.[108] In the end, the government decided to deem the troublemakers prisoners of war and began shipping segments of the group to the Petawawa POW camp in Ontario. Technically, the BCSC had no power to send individuals to "internment camps"—such could be done only by order of the Ministry of Justice under the Defense of Canada Regulations. Had the internees been informed of their right to appeal under the regulations, they could have more easily challenged their confinement, if they had wished to.[109] The difficult situation of the protesters was vividly demonstrated in mid-May by an incident at the Immigration Shed. Army troops who had replaced RCMP officers guarding those marked for internment had forbidden the resisters' friends and families to approach the building or send in food to supplement the meager rations, and the BCSC refused to meet with them to hear their grievances. The resisters inside staged a hunger strike, then exploded in protest and vandalized part of the center. Army troops were commanded to intervene forcibly to restore order, shooting in tear gas. As a result of the disturbance, dozens more Nisei were sent to POW camps, but these internments only strengthened the movement.[110]

By June the government's policy was a shambles. Hundreds of resisters inspired by the Nisei Mass Evacuation Group had refused road service, with most demanding internment instead, while shipments of new laborers to road work camps had all but dried up. Issei and Nisei men who had already been sent to the road work camps were growing increasingly restive, and a wave of strikes and sit-downs broke out among workers in Gosnell, B.C., and in Alberta. Although the camp administrators warned they would intern any strikers, it was an empty threat—Austin Taylor reminded Ottawa that the workers could make a higher hourly wage in POW camps than through road labor. Meanwhile, national defense officials complained that the camps were located too close to Canadian national railroad tracks, making security a serious concern. (In one of the very few instances of actual coordination of policy, General Alexander, the commander-in-chief of Canada's Pacific Command, consulted with the Western Defense Command in the United States regarding the selection of areas near railroad lines from which Japanese Canadians should be excluded.) A report by an RCMP investigator, delivered in early June, also stated that the camps were a security risk—the officer insisted, with some exaggeration, that enemy alien laborers not only were physically unfit but deliberately worked slowly to prevent completion of a road that would be part of the war effort against their Japanese homeland.[111] It was then that Jintaro Charlie Tanaka, a naturalized Issei who had obtained a position as counsel to the Spanish consul, stepped in to propose a compromise. Young, single men would be assigned to staff the road labor camps, as long as older, married men could be permitted to rejoin their families and settle in communities established by the BCSC outside the West Coast. BCSC director Austin Taylor endorsed Tanaka's plan, but it took three further weeks and the ongoing strikes at road work camps to force Ottawa to consent to negotiations with representatives of the resisters. Finally, in early July, agreement was reached.[112] Married men began to leave the road labor camps, and soon barely 500 workers, generally single men, remained.[113] It would not be so simple to undo the damage done to the resisters. Even though the issue over which they had protested had been resolved, the 758 Nisei "troublemakers" who had been interned as prisoners of war were not permitted to join their families in the "interior settlements." Many of them were incarcerated for the rest of the war, first at Petawawa, later at Angler, Ontario.

THE DEVELOPMENT OF MASS CONFINEMENT IN THE UNITED STATES

While the Japanese Americans were removed and confined in assembly centers, the War Relocation Authority prepared their transfer inland. As soon as the WRA was established in March 1942, Director Milton Eisenhower journeyed to San Francisco to meet with army and civilian officials there. Eisenhower's original plan was to arrange for the orderly individual release of the Japanese Americans once they were removed, and then their progressive resettlement and absorption by communities outside the West Coast. On April 7, 1942, he met with a group of western governors and state officials during their conference in Salt Lake City. All the governors present, led by Utah Governor Herbert Maw, warned Eisenhower of widespread anti-Japanese sentiment in their states. They refused to accept any Japanese American migrants, except under armed guard, and warned of widespread bloodshed if Japanese Americans were freed or resettlement attempted.[114]

Shocked by the resistance, Eisenhower changed course and proposed that Japanese Americans be removed to the interior of the country and placed in "war-length" confinement centers where they could be "protected" by the federal government.[115] He likewise refused requests for transportation of Japanese American farm labor to fill shortages. He admitted that the army had raised no objection to private employment, assuming that state governments were prepared to assure transportation and protection for the workers and to pay a prevailing wage. However, he insisted that "a wide dispersal" of workers might lead to trouble, and he declined to grant permission for the transfers. The WRA soon began scouting out locations for camps, using the guidelines developed in connection with the army. Although the camps were consciously designed for keeping inmates in long-term custody, the War Department and the WRA swiftly agreed that the phrase "concentration camps" would be strictly forbidden as too negative (and embarrassing) and agreed instead to refer to these facilities by the euphemism "reception centers" or "relocation centers." Meanwhile, to evade the implications of detaining American citizens, the army coined the official term "nonaliens" to describe the Nisei's status.

This policy shift did not take place without a certain awkwardness and denial within government circles. Mass incarceration of citizens was likely unconstitutional, as a legal opinion issued by the Interior Department's solicitor soon afterward contended:

> It is doubtful whether [Executive Order 9066 and consequent proclamations] furnish a legal basis for the involuntary retention of Japanese within relocation areas situated inside or outside the West Coast military area. . . . If it is thus concluded and demonstrated by the very acts of the military authorities that no danger attaches to the presence of large of West Coast Japanese outside military areas, the retention of other West Coast Japanese within relocation areas situated outside the West Coast military area would constitute *a clear and unjustifiable discrimination.*[116]

WRA Solicitor Philip Glick emphasized the feeling of government illegality when he told a meeting at the agency's Washington office in the summer of 1942, "Many of the members of the WRA staff are walking around these days with heavy constitutional consciences."[117] However, the bureaucrats could devise no better means for protecting Japanese Americans while inspiring a sense of security among the public.

President Roosevelt and Secretary of War Stimson, when consulted on the new policy, readily approved it. Rather than formally suspending habeas corpus or altering the legal authority that the WRA already enjoyed in order to make possible the indefinite confinement of citizens, the White House decided to designate the camps as defense areas within the purview of military authority and continue to hold Nisei under Executive Order 9066. Yet they too were aware that the policy had taken on a life of its own, distinct from its (ostensible) origins in regard to national security. When Canadian Prime Minister W. L. Mackenzie King met Roosevelt for a Pacific War Council in late June, FDR told him that he did not believe seriously that any Japanese attack on the Pacific Coast was plausible.[118] Two weeks later, Stimson was alarmed by a report from General DeWitt that Governor Culbert Olson of California wished to keep Japanese Americans in assembly centers so that they could be brought in for labor on the fall harvest. In a letter to the president in which he referred sarcastically to Olson as "that great patriot," Stimson complained bitterly that Californians, having rushed madly to get "the poor Japs" out of their state, now wanted to keep them further for their own convenience. Stimson stated instead that permanent relocation of Japanese Americans away from the coast should proceed, as it would represent "the permanent settlement of a great national problem."[119] As Stimson remarked to a critic of the government policy who urged individual hearings, "The evacuation once accomplished is not easily undone."[120]

In June 1942 Milton Eisenhower resigned as WRA director. He later stated that the pressure of the job and the gravity of the injustice of confining innocent Japanese Americans preyed on his conscience. In his farewell report to the president (and simultaneously in testimony before Congress), Eisenhower expressed his personal judgment that the Nisei were "80 to 85 percent loyal" and that the majority of Issei were at least "passively loyal." Nevertheless, Eisenhower recommended that the Japanese Americans be confined for the remainder of the war, then be divided up, with the pro-Japanese being sent to Japan, and the pro-American being aided to re-enter the larger society.[121] There was a moment of contention over who would be named the new WRA director. Interior Secretary Harold Ickes nominated his deputy, Indian Affairs Director John Collier. Clark Foreman, a liberal southerner and former director of the Julius Rosenwald Fund, obtained Mrs. Roosevelt's endorsement for his candidacy.[122] However, on Eisenhower's recommendation, backed by Budget Director Harold Smith, the post fell to Dillon Myer, another Agriculture Department specialist (one less visibly disturbed by the assignment than his predecessor).[123] Myer would be responsible for establishing WRA policy as the Japanese Americans were moved into the camps. He remained WRA director, despite continual sniping from anti-Japanese American forces, for the remainder of the agency's existence.

THE JOURNEY EAST

Starting in mid-1942, as the War Relocation Authority oversaw the construction of more permanent camps inland, the 110,000 Japanese Americans in the WCCA's assembly centers gradually began to be transferred to WRA camps. Those confined at Manzanar did not have to move since it passed directly from WCCA control to that of the WRA. Otherwise, a WRA camp was generally designated to correspond to each assembly center—Topaz for Tanforan inmates, Minidoka for Puyallup, etc.—so most of those who had been in the same Assembly Center found themselves in the same WRA camp as well. However, because there were more assembly centers than camps, contingents of people from different regions and backgrounds were thrown together in the camps.

For most Japanese Americans, the journey from assembly center to camp was a multiday cross-country train trip. (According to Motumu Akashi, then a young boy, one Nisei wit dubbed the train transporting them "the Orient express.")[124] Once transfer began, trainloads of several hundred inmates would leave each night, often in the midnight hours. These voyages were long and exhausting—especially for the 20,000-odd inmates being sent to the WRA's two camps in Arkansas. They were crowded together in the railroad cars, which were mostly antiquated parlor cars pressed into service, with old-fashioned fittings and velvet seats. The Japanese Americans sat on straight-backed seats beside closed windows with drawn curtains—army officers were afraid that if whites along the trains' route could see the travelers, they would throw stones at the trains. In the summer heat, the air in the closed railway cars was stifling. There were no sleeping facilities, and armed military guards watched over the involuntary passengers constantly to prevent escape. Only when the train stopped at stations could they emerge, in groups under guard, to go to the bathroom. Once the trainloads of Japanese Americans finally arrived at their destination, requisitioned buses took them the rest of the short distance behind the gates of the camps established to hold them.

The migrating Japanese population moving east was topped off by the arrival of the 1,037 Japanese American "voluntary evacuees" who arrived in successive shiploads from Hawaii. These people were primarily Issei who had been interned on the islands, plus their families.[125] Meanwhile, several hundred Japanese Americans who had not been sent to the assembly centers (mainly those in the eastern California section of Military Area 2) were rounded up by the army and prepared for removal directly to the WRA camps.

THE DISPERSION OF THE CANADIAN JAPANESE

Even as it responded to the challenge of the Nisei Mass Evacuation Group, the BCSC looked for ways to move Japanese Canadians away from the coast. The Alberta Sugar Beet Association offered some assistance. Desperate for workers, on March 31 its lobbyists had asked Labour Minister Humphrey Mitchell to send them Japanese to cultivate sugar beets. With the approval of the commission, representatives of the association traveled to Vancouver to recruit inmate labor. The commission announced specifications for employment, including housing with adequate furniture, stoves with wood or coal for heating, and clean drinking water, but had no power to enforce them. Nevertheless, since sugar beet farming guaranteed that families would not be separated, there was a rush among Issei and Nisei to sign up for farm labor. By June 25 some 3,879 people had left for sugar beet farms in Alberta, Manitoba, and southwestern Ontario. Alberta's government objected to the "importation" of the Japanese workers. As a result, in May 1942, the federal government signed a written agreement saying that it would be responsible for all the workers' health and education costs and would guarantee they would leave the province after the end of the war. (A similar agreement was rapidly concluded with Ontario, and with Manitoba's government a month later). Issei and Nisei would remain in the three provinces as an exploited source of labor, sheltered in often substandard shacks and put to long hours of backbreaking work without overtime pay. Japanese Canadian workers employed by unscrupulous sugar beet growers were hobbled in their struggle for better conditions by legal restrictions on their movement. Even after appeals to the BCSC led to regulations permitting them to change employers, widespread prejudice limited their options—particularly in Alberta, whose three largest cities voted ordinances banning Japanese Canadians from settling there.[126]

Meanwhile, in part through the brokering of Etsuji Morii (who left Vancouver in April for such a place himself), groups of Issei and Nisei were invited by the BCSC to move on a "self-supporting" basis to places in eastern British Columbia, including Christina Lake, Bridge River, Minto City, Lillooet, and McGillvray Falls. Some 1,150 Japanese Canadians—generally those with more means—agreed to assume full responsibility for all the expenses of their moving, housing, and living. Taking their families and household possessions, they chartered trains and traveled to the "self-supporting sites." Although forbidden to buy property, they established themselves on farmland leased from the government or private sources (or held in the name of non-Japanese associates). At the same time, those Japanese Canadians who had family or other sponsors for employment outside the West Coast were encouraged to apply to BCSC for special permits to accept approved employment. Approximately 1,350 did so in the following months, most to take farm labor in eastern British Columbia or Ontario.[127] Several dozen Nisei women relocated to cities such as London, Ontario, Toronto, and Montreal, where they were assigned jobs as domestic laborers, helping ease wartime shortages.

Nevertheless, the majority of Japanese Canadians were forced into concentration camps, known as "interior housing," in former mining settlements in eastern British Columbia's Slocan Valley. The BCSC decided on this location because there was abandoned housing available, from the days when these had been "boom towns," and they hoped that Japanese Canadian settlement could revive the economy of the desolate region. The last Japanese inmate left Hastings Park on September 30, and the Pacific Coast was officially closed to Issei and Nisei, apart from a few hospital patients, plus approximately one hundred ethnic Japanese in mixed marriages and their children. Unlike in the United States, spouses of whites were exempted from removal irrespective of gender, but spouses of non-whites (i.e., Chinese) or immigrants were not exempted.[128]

THE REMOVAL OF JAPANESE IN MEXICO

As mentioned, the outbreak of war in the Pacific led numerous Latin American nations to declare war on Japan. The extent to which their leaders had their eyes on Washington can be inferred from their coordination of policy regarding people of Japanese ancestry. Brazil, which had the hemisphere's largest Japanese population, resisted all cooperation with the United States. Conversely, the closest Latin American nation, Mexico, was among the first to take arbitrary action against citizens and residents of Japanese ancestry, albeit on an independent basis. Mexico had been a choice spot for Japanese immigration during the early part of the century—thousands of laborers were recruited for work on coffee plantations in the southern states of Oaxaca and Chiapas. As the work dried up and they completed their contracts, many of them migrated north to work in sugar plantations or coal mines—some of them hoping to pass illegally from Mexico into California. In the 1920s, after the end of the Mexican Revolution, vibrant communities of cotton farmers, fishermen, small merchants, and gamblers established themselves in Mexico's northern regions of Baja California, Sonora, and Sinaloa, while smaller communities emerged in Guadalajara and Tampico. Immigrants in Tijuana operated restaurants, opened businesses, and bought land. Nearly a thousand ethnic Japanese, mainly professionals and traders, admitted under a special 1927 immigration law, took residence in the Mexico City area.[129] During the 1930s the position of Japanese residents of Mexico became increasingly difficult. Fishermen were hindered by discriminatory state and local regulations, Japanese farmers in Mexicali were evicted after the government seized 10,000 acres of land in 1937, and Issei and Nisei in the capital experienced job discrimination. Their presence was also made uneasy by efforts of the Japanese Foreign Ministry to recruit them for intelligence networks.[130]

The coming of war between the United States and Japan led to harsh official action by Mexico against its residents of Japanese ancestry. In mid-1941 Mexico's government banned export of strategic goods to Japan, and it broke off diplomatic relations with Tokyo after Pearl Harbor (although Mexico did not officially declare war until May 1942), at which time it froze all bank accounts of Japanese nationals and imposed travel restrictions. West Coast Mexican elites and nationalists soon showed signs of the same sort of fears about Japanese invasion, and local Japanese subversion, as their Anglo neighbors. At the beginning of 1942, for example, the executive committee of the Union of Mexican railroad workers in the western part of the country submitted a written report containing purported plans, based on "trustworthy information," for an upcoming Japanese raid against Mexico, to be made in conjunction with action by ethnic Japanese fifth columnists. "The activities of fifth columnists will be to blow up bridges and destroy roads, to prevent help from arriving from the United States." The document urged the concentration of all

Germans, Italians, and Japanese living in the western part of the country into camps to be established in Yucatan or near the American border, where they could be closely watched.[131] Meanwhile, in mid-February Colonel Loaixa, governor of Sinaloa, insisted that Japanese agents, acting in the guise of simple fisherman, had mined Mexico's territorial waters. Although this was hotly denied by General Garay, the Mexican Army's chief of staff, it contributed to the larger belief that Japan was organizing an invasion of Mexico preparatory to a direct attack on the United States.[132]

In response to the pressure—and with the approval, if not the direction, of Washington—the Mexican government felt obliged to take drastic action.[133] Over the first weeks of 1942, raids were carried out on Japanese communities in Mexico City. Numerous Issei were arrested without charge and sent to an internment camp at Perote. Meanwhile, on January 2, 1942, the government ordered all residents of Japanese ancestry in Baja California to leave the state. Some 2,800 Mexican Japanese, including the bulk of the remaining landowners in the Mexicali region, were forced to fill out "voluntary relocation applications" and move at least a hundred miles from the coastal and border areas at their own expense. They were given barely ten days to settle their affairs—only a few of their Mexican wives and mixed-race children were permitted to stay. Their fishing boats and farms, including the rich cotton plantations, were taken over by local Mexicans, with no official compensation offered.[134]

Most of the refugees took the long slow journey from the coast—a five-day trip—and settled in the capital district or in Guadalajara. Soon, more immigrants and their children, chased out of Sonora by government authorities, came to join them, and in early March the area around Manzanillo, in the state of Colima, was emptied of Japanese. Ultimately as much as 80 percent of the Mexican Japanese population was uprooted. As one refugee recalled:

My family, plus five or six other families, put together their resources and hired a truck and a driver to take us all the way to Mexico City. . . . In retrospect, we must have looked like cattle in back of that truck. We ate and slept aboard the truck most of the time in order to save time and money. Upon our arrival in Mexico City, we stayed at what I would like to refer to as the "clearing house." New arrivals were allowed to stay there for a short time. The men went out daily job-hunting, but jobs were scarce. At night, this place was "carpeted" wall-to-wall with people sleeping on the floor.[135]

Members of the existing Japanese community in Mexico City, who were less affected by the official actions, transformed the defunct Japanese consulate and Japanese Associations into a "Co-Prosperity Society" (Kyoekai), which worked to aid the distressed migrants, as well as locals fired from factory jobs. Some 350 people were established on a ranch in Batan donated by a community member. Another 500 people, who had no other means, were sent to a refugee camp in Temixco established by order of President Miguel Avila Camacho, where they grew crops to feed themselves.[136] Most of the refugees were able after a period of time to find housing and some sort of employment, and they were later permitted to open Japanese schools for their children, but they lived in privation, with no government assistance and limited aid from the Kyoekai.

INTERNMENT OF THE LATIN AMERICAN JAPANESE

The Mexican government's arbitrary removal and internal exile of its ethnic Japanese residents was mirrored in the experience of the "Latin American Japanese" who were taken and deported to the United States during the war. This hemispheric prisoner exchange program had its origins in the late 1930s, at which time Washington grew concerned for the security of Latin America, which it considered a "soft underbelly" for Axis penetration.[137] The approach of war heightened these fears. In April 1941 President Roosevelt proposed that Japanese residents on Latin America's Pacific coast be interned in case of war on bases in the Galapagos Islands.[138] In a speech in October 1941, he charged that U.S. agents had obtained a "secret map" showing plans for Nazi conquest of South America and division of territories.[139] A central focus of concern was the defense of the American-controlled Panama Canal and the surrounding Canal Zone from sabotage in case of war. In a national radio address in September 1941, Roosevelt accused the Nazis of preparing "footholds and bridgeheads in the New World," including building air bases in Colombia within range of the Panama Canal.[140] In November 1941, hoping to drive Japanese residents away from the Canal Zone region, Panama passed a law forbidding all Asians from engaging in or continuing commerce, and seized the businesses of local Japanese.[141] At the same time, American diplomats orally agreed with Panamanian officials that if war broke out, all Japanese aliens in Panama would be rounded up and interned. As mentioned, in the wake of the Pearl Harbor attack

Panamanian police proceeded to round up all 171 Japanese residents, using funds provided by the U.S. War Department, and they opened a camp.[142]

Following the Pearl Harbor attack, the U.S. secretary of state and the foreign ministers of six Latin American republics met at Rio de Janeiro and established an Emergency Advisory Committee for Political Defense. The committee recommended the detention and expulsion of all "dangerous" Axis nationals in the region and pressured the remaining Latin American nations to embargo all Japanese-owned businesses on the State Department's Proclaimed List of Blocked Nationals and to control Japanese residents.[143] The Latin American governments initially resisted, claiming that they lacked the resources to establish efficient security programs and house internees. The State Department offered to finance construction of internment camps, based on the Panamanian precedent, or make its own detention facilities available.[144] One such camp, built to hold German and Japanese aliens, was opened at the Isle of Pines, Cuba, in April 1942.[145] State Department officials soon complained that German aliens were bribing jailers to release them and decided that it was safer and more efficient to take custody of internees and bring them north than to operate individual camps scattered through Latin America.[146] Ultimately, twelve Latin American countries received assistance from the United States in deporting German or Japanese enemy aliens. State Department authorities agreed to take all those whoever the Latin Americans claimed represented a danger. The Japanese Latin Americans were arrested by local police and deported without any hearings or due process. They were placed on U.S. military transports, guarded by American soldiers, then sent first to a temporary camp in Panama, where they were stripped of their passports. They then were moved on to the United States. Lacking any substantive legal basis on which to hold these involuntary entrants (except arguably a 1798 act that allowed custody of dangerous enemy aliens but had never before been enforced), the government devised a plan to charge them with entering the country illegally. Edward Ennis, director of the Justice Department's Alien Enemy Control Unit, later stated that "in March or April 1942" the State Department had asked the attorney general to take temporary custody of Latin American "alien enemies" pending their repatriation to German, Italy, and Japan.[147] The Justice Department placed them in internment in the "family internment center" at Crystal City, Texas, a camp run by the Justice Department's Immigration and Naturalization Service.

Although the State Department, for its part, instituted the internment program in the interests of hemispheric security, and originally intended to take custody only of German aliens, its purpose gradually shifted. As Japan conquered large areas of Asia and the western Pacific during early 1942 and diplomats grew aware of the extent of the American population under Tokyo's control, they became interested in prisoner exchanges. However, the massive refusal of Japanese soldiers on battlefields to surrender as dishonorable meant that the number of Japanese POWs available for exchange was small. It was then that the idea of using Latin American Japanese, especially those who had requested repatriation to Japan, as prisoners for exchange took hold.[148] Using the Swiss and Spanish governments as conduits, the State Department negotiated a series of prisoner exchanges, which resulted in the repatriation of Japanese diplomats and private citizens whose return was demanded by Tokyo, in exchange for American citizens. By August 1942 the United States had sent off 1,100 Japanese nationals to Japan, and in December Army Chief of Staff George Marshall called for the deportation to the United States of 1,000 more Latin American Japanese (plus 250 Germans) to use as exchange for American civilians interned by Axis nations.[149] The exchange process, however, proved cumbersome. The United States was limited in the resources available for shipping and internment of Latin American Japanese, and Japan insisted on selecting the individuals it would accept. After September 1943 exchange ship voyages were halted entirely because Japan refused to assure safe passage for repatriates in a war zone.[150] Still, the desire to effect further trades led the State Department to continue accepting Japanese Latin Americans. Indeed, as a result of its interest, the State Department not only confined Japanese diplomats and repatriates from Latin American nations but became complicit in their deportation of private individuals, even citizens. As Edward Ennis put it, many of those taken "were not security problems but the police authorities of our good neighbor nations took the opportunity to get rid of them for their own reasons."[151]

The chief culprit was Peru, whose government ultimately provided some 80 percent of those deported. The Peruvian government had a particular self-interest in getting rid of ethnic Japanese. Thousands of Japanese had come to Peru as temporary workers in the early twentieth century, notably after the cutoff of immigration to North America in the 1920s, and had remained as settlers after their labor contracts terminated. Peruvians had grown increasingly hostile toward the newcomers, many of whom stayed in closed Japanese social and religious groupings and refused to learn Spanish or take Peruvian citizenship. The economic success of the Japanese bred envy and resentment by local competitors, especially during the Great Depression. The government responded to its citizens' complaints in the late 1930s by enacting harsh legislation cutting off immigration and limiting access to citizenship for Peru's 20,000–25,000 Japanese residents, even the native-born.[152] In May 1940 tensions fanned by nationalist politicians and unscrupulous journalists boiled over into two days of anti-Japanese rioting in Lima. Issei-owned business were pillaged and destroyed, and hundreds of Issei and Nisei were left penniless.

With the coming of war (although Peru remained formally neutral until 1945), existing resentment of ethnic Japanese flared up once more, buttressing popular anti-Japanese measures. All Japanese-owned properties of any size, including five Japanese schools, were confiscated. Even as Peruvian government officials discussed means of expelling all residents of Japanese ancestry, Peruvian Japanese were ordered to leave the Pacific coast and remove to the interior. Some five hundred Japanese aliens signed up with the Spanish Embassy to request repatriation to Japan.[153] Thus, when the United States offered Peru the chance to turn over Japanese diplomatic officials and Axis nationals whom it regarded as "dangerous," the Peruvians were quick to take advantage. In early 1942 the Americans accepted responsibility for the five hundred repatriates, plus Japanese diplomatic and consular officials. Meanwhile, diplomat John Emmerson began working with Peruvian officials to produce lists of "dangerous" aliens and their families for deportation. Emmerson's efforts notwithstanding, the Americans lacked facilities for verifying whether those on the lists in fact posed any threat, and thus assigned priority on the basis of an individual's community leadership or influence. Peruvian officials motivated by greed or racial hostility, using distorted or invented intelligence, haphazardly listed Japanese as "dangerous" (or were inspired by bribes to protect others in similar categories by accepting poorer residents as proxies). Emmerson himself later confessed that during his time in Peru, he had found no reliable evidence of any planned subversion.

As the deportees arrived in the United States and were confined in Crystal City, they were examined by Justice Department officials, who registered objections to the wholesale shipments of internees who did not appear dangerous and refused to continue involuntary internment of internees without specific proof of danger. The State Department objected, on the grounds that it could not violate abrogate a deal made with the government of a sovereign state at the request of an agency that had no role in foreign policy. After several months of debate, the Justice Department finally stated that it would have nothing further to do with the program. The State Department then proposed that the Justice Department assist in selection of internees. Thus, in January 1943 the Justice Department sent Raymond Ickes (brother of Interior Secretary Harold Ickes) to South America to help assure a smaller and fairer process. Ickes condemned Peruvians for sending "lots of Japanese to the States merely because Peruvians wanted their businesses and not because there is any evidence against them."[154] Nevertheless, he was unable to persuade the American Embassy to suspend the program, and the deportations continued through late 1944, by which time 2,264 Issei and Nisei had been transported and interned.

CONCLUSION

The Japanese attack on Pearl Harbor mobilized or rationalized anti-Japanese sentiment throughout the Pacific Rim. Despite the lack of hard evidence linking Issei and Nisei with any disloyal conduct, they became handy stand-ins for the Japanese enemy in the public mind. The resulting suspicion of people of Japanese ancestry, which drew on pre-existing social and economic hostility toward them as a minority group and was further inflamed by the efforts of nativist and commercial interest groups, manifested itself in popular pressure for their removal from coastal areas and seizure of their property.

Yet if the demands for mass action were founded in popular opinion, the enabling force behind mass exclusion throughout the Americas was the U.S. government and its agencies. Besides confining 110,000 of its own citizens and long-term residents, many times the combined figure for all the other countries, the Americans pressured Latin American governments to control their ethnic Japanese populations. At the same time, anti-Japanese forces in Canada and Mexico buttressed the case for removal by appealing to solidarity with the United States and coordination of defense policy, and the Peruvians made use of Yankee concerns over security to banish individuals whose success had aroused resentment. Yet, perhaps surprisingly, the U.S. government was less harsh and punitive in its policies than the others. While Canada and Mexico ordered Japanese residents from the coast in hurried and arbitrary fashion, the United

States attempted to develop orderly procedures for evacuating Issei and Nisei. Similarly, while the measures taken by Washington, D.C., to protect the property of those it took from their homes were inadequate and led to considerable losses, at least the Americans did not appropriate or confiscate their possessions. Unlike the other governments, the U.S. government paid the expenses of confinement. Japanese Canadians at Hastings Park envied their American counterparts, who were migrating in intact family groups to facilities constructed by a federal agency for their use. Under the banner of the Nisei Mass Evacuation Group, they organized a widespread protest campaign, and suffered punishment, simply in order to obtain the government's pledge to allow them similar treatment.

The only area with a sizable ethnic Japanese population that escaped mass removal was Hawaii. In that case, it may well have been the large local Japanese population that played a decisive role in stalling the policy. Whereas ethnic Japanese elsewhere were a small and isolated minority whose racial difference and economic success made them easy targets for reprisal, Japanese in Hawaii were almost 40 percent of the territory's population, and they formed the backbone of the its workforce. Nisei were a central group in the islands' society and had existing relations with other groups. Thus, while some voices, mainly outsiders or newcomers to Hawaii, called for mass removal of the local Japanese, the territory's established white leadership was anxious to retain them. Furthermore, the unusual power granted the military as part of martial law both reassured those charged with territorial defense, notably Commanding General Emmons, and made it possible for him to deflect the strongly expressed will of President Roosevelt and Navy Secretary Knox that Japanese must be removed. The trust that Emmons and his associates offered the local Japanese was amply rewarded. They made impressive contributions to the war effort, through both military service and patriotic efforts on the home front. At the same time, as we shall see, the military did not scruple to make use of the presence of the local Japanese in more negative ways, to maintain control of the territory in the face of demands by civilian governors.

[4] THE CAMP EXPERIENCE

THE WRA CAMPS

The new locations for the Japanese Americans expelled from the West Coast were the ten camps, officially known as "relocation centers," that were established by the WRA. The first one to open was the former assembly center at Manzanar, which the WRA took over on June 1, 1942, and transformed into a long-term facility with the addition of new barracks and equipment. The WRA also assumed direction of the Poston assembly center project, then being constructed by contractor Del Webb on the Colorado River Indian reservation in Arizona, and turned it into a camp. While these camps were being filled, the WRA oversaw construction of eight further camps. Like the first two, the majority were established in desert areas of the West: Minidoka in Idaho; Amache (also called Granada) in eastern Colorado; Topaz in central Utah; Tule Lake in northeastern California; Gila River in southern Arizona; and Heart Mountain in Wyoming. In addition, the WRA adapted two former Civilian Conservation Corps camps in Arkansas, named Rohwer and Jerome, for use in confining Japanese Americans.

Poston, the largest camp, had a somewhat separate origin and development from the other camps. It grew out of a deal made in March 1942 between WRA Director Milton Eisenhower and John Collier, director of the Bureau of Indian Affairs (BIA). Collier, famous for his progressive reforms in governing Native American communities (and an unsuccessful aspirant for directorship of the WRA), agreed to let the government build a center on the Colorado River Indian reservation in Arizona, over which the BIA had jurisdiction, so that he could turn it into a showplace of community planning, complete with experimental farm cooperatives, schools, and cultural life. Collier secured Eisenhower's promise that the Indian Bureau would be granted full authority over the center—he warned the War Department that he wanted nothing to do with the project if it were to be just another concentration camp[1]—and justified the center's foundation to the Native American residents on the grounds that Japanese American farmworkers would irrigate the land and develop the local economy. Indeed, it was only with the arrival of the Japanese Americans that electric power came to the reservation.[2] To help develop his model community, Collier recruited director Wade Head and a staff of expert social scientists, notably the psychiatrist Alexander Leighton, to run the camp and to use it as a study site, adapting methods of conflict resolution to camp life and training Nisei for future service as social analysts.[3] (Collier also persuaded the famed Nisei sculptor Isamu Noguchi, who as a New York resident was exempt from Executive Order 9066, to volunteer for confinement at Poston in order to teach arts and crafts and design parks and buildings. Noguchi swiftly became disillusioned with the project after his arrival and secured his release after a few months).[4]

Following Eisenhower's departure from the WRA, Dillon Myer abrogated the deal with Collier. Deliberately abandoning a humanitarian operation that he feared would lead to administrative problems and permanent dependence on government aid among Japanese Americans (on the model of Native Americans on reservations), Myer insisted that the camps be run in uniform fashion and that emphasis be placed on swift resettlement rather than on permanent residence. After a struggle for power in mid-November 1942, during which Collier and Myer traveled to Poston in rapid succession and made opposing public presentations to the inmates, the WRA's policy prevailed, and Poston was ordered to be run in conjunction with the other camps. The WRA took over formal control of Poston in mid-1943.[5]

APPEARANCE OF THE CAMPS

The ten "relocation centers" bore many similarities. All were located in desolate and fairly unpopulated areas (at the height of occupancy, for example, Poston and Heart Mountain represented the third largest population centers in their respective states). In the western camps, temperatures ranged from well below zero in the dead of winter to 120 degrees Fahrenheit (49 degrees Centigrade) in the summer. The Arkansas camps were situated in warm, swampy areas. The dry air and high altitudes of the western camps were uncomfortable to residents. The hard-baked desert earth turned to rivers of mud in rainy seasons and otherwise broiled easily into dust. Dust storms were frequent occurrences. One inmate recalled, "The sandstorms were devastating. We were told to get under the bed or some way hide ourselves because you couldn't see [anything], and to cover your nose and mouth. Even so, the dust left a terrible residue. So we'd have to spend time cleaning up."[6]

As with the assembly centers, all the camp designs were based on military models. Blocks of residential barracks surrounded a central kitchen/ mess hall, with communal latrines and laundry and shower facilities constructed nearby. Other buildings, designed for use as school buildings and auditoriums, were added.[7] In some cases the camp was divided into units, whose inhabitants banded together into distinct communities.

Once they arrived at their destinations, the new inmates (known in official parlance as "residents") were assigned housing in the different blocks and received medical checkups and vaccinations. They were granted a minimal clothing allowance, although deliveries did not always arrive as promised. Within the camps, each family was assigned a single room measuring sixteen feet by twenty feet (in a few cases twenty by twenty-five), while single inmates shared rooms with strangers. Barracks were constructed of green lumber faced with tarpaper, with no interior wall coverings.[8] As a result, they provided inadequate shelter against the extreme temperature conditions, even with the addition of a pot-bellied stove to provide extra warmth for each family section. Despite the efforts of inmates to plug the spaces between the wall planks with newspaper, dust blew easily through the cracks during storms, covering everything inside with a layer of sand. Parents hung sheets to make partitions, but privacy was still difficult to obtain, and the thin walls of the rooms were no barrier to noise from other rooms. There were no closets assigned, so families lived out of their suitcases. Inmates scavenged or stole discarded lumber and building materials in order to construct furniture and housewares for themselves and their families—beds, bookshelves, tables, chairs, and *geta* (raised Japanese clogs) for crossing muddy unpaved paths between buildings. (Many of these objects, often finely crafted in Japanese style, have since become coveted collector's items.)

The only running water was in the bathrooms, which contained rows of rough wooden toilets without partitions, plus sinks and laundry facilities. Shower rooms, like toilets, were sex-segregated but otherwise lacked privacy. Thus, performing intimate functions became an ordeal of shyness and humiliation for the mass of Nisei in the awkward teen years and for those, especially older women, not accustomed to displaying their unclothed bodies in public. Such people waited until the midnight hours to visit the bathroom. Because of the cramped space in the barracks, many younger people spent their entire day outside the residences and came back only to sleep. Young married couples or courting pairs would comandeer unused ambulances or take refuge in the laundry rooms, seeking privacy amid the laundry hanging out to dry to "hug and kiss between the sheets," as one inmate later termed it.[9]

Although the interior of the camps was controlled by the WRA security forces and by inmate police, each camp had a barbed wire fence on its perimeter, which was ringed with guard towers patrolled by army sentries who could be called inside to intervene in an emergency. The government insisted that the guards were present to protect the inmates. However (as Japanese Americans did not fail to note), their gun emplacements pointed into the camp, not outside, and the inmates were kept from leaving. On numerous occasions, trigger-happy guards shot at inmates whom they believed moved "too close" to the fences. In at least two documented cases, those of Topaz inmate James Hatsuaki Wakasa in 1943 and Tule Lake inmate Soichi James Okamoto in 1944, Japanese American inmates were killed by sentry fire.[10]

LIFE IN CAMP

Living conditions for the inmates varied across the different camps and at different times. Food, especially at first, was of poor quality. Camp cooks were inexperienced at boiling rice in the high-altitude mountain regions, or dealing with local hard water supplies, with the result that meals were improperly cooked. One inmate recalled, "There was dysentery at the beginning, sanitation was so bad. . . . When the wind blows, the sand goes in the kitchen, in pans, and the hot rice. On the top of the rice they put Jell-O, since we had only one plate to eat out of, so it all melted together."[11] As at the assembly centers, camp food budgets were consciously kept low— under the army standard of 50 cents per day—in order to forestall criticism of "coddling."[12] Although for reasons of administrative efficiency WRA officials ordered food through the army quartermaster, they were required to follow civilian rationing requirements. As a result, except on special occasions, there was no meat except for Vienna sausages and organ meats, and the food was generally unappetizing and unhealthful. One Nisei recalled, "When we lived at camp, the diet at the beginning was really terrible—just starches . . . and hardly any vegetables or fruits. . . . I remember having breakfast, oatmeal, and it was full of those little black bugs."[13] Menus slowly improved once inmates began growing vegetables for camp consumption and receiving packages from the outside to supplement the inadequate food supplies offered. Still, Eleanor Roosevelt told her daughter after a 1943 visit to Gila River, "The day I was at the camp in Arizona, there was no sugar, no butter, and no coffee. They had fish and a green vegetable for lunch and again for supper."[14] There were widespread reports of sugar and other scarce food stores being appropriated and sold on the black market by corrupt WRA employees.[15]

Medical care, similarly, varied widely in quality. On the one hand, facilities were primitive, especially at first. Although Japanese American doctors worked long hours and served with dedication, there were not enough physicians or trained health-care staff to care for the entire inmate population, and other physicians were impossible to secure in wartime.[16] The 200-bed hospital and single ambulance provided for each camp meant chronic shortages of hospital beds and medical supplies. In addition to nausea and other ailments from the poor food, inmates suffered epidemics of pneumonia and influenza, while untold others died of preexisting conditions such as asthma and heart ailments, which could not be properly treated in the spartan camp conditions.[17] Inmates were often forced to rely on alternative medications and on community health-care providers such as midwives.[18] On the other hand, health care and medicine were provided free of charge. Even such limited facilities as were provided represented a gain for many inmates, especially Issei women, who had not had access to affordable and accessible health care, and particularly dental care, for many years.

Schools were another area of camp life that varied widely. Although education was not initially considered part of camp functions, the WRA realized that it could not violate compulsory school attendance laws, so nursery, elementary, junior high, and high schools were formed in each camp once mass confinement was executed. Expenses for education ultimately made up a large share of WRA budgets. At first, classes were conducted in unused barrack and recreation hall spaces, with students sitting on the floor or standing. Gradually, schoolrooms with blackboards and rough desks were constructed. Textbooks were provided, usually by the state in which the camp was located, but laboratory and shop equipment was almost totally lacking. Thus, students in typing class at different camps were forced to practice on blocks of wood with paper circles, as they were not furnished typewriters. The schools boasted a wide variety of sports teams (although finding visiting opponents and organizing matches outside camp was difficult), service clubs, and student government groups. High schools in the camps also produced newspapers (such as *The Desert Sentinel* at Gila River's Butte High School) and school yearbooks complete with photos and advertising. In accordance with the WRA's "Americanization" program, there were patriotic exercises in schools, such as daily flag saluting. Curricula were designed in accordance with standards of the state in which the camp was located, and all except Tule Lake were accredited. Finding licensed teachers remained a problem. Although the WRA hired educational specialists such as Dr. Miles Cary and Dr. Rachel DuBois, and dozens of whites (and a few African Americans) arrived to teach in camp schools, much of the teaching was carried on by inmate teachers, who were hurriedly trained and accredited. While this meant that students were exposed to highly talented and motivated Nisei teachers—scientists, engineers, and artists who had their first opportunity to use aspects of their training in a professional setting—the vast majority of those set to teach had incomplete college degrees and little or no classroom experience, and all earned low pay.[19]

Camp administrations offered jobs for all those willing and available to work—not just teachers. In part from WRA ideological principle, in part because of outside labor shortages, the inmates ultimately composed a predominant fraction of the camp labor force. Wages ranged from $12 per month for unskilled labor to $19 per month for professionals—as in the assembly centers, pay was kept deliberately lower than army privates' wages to avoid public outcry. In a sense, as was pointed out at the time (and more recently by historian John Howard), the camps represented a kind of American-style socialist regime.[20] The inmates were paid a similar wage for their work, offered identical living facilities, and provided basic (if inadequate) medical care free of charge. Private enterprise was forbidden in the camps, though the WRA sponsored the formation of agricultural collectives, and provided for formation of cooperative enterprises to run stores and canteens (individual entrepreneurs did open barbershops and personal service operations within the cooperatives). The success of these cooperatives was relative: they dealt mostly in products such as soft drinks and chewing gum, rather than necessities, and they enjoyed a literally captive audience—white officials did not take the opportunity to share in them. For large purchases, inmates made heavy use of mail-order catalogues. They also engaged in a variety of black market sales and other illicit activities, reportedly including even prostitution rings. Again, Nisei professionals such as teachers and social workers, who had been unable to find jobs in their field on the prewar West Coast due to entrenched racial prejudice, were able to gain valuable experience in camp that would aid them in securing postwar employment. Nisei women, in particular, were able for the first time to occupy community and professional leadership positions in large numbers.[21] Still, the poor labor conditions upset inmate workers, and the disparities between the pay and living conditions offered inmate professionals and those given Caucasians doing the same jobs were a simmering source of resentment within the camps.[22]

To pass the time, the inmates undertook an increasingly thorough organization of their community life, especially in the areas of athletics and cultural activities. Inmates organized sports teams and volunteered to teach classes in arts and crafts. Japanese art forms, such as calligraphy, gardening, woodworking, dance classes, flower arranging, tea ceremony, folk music, and scroll painting, flourished. Inmate artists produced paintings, drawings, and sculpture, and writers and poets remained busy. Some camp newspapers featured literature sections, while inmate poets put out pamphlets such as *Poston Bungei*. A group of writers and artists in Topaz, led by artist Miné Okubo, produced a notable literary magazine, *Trek*. Libraries, stocked by donations from inmates and outside sources and staffed by volunteers, became visible centers of community life. These developments were encouraged in part by WRA administrators who feared the impact of boredom on the inmates and saw formation of such leisure activities among young Nisei as baseball teams, Boy Scout troops, Red Cross chapters, and swing bands to be tools for "Americanization." Several camps, such as Minidoka, had swimming holes, and youngsters enjoyed toy boat races. There were also such typically American activities as jazz concerts, sock hops, plays, and exhibitions. In other cases inmates were forced to organize amid administration opposition or indifference, demonstrating their agency by raising money, demanding facilities such as auditoriums and access to materials in order to do their projects.[23]

Religious life in camp was also rich. Worshipers flocked to Sunday Christian services, both Catholic and Protestant (some, drawn perhaps in part by boredom, attended services by different sects in rotation). Outside ministers were allowed to visit to conduct weekly services, and inmate prayer and Bible study groups also appeared. Some of the religious activity may have been a tribute to the conscientious support of non-Japanese ministers and congregations. The American Friends Service Committee (with the assistance of a donation from Eleanor Roosevelt) organized emergency programs for evacuees and continued to offer various forms of support. Rev. Herbert Nicholson became well known for his many trips to the camps to offer support to Japanese Americans. Rev. Emery Andrews, who had been the pastor of the Baptist Church on Bainbridge Island, moved with his flock to Minidoka. Outside church groups and YMCAs, many of whom were alerted to the plight of the inmates by the American Friends Service Committee and the Federal Council of Churches, sent clothes and supplies and school equipment for the inmates, and organized donations to give Christmas presents to all center children.

Meanwhile, followers of the different Buddhist sects, who represented the majority of confined Issei and Nisei, shared space or constructed their own temples. There they organized regular services, much to the dismay of camp officials disdainful of such "heathenism."[24] With the arrival of a contingent of interned Buddhist ministers from Hawaii, the Topaz camp became the wartime headquarters of the Buddhist Churches of America. Curiously, a later survey found that, in general, Japanese Americans who identified as Buddhists were far less unhappy and bitter over their camp experience than those who identified as Christians. It is not clear whether this reflected the influence of Buddhist teachings or the more Japanese-identified and less assimilated nature of Buddhist communities, which made their members more resigned to treatment as a hostile foreign group.[25]

PSYCHOLOGICAL IMPACT OF CONFINEMENT

Camp life had a paradoxical effect on the inmates. On the one hand, despite the hardships involved in confinement and the often harsh surroundings, the inmates had a more leisured existence than in their prewar lives. As one inmate put it, Issei who had toiled on farms and in canneries finally had some rest and refreshment after forty years of "drudgery" and could express their artistic and horticultural creativity.[26] Issei women in particular, relieved of most housework as well as farm labor, were able to devote themselves for the first time in years to hobbies such as knitting and crocheting or to take classes in Japanese calligraphy and dance. One younger woman—amazed to see men doing cooking and dishwashing—called the experience a "camping vacation" for the women.[27] Similarly, many children, surrounded by playmates of their age group and absorbed in school and athletic activities and making friends, enjoyed their time. One older Nisei later recalled, with a mix of nostalgia and envy, that the young Nisei "were carefree. They had not a worry in their lives because they had a roof over their heads, they didn't have to cook, wash dishes, clean house, or work for a living. The government took care of everything, and if you didn't have clothes, the government would furnish you clothes. So some of those younger people, kids who were in grammar school, junior high, and high school, during those evacuation years, really had the best years of their lives."[28]

Yet the injustice of being dispossessed and confined unjustly, and the boredom and futility of camp existence, preyed on the inmates. One young inmate later recalled, "Camp was demeaning. I felt like I was a piece of shit, actually. As kids we made the nest of what was available, but deep down it still felt like I was filthy. I was never cleansed of that feeling."[29] Meanwhile, camp life worked to break down the patriarchal family structures of precamp Japanese American communities.[30] Nisei youth, freed from dependence on their parents and stifled in their cramped home quarters, spent large amounts of time with their own peer group. In particular, many Nisei teenagers ate with their friends in the communal mess halls rather than with their families. This may have actually promoted their development and maturity—it is too easy to read alternate family patterns as pathological.[31] Yet the impact on the Nisei of the camp experience, combined with uncertainty over the future and a lack of positive outlets for expression of their malaise, was also apparent in the rise of gang activity and juvenile delinquency. Conversely, Issei fathers, stripped of their property and their secure role as community leaders, lost their moral and economic authority over their children. Many anecdotal tales of psychological difficulties, alcoholism, and spousal and family abuse by Issei attest to the isolation and trauma they experienced.[32]

The cramped conditions and lack of personal space within the camps also accentuated the cultural and ideological differences between generations. Factions likewise divided along regional, socioeconomic, and even residential differences. Issei took out their bitterness over their loss of self-respect and community influence (which was compounded by their initial exclusion from eligibility for election as council representatives) on the Nisei, for what they considered arrogance and bad management. Reports spread of Issei taunting Nisei, "Of what use is your American citizenship now? We're all in this together and you have no more rights than we."[33] At the same time, a number of Issei took refuge in a sentimental feeling of association with militarist Japan, a land most of them had not seen for decades. "They imagine they will be hailed as silent martyrs of circumstance by their homeland when victory is signed on the dotted line, and perhaps they will be rewarded with political or economic plums."[34] Anti-administration sentiment predominated, and JACL leaders and others who worked with camp administrations or showed themselves too openly progovernment found themselves accused of being traitors and collaborators. With the quiet support or acquiescence of the majority, groups of pro-Japanese inmates (among whom Kibei were prominent) formed gangs to pursue terror campaigns marked by threats and organized beatings of JACL supporters and those they suspected of being *inu* (dogs, i.e., informers).

RIOTING AT POSTON AND MANZANAR

For the most part, the Japanese Americans confined by the WRA did not revolt against the government. Given their powerless state, they had little choice but to follow official orders. In the majority of cases, the primary interest of the inmates was not in challenging the system but in holding their families together, educating themselves, and generally making the best of their situation. Indeed, official reports noted the Japanese Americans' rapid and determined adjustment to their situation and praised the inmates as predominantly cooperative and orderly.[35] Yet, as WRA leaders recognized, the injustice of incarceration and the unnatural life facing Japanese Americans within the camps bred widespread bitterness and discontent.[36]

This discontent, which marked the entire history of the camps, mostly inspired inmates to apathy and cynicism toward authority. However, it also inspired inmates to engage in different forms of protest and resistance. Defining resistance in the context of the WRA camps is a difficult and contested business. As is demonstrated by the case of the loyalty questionnaire and the "no-no boys" (which will be discussed presently), it is not always easy to judge how much the actions of Japanese Americans were intended as conscious acts of rebellion against oppressive authority, and how much they resulted from frustration, confusion, nihilism, survival instincts, or sympathy for the Japanese enemy. Certainly, many inmates expressed their opposition to WRA policies on an individual and indirect level (learning Japanese language, spreading rumors, stealing supplies in order to furnish family barracks, etc.). None of these actions, however, vitally affected the operation of the camps or public perceptions of Japanese Americans. A smaller number expressed their ideas more openly, either within officially established channels (petitioning camp administrators, participating in inmate self-government, writing editorials in camp newspapers, sending letters to the White House) or in letters to outside sympathizers. The impact of these was more perceptible but difficult to determine.

Finally, in a few instances inmates joined in mass actions, organized and otherwise, that collectively expressed their resistance and reshaped policy. The first such notable incident was the Poston strike of November 1942. As the inmates at Poston sweltered during the hot summer of 1942, awaiting mosquito netting that never came, conflict erupted between different factions. Issei angry over their exclusion from leadership faced off against Nisei on the council, some of whom were JACL members, while Nisei considered pro-administration were targeted for gang violence as informers. On November 14 Kay Nishimura, a Kibei, was badly beaten by a mob of hooded assailants. Authorities immediately arrested fifty suspects, including members of a judo club, but the following night another beating took place. Seeking to halt the wave of violence, FBI agents ordered the arrest of two popular judo club leaders, George Fujii (Nishimura's former brother-in-law) and Isamu Uchida, and charged them with assault. The FBI's heavy-handed action provoked widespread anger. Rumors spread that those charged would be tried outside camp, where they could not hope for a fair trial. Meanwhile, on November 17 WRA Director Dillon Myer made a surprise visit to camp. He announced to administration officers that Poston would be run exclusively as a temporary camp, despite Indian Bureau promises of land and model communities (reaffirmed in a speech at Poston earlier that month by BIA director John Collier), and all the work that had been done to build them. Myer's comments threw the camp into confusion and added fuel to the fires of discontent.

The following morning, November 18, a crowd of some thousand inmates from Unit 1, joined by the Poston Community Council, demanded the release of Fujii and Uchida from custody. A committee of inmates

called on Poston Director Wade Head to ask for their release and for redress of other grievances, but Head, who was about to leave with Myer
for meetings in Salt Lake City, refused to intervene. As word of Head's departure spread through camp, crowds formed around the police station
and camp stockade to prevent the detained inmates from being taken out
of camp. The Community Council and Issei Advisory Council resigned.
Issei leaders appropriated a nearby mess hall for public meetings, and
those who refused to speak Japanese were shouted down. An Emergency
Executive Council composed of both Issei and Nisei was formed, and it
declared a general strike in support of the jailed men. The resulting work
stoppage paralyzed Unit 1 and spread to parts of Units 2 and 3. The strike
lasted for a week, during which time inmates refused to work and WRA
administrators, temporarily deprived of the project director, remained
outside the disputed area. Shifts of inmates stood watch at barricades
around the jail to make sure the prisoners were not removed from camp,
raised flags with symbols of their blocks, marched and chanted Japanese
slogans, and played Japanese military songs over loudspeakers. Although
project social analysts Edward Spicer and Alexander Leighton talked Acting Director John Evans out of summoning armed troops, as other WRA
officials proposed, they were unsuccessful in their attempts to calm the
strikers. As the days passed and the strikers tired, the protests began to
wind down, and negotiations began between administrators and inmates
with the endorsement of the project director. The results of this unprecedented dialogue were a new level of understanding and some conces-
sions made to the inmates—the Issei were granted a voice in administration, one suspect was released, and the other was set for trial by a camp
court—while the administration extracted the promise of a halt on attacks on suspected informers.[37]

The disturbance at Manzanar occurred a few weeks after that at Poston,
and while its causes were similar, its results were not.[38] As at Poston, there
was conflict between inmate factions. In this case, the governing faction
was dominated by the Manzanar Citizens Federation, composed of JACL
members and progressive intellectuals. They were denounced as tools
of the camp administration by members of a Kibei group that formed
around Joseph Kurihara, a Nisei World War I veteran embittered by removal, as well as by a radical (largely Kibei) Kitchen Workers Union.
Gang members organized terror attacks on JACL members. In November 1942 the Kitchen Workers Union, led by Kibei activist Harry Ueno,
accused white kitchen workers of stealing sugar and demanded an in-

quiry into administration graft. During the first week of December, Fred Tayama, a prominent JACL member, attended a JACL conference in Salt Lake City, where he endorsed the opening up of military service to Nisei. On his return to camp on December 5, 1942, Tayama was beaten by a group of assailants. On the basis of identification by the victim, Harry Ueno was arrested for assault. Because of Ueno's previous accusations of pilfering, the arrest appeared politically motivated.

As at Poston, the camp administration agreed under pressure to try Ueno in camp but called in return for an end to beatings of informers. However, a mob, including a visible contingent of demonstrators performing Japanese chants and marching with Rising Sun flags, rejected the deal and assembled to demand Ueno's immediate and unconditional release. Agitators called for violence against JACL members and others on a "death list"—one group surrounded the camp hospital in order to attack Tayama but was restrained from entering. When the mob gathered around the stockade where Ueno was being held, project director Ralph Merritt declared martial law and called in security forces from the camp perimeter. The military police fired tear gas and shots into the crowd, killing one man and wounding several others, one of whom later died as well. The shootings were foolish and further strained tensions. As one inmate noted soon after, "When the MPs fired several of the casualties were among the ranks of the onlookers who were neither demonstratively supporting nor opposing the storming of the bastille."[39] The descriptions of pro-Japanese mobs and the fact that the disturbance occurred near the anniversary of the Pearl Harbor attack led the *Los Angeles Times* and other anti-Japanese West Coast newspapers to publish distorted accounts of the "Manzanar Riot."

The two incidents have given rise to a historical debate. Brian Hayashi describes the "riots" as inchoate in their purposes and driven by large-scale support for the Japanese enemy, as the Japanese marching songs and chants indicate. Hayashi states that most "average" Manzanar Japanese in the fall of 1942 had a prisoner-of-war mentality and supported Tokyo in the belief that Japan would win the war and take care of them afterwards. (Though he does not say so, Hayashi presumably means most Issei, since his evidence appears to derive entirely from Issei sources.)[40] While such ideas were indeed present, other historians, such as Paul Bailey and Arthur Hansen, argue persuasively that ideological considerations were not important in the Issei resistance.[41] While Bailey and Hansen agree that the Issei, particularly in their straightened circumstances, may have felt nostalgia for a Japan they had long ago given up, the incidents can more accurately be described as part of the Issei wish to regain their naturally dominant role in Japanese communities, and the larger community's struggle to preserve its cultural autonomy. Jeanne Wakatsuki Houston, a child inmate at Manzanar, shared their view, insisting that the generalized psychological demoralization that she saw in her own Issei father was at the root of the incident: "It was the humiliation. It brought him face to face with his own vulnerability, his own powerlessness. He had no rights, no home, no control over his own life. This kind of emasculation was suffered, in one form or another, by all the men interned in Manzanar. Papa's was an extreme case. Some coped with it better than he, some worse. Some retreated. Some fought back. . . . Looking back, what they now call the December Riot seems to have been inevitable."[42]

SELF-GOVERNMENT AND LIBERTY IN THE CAMPS

The WRA's policy toward Japanese Americans was a complex mix of authoritarian control and promotion of democratic living. In certain respects, the camps resembled prisons. As at the assembly centers, guards were authorized to conduct warrantless searches of living quarters. FBI agents maintained surveillance of camp activities and reported on "disloyal" activities. Numerous items, including cameras and radios, were initially declared contraband and taken from inmates (Manzanar Director Ralph Merritt bent the rules for famed photographer Toyo Miyatake by allowing him to take pictures on condition that he use a Caucasian assistant who actually pulled the camera switch). This policy was widely ignored and ultimately relaxed, but inmates whose equipment was confiscated did not always get it returned. Incoming and outgoing mail, especially from enemy aliens in Justice Department camps, was read and censored. In one woman's words, "A letter from my dad was censored with words or phrases cut out like crossword puzzles."[43] Entry into or exit from the camp was forbidden without a special pass or permit. As time went by, the restrictions on mobility were eased as well. Individuals were authorized to leave the camp on passes in order to walk or drive to nearby towns to pick up supplies, while teachers and Boy Scout leaders were authorized to guide children on nature walks and rock-finding expeditions.

Nevertheless, outside friends and Japanese Americans released from camp frequently had difficulty getting permission to see inmates. Even Nisei solders were sometimes forced to speak to their families through the fence or even break into and out of camp to visit with them.

Inmates were closely monitored, both by the FBI and by government social scientists, who viewed the camps as a marvelous laboratory for studying the social interaction and readjustment of a minority group. Groups of "community analysts" moved into the different camps. First, John Collier and Wade Head hired a team of social scientists as part of their plans for model community-building at Poston. After the social scientists were credited with reducing tensions, the WRA hired community analysts for the other camps. Their assignment was to report on inmate opinion and attitudes, based on information from "informants," with the goal of accumulating data and aiding conflict resolution. In addition, the Japanese Evacuation Research Study, a private research project directed by sociologist Dorothy Swaine Thomas of the University of California, sent teams of social scientists (many of whom were themselves Nisei) to the camps as reporters.

The government's community analysis policy was meant to be benign, and to help administrators respond positively to inmate needs. Many of the community analysts were genuinely sympathetic to Japanese Americans and anxious to improve their lot. A WRA analyst at Manzanar, Morris K. Opler, was so enraged by the confinement of the Nisei that each evening after finishing his government work he ghostwrote the JACL's *amicus* brief in *the United States v. Korematsu* Supreme Court case that challenged the constitutionality of removal. Yet the line between reporting on daily inmate life and attitudes, on the one hand, and performing official surveillance or informing on anti-administration activities, on the other, was a thin and difficult one, especially for the incarcerated Nisei reporters. It was difficult for even well-intentioned social workers not to be torn between their wish to be useful and accurate and the almost inherently compromised nature of their assignment. The analysts were put in the position of being, in WRA advisor Hugh Anderson's terms, "constructive evacuee spies" and would face criticism as a result from later generations of social science scholars, who did not face the same dilemmas. [44]

At the same time, from democratic principle mixed with its mission of encouraging "Americanization" of the inmates, the WRA concentrated on establishing a measure of inmate self-government through elected block councils, to which representatives were elected from each block.

At first, membership on the councils was restricted entirely to American citizens, but this restriction provoked widespread outcry among Issei; by mid-1943 the aliens too were made eligible for election. The councils were responsible for planning space utilization and deciding how much land would be reserved for food production, controlling profits from community enterprises, and running the local mess hall (good chefs being at a premium, kitchen workers sometimes threw their weight around). The councils were also responsible for maintaining order and resolving disputes between inmates, and they operated courts to try inmates for offenses according to laws and constitutions they drafted.[45] The councils helped make work schedules run smoothly. They had no power over the WRA, however, and were often ineffective in representing inmates against the administration or in petitioning for redress of grievances. In historian Sandra C. Taylor's words, the WRA's inmate self-government policy provided Japanese Americans with all the external trappings of democracy—except freedom.[46]

The odd mix of government control and democracy was perhaps starkest in the area of publishing, a large area of inmate enterprise. Each camp had a daily newspaper. Some were distributed in mimeograph form; others (such as the *Manzanar Free Press*) on newsprint. The camp newspapers were the main source of information for confined Japanese Americans, although the inmates also received subscriptions of outside newspapers, including the JACL organ the *Pacific Citizen* and the three ethnic Japanese newspapers in the "free zone" that continued to publish (albeit under strict government control): *Utah Nippo* in Salt Lake City, and *Colorado Times* and *Rockii Nippo* (later *Rocky Shimpo*) in Denver.[47] Many of the writers and editors of the camp newspapers, such as Chiye Mori, Eddie Shimano, Bean Takeda, Bill Hosokawa, Hisaye Yamamoto, and Kiyoshi Conrad Hamanaka, were veterans of the prewar Japanese vernacular press and the assembly center newssheets, and they helped give the camp newspapers a professional look. There has been a lively historical debate as to the extent to which the different camp administrators limited freedom of the press. In Takeya Mizuno's phrase, the press was "free from censorship" but was published under the "supervision" of center directors and WRA officials.[48] This meant that the administration laid out ground rules and reserved the right to exert pressure on inmates, who responded with self-censorship. As one former inmate recalled, "We knew what we could and could not print."[49] One Nisei editor complained that the only thing free about the *Manzanar Free Press* was its purchase price.[50] Conversely, Bill Hosokawa, who served as editor of the *Heart Mountain Sentinel*, has insisted that he saw no official interference with newspapers.[51] Sandra Taylor notes that Topaz camp authorities directly censored newspaper coverage on only one occasion, but that they controlled press coverage through their selection of newspaper employees.[52] Paul Bailey asserts that inmate journalists were "under the hard heel of camp management," and that as a result, "Much of what they know, the camp journalists could never record."[53] Yet, an examination of the *Poston Chronicle*, reputedly the most unfettered of the camp newspapers, also reveals some forthright criticism of the WRA for paying higher wages to Caucasians than Nisei for the same jobs, plus articles by Bob Hiratsuka, referring to the relocation centers as "concentration camps" and Poston as "this man made hell on Earth."[54]

Finally, the WRA was inconsistent in its reaction to inmate protest. On the one hand, managers at Poston were able to keep lines of communication with inmates and negotiate mutually beneficial reforms. Conversely, WRA officials at Manzanar were badly shaken by the disturbances there and harshly punitive toward those whom they labeled "troublemakers." Following the declaration of martial law in December 1942, security guards seized a group of sixteen inmates implicated in the disturbances and put them in isolation at a facility in Moab, Utah. (Another group, composed of the JACL members and pro-administration Nisei on the "death squad," was removed temporarily to Death Valley before being released.) A few weeks later, in January 1943, the sixteen were transferred from Moab to a new penal colony, dubbed an "isolation center," created in an old Navajo reservation school at Leupp, Arizona. In the months that followed, some forty more Japanese Americans suspected or accused of various offenses (notably conspiring in beatings of other inmates considered too friendly to the administration) were likewise confined there as "troublemakers." The WRA was aware that insufficient proof of their guilt existed, and also that if they were tried in camp, other inmates would be frightened to testify against them or convict them. Thus, the inmates remained in custody at Leupp, separated from their families, for up to eleven months, even though they had been convicted of no offenses and had been promised "speedy hearings." In late 1943 Dillon Myer and WRA leaders, realizing that if news of the secret facility at Leupp spread it would reflect badly on the agency, hastily liquidated the center and moved all the inmates to the new segregation center it had created at Tule Lake for those adjudged "disloyal" (about which more below). Once at Tule Lake, ten recalcitrant inmates were immediately isolated in a stockade, where they remained for weeks.[55]

THE CANADIAN CAMPS

Beginning in April 1942, the British Columbia Security Commission carried out plans to remove Japanese Canadians from the West Coast to the interior of the country. As noted, some Issei and Nisei were recruited for jobs on sugar beet farms, while others were able to use their own funds and relocate to "self-supporting projects"(a misnomer, since all Japanese Canadians were required to live off their own funds) or were given special work permits to relocate outside the restricted zone. A small number, less than 945, carried on the work of the road labor camps, while some 700 Issei and Nisei who had earlier protested official policy remained interned as POWs. However, a large majority of West Coast Japanese Canadians—some 11,000 people—were slated for mass confinement. Families were removed from Hastings Park or Vancouver and permitted to take with them only 150 pounds of baggage per adult and 75 pounds per child. They were placed on Canadian Pacific and Canadian National railroad cars and sat on hard wicker seats during the approximately 500-mile trip inland. Their destination was the "ghost towns" of the Slocan Valley, a group of old and largely abandoned mining settlements located amid attractive natural scenery of forests and mountain streams. There they were soon joined by some 1,000 men who had been released from road labor camps.

Within weeks, the Japanese Canadians were crowded into five "ghost towns" scattered through the valley: Kaslo, Greenwood, New Denver, Sandon, and Slocan City (the latter composed of the "satellite" towns of Bay Farm, Popoff, and Lemon Creek). In addition, there was one American-style camp built from scratch on abandoned ranchland near the town of Hope (which lay, however, inside the excluded zone). Once completed, it was dubbed Tashme, from the initials of the last names of the three BCSC members. At first the BCSC divided inmates among different settlements based on religion, with Catholics being sent to Greenwood, Anglicans to Slocan, United Church (Protestant) members to Kaslo, and Buddhists to Sandon. As the population grew, the BCSC began to assign space as it became available. Nevertheless, each area retained a prominent de-nominational focus.[56] In the end, some 12,000 Japanese Canadians would remain confined in family groups in these camps, which the Canadian government officially referred to as "interior settlements" or "relocation centers." Unlike in the WRA camps, there were no barbed wire fences or guards in watchtowers controlling the Japanese Canadian inmates. How-ever, their movements were tracked by the RCMP, and the rugged moun-tain terrain and the largely unfriendly local population they encountered made any substantial movement difficult. Until mid-1943 no Issei or Ni-sei were permitted to travel without special authorization, and even after that, those wishing to change residences or travel more than fifty miles from camp were required to obtain a pass.

The BCSC did not make extensive preparations for the operation of the camps, which its leaders clearly conceived of as a temporary measure until resettlement in the East could take place. In any case, the severely limited funds provided to the BCSC meant that its directors could not provide large-scale services. Housing was an immediate problem. The BCSC later claimed in its official report that sufficient housing was avail-able in the "ghost towns," yet the amount of work that needed to be done to make these long-abandoned houses habitable was considerable.[57] There was also need for new housing. As a result, the first contingents of Japa-nese Canadians sent to the Slocan Valley included construction workers, masons, and plumbers. After reaching their destination, these men were assigned to cut the abundant wood surrounding the towns and to use it to rebuild old housing and to construct 1,100 new houses at Tashme and Lemon Creek. While they worked feverishly to build shelter, they and other inmates were housed in tents (or, in one case, in an abandoned hockey rink). The completed houses were windowless and cramped. One former inmate described her family's house in Rosebury:

> Our shack, number 208, was 14 by 28 feet divided into three tiny rooms. It had a camp stove, a small two-burner kitchen stove, and a wooden sink. It had no electricity, and the communal water tap was outside. The shack had only green shiplap boards for the outside walls, no inner walls and a roof but no ceiling. In the small rooms, beds had to be pushed against the walls, and on winter mornings the bedding was stuck frozen to the wall. The cracks in the wall and the floor were stuffed with whatever was available to keep out the cold.[58]

Inmates huddled in the communal kitchens, amid the relative warmth of the cooking stoves—the builders did not receive shingles or materials for insulation, and the houses did little to keep out the bitter winter chill of the mountains. A Nisei clergyman recalled an occasion when an inmate put a hot-water bottle in his bed, only to find it frozen by morning.[59] Most of the Japanese Canadians, living in coastal British Columbia, had little or no experience of snow. While it made for beautiful landscapes, it also complicated their lives. As one inmate recalled, "everything was wet in the house. You know, condensation. They build up the stove until it was very hot and then the heat would work on the outside snow and it would drip, drip, drip. Clothes got ruined. Blankets wet. . . . It was awful."[60]

BCSC supervisors and a skeleton administrative staff directed the operations of each of the camps except for Tashme, which was effectively self-administering. Administrators provided the inmates with the housing, once completed, and with stoves and bunk beds. The government also paid for fuel, offered limited mail service (with correspondence heavily censored), and provided medical care—such limited care as could be provided by inmate nurses and physicians working with scanty supplies and facilities buttressed by scattered regional health care professionals. A hundred-bed tuberculosis hospital for Japanese Canadians opened at New Denver, and small infirmaries opened in the other camps.

The contrast between the official resources allocated to Japanese Americans in the WRA camps and those granted their Canadian counterparts was striking. First, there was no food provided for inmates in Canada. While the BCSC started a few small-scale farms and the authorities permitted inmates to start private garden plots, they did not pay cultivators or produce the kind of dietary supplement of fresh fruits and vegetables that Japanese American farmers did. In addition, there were no communal dining halls, with the result that Issei and Nisei wives and mothers spent much time in cooking and cleaning. Unlike the WRA, the BCSC did not fund camp newspapers, so the only source of information the inmates had was the censored tri-weekly issues of the *New Canadian*. Its editors walked a fine line, protesting injustice while avoiding being shut down.[61]

Education proved a particularly thorny problem. Canadian provinces were obligated to provide free primary and secondary education to all residents, but British Columbia's government (and that of Alberta) rejected their mission of providing for the Japanese Canadians. The BCSC reluctantly undertook to provide schooling up through eighth grade for children in the camps and built rough school buildings in all the camps.[62] However, even more than in the United States, the schooling was slipshod and poorly funded—barely twenty dollars per student per year. Under the direction of Hide Hyodo, the only Nisei teacher hired in prewar British Columbia, 120 Nisei college and high school students, especially women, were pressed into service to design curricula and lead classes. While parents banded together to buy supplies, they had little spare capital for equipment. Those who wished to attend high school were therefore relegated to using paid correspondence courses. Eventually, a coalition of church groups joined together to open free kindergartens and high schools in the camps (plus a Catholic Mission school at Greenwood). However, these schools also suffered from poorly trained teachers and lack of typewriters and sports equipment.

Japanese Canadians struggled to deal with their difficult situation in the camps. Boredom, mixed with the stress of adaptation and resentment at being exiled without charge from their homes, took a heavy toll, especially at first. In particular, Issei fishermen and farm couples who had worked for years found themselves stripped of their livelihoods and their stature. Inmates struggled to organize community parties, dances, sports activities, and (in Tashme) Boy Scouts. Christian groups formed congregations (as well as schools) with the aid of different clergy—Rev. Kosuburu Shimizu, a United Church minister, reconstituted his Vancouver congregation in Kaslo.[63] The Buddhist majority, which could not draw on similar support from white coreligionists, struggled to build temples and create makeshift facilities in the camps.[64]

Employment became a vital necessity, both to relieve stagnation and build up the camps and out of economic need. Although the Japanese Canadians in the "ghost towns" faced more restrictive conditions than those of the "self-supporting communities," they were equally required to be self-supporting. The vast majority of inmates were forced to purchase, out of their earnings or savings, their own clothes, food, and supplies, generally at the inflated prices charged by local shopkeepers. However, the only available jobs offered low wages (although rather higher than those in WRA camps) and were often uninteresting. Issei and Nisei men earned salaries between 22.5 and 40 cents per hour for outdoor tasks such as construction labor or cutting wood (in the summer of 1943, the government opened a saw mill and employed inmates to cut firewood to send to Canadian cities hit by wartime coal rationing).[65] Skilled professionals hired by the government to take care of education and social welfare services earned between 30 and 75 dollars per month. One inmate recalled, "You couldn't do anything but work for the government. Cutting wood. On the roads. . . . The pay was just enough to live on. I think it was 30 cents an hour. . . . Just living took anything you made. Some people stopped using sugar and sold their ration tickets."[66] Only those aged and ill or those with children who were deemed unable to work and had no resources of their own (less than $260 total assets per adult) were supported by provincial relief funds.

The BCSC recognized that conditions were inadequate and warned of the danger of potential reprisals by Japan against allied prisoners if steps were not taken. Responding to complaints by Japanese Canadians and the Spanish consul, a royal commission (made up of four white Canadians) was selected at the end of 1943 to report on conditions in the camps. Commission members were given a minimal budget, held no public hearings, and spent only two days in the camps, far less than in Vancouver. Based on an examination of the dilapidated housing standing in Vancouver's abandoned Japantown and in Steveston, which by then had been left vacant for almost two years, the commission determined that housing in the camps was equivalent to prewar community standards, and added that since the inmates received free housing and fuel, the low pay they received was adequate. The main reform the commission called for was assumption of school fees by provincial governments. Its report, issued in March 1944, attracted little attention, and commentators denounced it as a whitewash by the government.[67]

PROPERTY COMMISSION SALES

The economic condition of Japanese Canadians was further weakened, and the bitterness of their exile exponentially increased, by the forced sale of their property and possessions. As mentioned, in March 1942 an Order in Council had given the custodian of enemy property responsibility for managing the property of all Issei and Nisei, on a generally voluntary basis. Over the following months the custodian leased most of the Issei-owned farms in the rich Fraser Valley and was also engaged in shipping household items requested by inmates in the camp.

Even before mass removal was ordered, however, the government undertook some forced disposition of property. As mentioned, after Pearl

Harbor, ethnic Japanese were officially forbidden to fish, and their boats were impounded under the War Measures Act and moored at New Westminster. Government ministers wished to put the boats back into operation, in order to maintain the province's food supply, and they recognized that the boats would soon deteriorate if they were not maintained. Once it became clear that Japanese Canadians would not be permitted to resume fishing, officials determined to sell the boats to non-Japanese. Thus, even as the Order-in-Council of January 14, 1942, excluded adult male Japanese nationals from the West Coast, a separate order, P.C. No. 288, provided for the appointment of a Japanese Fishing Vessel Disposal Committee to supervise sales. The committee was formed of a judge, a naval officer, and a Japanese Canadian, Kishizo Kimura. During the spring of 1942, the committee surveyed the boats and sold them on the open market to white British Columbians. Kimura managed to persuade his fellow boat-owners to allow the government to take 1 percent of the sale prices as a fee for arranging the sales. At the same time, the government allocated eighty thousand dollars to fix boats that had been damaged in transport and to indemnify their owners for the theft and vandalism they had been exposed to while in official custody. By July 1942, when the custodian of enemy property took over the committee, most sales had been transacted. The prices the committee obtained for the boats gave rise to numerous complaints. In part due to the neglect they had suffered through months of idleness, the boats were appraised at less than the prices that the Japanese Canadians had purchased them (and those at Depression prices, not inflated wartime ones). The oversupply created by the mass sales in turn led to a buyer's market, from which white purchasers were able to obtain boats at even less than the appraised value. Meanwhile, as in the United States, cars owned by Issei and Nisei and stored by the government were sold after a few months, often at greatly reduced prices—prices which were also further reduced by the fee claimed by the property custodian. Nevertheless, there was a general recognition by Japanese Canadians and sympathizers that these sales were necessary to avoid the boats and cars being put permanently out of commission, and that the government had acted with a degree of good faith.[68]

Any such good faith was absent, however, in the case of agricultural and personal properties. Ian Mackenzie, who had been the chief instigator of Japanese Canadian removal, was also the prime mover in arranging the sale of the rich farmland that they had painfully acquired in prewar decades. As minister of Veterans and Pensions, Mackenzie wanted to make it possible for white army veterans to acquire land cheaply, to assure postwar economic stability. He was also well aware that depriving Japanese Canadians of their property would help prevent them from ever returning to the Pacific Coast, a goal of enormous concern to his white constituents. Thus, in mid-1942 Mackenzie introduced a bill in Parliament to establish a Veterans' Land Act (VLA) program. At Mackenzie's suggestion, on June 28, 1942, Gordon Murchison, administrator of the Soldier Settlement Board, which would run the program, took over responsibility for the 939 Japanese-owned farms held by the government. He had his department appraise the "alien" properties. Mixing anti-Japanese prejudice—Murchison was convinced that Japanese Canadians had been moved because they posed an actual security threat—with his departmental self-interest in securing a good deal for the soldiers, Murchison and his staff deliberately undervalued the farmland and structures—they refused, among other things, to take account of new improvements or the value of the current crops planted by tenants.[69] Meanwhile, to make sure that the land was preserved until the Veterans' Land Act could become law, Mackenzie and his colleague Thomas A. Crerar, minister of mines and resources, obtained an order in council freezing any sales of Japanese-owned farms. Once the VLA was enacted in the fall of 1942 and the land surveys completed, Mackenzie put pressure on Norman McLarty, secretary of state, to approve a new Order-in-Council permitting the custodian of enemy property to undertake forced sales of the Japanese Canadian property. His plans were echoed by Vancouver's city council and by influential West Coast lobbying groups, and seconded by the Vancouver representative of the property custodian, G. W. McPherson. McPherson, who harbored strong anti-Japanese prejudices of his own, hoped to clear Powell Street Japantown, where many houses had fallen into disrepair, in order to promote the economic development of downtown Vancouver. He petitioned Ottawa to allow him discretion to sell off property, asserting falsely that his chief interest was in disposing of small numbers of unprofitable holdings.

Mackenzie's scheme received a further boost from Labour Minister Humphrey Mitchell and his department. With the removal of Japanese Canadians from the West Coast completed, the BCSC lost its formal raison d'être, and by the time Austin Taylor resigned in November 1942, it had begun winding down its affairs—it was officially dissolved by Order-in-Council on February 5, 1943. The Labour Department then gradually assumed responsibility for Japanese Canadians. Department officials were aware of the financial difficulties of the Japanese Canadians in the camps. However, the department felt unable to provide higher wages or funds for them because of popular complaints, echoed by racist newspapers and by the Conservative opposition, about "coddling" of the inmates. Such sales appeared to department bureaucrats to be a useful way to provide relief to hard-pressed Japanese Canadians without having to use taxpayer funds.[70]

Bowing to the interdepartmental pressure, McLarty brought up to the cabinet's Committee on Japanese Questions the question of amending the enemy property custodian's powers. On the strong recommendation of Mackenzie, the committee readily granted official approval, and on January 23, 1943, an Order-in-Council was issued to permit forced sales. At first the new regulations did not attract much attention—McPherson had presented the change as a minor administrative reform, and most people probably considered it that way—although Professor H. F. Angus (prompted by Rev. Howard Norman of the Vancouver Consultative Council, a liberal church group) immediately wrote Prime Minister Mackenzie King a letter of protest, which remained unanswered, asserting that the provision was reminiscent of the notorious Nuremberg Laws under which the Nazis had seized Jewish property.[71] In late March 1943 McPherson publicly announced that he intended to dispose of all Japanese Canadian property in his care, personal possessions as well as land. The news attracted significant outrage. The *New Canadian*, defying wartime censorship, took the step of criticizing the government's action, calling it "the last straw which can be added" to the already intolerable burdens of Japanese Canadians. On March 31 a group of prominent Issei set up the Japanese Property Owners' Association to fight the action. The association soon had chapters in all the camps. After organizing surveys and determining that the vast majority of property owners opposed the sales, the association determined to bring legal challenges to the government's actions.

In order to proceed with the sales, the government established two bodies, the Rural Advisory Committee to consider bids on agricultural land and the Greater Vancouver Advisory Committee to sell urban housing and stores. Ivan Barnet, the Vancouver VLA representative, made an offer of $750,000, using secret (and doubtless fictitious) appraisals, for properties that had been collectively assessed for taxes at over $1,200,000. The Rural Advisory Committee did a random sampling and determined that Barnet's estimates were low—less than 70 percent

of the real value of the farms. However, committee members then expressed interest in selling the lot for $850,000, at which point the com-
mittee's lone Japanese Canadian representative, Yasutaro Yamaga, a Fraser Valley farmer and community historian greatly respected within the
Japanese community, promptly resigned in protest at the inadequacy of
the offers.[72] The Department of External Affairs also expressed its opposition to the sales. In a memo calling for an interdepartmental meeting, they reminded colleagues that the U.S. government had stored the
properties of Japanese Americans and not despoiled them without their
consent.[73]

Despite these expressions of opposition, on June 23 the sale was
registered—the 769 properties and their rental income were taken over
by the VLA for $850,000. Although this deal removed a large fraction of
the available property, smaller transactions continued over the next four
years. The custodian disposed of inmates' personal property and housewares at fire sale prices, and white British Columbians enjoyed bargains.
Not only did the custodian's VLA sales amount to a heavy loss of assets
for Japanese Canadians, but even such funds as resulted were not placed
under their control. Rather, the government held the money without interest in escrow accounts for those in the camps and limited their with-
drawals to $100 per month. Nor did Japanese Canadians reap much ben-
efit from the proceeds of the sales once they received them. Those in the
camps were forced to use the funds to pay for their confinement, rather
than receiving government aid.

The Japanese Property Owners' Association attempted in vain to stop
the sales and advised property owners not to cash checks from the sales
in order not to give the appearance of consent. In July 1943 J. A. McLennan, a white attorney hired by the association, brought Petitions of Rights
in Exchequer court on behalf of three plaintiffs—a Japanese national, a
naturalized Issei, and a Nisei. The overtaxed court was slow to act on the
cases. They did not go to trial until May 1944. They then bogged down
over the technical question of whether the custodian could be sued as
an officer of the crown.[74] The court did not hand down a decision until
September 1947, when Justice Joseph Thorson dismissed the cases. In his
opinion, he noted that the government's authority under the War Measures Act was unlimited, and he declared that the custodian was not an
officer of the crown. To add insult to injury, the Japanese Property Owners' Association, whose members had suffered the loss of their primary
capital, was assessed a further $1,800 in court costs.[75]

RESETTLEMENT AND LOYALTY HEARINGS

As noted, U.S. War Relocation Authority Director Milton Eisenhower determined in the spring of 1942 that a policy of individual "relocation" (i.e., resettlement) of Japanese Americans following their removal from the West Coast was not realistic. He rejected calls by libertarian groups for the institution of loyalty boards, like those created for German and Italian aliens, to conduct hearings so that innocent Japanese Americans could be released. Not only did the FBI insist that it did not have the resources to devote to such hearings, but WRA administrators argued (ironically, in retrospect) that setting up hearings for Nisei would be a dangerous precedent for examining the loyalty of American citizens.[76] Still, Eisenhower and his advisors were unhappy with the idea of mass incarceration in camps, on both humanitarian and constitutional grounds. Their unhappiness increased as it became clear that the camps were damaging to the inmates' well-being. As a result, by the time Eisenhower departed the WRA in June 1942, he and his associates had already begun formulating plans for permitting individuals to leave camp.

The planning accelerated after Dillon Myer took over as WRA director. Myer was adamant that the camps be considered only a temporary expedient—not the kind of pioneer communities John Collier advocated—and insisted that the mission of the WRA should be one of "all-out relocation," that is, to resettle the inmates outside as soon as possible. Still, the WRA and its allies faced significant obstacles to implementing resettlement. General DeWitt maintained that it was impossible to distinguish a loyal from a disloyal "Japanese" and refused to permit any people of Japanese ancestry to return to the West Coast excluded zone. (In mid-1942 DeWitt read a report by Kenneth Ringle, who recommended that Kibei, whom he considered a potentially dangerous group, be segregated from the rest of the Nisei. Although Ringle's goal was to reduce general hostility to the mass of Nisei and make possible their release from confinement, his report only solidified DeWitt's belief that all Japanese Americans posed a danger to security).[77] The option of resettlement outside the Western Defense Command remained open, but even that was controversial. The government's own action in removing and confining West Coast Japanese Americans, reinforced by sensational newspaper coverage, left most Americans convinced that the Issei and Nisei were treacherous and disloyal, and they expressed widespread hostility to any idea of opening up the "relocation centers." In the face of this opposition, the WRA remained concerned about the safety of Issei and Nisei if they were released—indeed, government officials generally refused to make official statements about Japanese Americans during 1942 for fear of stirring up further opposition.[78]

In the end, WRA officials decided that the way to proceed would be to devise a system of "furloughs" or parole. These would permit individuals to obtain leave while maximizing the appearance of security and avoiding public antagonism toward Japanese Americans. The first leaves granted were for transfers by Nisei college students: they symbolized the positive, Americanized side of the community and they were most visibly handicapped by being removed from school. Beginning in the first weeks after Executive Order 9066 was signed, a group of West Coast college presidents, led by Remsen Bird of Occidental College and Robert Sproul of the University of California, had made various efforts to resettle students outside the West Coast. As a result, some 630 students who found sponsors outside the West Coast were able to transfer before the exclusion orders went into effect and thereby avoided being confined in camp.[79] On April 24, 1942, Sproul wrote a letter to President Roosevelt proposing a new plan for the creation of a program of federal scholarships to allow American citizens faced with confinement in camp to relocate to other campuses and continue their education. This way, he explained, the loyalty of these future community leaders and their faith in democracy would be preserved. California Governor Olson followed with a note endorsing the plan.

Roosevelt (under prodding from his wife, Eleanor, who had already spoken privately in favor of student relocation) responded on May 25 with a letter drafted by John Studebaker of the U.S. Office of Education. The president expressed his approval of the plan and its underlying rationale. "I am deeply concerned that the American-born college students shall be impressed with the ability of the American people to distinguish between enemy aliens and staunch supporters of the American system who happened to have Japanese ancestry."[80] Yet Roosevelt did not promise any funding. WRA officials quickly determined that in the face of widespread hostility toward Japanese Americans, they could not rely on public funds for student relocation; any such involvement would, as Dillon Myer bluntly put it, "sink the program."[81] Instead, with the consent of the War Department, the WRA called on Clarence Pickett, head of the American Friends Service Committee (which had opposed removal), to supervise the creation of a voluntary agency, the National Japanese American Student Relocation Council, under the direction of President John Nason of Swarthmore College. The agency raised private funds for scholarships to allow Nisei college students to enroll at institutions outside the West Coast and supervised their transfer. In order not to arouse public protest, enrollment was at first limited to U.S. citizens who had never been to Japan, though ultimately this rule was dropped. The program helped some 3,713 Nisei students—a number greater than the total Nisei college student population in 1941—to relocate to colleges and nursing schools and to pursue their education.[82]

Another early group of departures was that of laborers detailed by the government for short-term agricultural work. Under this program (actually started under the WCCA), local governments could hire groups of Japanese American laborers if they offered to pay prevailing wages and provided transportation and security. At first the program remained very small—only about 1,500 workers were recruited during the spring of 1942, despite widespread labor shortages and heavy demand—due to fears of violence and lack of volunteers. During the fall of 1942, however, sugar beet companies in the Rocky Mountain states, following the Canadian example, sent delegations to the WRA, which hired agents to oversee recruitment of inmate workers. The better pay and freer conditions were popular, and by the end of October some 10,000 inmates had signed up for work in the sugar beet harvest. They were widely credited with saving the year's crop. Once their job was completed, all were immediately returned to confinement in the camps.[83]

Even as students and seasonal workers began to leave the camps, WRA staffers devised procedures for issuance of "leave permits." As with the college relocation group, initially only American citizens who had never lived or attended school in Japan were eligible. Under this program, which went into effect on July 20, 1942, an inmate who was able to secure sponsorship by an outside employer not located in an excluded area could apply to the project director for permission to leave camp.[84] The project director would then, through an elaborate bureaucratic process, petition the WRA regional director, who would consult the FBI to see if there was derogatory information on the applicant in its files. If not, the regional director could then send the matter up to the WRA director, who would make the final decision as to whether to issue a "leave permit." Also, the director was empowered to order the inmate back into a camp at any time if he believed it necessary, although WRA lawyers were well aware that no legal basis existed for rounding up a U.S. citizen once released outside a military area.[85]

Although the WRA's leave policy was intended to allow for release of inmates, it not was only extremely cumbersome but was premised from the outset on the essential untrustworthiness of Issei and Nisei.[86] Worse, WRA officials, overly afraid of inflaming public opposition, were far too cautious. Thus, the policy was not widely announced, and many inmates never learned of its existence. There were further difficulties with the military. Although many of the jobs open to the inmates were located in the industrial areas of the East Coast, the Eastern Defense commander, General Hugh A. Drum, expressed reluctance to allow Japanese Americans to enter the area. Thus, while relocation to the East was not absolutely forbidden, it was all but ruled out in practice. As a result, only eleven applications were processed in the ten weeks that followed.[87]

The obvious failure of the policy caused an internal debate within the WRA. A set of employees led by Thomas Holland and Robert Frase (supported by outside liberal groups) argued that the only expedient and just way to manage resettlement was to open the camps without restrictions and assist people to find homes outside the West Coast. Another faction argued that without proper screening the WRA would be releasing dangerous people, and in any case opposition to Japanese Americans meant that their release would lead to bloodshed. Although Director Myer wavered, he ultimately decided in favor of screening, especially after the office of Solicitor General Charles Fahy sent word that the Justice Department would not endorse completely opening up the camps but would help defend in court a liberalized furlough procedure. Thus, in October 1942 the WRA produced a somewhat more flexible leave process. In contrast to the first one, all Japanese Americans were made eligible for release, and release was made a "matter of right," *but only* where the individual inmate posed no identifiable danger to security, had a job promised, and attracted no opposition from the surrounding community. Under the terms of the leave, the WRA required paroled inmates to remain in contact with "leave officers," in case return to the camps was required. (This last requirement was clearly unenforceable as well as unconstitutional, as WRA Solicitor Philip Glick recognized, but he claimed it was vital for bookkeeping and statistical purposes.)[88] Those who could not meet these requirements remained in confinement.

The new policy did not bring about an immediate exodus from the camps. However, its timing coincided with that of other events that worked in favor of resettlement. In particular, as we will see in chapter 5, toward the end of 1942 the army decided to create a segregated all-Nisei combat unit for active service in Europe. To prove to Nisei that they were not being recruited simply as cannon fodder, the White House also agreed to permit properly cleared American citizens to work in war plants. The opening up of wartime service to the Nisei was accompanied by the issuance of a public letter, dated February 1, 1943, and signed by President Roosevelt, that endorsed the army's action and added an eloquent tribute to equal rights: "No loyal citizen of the United States should be denied the democratic right to exercise his citizenship, regardless of his ancestry. The principle on which this country was founded and by which it has always been governed is that Americanism is a matter of the mind and the heart; Americanism is not, and never was, a matter of race or ancestry."

Roosevelt's intervention, although designed to justify a politically expedient goal and limited in its purpose and reach, put the prestige of the presidency for the first time behind the loyalty of Japanese Americans and turned the government's focus toward resettlement.[89] A further indication of White House backing was the involvement of First Lady Eleanor Roosevelt. Mrs. Roosevelt, who had expressed cautious support for Japanese American loyalty during 1942, actively encouraged resettlement. In April 1943 she made an impromptu (and unguarded) tour of the Gila River camp and reported in her syndicated column on the brave efforts of Japanese Americans to build their lives amid the difficult surroundings. Immediately afterward, she traveled to Los Angeles, the center of anti-Nisei sentiment, and publicly spoke up in favor of resettlement. "The sooner we get the young Japanese out of the camps the better. Otherwise if we don't look out we will create another Indian problem. I think it is bad to institutionalize anybody."[90]

To support mass relocation, the WRA established a set of regional field offices in the East, South, and Midwest and hired employment and social welfare workers to find jobs and intercede with community leaders on behalf of the inmates. At the same time, recognizing that the success of resettlement depended on improving the public image of Japanese Americans, WRA officials worked in collaboration with the Office of War Information (OWI) to issue press releases and create positive propaganda, including speaking tours by Nisei war hero Ben Kuroki and by Joseph Grew, former U.S. ambassador to Japan. Paradoxically, the WRA's focus on presenting a benign public face of Japanese Americans to enable resettlement, a mission that went far beyond its original assignment, led its officials to manufacture images of happy, cooperative camp populations while stifling actual protest and dissent within the camps. It also fostered the development of a sometimes coercive policy of "Americanization," that is, Japanese assimilation to white American values.[91]

THE LOYALTY QUESTIONNAIRE

It was in the process of establishing procedures for resettlement that the WRA made a fatal blunder. Once the War Department decided to accept Nisei soldiers, it advised the WRA that a joint board of military officers would be formed to determine the loyalty (and hence admissibility) of those Nisei who wished to enlist. The examination would consist of a loyalty questionnaire, testimonials from witnesses (generally white Americans) as to the individual's character and views, and information from FBI and military intelligence agency files. WRA administrators jumped at the chance to associate their leave clearance efforts with those of the Army, whose involvement and seal of approval would both assure greater security and offer the WRA better political cover for the policy. Therefore, they requested and received the War Department's consent to have the board undertake a comprehensive examination of the loyalties of all the inmates, so that all but the dangerous could be cleared. In the process, the unquantifiable and amorphously defined concept of "loyalty" became a stand-in for security.

The leave examination procedure itself was tragically flawed. The WRA ordered all Japanese Americans seventeen and older to fill out the questionnaire, with no real consultation or explanation of the purpose of the form or how the information regarding "loyalty" would be used. They thus further inflamed the suspicions of the inmates. Even among those who understood the goals of the questionnaire, many inmates, especially older Issei stripped of their life possessions, had no means or intention of resettling outside the West Coast amid unknown and potentially unfriendly surroundings. They thus naturally resisted a procedure they feared would cast them and their families adrift. When Japanese Americans refused to fill out the questionnaire, camp authorities interpreted this as a show of disloyalty and improperly pressured them with threats of arrest. The flaws in the loyalty procedure also reflected the logical and practical impossibility of determining individual attitudes, especially under such trying circumstances. Each inmate's loyalty was judged on the basis of subjective interpretation of the questionnaires, and a shifting point system based on arbitrary or irrelevant factors such as the individual's religious affiliation or whether the individual held money in Japanese banks. The examiners provided by the Army Provost Marshal General's Office, moreover, judged the inmates according to harsh, racially biased standards—their training manual warned them to be extremely cautious in endorsing the loyalty of "the Japanese," irrespective of citizenship, since they were "disassociated from American life" and well known for "deceit" and widespread "disloyalty."[92]

Moreover, the questionnaire itself, devised for those seeking to enlist in the army, was hastily assembled and badly designed to assess the entire population. Two questions in particular became notorious for the anguish and trial they caused Japanese Americans. Question 27 asked, "Are you willing to serve in the Armed Forces of the United States on combat duty, wherever ordered?" Nisei men, who feared that a positive answer would trap them into joining up, were reluctant to answer. Even worse, question 28 asked the inmates whether they were prepared to swear unqualified allegiance to the United States "and foreswear any form of allegiance or obedience to the Japanese emperor, or any other foreign government, power, or organization." (Since the Issei, Japanese subjects barred from naturalization in the United States, could not renounce their allegiance to Japan without becoming stateless, the provision violated international law and was thus eventually changed in the case of noncitizens to ask whether they would "abide by" American law.) Not only did many Nisei feel insulted at being asked to swear absolute loyalty to a government that had violated their citizenship rights, but they feared that agreeing to foreswear allegiance to Japan and the emperor would be an admission that they had ever actually held any such allegiance. As one Nisei subsequently put it, "It was like being asked, 'Have you stopped beating your wife?' The question itself implied guilt."[93]

THE LEAVE PERMIT SYSTEM

Despite these obstacles, some 85 percent of inmates overcame their suspicions and answered "yes" to both questions. If the Joint Board did not then find reason to question their loyalty, they became eligible to seek employment and, if they found it, to apply for a "leave permit" to be released from camp. Those granted leave permits received a $25 allowance and a train ticket to their destination. In exit interviews WRA officials not only required departing inmates to promise to keep the government informed of their addresses, but they paternalistically reminded them of their duty to abandon their ethnic characteristics, "assimilate" into their new communities, and avoid congregating in groups with other Japanese Americans. As Miné Okubo described: "After plowing through the red tape, through the madness of packing again, I attended forums on 'How to make Friends' and 'How to Behave in the Outside World.'" . . . I received a train ticket and $25, plus $3 a day for meals while traveling; these were given to each person relocating on an indefinite permit. I received four typewritten cards to be filled out and returned after relocation, and a booklet, 'When You Leave the Relocation Center,' which I was to read on the train."[94]

In the end, only 17,000 inmates, less than 15 percent of the total, were able to leave the camps during 1943, and a similar number followed in 1944. Many Nisei were reluctant to leave their families in confinement and settle in new (and potentially hostile) communities when at least in the camps they had work and security. In any case, the leave clearance procedure was so slow and cumbersome that sometimes the outside jobs for which application was made were filled by the time the permits were granted. By the beginning of 1944, the Joint Board was dissolved, the victim of differing visions of Japanese Americans within the government. The WRA then organized its own examinations in order to determine which inmates could be released from camp and resettled outside. The Army Provost Marshal General's Office, conversely, took on the task of determining which inmates were loyal enough to take employment in defense plants or other sensitive industries (including attendance at universities doing defense-related research).[95]

At first, the resettlers were primarily Nisei in their late teens or twenties who were going out on their own for the first time and leaving the camps to join the army, go to school, or accept employment. Slightly more men than women left camp, but since those joining the army were virtually all male, the majority of those who relocated for jobs were female.[96] As soon as they established themselves, these initial resettlers were joined by small groups of other migrants—generally siblings and friends, in some cases parents and older relations. Although some Japanese Americans resettled on farms or in small towns, most wartime migrants moved to the urban Midwest (especially Chicago, which had some 22,000 Japanese American residents by the end of the war) or the Northeast—several thousand, mostly after resettling elsewhere and then moving on, found their way to New York.[97]

The resettlers generally enjoyed their new freedom outside camp, and they generally found less prejudice in their new communities than they had on the West Coast, but they still faced great challenges.[98] Already scarred by the camp experience, they entered their new communities with little in the way of resources or contacts, and were forced by poverty and housing discrimination to move into or next to ghetto areas. Very often they represented the first sizable population of Japanese ancestry in their new homes. One Nisei who moved to Chicago later recalled, "One day when [friends and I] went shopping, a bunch of women on the street started yelling. It was like they thought Japan had invaded Chicago, and they were scared and running away from us. It gave us a funny feeling."[99] Only a few Nisei were able to secure jobs in defense plants, and there is evidence of a measure of job discrimination against them. Most lacked the resources to start their own businesses.[100] Instead, to make a living they were forced to take jobs such as domestic labor, whose requirements and salaries were on the average well below their level of training and education.[101] Yet, because of their head start in working and the availability of educational opportunity, one study found that Nisei who resettled had greater average long-term economic success (even if they subsequently returned west) than those who remained in camp.[102] Although they were warned by the War Relocation Authority and the FBI to fit in as much as possible and to avoid other Japanese Americans as a condition of their parole from the camps, they were brought together into ethnic communities both by internal factors such as religious observance and the need for community and by external factors such as racial prejudice and housing discrimination.[103]

WARTIME RESETTLEMENT BY JAPANESE CANADIANS

Canadian policymakers faced similar dilemmas regarding resettlement as their neighbors further south but differed in both their approach to the question and their means. Caught between the urge to resettle Issei and Nisei, on grounds of both principle and economy, and the difficulties of assuring security and avoiding hostile public reaction, Canadian officials offered only limited efforts to assure release from confinement. In June 1942 the British Columbia Security Commission persuaded the municipal government of Winnipeg to permit Nisei domestic laborers to migrate and secured them housing through the local YWCA. The BCSC tried to persuade other towns in western Canada to lift their bans on Japanese settlement, but many refused to permit Japanese laborers even to relieve desperate shortages. The situation was not much better in Ontario, although Premier Mitchell Hepburn hired 350 Japanese Canadian workers for his farm.[104] Meanwhile, the BCSC sent Mrs. C. V. Booth, a Labour Department staffer, to tour eastern Canada and report on possibilities for resettlement, and set up offices in Lethbridge, Schreiber, Montreal, Toronto, and Winnipeg to locate jobs for "self-supporting" Japanese Canadians. After the BCSC was dissolved in early 1943, these offices were taken over by George Collins, the Department of Labour's placement commissioner, who commissioned a plan for "reallocation" of Japanese Canadians to go east. Ernest Trueman, a former missionary, was hired to help arrange the resettlement of migrants in Ontario.[105]

This tension between economy and security continued to express itself in official policy. On the one hand, the authorities repeatedly maintained, when it suited them, that the settlements were temporary and transitory facilities and that dispersion outside the West Coast was the main goal. Thus, when the Spanish consul complained that families in Rosebury were living without running water, government officials refused to install pipes, on the grounds that if families did not like the facilities provided, "These people have the opportunity of moving to eastern Canada to private employment."[106] At the same time, Canadian authorities utterly failed to develop a realistic policy to persuade those confined in the ghost towns and camp facilities to move east. Instead, the government embarked on a futile policy of coercion. The February 5, 1943, order-in-council that dissolved the British Columbia Security Commission gave the Department of Labour full authority to resettle or move any Japanese Canadian. Labour Minister Humphrey Mitchell resolved to use National Selective Service provisions to send unmarried Canadian citizens to relieve labor shortages in rural Ontario. Nisei in the camps were outraged by the plan and sent Mitchell petitions arguing that a government that had stripped them of their citizenship rights could not now declare them Canadian citizens for the purposes of forced labor.[107] All but a handful of Nisei ignored their conscription notices, thereby forcing Mitchell to transform the program to a voluntary one by the end of the year.[108]

In the end, only a small fraction of Japanese Canadians went east before the end of the war. Not only did the government not offer sufficient logistical support or any financial assistance for mass resettlement, it placed burdensome restrictions on it. The Department of Labour required Japanese Canadians wishing to migrate east to have a job offer at their desired destination to obtain a permit, and until the end of 1943 it refused to permit single Nisei men to take jobs. Those wishing to travel outside the excluded zone had to first obtain a RCMP travel permit— a cumbersome process—and to submit to official restrictions on their activities even after they moved. Most notably, Justice Minister Louis St. Laurent was granted authority over licenses for "enemy alien" business operations, which covered both Issei and Nisei, and he generally denied any such authorization. There were also limitations on Issei and Nisei purchases of houses or farm property, though this was for many the only way to assure decent lodging amid wartime housing shortages and prejudice. Thus, for the Japanese Canadians, as one commentator put it, "going east was tantamount to being prisoners on probation, enjoying none of the rights of citizenship such as acquiring or leasing property and launching businesses."[109] There were local restrictions as well. As mentioned, many Alberta towns banned Japanese Canadian settlement. The town of Chatham, Ontario, where families of sugar beet workers migrated, passed a resolution in 1944 against settlement by ethnic Japanese.[110]

Some seven hundred ethnic Japanese (including a number of individuals who originally took jobs in farms and logging camps in rural Ontario) resettled in Toronto in the months after evacuation, while another four hundred moved to nearby Hamilton. In mid-1943 the Toronto Board of Control, fearing that Japanese Canadian resettlers would form a new ghetto, protested their continued arrival. The federal government agreed to establish a system whereby Issei and Nisei newcomers were required to obtain a residence permit to settle within Toronto's city limits. This permission was granted sparingly, although those who settled in outlying areas were able to enter the city freely during the day. Nisei were also denied licenses to operate businesses downtown.[111] Instead, the newcomers were settled in domestic service, restaurants, and garment factories (many of them within the Jewish community) until they could find less menial employment on their own. Church groups in both Ontario cities set up charitable organizations to help the resettlers. An umbrella welfare and lobbying group, the Co-operative Committee for Japanese Canadians, was formed in Toronto in 1943. Meanwhile, representatives of the local Nisei community formed their own group, Japanese Canadian Citizens for Democracy (JCCD). Toronto's elite newspaper, the *Globe and Mail*, for its part, took a hostile position, describing Japanese Canadians as guilty of widespread subversion, perennially disloyal and incapable of assimilation. In November 1943 it formally advocated the wholesale deportation of all those of Japanese ancestry to Japan.[112]

The one place where Japanese Canadian migrants were welcomed without official obstacles was Montreal, where some six hundred wartime migrants settled and where a few newcomers were even able to open businesses.[113] As in Toronto, various church groups (many of them Catholic) and individual Jews aided the resettlers.[114] Yet even in Montreal there were also expressions of prejudice and discrimination. In October 1944 McGill College (which was notorious for its longstanding discriminatory policies against Jews and other minorities) became the first Canadian university officially to close its doors to Japanese Canadian students, on the grounds that since they were not admissible for military training, educating them would be a waste.[115] The English-language newspaper *Montreal Star* editorialized in May 1944 that the Japanese Canadians were spies for Tokyo and proclaimed the need to deport the entire Japanese Canadian population "lock, stock and barrel."[116]

Most egregiously, even as it pushed dispersion and resettlement, the Canadian government acted to brand Japanese Canadians nationwide as second-class citizens. One of the few positive aspects, at least for Nisei and naturalized Issei, of resettlement outside British Columbia was escaping the legal discrimination that they experienced there, which was crystallized in the race-based disenfranchisement of citizens of Asian ancestry. In 1944 a new Soldier Vote bill was introduced in Parliament, which made it possible for Canadian soldiers serving abroad to vote. One clause of the bill, however, provided that all those whose "racial origin" was that of a country at war with Canada would be barred from suffrage. After it passed the House of Commons, a pair of senators objected that this amounted to Nazi-style racial hatred. Prime Minister King and the cabinet then agreed that the government should not exclude those who had the right to vote before the war, as long as it did not enfranchise those who did not have such rights. Therefore, the government endorsed a provision that disqualified the Japanese Canadians who had moved from British Columbia after the start of the war from voting in federal elections. King defended the amendment on overtly racist grounds, insisting, with a patent lack of logic, that to allow the Japanese who had not previously voted access to suffrage would be an act of "racial favoritism" toward a race with whose country Canada was at war.[117]

SEGREGATION IN THE UNITED STATES

Not all the inmates in WRA camps made the "correct" responses to the government's loyalty questionnaire during 1943. Some 10–15 percent of the inmate population answered "no" or qualified their answers on the loyalty form. How much the actions of these inmates, termed "no-no boys," were inspired by ignorance, confusion, anger, protest, support for Japan, or fear of being separated from family is unknowable. Since "no-no" boys were disproportionately draft-age males, concern about being forced into the army may well have been an important factor. Furthermore, the conditions in the different camps and the responsive or authoritarian temper of their individual administrations were reflected in the broad variations between them in the number of inmates who answered "no-no," qualified their answers, or refused to fill out the loyalty questionnaire altogether. Outside pressures also played a role: pro-Japanese or disaffected inmates pressured others to answer "no," while pro-administration forces pushed for "yes." In any case, what is clear is that the decision caused enormous disruptions among Japanese Americans and divisions within families. Japanese Americans remained marked for decades, in their careers, material circumstances, and social relationships, by their answers on the loyalty questionnaire. In addition to the "no-nos," there were those who requested repatriation to Japan. Disturbingly, while during 1942 only some 2,200 inmates, almost all Issei and their underage children, had formally requested postwar deportation or repatriation, some 2,500 inmates—two-thirds of them U.S. citizens—made such requests during the registration period, and an even larger number did so during the months that followed.[118] All these inmates were judged "disloyal" and thereby became ineligible for leave clearance,

The results of the questionnaire, as equivocal as they were, soon brought attacks against the WRA. Congressional critics such as Kentucky Senator Albert "Happy" Chandler and the Dies Committee separately held hearings in mid-1943 during which they publicized absurd charges of inmate "coddling" and subversion. They interpreted the large number of "no" responses to questions 27 and 28 as proof of widespread inmate disloyalty and subversion and demanded that those judged "disloyal" be segregated and lodged in a high-security facility. Myer refused, arguing that it would harm morale to punish some inmates if there was no reward for others—better to release as may people as possible and handle the rest. Yet many camp administrators favored a crackdown on hostile inmates and "troublemakers," and the WRA's political position in the wake of the congressional attacks was weak.

In March 1943 the WRA director wrote Secretary of War Stimson to warn him that the continued existence of the camps was having a negative effect on inmate loyalty and morale. Noting that large-scale resettlement of "loyal Japanese" was now possible, he pressed Stimson to lift West Coast exclusion—it was obvious that resettlement outside the West Coast would lag as long as Japanese American loyalty remained tainted by such exclusion. Myer's demands placed the secretary of war in a dilemma. By agreeing to the Joint Board hearings, the War Department had effectively conceded that the loyalty of Japanese Americans could be determined. Japanese Americans judged loyal could not logically then be barred from returning to the West Coast, especially as American victories in the Pacific made any possibility of Japanese invasion increasingly remote. Yet Stimson and McCloy were well aware that General DeWitt and California politicians were dead set against permitting the return of Japanese Americans, and that return might weaken the constitutional defense of the original removal. Hoping to buy time, the War Department thus parried Myer's thrust. Insisting that the trauma and demoralization that Japanese Americans faced in camp were fomented by "troublemakers," Stimson retaliated by demanding that the WRA undertake a segregation policy before he would consider opening up the West Coast. Myer replied with exasperation that if such a process were as easy as Stimson described, then the army could have carried out such segregation itself in the assembly centers. Nevertheless, Myer knew that army cooperation was necessary for successful resettlement. Thus, the WRA director reluctantly agreed to segregation of "disloyal" inmates. Ironically, even after segregation, the vast majority of the "loyal" Japanese Americans remained confined in the other camps, unwilling or unable to resettle outside of the West Coast.

The WRA designated Tule Lake as the "segregation center," since it had had the highest number of "no-no boys," and transformed it into a high-security center. Beginning in mid-1943 WRA officials supervised the transfer of some eighteen thousand "no-nos" (as well as all but a handful of renunciants) to Tule Lake, and an exchange of "loyal" inmates from Tule Lake who were assigned to be scattered around the other camps. However, many of these "old Tuleans" were reluctant to pull up stakes and start up again in a new camp. They refused to leave, with the result that they were mixed in with the "disloyals" in overcrowded quarters. Tule Lake after segregation was overcrowded and grim. Conditions resembled those of a prison camp, with constant surveillance by guards and reported beatings of inmates. In late October 1943, aroused by the death of a laborer in a traffic accident, a group of farmworkers organized a work stoppage, hoping to draw official attention to the dangerous working conditions and insufficient food given the inmates. Camp Director Raymond Best agreed to receive an inmate delegation for negotiations. On November 1 Dillon Myer visited Tule Lake and spoke before an angry crowd, promising inquiries and better conditions. The crowd dispersed peacefully. However, disgruntled WRA employees, angered by the unrest, spread lurid tales of Myer's being "kidnapped" by inmates. Three days later, a group of inmates spotted a convoy of trucks leaving the camp. Fearing that the trucks were carrying away food grown at Tule Lake to other camps, the enraged inmates tried to block the trucks from moving. They ran into a group of WRA security police, and a brawl ensued. One guard was beaten by inmates, while several inmates were roughed up by police. Although the conflict quickly abated, Director Best panicked and called in army troops from the camp perimeter. The following day, tanks and armed guards took over the camp, and the army declared martial law. The camp remained under military rule for two months. A total of 350 inmates, some as young as fifteen, were summarily locked in a "stockade," a confined jail space permitting only visual contact with the outside (even that was later taken away). They remained confined without charge for months. A group of 199 inmates launched a one-week hunger strike to pressure the administration to release them from imprisonment, but were unsuccessful. In April 1944, the majority of inmates were released back to the camp, but one set of inmates remained in the stockade until August. Only when ACLU lawyer Ernest Besig threatened to bring habeas corpus suits and embarrassing publicity did the WRA agree to their release. [119]

Although the inmates involved in the Tule Lake incident had apparently little in the way of underlying ideological goals beyond feeding themselves and protesting unsafe conditions, their actions triggered enormous changes. First, the incident was quickly seized on and blown up by the anti–Japanese American press on the West Coast, whose editors wished to forestall as much as possible the return of Japanese Americans to their homes. Although in theory Tule Lake was supposed to house the "disloyal" Japanese precisely so that the loyal could be released, editorials in the Hearst Press and the *Los Angeles Times* charged that the riot was proof that no Japanese American could be trusted or—more importantly in their eyes—permitted to return to the West Coast. Writer Carey

McWilliams, decrying the manipulation of the news in the press campaign, later remarked acidly that the only riot took place, not in camp, but in California newspapers.[120]

The West Coast press accounts pushed the White House into damage control mode and led to a reshaping of government policy. Although they rejected harsh punitive action against the Tule Lake inmates, since it could rebound against Americans held by Japan, President Roosevelt and Attorney General Biddle agreed that a bill to permit "disloyals" to renounce their citizenship would make control of recalcitrant Nisei inmates easier on constitutional grounds and would make it possible for the government to expel them to Japan after the war. The new act, the first-ever denationalization law of its kind, was swiftly passed by Congress and signed into law in July 1944. While designed to give political cover to resettlement by "loyal" inmates, the law would eventually create lasting misery.[121]

The passage of the law in turn lent additional force to the arguments of the "resegregants," a faction of hard-liners, predominantly Issei and Kibei, who had reacted, first to their confinement in the camps, and then to the harsh conditions at Tule Lake, by pushing a pro-Japan agenda. Although Dillon Myer blamed the rise of the "resegregant" movement on a group of Hawaiian Nisei who had been removed from the islands as security risks, the truth was more complex.[122] In fact, one major organizer of the resegregants, Mr. Akashi, was a West Coast Issei who had been a staunch patriot and defender of the American system in prewar years. Embittered by his unfair treatment, he helped found two pro-Japanese organizations, the Sokoku Kenkyu Seinen Dan (Young Men's Association for the Study of the Motherland) and the Sokuji Kikoku Hoshi Dan (Society for Immediate Return to Serve the Motherland) once confined at Tule Lake.[123]

Amid the waves of wartime anti-Japanese prejudice, it was plausible to believe, as many did, that the Issei and Nisei had no future in America, and that they should therefore concentrate on being Japanese. Also, many resegregants were convinced by pro-Japanese propaganda of Tokyo's inevitable victory in the war and hoped to be rewarded for their patriotism afterward. Thus, within the camp, the resegregants organized Japanese military exercises, taught martial songs, displayed rising sun flags, and instituted Japanese-style schools with daily bowing to the emperor. Through the months that followed the passage of the denationalization law, pro-Japanese thugs coerced other Nisei in the camp to renounce their American citizenship and organized beatings and harassment of those who resisted as traitors.

ANGLER CAMP

The "troublemakers" among Japanese Canadians were interned by the government in Angler, Ontario (some were held first at Petawawa). The origins of these 750-odd Issei and Nisei men, and the cause of their being sent to Ontario, varied considerably. Some were Issei who had been taken into custody as potential dangerous in the wake of Pearl Harbor. Others were members of the Nisei Mass Evacuation Group who had resisted going to road work camps or requested internment during the Hastings Park period. Others had been arrested for being recalcitrant. For example, two men working at a road labor camp in Alberta who refused to work after their crew members were injured by falling rocks were taken into custody and sent to the POW camp.[124] Takeo Nakano, an Issei from Woodfibre, had a particularly tragic tale. After being released from a road camp, he had gone to rejoin his family. When he reached the "ghost towns," however, he was assigned to live in the Slocan camp, where authorities claimed they had need of workers. Nakano protested, saying that he had been promised he could join his family in Greenwood. When he was sent to Slocan nevertheless, he and fourteen colleagues refused to work unless they were reunited with their families. All were summarily taken way, sent to jail in Vancouver, and removed from there to Angler.[125]

If these men's origins were diverse, they were given largely identical treatment. The camp was surrounded by armed guards and barbed wire fences. In a powerful demonstration of official terror, as part of the clothing they were issued, each inmate received a uniform with a large red circle on the back, resembling the rising Sun on the Japanese flag. While this was supposedly to identify them more easily in case of escape, the prisoners were conscious of the resemblance of the marker to a bull's-eye, which seemed to invite prison guards to shoot them in the back. Indeed, in July 1942 guards actually shot bullets into the huts at Petawawa, forcing inmates to seek cover. Confined to a small area and separated from their families, the inmates were housed in unpartitioned bunks in four double-winged huts constructed of tarpaper-covered wood, where they struggled against the lack of privacy and the frigid winter weather. Their sending of mail was limited to four postcards plus small letter sheets per month, and the contents were censored. There was little available to them in the way of libraries or school facilities, although the Red Cross donated some books, cigarettes, and recreational equipment, and a recreation hall was eventually opened to provide movies, music practice, and judo instruction. In theory, these internees (uniquely among confined Japanese Canadians) were not required to be self-supporting, but were guaranteed minimum support by the Geneva Convention. They also received a monthly allotment of fifty dollars through the Spanish consul (according to one source, from his own pocket), plus food packages and aid from inmates in the "ghost towns."[126] However, because of supply problems, as well as the sometimes vengeful attitude of government authorities, food and cigarette rations remained meager, even with the addition of supplies of tea, miso, and shoyu sent from Japan via the International Red Cross. In summer 1942 a canteen opened to permit prisoners to use their own funds, plus allotments, to buy tobacco, chocolate, stationery, and other goods.[127]

In November 1943 the Angler camp administration decreed that inmates would be required to chop wood in the surrounding area to provide their own fuel for heating. When the internees protested that they were civilians not required to work and did not have any training or expertise in chopping wood, their privileges were temporarily suspended and their food rations were further reduced.[128] Uncertainties as to the legal status of Nisei and disputes over their rights made for difficulties and provoked further conflict. The Canadian government decreed that Nisei prisoners were not covered under the Geneva Convention. Thus, when Issei prisoners met with the Spanish consul, as representative of the protecting power, Nisei prisoners were barred from joining them.

As at Tule Lake, pro-Japanese forces struggled for supremacy inside the camps with loyalists. The Issei who had requested repatriation were joined by a Canadian Citizenship Renouncement Group, composed predominantly of Kibei (Kika). They argued that since the Nisei were dual citizens who had been stripped of their Canadian citizenship rights, they would be better off disclaiming that citizenship entirely and concentrating on being real Japanese instead of pseudo-Canadians. In response, a number of Nisei wrote to the Canadian government to renounce their citizenship. However, Canadian officials decreed that as native-born British subjects, they could not legally do this. The Issei militants, like their counterparts south of the border, were inspired by Japanese propaganda to claim that if the Nisei remained in confinement, they would receive $25,000 compensation for their suffering once Japan won the war, and there would be a place for them in the victorious postwar Japanese empire.[129] Both groups dissuaded other prisoners from signing up for "work leave" to get out of camp. Members of the former Nisei Mass Evacuation

Group supported remaining in Canada, but even they were split over whether to accept immediate employment outside camp and send for families, or to remain inside to protest the undemocratic treatment they had received. In the end, some 430 of the original 750 internees remained in Angler through the end of the war.

THE JUSTICE DEPARTMENT CAMPS

The ethnic Japanese aliens held in custody by the U.S. government during the war were housed in a network of camps managed in cooperation with the War Department by the Justice Department's Enemy Alien Control Division, in part using facilities maintained by the Immigration and Naturalization Service. Since the internees were frequently shuttled from place to place with no evident pattern, it is difficult to generalize about their experience. As mentioned, mainland Issei detained after Pearl Harbor were held in stations run by the INS throughout the nation. Ironically, the immigration station at Ellis Island, New York, past symbol of welcome to immigrants, became a holding center for aliens taken into custody on the East Coast. Groups of Issei arrested on the West Coast during early 1942 were sent to a camp at Santa Fe, New Mexico. Others were sent to a camp at Kenedy, Texas. Meanwhile, the Justice Department held a handful of Issei women in a camp at Seagoville, Texas. A group of thirty-two Issei and Nisei from the town of Clovis, New Mexico, were arrested after Pearl Harbor and held—the citizens quite illegally—at Old Raton ranch, an abandoned Civilian Conservation Corps camp in New Mexico.[130] By April 1942 about a thousand Issei, as well as German and Italian nationals, had been detained by the army at Fort Missoula, Montana. Another thousand were held at Fort Abraham Lincoln, near Bismarck, North Dakota.

It was during their initial confinement that these arrested enemy aliens (Japanese as well as German and Italian) were granted hearings by hearing boards assembled for the purpose. During these hearings, they were forbidden to have attorneys or to testify other than by answering questions, but they were permitted to present evidence to prove their loyalty—including witnesses, if available. If, as in most cases, the hearing boards determined that the aliens did not pose a threat, they were released—however, unlike German and Italian aliens, who were liberated entirely from custody, released Japanese aliens were sent to join their families in the WRA camps. Those aliens whom the boards deemed dangerous were scheduled for long-term internment. In some cases, they remained at their initial detention centers, while others were moved. (Santa Fe was emptied of its Japanese alien population, only to be mobilized subsequently to house renunciants from Tule Lake and their families who were being deported to Japan.) Army-run camps at Fort Livingston, Louisiana, and Lordsburg, New Mexico, were created to house this overflow. The migration was marked by tragedy: on July 27, 1942, as a trainload of Issei arrived at Lordsburg and were marched into camp, two men too ill to walk were shot to death by a sentry under suspicious circumstances.

By April 1943, a total of 5,166 Japanese aliens in Hawaii, Alaska, and the U.S mainland (plus 477 U.S. citizens of Japanese ancestry) had been arrested, of whom some 2,980 were still being held or interned.[131] Lordsburg itself held up to 2,500 internees at one point, before they were again dispersed. As mentioned, conditions in the camps differed—Lordsburg was in a mountainous desert region, while Fort Livingston was in a swamplike area—but their facilities were similar and indeed bore a general resemblance to those at the Canadian POW camps at Petawawa and Angler. The army camps were made up of barracks surrounded by barbed wire and sentries. Each included gardens for growing food, recreational centers, and sports activities—army engineers built an athletic field for the inmates at Lordsburg. Mail was censored and visitors forbidden, apart from the official visits of the Spanish consul. However, most of the cooking and other internal tasks in the American camps were assigned to the prisoners themselves. As in the case of the Japanese Canadians at Angler, there was some uncertainty over the status of the internees under the Geneva Convention, and disputes broke out when prisoners at Camp Livingston resisted administration orders to chop wood for fuel without pay. Unlike in Ontario, however, the U.S. internees accepted a compromise under which they agreed to chop wood, but for their exclusive use.[132] In 1943 the INS took over an old CCC camp on the Lochsa River in Idaho, which had been run as part of the federal prison at Leavenworth, Kansas, and renamed it the Kooskia Internment Camp. The INS recruited Japanese aliens from the larger internment camps to do paid road labor extending the Lewis and Clark Highway.[133]

Beginning in early 1943, the army and the Justice Department devised a new policy, by which Issei men in custody could be joined by their families from the WRA camps. The installation at Crystal City, Texas, was designated as the family internment center. Beginning in March 1943, families who accepted "voluntary internment" alongside their fathers were brought into the camp and thrown together with German alien internees and their German American families, plus the shiploads of ethnic Japanese and German Latin Americans who had already been placed there. Because of the presence of family groups, Crystal City's structure was unique among the internment camps. Families were housed in various kinds of individual residences—Japanese were generally placed in wooden cabins dubbed "victory huts"—with iceboxes and running water. Food rations were provided, including a daily milk ration delivered for children, plus medical care.[134] A central commissary was set up, as were community washrooms and showers.[135] Each adult was given a set of chores to perform, such as gardening or delivering ice, and could volunteer for additional work as well at a rate of eighty cents per day.

Daily life in Crystal City was much like that in the WRA centers. Internees struggled against boredom, psychological trauma, and internal discord. However, unlike in most other camps, Japanese Americans were not held in isolation but had contact with other groups who were also confined. Most distinctive was the network of schools set up to educate several hundred children. Because of the separate interests of internee groups, which reflected a diversity of attitudes toward the U.S. government and American culture as well as the internees' predicted postwar needs, diverse programs were established.[136] For example, almost all the ethnic German parents, disillusioned with the United States by their internment and subjected to pressure by pro-Nazi internees, sent their children to a German-style school. The Latin American Japanese children, who spoke little English and whose families could logically expect postwar deportation, were sent to a Japanese school, as were some Nisei from Hawaii who had attended prewar Japanese schools. The curriculum of the school, following Japanese models, featured not only academic subjects but also flower arranging and etiquette classes. Japanese educators emphasized honor and loyalty through martial arts, *sushin* (ethics) courses, and patriotic festivals such as the emperor's birthday. Mainland Nisei children, plus a few German children, attended an American-style public school run by white teachers from the local community. It inculcated democratic values and encouraged Nisei children to develop and express their citizenship. The school's mission and activities, notably its holding of a high school prom, led to angry protest from partisans of Japanese ancestral customs, and to divisions within the community.[137]

CONCLUSION

It is difficult to speak in general terms of the enormous and bewildering variety of camps established by the American and Canadian governments during the war to hold different classes and nationalities of ethnic Japanese, and of the treatment of the people in them. Many of the arrangements were improvised and haphazard. The legal regimes and authority under which they operated were also in many instances confused. The Issei, as foreign nationals, were able to claim the minimum standards and protections of the Geneva Convention. Ironically, the protections were applied more strictly to those confined in internment camps, who otherwise faced the most stringent restrictions on their liberties, than to those in the WRA camps or the Canadian ghost towns, who had not been deemed to represent an individual danger. More paradoxically still, because the arbitrary treatment of citizens was such a largely unprecedented—and constitutionally contradictory—phenomenon, the Nisei could claim no similar protections under the Geneva Convention or other act of international law.

The comparison between the experience of Japanese Canadians in the ghost towns and that of the Japanese Americans held by the WRA is nonetheless illuminating. In most respects, the Canadians faced far harsher conditions. They faced a more extreme climate, had less choice of jobs, and were more isolated from the outside world. Most importantly, Canada's government provided only a fraction of the funding that the Americans did—about one-third, according to one estimate on a per inmate basis—and Japanese Canadians were required to eke out an existence largely on their own funds. The publicly funded mess halls, clothing allowances, high schools, music and crafts programs, and consumer cooperatives operated by the American government had no counterpart in Canada. The structures put in place by the WRA to provide practical and financial assistance to resettlers, especially college students, and to advocate for them in their new homes were not copied by the Canadians, who developed a coercive resettlement program and refused to grant business licenses and residence permits. Furthermore, while Japanese Americans lost the lion's share of their property during removal and afterward, the outright confiscation of Japanese Canadian properties, and the dissipation of their assets in forced sales, were so glaringly unjust as to arouse anger and opposition from whites as well as Issei and Nisei.

Still, what is most telling is the overall identity of the camp experience, irrespective of material conditions. The same signs of apathy and family breakdown appeared among Issei and Nisei on both sides of the border, and similar doubts about resettlement were expressed. Some previously patriotic inmates denounced their governments and associated themselves with Japan, and factions of Nisei sought to renounce the citizenship that had failed to protect them. Inmate unrest was so pronounced in the WRA camps that it led the U.S. government to a unique and destructive official policy of segregation of "no-no boys," even as the Canadians interned groups of Nisei and "troublemakers" alongside aliens at Camp Angler. A similar sense of betrayal, matched by a practical wish to prepare as best as possible for postwar conditions, led many ethnic German and Japanese families at Crystal City to reject U.S. public school models for their children, and to educate them in the style of their past homelands. These patterns suggest that, while the official support given Japanese Americans may have helped them recover more rapidly, in both moral and financial terms, following evacuation, no official treatment, however humane, could erase the essential wound caused by their arbitrary confinement.

[5] MILITARY SERVICE AND LEGAL CHALLENGES

IN SPITE OF THE LIMITATIONS ON THEIR FREEDOM DURING World War II, Japanese Americans were active in pressing for fair treatment, and they were ultimately able to impact decisions about official policy on a national level. The two most visible areas in which the Nisei, with their non-Japanese allies, fought to restore their group's constitutional rights were military service and the courts. The enlistment of up to 33,000 Nisei soldiers from Hawaii and the mainland in the U.S. Armed Forces during the war years, especially those who volunteered for military service from camp, rebutted widespread public images of Japanese Americans as disloyal or suspect and furnished graphic and enduring evidence of the loyalty and good citizenship of the entire group.[1] The outstanding combat record of the all-Nisei, segregated 100th Battalion/442nd Regimental Combat Team and the Nisei interpreters in the Military Intelligence Service, compiled at the horrid cost of thousands of battlefield casualties, encouraged government officials to push the release of inmates from the camps. In contrast, the protracted refusal of the Canadian government to permit enlistment of Japanese Canadians badly damaged the group's standing, though it saved many of their lives. A different kind of heroism was demonstrated by the members of the Heart Mountain Fair Play Committee (FPC) and other draft resisters. These Nisei refused on principle to fight until the government that had confined their families restored their civil rights, and they bravely stood up in defense of their constitutional rights at the price of prison and widespread obloquy.

The resisters movement, in turn, overlapped with a larger series of legal challenges to government control of civilians, both Japanese Americans confined under Executive Order 9066 and those subject to martial law in Hawaii. The cases of the Nisei plaintiffs who resisted curfews and evacuation in early 1942 made their way slowly through the federal courts in the months and years that followed. Meanwhile, the presence of Japanese Americans in the territory of Hawaii was a principal element in the institution of military rule. Even in legal cases brought by non-Japanese against the imposition of military tribunals, the Nisei might be considered the "silent defendants" who remained a leading object of controversy.

NISEI SOLDIERS

There were few mainland Nisei in the tiny American army of the 1930s—various Chinese American and Japanese American volunteers were reportedly refused enlistment by prejudiced military recruiters.[2] When in September 1940 President Roosevelt signed the Selective Training and Service Act, many Japanese Americans feared that as a result of the tensions in the Pacific they would be excluded from military service. However, they were included on an equal basis, and in the year that followed some three thousand Nisei on the West Coast and in Hawaii were inducted into the army—unlike their African American counterparts, these Nisei were mixed into white units. Their unblemished service record and the warm community approval for their efforts led many white Americans (notably Eleanor Roosevelt, who had not been previously engaged with Japanese Americans) to affirm their faith in the group's loyalty. Forty-five Nisei (including Kibei) enrolled as students and instructors in the Fourth Army Intelligence School (later known as the Military Intelligence Service [MIS] Language School), which opened in November 1941 at the Presidio in San Francisco.[3]

Following the Japanese attack on Pearl Harbor, Japanese Americans became suspect in the eyes of the American military. West Coast Nisei who rushed to volunteer for the U.S. Army following the attack were refused. In February 1942 the War Department reclassified the status of all draft-age Nisei as "4-C" (enemy alien) and formally barred their enlistment. The government similarly dismissed a proposal by JACL leader Mike Masaoka (presented in a last, desperate bid to forestall mass evacuation) for the creation of a "suicide squad" of Japanese American soldiers who would demonstrate the group's loyalty by undertaking perilous missions.[4] As noted, the Nisei ROTC troops in Hawaii who had been formed into the Territorial Guard were summarily discharged, although they succeeded in organizing the Varsity Victory Volunteers.[5] The Hawaiian Nisei in the 298th and 299th Battalions were confined to base and ultimately transferred to Camp McCoy, Wisconsin—more to keep them from away from the Pacific theater than to assure their training.

Individual Nisei who were already serving in Army units were either discharged or retained after Pearl Harbor, generally according to the wishes of their commanding officers. Some of the few Nisei GIs who remained, such as Sergeant Ben Kuroki of the Army Air Corps and Sergeant Frank "Foo" Fujita, a POW in Asia, later distinguished themselves for heroism.[6] Meanwhile, those working as instructors or translators at the MIS language school (which was kicked out of the Presidio in the spring of 1942 and ultimately relocated to Camp Savage, Minnesota) began to compile a fine record. An initial group of Nisei translators, including the brothers Tadao and Takashi Kubo, served at the battle of Guadalcanal in October–November 1942.[7] There they uncovered a document that accurately listed all imperial navy ships and air bases with call signs and code names. Soon after, the MIS staffers translated a set of Japanese battle plans for the Philippines.[8]

In the summer of 1942, as West Coast Japanese Americans were being removed and transported, first into assembly centers and then into the WRA camps, the War Department undertook a study of whether Japanese Americans should be permitted to enlist, in view of the urgent need for military manpower. Asked for his views on the subject, General DeWitt responded in July with a memo that demonstrated his continuing and excessive aversion to all Japanese Americans. DeWitt stated in his response that Japanese Americans were not trustworthy. If the army accepted Nisei soldiers at all, it should ban all Kibei and restrict the rest to service in labor battalions, to be sent to exclusively the European front. If, however, the army decided not to accept any Nisei soldiers (which DeWitt strongly implied was his preference), all Nisei already in the military should be discharged and sent to the camps, and then the entire ethnic Japanese population should be expelled from the country after war's end.[9] In large part as a result of DeWitt's memo, in September 1942 the army's General Staff, led by Deputy Army Chief of Staff General McNarny, issued a formal recommendation against the enlistment of any Nisei in the armed forces, although Col. Kai Rasmussen was authorized to tour the WRA camps in order to recruit some 150 new civilian language school teachers and specialists for the MIS Language School.[10]

At this juncture, an unusual coalition came together in support of Japanese American soldiers. On October 2, 1942, Elmer Davis, director of the Office of War Information, and his associate, former WRA director Milton Eisenhower, wrote President Roosevelt proposing that loyal Americans of Japanese ancestry who had been suitably screened be permitted to enlist in the army and navy, and that the president make a public announcement in support of Japanese American loyalty. Such moves, Davis and Eisenhower stated, would counter the declining morale of Japanese Americans in the camps and refute enemy accusations that the United States was fighting a racial war against all Asians.[11] WRA Director Dillon Myer and JACL Secretary Mike Masaoka strongly seconded the call for recruitment of Nisei soldiers. In October 1942 the JACL sent a petition to the president calling for the draft to be reinstated for citizens of Japanese ancestry, while Myer lobbied McCloy and FDR's close advisor Harry Hopkins to open military service.[12]

Roosevelt expressed cautious interest in forming noncombat battalions of Nisei troops, and he asked for the opinion of his chief advisors. Navy Secretary Knox, citing widespread opposition to Japanese Americans among navy officials, immediately recommended against the idea. Knox's views prevailed, and Japanese Americans remained barred from naval service throughout World War II. However, the Army General Staff's recommendation against Nisei enlistment (of which the president may not have been aware) was overridden by the War Department's chiefs. On October 15, 1942, Assistant Secretary of War McCloy wrote to Secretary of War Stimson to recommend that Nisei be allowed to serve. McCloy insisted that the vast majority of the Nisei were innocent and had been unfairly classed with the disloyal few. Permitting them to enlist would redeem their loyalty.[13] Bolstered by McCloy, Secretary Stimson informed the president that the War Department favored Nisei enlistment. It would improve the U.S. image to have soldiers of Asian ancestry fighting among its troops, he stated, while the Nisei soldiers would make good fighters. Stimson also maintained that the soldiers' presence would serve a powerful psychological function by demonstrating Americans' trust in the loyalty of Japanese Americans. This would grant all those in the camps a special measure of self-respect, aiding their eventual postwar assimilation. For this reason, Stimson argued that organization of a labor battalion, as DeWitt proposed, would be a "faint-hearted compromise" that would defeat the purpose of opening up the military to Japanese Americans.[14]

McCloy quickly set about securing endorsements from army commanders for the plan. He first obtained the concurrence of General George Marshall, the army's chief of staff.[15] In December 1942 McCloy traveled to Hawaii. There he secured Hawaiian Commander General Delos

Emmons's endorsement of Nisei recruitment. McCloy's and Emmons's determination to give the Nisei the chance to prove themselves through armed combat was reinforced by the efforts of the Varsity Victory Volunteers. In the first days of 1943, the War Department submitted a plan calling for the recruitment of a new unit, the 442nd Regimental Combat Team, to be formed by 3,000 volunteers from the camps and 1,500 from Hawaii.[16]

FDR did not take any active steps to promote the idea of Nisei soldiers during the fall of 1942. However, Roosevelt was susceptible to Stimson's arguments, particularly regarding the public relations boost Nisei soldiers would give the allied war effort—the president told his secretary of war that he was ready to create special "nationality" units when there was a propaganda advantage to be gained from them—and in January 1943 he approved the plan put together by the War Department.[17] Roosevelt and his advisors decided to form a separate all-Nisei unit, on the model of the segregated units the military maintained for African Americans, which would be led by white officers. Although the War Department insisted that the reason for the segregation was solely to maximize the unit's visibility (and hence value in proving Nisei loyalty), army commanders also wished to avoid sparking racial tensions through formation of mixed units.[18] To assure the loyalty of army volunteers, the Army Provost Marshal General's Office set up a joint army–navy hearing board. (It was this board that the WRA then commissioned to examine the loyalty of all confined Japanese Americans, as part of the "leave clearance" procedure.) The proposed action, especially the establishment of the joint board, aroused spirited protest from General DeWitt, who argued (quite logically) that once the War Department conceded that the loyalty of Japanese Americans could be determined, it would undercut the army's original rationale for evacuation and exclusion of all Japanese Americans from the West Coast.[19]

On January 28, 1943, Stimson publicly announced the creation of the new unit, referring to Nisei loyalty as "a voice that must be heard." (Three days later, on February 1, President Roosevelt followed with his statement about Americanism being a matter of the "mind and heart" rather than of race.)[20] With the blessing of the WRA and strong support from the JACL—whose chief power-broker Mike Masaoka immediately volunteered for the 442nd and was sent to organize its public relations squad[21]—army recruiters toured the camps. In addition to their appeals to the patriotism of the inmates, army officials publicly threatened to institute a draft to raise troops if not enough Nisei volunteered.[22] Still, many Nisei men were reluctant to leave their families amid the difficult conditions and uncertain future of camp life. In addition, the army and the WRA underestimated the depths of anger and resistance that the government's actions had inspired among inmates. In private conversation and public meetings, inmates denounced the segregated combat unit as a further example of injustice and scorned those who joined. In some cases, the families of volunteers were ostracized by camp neighbors.[23] Religious bigotry may also have played a role in heightening suspicions of the new unit. Assistant Secretary McCloy approved only Christian chaplains for the 442nd and initially rejected the JACL's request for Buddhist chaplains, on the grounds that the widespread ignorance and loathing of Buddhism in America might compromise the unit's public image.[24] For whatever reason, only about 1,700 Nisei men from the camps made the difficult decision to enlist in the initial months, less than one-half of Dillon Myer's projected total. In contrast, some 10,000 Nisei from Hawaii, including the members of the Varsity Victory Volunteers (who received priority status for slots), rushed to volunteer, and most were forced to wait. The pool from Hawaii was so numerous—2,686 were accepted in the initial cull—that there was sufficient manpower for the new unit.

Once inducted, the Nisei volunteers of the 442nd Regimental Combat Team (who soon dubbed themselves the "Go For Broke" Battalion) were sent for extensive training at Camp Shelby, Mississippi, beginning in March 1943. Unaccustomed to a segregated society, the Nisei soldiers remained in some confusion about where they fit in, even after their commanders instructed them to use the "white" facilities. Earl Finch, a rancher in nearby Hattiesburg, soon befriended the Nisei soldiers, sponsoring sports teams and social outings, and won himself national attention as a champion of fair play.[25] The units slowly coalesced, though at first there was great friction between the Hawaiian recruits and the mainlanders, whom the Hawaiians dubbed "kotonks":

> Both sides, especially the Hawaiian side, looked upon the others with some, I would say, distrust. For one thing it was easy to note that the mainland Japanese spoke a better brand of English. We, for the most part, spoke pidgin. . . . [F]ights became commonplace. It got so bad at one stage during the early days of our training, senior officers of the regiment seriously discussed the possibility of disbanding the regiment, that if we could not work together, how can we ever consider going into combat together?[26]

Already at Shelby were the more experienced Hawaiian Nisei troops of the 100th Battalion (who had previously trained in Wisconsin and Louisiana). In the late summer of 1943, however, they were called for overseas duty. After a short stretch in North Africa, the 100th was sent into combat in Salerno, Italy, that September. In fighting over the next six months, the 1,432 soldiers in the unit distinguished themselves for bravery under fire and suffered heavy casualties, reducing their numbers to 521 men. For their bravery, they received 900 Purple Hearts (and hence the nickname "Purple Heart Battalion").[27]

In January 1944 the army announced that the military draft would be officially reopened to Nisei. Swallowing whatever misgivings they may have had, over 10,000 draft-age Nisei men from the camps entered the army and courageously went off to fight in the 442nd Regimental Combat Team and other units.[28] Beginning in February 1944, groups of soldiers from the original volunteer contingents of the 442nd, following their training at Camp Shelby, were shipped to Italy to replace casualties from the 100th Battalion. The rest of the 442nd reached Italy in June 1944 and were deployed on the road to Rome, where they joined and were officially merged with the remaining troops of the 100th. In July 1944, after the Nisei troops fought in Belvedere and Livorno, Italian Theater commander General Mark Clark awarded the 100th a Presidential Unit Citation and the other units a commendation. In September 1944 the troops of the 442nd succeeded in crossing the Arno. The heavy fighting cost them 1,272 casualties, almost one-fourth of the unit's forces.[29] Following the Tuscan campaign, the 442nd was sent to the Vosges Mountains in France. In three days of heavy fighting, the Nisei took the town of Bruyères. Soon after, during the Battle of the Bulge in December 1944, the 442nd was ordered to rescue a trapped Texas battalion, the "Lost Battalion." Over a period of two weeks, the soldiers broke through to relieve the battalion, then took the ridge the Lost Battalion had originally been sent to secure. The total casualty list for this fighting was some 2,000, including 140 killed, a higher figure than the total of those soldiers whom the Nisei managed to save. By this time, the 442nd had lost half its strength, and its remaining troops were pulled off the line to rest while its ranks were refilled with newly trained Japanese American conscripts. In March 1945 the 442nd, removed to Italy, joined an offensive in the Appenines. Shortly after, the 522nd Field Artillery Battalion, a unit of the 442nd that was later attached to the 7th Army, participated in the liberation of the Munich area (where it was partly responsible for liberating the Dachau extermination camp).[30]

Once military service was opened to Nisei, further volunteers were sent to the MIS Language School as instructors or students in Japanese translation. Ironically, it was the Kibei, whom military and intelligence authorities had considered the most suspect and recalcitrant group among the camp population, who formed the backbone of the language specialists. Unlike most U.S.-educated Nisei, the Kibei were fluent in Japanese, and this proficiency, augmented by their recent residence in Japan and familiarity with modern slang, made them the most effective Japanese-language interrogators and interpreters. The MIS staffers were deployed throughout the Pacific theater. There they studied captured enemy plans and documents and interrogated Japanese prisoners. One group of Nisei served with the marine corps unit "Merrill's Marauders" when it landed behind enemy lines in Burma. According to the estimate of General Willoughby, director of intelligence for General Douglas MacArthur, the work of the Nisei MIS shortened the Pacific War by two years and saved a million lives.[31] Japanese Americans also participated in noncombat military positions. Nisei women joined the Women's Army Corps or became army nurses. A number of Nisei and also Issei (who remained barred from the army until the last months of the war) joined the Office of Strategic Services as overseas intelligence and propaganda officers in China and India.[32]

The work of the Nisei MIS and OSS staffers was largely in top secret and classified assignments and thus remained unknown for decades after the war. Conversely, the exploits, first of the 100th Battalion and later of the 442nd, were accompanied by strong public relations campaigns by the WRA, the Office of War Information, and the War Department on behalf of the patriotism of Japanese Americans. The OWI (which had previously filmed a documentary, *Japanese Relocation*, that presented an idealized image of camp life) put together a special documentary film, *Nisei Soldiers*. Numerous non-Japanese soldiers wrote letters to newspapers and political representatives defending the loyalty and the civil rights of Japanese Americans. Secretary of War Stimson publicly referred to the bravery of Nisei soldiers in defending release of inmates from the camps and referred to an attack on a Nisei soldier as "an inexcusable and dastardly outrage."[33] President Roosevelt himself (who had spoken slightingly of "Japs" as inherently untrustworthy in speeches on the Pacific Coast during the summer of 1944)[34] made a nationally broadcast radio address on Columbus Day in 1944 in which he praised the "combat teams composed of Americans of Japanese ancestry who come from Hawaii" who were giving the lie to Nazi theories of racial superiority.[35] The following month, Roosevelt stated during a press conference that the government's interest in hastening release of Japanese Americans from the camps was "actuated" in part by the achievements of the "Japanese" battalion in Italy, which he called "one of the outstanding combat battalions we have."[36]

CONSCRIPTION AND DRAFT RESISTANCE

Despite the proud achievements of the Nisei soldiers, the reopening of conscription left lasting scars on the Japanese community. Although in his February 1943 public statement President Roosevelt had described the formation of a volunteer unit as a "natural and logical step" toward restoring normal selective service requirements, and the army continued to permit Nisei volunteers to enlist in the 442nd, the War Department did not reinstate conscription for Japanese Americans during 1943. Department chiefs believed that an all-volunteer unit would have the strongest impact on public opinion. They also realized that maintaining Nisei conscripts in a racially segregated force, as the army staff insisted be done, would further insult Japanese Americans, even those who had accepted a separate volunteer unit for the sake of visibility. Similarly, many Japanese Americans agreed with the argument of OWI Director Elmer Davis that it would not be fair to draft people whom the government had arbitrarily confined.[37] However, soon Assistant Secretary McCloy, facing acute manpower shortages and fortified by reports of the success of the 100th Battalion, pushed for drafting of Nisei men. WRA and JACL leaders, who considered military service the key to restoring full citizenship to Japanese Americans, lobbied in support of the move. By the end of 1943, the army officially resolved to reopen selective service to Japanese Americans, both inside and outside camp.[38]

Secretary Stimson announced the new policy on January 20, 1944. It caused an immediate storm of protest within the camps. Public speakers and petitions decried the injustice of drafting Nisei to fight for a government that deprived their families of their civil rights. In the weeks that followed, approximately three hundred Nisei from the various camps refused induction into the army, stating that they would agree to fight once their full rights were restored, but that they refused to serve while their families remained imprisoned. Families divided over whether their sons and brothers should resist induction. A group of Issei women, the Mothers' Committee of Topaz, mobilized (with help from some Issei men) to draft a petition and statement, which they sent, along with an eloquent letter, to Chief Justice Harlan Stone. The letter deplored the injustice perpetrated on their sons by the draft and called for the restoration of full civil rights to the Nisei.[39] Meanwhile, a Mothers' Society organized at Minidoka collected over a hundred signatures for a petition that was then sent to Eleanor Roosevelt. Tactfully asking the First Lady's guidance, the petitioners proposed that drafting of Nisei be suspended until they could "regain their confidence." The petitioners asserted that Nisei had volunteered in large numbers before the war but had been deeply wounded by the stripping of their citizenship rights. "When they, the Nisei, consider the purpose of this war and then think about the treatment they are receiving at present, they discover the existence of a great paradox. They are dejected, and have lost their firm, unshakable faith and spirit. To think of sending them in this condition to the front, we, as mothers, considering the past and the future, feel an extreme and unbearable anguish."[40] Mrs. Roosevelt politely but firmly declined to intervene, arguing that the draft might be "the one thing that will make this nation see" the cause of fair treatment.[41]

The center of draft resistance was the Fair Play Committee at Heart Mountain. The FPC originated with Kiyoshi Okamoto, a Hawaiian-born Nisei in his mid-fifties (and, ironically, past vice-chair of a Nisei Democratic Club) who had been embittered by removal.[42] During 1943 Okamoto had distinguished himself among inmates by offering challenges to official policy and by his forthright opposition to Nisei enlisting in the army.[43] Inspired by Okamoto's arguments and his example, a circle of young Nisei inmates led by Sam Horino and Frank Emi organized the FPC as a forum for discussion of camp conditions and the injustice done to Japanese Americans by the government. The reopening of selective service to Japanese Americans led these Nisei to draw the line, and once the news of conscription reached Heart Mountain, the FPC issued a public manifesto. They were careful to make clear that they were not afraid to fight for their country:

> We, the members of the FPC are not afraid to go to war—we are not afraid to risk our lives for our country. We would gladly sacrifice our lives to protect and uphold the principles and ideals of our country as set forth in the Constitution and the Bill of Rights, for on its in-

violability depends the freedom, liberty, justice and protection of all people including Japanese-Americans and all other minority groups. But have we been given such freedom, such liberty, such justice, such protection? NO!![44]

FPC activists argued that until Japanese Americans had their constitutional rights restored and discrimination within selective service was ended, they should refuse to register or take physicals for the draft, and denounced those who did as collaborators.[45]

Heart Mountain Director Guy Robertson responded to the FPC campaign by banning its meetings, removing FPC leaders Kiyoshi Okamoto and Sam Horino to Tule Lake, and threatening all draft resisters with arrest and prosecution. The FPC attempted to publicize its case outside the camp by providing bulletins to Japanese American periodicals, However, while the camp newspaper *Heart Mountain Sentinel* ran letters by Frank Emi, the only newspaperman to publish the FPC's manifestos was editor James Omura of *Rockii Shimpo*.[46] Ironically, it was a non-Japanese outside newspaper, the Cheyenne *Eagle*, that published the strongest statement in support of the resisters.[47]

Ultimately sixty-three draft resisters from Heart Mountain were arrested and brought to trial. In addition, seven leaders of the Heart Mountain FPC were indicted on charges of conspiracy to oppose conscription, as was *Rockii Shimpo* editor James Omura.[48] Meanwhile, the government set up group trials for draft resistance at two other camps, Minidoka and Tule Lake, although the individuals at those camps had not worked together. These Nisei persisted in the face of open hostility from the JACL, which publicly supported their prosecution. At the behest of the JACL, Minoru Yasui, who had previously challenged mass removal before the Supreme Court, traveled to camp to talk them out of pursuing their case.[49] Similarly, American Civil Liberties Union leader Roger Baldwin stated publicly his refusal to support the draft resistance movement. Baldwin admitted that the resisters had a strong moral case but countered that they had absolutely no defense in legal terms.[50]

The defendants from Heart Mountain were the first to be brought to trial, on May 8. Judge T. Blake Kennedy, who had a history of racist opinions, waved aside all the resisters' arguments on the unconstitutionality of their confinement. Convicted six weeks later, they were each sentenced to three years in federal prison for draft evasion. In addition, in November 1944 a jury in Cheyenne convicted the leaders of the Heart Mountain FPC of conspiracy to oppose conscription, though James Omura was acquitted of all charges. (The conspiracy convictions were later set aside on appeal).[51] The Minidoka draft resisters were brought to trial in September, in a series of thirty-three hurried proceedings over eleven days, before judge (and former governor) Chase Clark, who openly avowed his anti-Japanese bias. Clark sentenced these defendants (plus five Nisei who pleaded guilty) to prison terms of eighteen months to three years for draft evasion.[52]

Only the resisters from Tule Lake escaped felony conviction.[53] Judge Louis Goodman, brought from San Francisco to Eureka, California, for the trials, was a newcomer to the bench who had no close connections in the community and no record of anti-Japanese feeling. After hearing the evidence, he found the defendants not guilty on due process grounds; it would, he said, be "shocking to the conscience that an American citizens who had been confined on the ground of disloyalty, and then, while so under duress and restraint, be compelled to serve in the Armed Forces, or be prosecuted for not yielding to such compulsion."[54]

After their trials, the convicted Heart Mountain and Minidoka draft resisters, as well as individuals from other camps who were brought to trial, were sent to prison. The acquitted Tule Lake resisters were restored to "freedom" at the camp. Once the war ended and the immediate passions associated with it dimmed, the case of the Nisei draft resisters appeared to many groups (although not the JACL) as an injustice, and they supported clemency. On Christmas Day, 1947, President Harry Truman signed a full pardon for all resisters. By that time all the Nisei but one had served his prison sentence, but at least the pardon restored their civil rights and indirectly acknowledged the justice of their cause. Despite the pardon, the brave constitutional stand of the draft resisters remained long hidden within Japanese American history, and those who had agreed to go to jail for their belief in democracy were shunned by others in the Nisei community. It would not be until 2002 that the JACL offered its own public apology for its opposition to the draft resisters.

MILITARY SERVICE IN CANADA

The differences between the wartime Japanese American and Japanese Canadian experience with regard to military service were glaring, and can be said to have had significant consequences for the postwar development of the respective communities. From the outset of the war, Canadian government officials demonstrated widespread hostility to Nisei military service. After Canada declared war on Germany in September 1939, the National Japanese Canadian Citizens League sent a telegram to Ottawa pledging its members' support, and numerous individuals went off to enlist in the Canadian Army, only to have their services rejected. In the two years that followed, twenty-five Japanese Canadian volunteers, most from the prairie provinces and the East and some of mixed ancestry, managed to join up—only three British Columbia Nisei were accepted, and one intrepid recruit, Jack Nakamoto, traveled all the way across Canada attempting fruitlessly to enlist until he was finally accepted in Quebec City.[55] However, the gates remained effectively closed, even though Japan and Canada were at peace and manpower was needed. As mentioned, when the Canadian government imposed conscription for military service within Canada in late 1940, Prime Minister Mackenzie King and his cabinet ordered an inquiry by the Standing Committee on Orientals and thereafter adopted the committee's recommendation that ethnic Japanese be exempted from the draft. Although the National Japanese Canadian Citizens League officially disclaimed any link between military service and suffrage rights, it was clear to all—and not least the British Columbia politicians who opposed civil rights for Nisei—that it was logically absurd to require military service from those denied voting rights.[56]

After Pearl Harbor, public sentiment in favor of exclusion of Nisei from military service was reinforced. University students were barred from military training, and even high schoolers were dismissed from cadet corps.[57] Although Nisei and their defenders continued to emphasize the contribution of Japanese Canadian soldiers during World War I, and there were reports that veterans would be exempted from road camp service, the past military service of community members did not end up sparing themselves or others from mass removal.[58] However, in spite of the various calls for their dismissal, none of the twenty-five Japanese Canadians already serving in the army was dismissed. In the following two years, these soldiers, plus a half dozen further recruits, began to compile a strong service record. Dave Tsubota of Montreal was among the Canadian troops who took part in the famous 1942 Dieppe raid. Taken prisoner by the Germans, he remained in a Nazi POW camp for over two years. Jim Ubukata, a biracial Nisei from Moose Jaw, served as a radar technician in the Royal Canadian Air Force as part of a unit that saw action in Europe. Brothers Harry and Minoru Tanaka both served in combat, Harry in North Africa, Sicily, Belgium, and Holland, and Minoru in France, where he was killed in action in 1945. A few other Nisei were detailed for teaching, as Japanese instructors at the School of Oriental and African Studies in England.[59]

The Canadian government did not reverse its ban on enlistment of Nisei soldiers until the beginning of 1945, and then only under pressure. In May 1944 the South-East Asia Command, responsible for coordinating the United Nations war effort in southern Asia, opened a South-East Asia Training Interrogation Centre to produce interpreters and translators. The unit was immediately plagued by lack of experienced Japanese language teachers. Since Canada had the largest population of Japanese-speaking British subjects in the British Empire, the British Army requested permission to recruit Japanese Canadians, and in mid-1944 Donald Mollison, a recruiting officer, traveled to Ontario to find Japanese speakers for intelligence work in Burma. Mollison assembled a group of twelve Nisei from London and Brantford, with the promise of enlisting them as corporals in the British Army. Although the Canadian Army did not object to the enlistment of Nisei by Great Britain, and the Cabinet War Committee even agreed that the Department of National Defense could begin sending enlistment questionnaires to Nisei prospects who requested them, Prime Minister King put off any action on the question until after Parliament had had a chance to debate on external affairs.[60] This delayed the matter indefinitely, and in the meantime the cabinet not only declined to allow Mollison's men to serve as Canadian soldiers but refused to guarantee that if they enlisted in the British Army they would be permitted to return to Canada.[61]

Finally, at the beginning of 1945, six months after Mollison had selected his troops, the War Cabinet reversed position—allegedly following a direct request from British Prime Minister Winston Churchill to Mackenzie King.[62] The original twelve recruits, plus twenty-three more, were inducted into the Canadian Army (as privates!) and "loaned" to the British, who sent them overseas for work with the Psychological Warfare Broadcasting Unit.[63] At first, the Canadians agreed that the British could detail up to a total of 100 Nisei as translators. This number was obviously insufficient, so on April 29 the cabinet agreed to recruit more Nisei translators, with a maximum quota set at 150, for duty in Asia.[64] While Prime Minister King acknowledged in response to a question in Parliament in April that the Nisei had been recruited by the British "for war purposes," the War Cabinet declared that all information on Nisei enlistment, including the identities and activities of the Nisei recruits, was classified as top secret—allegedly for security purposes, but in fact to avoid the political repercussions of Nisei soldiers on public opinion in British Columbia.[65] Even after the war ended with V-J Day in August 1945, the Privy Council maintained the ban and had an article on Nisei GIs censored.[66] Due to such secrecy, plus the Canadian government's harsh treatment of ethnic Japanese residents, recruitment was not brisk. According to the Department of National Defense, only 119 Japanese Canadians were on active service between December 7, 1941, and V-J day, and 112 translators were still in service in November 1945.[67] In September 1945 Thomas Shoyama, well-known editor of the *New Canadian*, volunteered for service as a linguist. His service lent publicity to the existence of Nisei soldiers. Many of the new recruits were sent to basic training in Ontario, then detailed to the S-20 Pacific Command Language School in Vancouver, then still officially closed to ethnic Japanese (and where the recruits faced various expressions of prejudice, including exclusion from a local movie theater). The Nisei eventually served primarily in the War Crimes Investigation units in the Far East. The presence and contributions of the soldiers ultimately instilled community pride and attracted some public notice and support.[68] Still, in comparison with the wartime service of Japanese Americans, the enlistment of the Japanese Canadians came, as one commentator put it, "too little and too late" to shape the group's fate.[69]

THE SUPREME COURT AND THE WARTIME INTERNMENT CASES

Military service—including the fight against conscription—represented the arena in which most Nisei claimed their citizenship rights and attempted to remake the government's policy from mass incarceration to liberation. However, from the beginning, a few brave individuals, with the aid of sympathetic lawyers, brought legal challenges to Executive Order 9066 and to their confinement. A series of these cases was ultimately heard by the United States Supreme Court. These cases pushed the government into a hostile and defensive posture. War Department chiefs, notably Assistant Secretary McCloy, feared the larger consequences if the Supreme Court found for the Nisei. As they saw it, the army would then be put in the position of acting illegally, its reputation would be tarnished, and its leaders would be hobbled in responding to future emergencies. In addition, many government officials feared that if Executive Order 9066 were overturned, Japanese American would immediately return en masse to the West Coast, where public opinion was extremely hostile and there were no structures in place to ease their transition, with the result being chaos or bloodshed. Therefore the Justice Department fiercely opposed the legal challenges before the Supreme Court, and War Department and Justice Department officials collaborated in deliberately withholding and manipulating relevant evidence regarding the evacuation in order to improve their chances of winning.[70]

The first cases to go through the courts were those of Minoru Yasui and Gordon Hirabayashi. Minoru Yasui was born in 1916, the son of a prosperous farmer in Oregon. Yasui studied law at the University of Oregon (where he also underwent military training and received a lieutenant's commission in the army reserve), but after being accepted to the bar he was unable to secure work in Oregon and instead took a job as an attaché with the Japanese Consulate in Chicago. In days following the Pearl Harbor attack, he resigned from his job and rejoined the army, but he was discharged on racial grounds within a few days. Meanwhile, his father was arrested as a potentially dangerous enemy alien and interned in Missoula, Montana (where he remained until 1945).[71] In the wake of these two traumatic events, Yasui decided to bring a test case to challenge the constitutionality of Executive Order 9066. On March 28, when the curfew ordered by General DeWitt against all West Coast residents of Japanese ancestry went into effect, Yasui arranged with a local attorney to defend him, walked the streets of Portland after dark, went to a police station, demanded to be arrested, and succeeded in having himself charged so he could bring his test case.[72]

Gordon Hirabayashi, born in 1918 in Washington and raised in a Japanese religious sect close to the Quakers, became active during his years as a student at the University of Washington with the campus YMCA and with the progressive pacifist group Fellowship of Reconciliation. In the spring of 1942 Hirabayashi decided to resist evacuation and wrote a statement of principles opposing Executive Order 9066 as a violation of his citizenship rights. With assistance from the Quakers and from state representative Mary Farquarson, who organized a defense committee, Hirabayashi visited a local FBI office in May 1942 and presented his statement, whereupon an agent arrested him (the FBI agent confiscated Hirabayashi's diary, which provided evidence of curfew violations; as a result, he was charged with both failing to report for evacuation and violating curfew).[73]

Two further cases that would reach the Supreme Court, those of Fred Korematsu and Mitsuye Endo, also arose once mass evacuation was put into effect. Fred Korematsu, a Nisei from Oakland, California, hoped to move to the Midwest with his non-Japanese girlfriend (and had plastic surgery performed on his face in order not to stand out in his new home). He thereafter sought to remain on the West Coast long enough to earn enough money for the trip, and he attempted to pass as Spanish-Hawaiian to avoid removal. However, he was discovered in nearby San Leandro and arrested. While in custody, he was visited by northern California ACLU director Ernest Besig, who offered to represent him in a suit against evacuation. After some hesitation, Korematsu agreed to act as plaintiff in a challenge to the removal policy.[74] Mitsuye Endo was one of a small group of California state Nisei employees who were dismissed from their positions in early 1942. Following her removal to the assembly center at Tanforan, Endo was contacted by ACLU lawyer James Purcell, who sought to challenge the arbitrary dismissal of Nisei state employees. She agreed to serve as a test case.[75] Purcell determined that the most rapid legal means to this end was to bring a habeas corpus case charging the federal government with unlawful detention that deprived Endo of her right to return to her job, and thus Purcell challenged her confinement through this circuitous route. Following Endo's transfer to Topaz, WRA solicitor Philip Glick personally visited her and offered her a "leave permit" to relocate outside the West Coast if she would drop her suit, but she courageously refused and remained in camp to pursue her case.[76]

In addition to these cases, two other legal challenges to removal were heard in the lower courts in 1942. Lincoln Seiichi Kanai, a YMCA secretary in San Francisco, who had publicly announced his opposition to Executive Order 9066, left the West Coast by car on June 1, 1942, in order to test the law and the state of public sentiment. Caught by the FBI at a YMCA convention in Wisconsin and arrested, he was brought back for trial on the West Coast and convicted of violating Public Law 503 by leaving a military zone without authorization. Kanai declined to appeal his conviction. A more substantial challenge to the constitutionality of General DeWitt's evacuation order was that of Ernest and Toki Wakayama. Ernest Kinzo Wakayama, born in Hawaii in 1897, was a veteran of World War I and an officer of the American Legion, while Toki was a California-born Nisei. While at Santa Anita Race Track Assembly Center, the Wakayamas petitioned for a writ of habeas corpus, though by the time it was filed on August 20, 1942, they had been moved to Manzanar. The attorney who assumed chief direction of the Wakayamas' case was A. L. Wirin, a progressive Jewish ACLU lawyer. (Warned by partners in his law firm that the labor union clients who provided most of their business would be unhappy about his defending "Japs," Wirin courageously left the firm and set up his own practice in order to take the case.) Joining with Wirin in the Wakayamas' defense was Hugh MacBeth, an African American lawyer in Los Angeles who had opposed removal. U.S. Attorney Leo Silverstein, with California Attorney General Earl Warren joining him, argued for continued confinement. In October 1942 the Wakayamas' petition was heard by a panel of three federal judges, Campbell E. Beaumont, J.E.T. O'Connor, and Harry Hollzer, sitting en banc. After repeatedly delaying consideration, despite the emergency nature of a habeas corpus petition, on February 4, 1943, Judge Hollzer granted the Wakayamas a writ of habeas corpus and set the case down for a full hearing. By this time, however, the Wakayamas no longer wished to proceed. Worn down by large-scale official harassment at Manzanar, allegedly including beatings, and ostracism by fellow inmates, they withdrew their suit and filed requests for "repatriation" to Japan.[77]

Once the legal cases were brought, the plaintiffs and their attorneys became enmeshed in legal and strategic disputes with the JACL and the ACLU, which would ordinarily have been expected to be their chief supporters. The JACL was taken by surprise by the cases, which violated the organization's policy of full cooperation with the government. As a result, the national JACL announced that it was "unalterably opposed to test cases to determine the constitutionality of military regulations" and refused moral or financial support, denouncing Yasui as a "self-styled martyr." The JACL's policy of nonassistance persisted until early 1943, when the Yasui and Hirabayashi cases, and later the Korematsu and Endo cases, went before the Supreme Court.[78] At the same time, the national ACLU was hindered by the vote of its board not to challenge the constitutionality of Executive Order 9066. Although the national ACLU did permit the northern California branch to take the Hirabayashi case in order to challenge the discriminatory application of the president's order to Japanese Americans, the line between acceptable and unacceptable legal argument was difficult to maintain, and the defense strategy suffered from a certain incoherence.[79]

Hirabayashi's and Yasui's were the first cases to be heard in court. (In a subtle sign of official racism, Hirabayashi's case was formally captioned *Kiyoshi Hirabayashi v. United States*, in spite of the fact that the defendant's legal first name was "Gordon.") Judge Lloyd Black instructed the jury to find Hirabayashi guilty if he disobeyed the law, without considering its constitutionality. The jury then convicted Hirabayashi of violating both the evacuation order and the curfew, and Judge Black imposed sentence on both counts, with the sentences to run concurrently.[80] Conversely, in the Yasui case, Judge James Fee found that the curfew violated the rights of American citizens. However, Judge Fee declared that Yasui had given up his American citizenship through his prewar employment with the Japanese Consulate and ruled that the curfew was thus enforceable against him as an enemy alien.[81] Both cases were quickly brought up for appeal to the Ninth Circuit Court of Appeals. In view of the importance of the questions involved, the appellate court certified for the Supreme Court the essential question of whether DeWitt's exclusion orders represented a constitutional exercise of the war powers of the president, and the Supreme Court agreed in late March 1943 to hear the cases.

As the two sides prepared their briefs, the government engaged in widespread manipulation of evidence, particularly with regard to the reasons for evacuation. As we have seen, General DeWitt had ordered mass removal because it was allegedly impossible to determine or trust the loyalty of any individual of Japanese ancestry. Once the War Department opened up military service to Nisei and created a joint board to screen the loyalty of Japanese Americans, the government could no longer make such a claim (which may have been legally unsustainable in any case). Instead, in lower court arguments Assistant Secretary McCloy and Justice Department lawyers adopted the stance that evacuation was necessary because, while Japanese American loyalty could indeed be determined, there was not sufficient time for such an operation in the emergency situation on the West Coast during the spring of 1942. However, in April 1943 General DeWitt sent McCloy a copy of the final report he had prepared on evacuation. In its pages DeWitt clearly stated that he had undertaken race-based evacuation of Japanese Americans because there was no way to tell a loyal from a disloyal "Japanese"—lack of time had not been a factor. (DeWitt and Bendetsen reminded McCloy that if time had been the chief consideration, the government could have undertaken loyalty examinations of Japanese Americans in the assembly centers and not spent millions of dollars building camps.) McCloy ordered DeWitt to recall and destroy all copies of the final report and then to rewrite it to match the new line the government had adopted. McCloy concealed both the existence of the report and the information it contained from the

Justice Department lawyers arguing the case, whom he considered insufficiently committed to defending the policy. However, military officials arranged for (biased and distorted) information in the report to be leaked to West Coast state officials for insertion in their *amicus curiae* (friend of the court) briefs supporting mass evacuation. At the same time, President Franklin Roosevelt was tipped off by his confidential advisor, attorney Morris Ernst, that the court was likely to (and ought to) overturn Executive Order 9066 in its decision, at least as applied to citizens. Roosevelt asked Ernst to put together a plan to impose martial law on the West Coast so that the government could keep Japanese Americans confined in such a case.[82] At the same time, President Franklin Roosevelt was tipped off by his confidential adviser, attorney Morris Ernst, that the court was likely to (and ought to) overturn Executive Order 9066, at least as applied to citizens. Roosevelt asked Ernst to put together a plan to impose some form of martial law in such a case so that the government could keep Japanese Americans confined.

The Hirabayashi and Yasui cases were argued before the Supreme Court on May 10, 1943. Six weeks later, on June 21, the Court issued its decision. By unanimous vote, it upheld DeWitt's initial race-based curfew order as an emergency war measure. (Since Judge Black had ordered Gordon Hirabayashi's prison sentences for disobeying the curfew and the evacuation order to run concurrently, the Court—exercising some breathtaking judicial hairsplitting—ruled only on the curfew and refused to discuss the constitutionality of the evacuation order.) The Court exercised an ordinary standard of review, with no extra scrutiny, and found the curfew reasonably related to the (unstated) purposes for which it was intended.[83] The Court based its approval of the curfew order not on any demonstrated act of sabotage or espionage but on acceptance of the military's uninformed stereotypes of people of Japanese ancestry as clannish and unassimilated, and thus dangerous: "Whatever views we may entertain regarding the loyalty to this country of the citizens of Japanese ancestry, we cannot reject as unfounded the judgment of the military authorities and of Congress that there were disloyal members of that population, whose number and strength could not be precisely and quickly ascertained."[84] On the same grounds, the justices then unanimously sustained Minoru Yasui's conviction but overturned the lower court judge's determination that Yasui had forfeited all his citizenship rights by working for the Japanese Consulate.[85]

Although the Court had upheld military action based on race in *Hirabayashi*, it did not explicitly uphold mass evacuation. The War Department and Justice Department thus turned to defending that policy from high court appeals, first in the *Korematsu* and then in the *Endo* case. Both cases remained long stalled in the lower courts. Fred Korematsu had been brought up for trial in September 1942. As expected, Federal Judge Adolphus St. Sure found him guilty of violating Public Law 503 by refusing to report for evacuation. However, on the excuse that he did not wish to send Korematsu to prison for his offense, Judge St. Sure imposed a suspended sentence, which under existing law was nonfinal and hence nonappealable. As a result, Korematsu's lawyers were forced to petition the court of appeals, and ultimately the Supreme Court, to obtain a ruling opening the door for an appellate review of the case before they could even argue the merits. Meanwhile, Mitsuye Endo's habeas corpus petition was argued before Judge Michael Roche in July 1942, and the lawyers submitted supporting briefs thereafter. However, although a habeas corpus petition is supposed to be an expedited proceeding, in which a judge rules quickly, Judge Roche deliberately stalled his decision for over one year, during which Mitsuye Endo remained arbitrarily confined. Finally, in July 1943, after the Supreme Court decisions in the *Hirabayashi* and *Yasui* cases, he issued an order dismissing Endo's petition but did not offer any explanation or grounds for his action.[86]

Once the courts determined that the *Korematsu* case was appealable, it was brought before the Ninth Circuit Court of Appeals, which, without holding further argument, affirmed the defendant's conviction in December 1943 under the logic of the Supreme Court's *Hirabayashi* ruling. The Supreme Court then agreed in March 1944 to hear the case. James Purcell and the ACLU lawyers defending the *Korematsu* and *Endo* cases hoped that they would be argued together before the Court, since it seemed obvious that the government had little chance of prevailing in the *Endo* case and the arguments presented in it might influence the justices to rule in favor of Korematsu as well. At the same time, the fact that both cases were forthcoming might push the government to take action to lift exclusion, so as to avoid being put in the position of acting illegally. After *Endo* was brought before the Ninth Circuit Court of Appeals, Judge William Denman, who hoped for a rapid resolution to the case, certified questions for the Supreme Court in April 1944, in hopes that it could be brought before the Court before its summer recess. However, citing the needs of the lawyers involved, the Court decided to put off argument on both cases until its fall 1944 term. It thereby escaped entirely having to rule on the government's actions during the 1944 campaign, when President Roosevelt (who had appointed seven of the nine justices) was seeking re-election.[87]

As in the *Hirabayashi* case, Assistant Secretary of War McCloy and Justice Department lawyers engaged in manipulation of evidence during the preparation of government's *Korematsu* brief. In early 1944 the War Department released the final report drafted by Bendetsen and signed by General DeWitt, which then became the central piece of official evidence. To justify mass evacuation, its authors resorted to use of distorted evidence and to outright deceit. Most importantly, the report made knowingly false allegations that West Coast Japanese Americans had engaged in widespread signaling of offshore Japanese submarines in the weeks after Pearl Harbor, leading to widespread attacks on American ships leaving the coast. FCC Chairman James Fly, who had conducted an investigation during the spring of 1942 and informed DeWitt that the army's signaling detection equipment and operators were defective and that its reports of signaling were false, shared his findings with the Justice Department lawyers. In accordance with their duty to inform the Court of the presence of false evidence, the lawyers then included a section in the completed brief describing the final report's misrepresentations. Under pressure from McCloy, seconded by Solicitor General Charles Fahy, who were dedicated to defending mass evacuation at all costs, the entire section was stricken and the brief was reprinted with no mention of the report's distortions except for an unobtrusive footnote that the Justice Department did not "rely" on it.[88]

Oral argument in both the *Korematsu* and *Endo* cases took place in October 1944. Over the following weeks, as the judges drafted their opinions, the fall presidential election passed. On December 18 the Court announced its decision. By a 6–3 margin, it upheld Fred Korematsu's decision, finding mass race-based evacuation to be a constitutional use of wartime presidential authority.[89] In his majority opinion, Justice Hugo Black (a longtime personal friend of General DeWitt) insisted that the army had removed Fred Korematsu not because of racial hostility but only because of the needs of security in a time of danger. He likewise insisted, through a tortured reading of the record, that since not all Japanese Americans who were evacuated went to the WRA camps, their detention was not at issue. "Regardless of the true nature of the assembly and relocation centers—and we deem it unjustifiable to call them concentration camps with all the ugly connotations that term implies—we are dealing specifically with nothing but an exclusion order."[90] Justices Frank Murphy, Robert Jackson, and Owen Roberts issued strong individual dissents. Jackson warned that the decision amounted to a bill of attainder against Japanese Americans and added that the Court's approval of arbitrary military power over citizens represented a "loaded weapon" for future use against civil liberties in times of danger.[91] Murphy called the majority opinion a "legalization of racism."[92]

In contrast to the sharp exchanges between the justices in *Korematsu*, the Court's unanimous ruling releasing Mitsuye Endo was brief and almost offhanded. In the *Endo* opinion, Justice William O. Douglas evaded all constitutional questions regarding the arbitrary race-based imprisonment of American citizens—the central fact of the government's policy. Instead, he merely found that nothing either in Executive Order 9066 or in the congressional legislation enforcing it granted the WRA or any agency the power to detain a concededly loyal citizen such as Endo. So cautious were Justice Douglas and the Court that his opinion did not even explicitly state whether Endo might return to her home and job on the West Coast, the subjects of her initial petition![93] Justice Owen Roberts rejected Douglas's logic in a concurrence, stating that the president had confirmed the action in his messages to Congress, and Congress had approved incarceration by funding the agency. Justice Frank Murphy added his own concurrence, explicitly connecting the confinement with the evacuation that the Court had just upheld in *Korematsu*.

Ironically, although the *Korematsu* decision has achieved classic status in the history of American constitutional law, it had little influence in the actual shaping of government policy toward Japanese Americans. In contrast, the *Endo* decision, which capped a long drawn out struggle within government circles over exclusion and the return of Japanese Americans to the West Coast, catalyzed a reorientation of official policy.

MARTIAL LAW IN HAWAII

Intimately connected to the confinement of U.S. citizens of Japanese ancestry was the denial of civil rights to all civilians, Japanese Americans and others, under wartime military dictatorship in Hawaii. Although there was no mass removal of local Issei and Nisei, their presence was central in the long legal and political struggle over military rule and the refusal of the army to restore civilian authority.[94] When Commanding General Walter Short first insisted, at the time of the Pearl Harbor attack, that Governor John Poindexter sign the proclamation for unlimited martial law in Hawaii, he assured Poindexter that it would be only a temporary measure, until the immediate crisis had passed—a "reasonably short time."[95]

Nevertheless, once granted extensive powers, the army proved reluctant to surrender any meaningful authority. The most recalcitrant figure was Colonel (later General) Thomas H. Green of the army Provost Marshal General's office, the military's chief executive officer. It was Green who drew up the martial law proclamation that bypassed the Hawaii Defense Act and gave absolute power to a military governor, and Green who created an organizational plan in the succeeding days that left Hawaii with a status resembling that of a conquered province. Over the ensuing months, Green drafted the military orders that regulated Hawaiian society. Rather than using the machinery of the existing civilian government, he confiscated relief funds granted by Congress and used the proceeds to hire civilian employees to carry out official functions.[96]

From the outset, a prominent feature of the martial law regime designed by Green was the imposition of military tribunals, erected under General Order 4. Although civilian courts were permitted to reopen a week after the attacks, they were restricted to civil cases. All criminal cases were tried by a network of military commissions and provost courts established by the military governor's office, allegedly based on the model of military courts-martial. In fact, these military tribunals, presided over by armed officers generally untrained in law, were classic examples of drumhead justice, unfettered by rules of evidence, presumption of innocence, or constitutional safeguards of fair trials. Juries were forbidden, and lawyers discouraged or even barred. Defendants were not given copies of the charges against them and were permitted only to look at the prosecution's copy of charge sheets. Furthermore, the suspension of habeas corpus meant that civilians could be held without charge. The tribunals frequently issued severe sentences, including fines and imprisonment, for misdemeanors and relatively trivial offenses, and the system had no machinery established for appeals. So seldom did the tribunals issue acquittals that defendants generally chose to plead guilty, whether or not they had not committed the crimes charged, rather than face the heavy penalties meted out to those who dared plead not guilty.[97] Of the 22,480 trials conducted in provost court in Honolulu in 1942–1943,

99 percent ended in convictions.[98] One official who heard 819 cases where defendants pleaded not guilty issued convictions in all 819![99]

The case of Sanji Abe furnishes an illustration of the embattled position of Japanese Americans under the regime. Abe, a World War I veteran and former Honolulu policeman, was the lone Nisei senator elected to the prewar legislature. Despite (or because of) his position, Abe seems to have been closely watched by the military authorities once war began. On August 2, he was arrested and charged with possession of a Japanese flag. Abe protested that he had never bought or flown any Japanese flag—the item in question (which Abe suspected had been planted) was found among other stage property in a theater of which he was part owner. He also pointed out that the military orders making possession of Japanese flags a crime were not issued until August 8, six days after his arrest. Army officials were thus forced to release him on August 19. Still, even after he publicly burned the offending flag, he remained under suspicion. As if to demonstrate in graphic terms the authoritarian power of the military, in September 1942 Green had Abe rearrested, this time without charge, and placed in "custodial detention," where he remained for nineteen months.[100]

There was little audible opposition within the islands to martial law or military justice. Neither the Hawaii Bar Association nor local business groups (who were delighted by the harsh curbs imposed on labor and the outlawing of strikes) took a contrary position. As late as December 27, 1942, the Honolulu Chamber of Commerce praised the government as "eminently fair and considerate of our civil rights."[101] The local press, subjected to official censorship and the influence of the army's propaganda apparatus, remained similarly supportive. As the *Hawaii Advertiser* editorialized in December 1942, "the community as a whole, business men, professional men and average citizens, do not desire complete elimination of martial law at this time."[102] Honolulu Mayor Lester Petrie, the chief civilian office holder, was an outspoken defender of military rule, arguing that essential functions could be assured only by the army.[103]

In July 1942 a new territorial governor, Federal Judge Ingram Stainback, was appointed, although his power was largely nullified under the military government. As the menace of invasion by Tokyo receded following the battle of Midway, he grew increasingly impatient over army control and attempted to negotiate a return to civilian rule. However, he made no headway with Green and the other military commanders, at least in part because of the issue of Japanese Americans. Green had already insisted to Assistant Secretary of War McCloy that if regular criminal courts reopened, the one hundred U.S. citizens of Japanese ancestry of doubtful loyalty who were being held on Sand Island would be able to file habeas corpus suits for their release. In any case, he noted, no Japanese American charged with a criminal offense could secure a fair trial in wartime Hawaii (irrespective of the presence of Nisei jurors), so military tribunals could better assure justice.[104] Navy Secretary Frank Knox, backed by Admirals Chester Nimitz and Ernest King, commanders of the Navy's Pacific Fleet, immediately protested any relaxation in martial law because of the danger posed by Japanese Americans, and "the large number of unquestionably pro-Japanese who are still at large" on Oahu.[105] Rebuffed by the military, on October 3 Stainback took office with a unilateral proclamation restoring civilian rule. He then named J. Garner Anthony as his attorney general. Anthony, a wealthy member of an elite local firm, had boldly published an article in the *California Law Review* during the spring of 1942 arguing that martial law was unconstitutional.[106]

Stainback and Anthony turned for help to Interior Secretary Harold Ickes, whose department exercised official oversight of the territory. Ickes (who had been privately outraged by the unjust treatment of Japanese Americans) was widely known to have been shocked and displeased by Poindexter's action in turning over all authority to the military.[107] Throughout 1942, Ickes had watched events in Hawaii closely, thanks to an agent, Ben Thoron, whom the secretary had sent in February 1942 to report on the situation. Ickes had also attempted without success to intervene with the War Department to curb the excesses of military justice.[108] Stainback and Anthony found Ickes strongly in agreement—although the secretary ordered Stainback to excise the part of his proclamation officially withdrawing Poindexter's declaration of martial law, on grounds that it was better to try for a negotiated settlement.[109] Ickes's undersecretary Abe Fortas held a series of conferences in August 1942 with Green and with Justice Department officials. Initially there was a spirit of conciliation and an accord was reached. Fortas proposed that civilian courts resume jurisdiction over all civil and criminal trials except for matters involving members of the armed forces and those employed by the military governor, which would continue to be heard by the military tribunals. The army delegates objected that Japanese Americans and other nonwhites could be called as jurors, and there was great risk that their racial hatreds or disloyalty would prevail over impartial justice. To calm such fears, Fortas agreed to grant the military governor authority to exempt any classes of persons from jury service.[110]

Upon his return to Hawaii, on August 31 Colonel (now General) Green issued General Order 133, which restored jurisdiction over ordinary criminal matters to the civil courts, while retaining the suspension of habeas corpus. However, he followed four days later with General Order 135, which "interpreted" the former order to forbid federal courts from trying civil or criminal cases challenging statutory provisions for the protection of the government, the war effort, or national security. Similarly, territorial courts were barred from trying cases based on local ordinances involving such matters as vagrancy, prostitution, and assault and battery against law enforcement officers.[111] This meant there was little change in practice. Emmons, while more flexible than Green, upheld these actions. Emmons insisted that the civilian governor must remain subordinate to the military, and that he must be the one to determine what powers to return to civilian control and when. Further air attacks on Hawaii, he told McCloy, were possible, even likely. Most important, he needed to control the civilian population. He made clear that the presence of so many Japanese American citizens and aliens, "some . . . disloyal and others of doubtful loyalty," made security an urgent consideration.[112]

Ickes was outraged by Green's actions, which he considered a violation of the spirit of Fortas's agreement. In a (barely) anonymous interview, Ickes complained that the military regime had "violated every guarantee of the Bill of Rights except possibly that of free worship."[113] He resolved to work for a more significant rollback of military rule. To build support in Congress, Ickes threw his support to Joseph Farrington, who was elected territorial delegate in November. Farrington was an outspoken opponent of martial law, which he claimed was detrimental to the war effort. Meanwhile, Ickes and Biddle began a new set of conferences with McCloy to find an arrangement. Both McCloy and Secretary of War Stimson believed that in the "fortress" of Hawaii, the local commander must have maximum authority. They pointed to newspaper reports (which they did not bother to mention were issued by a censored press dependant on the goodwill of the military governor's office) that martial law in Hawaii was popular with all except "the politicians."[114] In December 1942 Stainback traveled to Washington, hoping to persuade the president to revoke martial law. He and Anthony joined Biddle (and occasionally Ickes) in a new series of negotiations with McCloy and Emmons—Green was present at

the initial sessions but was thereafter excluded. The army refused to surrender any real authority. It was clear to observers that their resistance
was fueled (or at least justified) by the fear of Hawaii's racial diversity, especially the local Japanese. One journalist noted, "Hawaii contains within
itself a highly explosive population condition which the military authorities feel can be controlled only by absolute military power."[115]

Although all the parties had hoped to shield President Roosevelt from
the debate, given the vast wartime burdens on him, once the two sides
reached obvious deadlock Biddle appealed to him to press the military, who he said were "now running Hawaii lock, stock, and barrel," to
turn back the civilian functions in the territory to Governor Stainback.
Biddle's assistant James Rowe, a former White House assistant, had already forwarded the president a memo enclosing Anthony's reports on
the army's police state tactics in Hawaii and strongly recommending that
he read them in full.[116] Now the attorney general sent the president reports of poor administration and curfew violations by the army and
complained of Green's arrogant and unyielding attitude—even McCloy
had agreed that he be replaced. Biddle warned that if conditions did not
improve, Republicans would have ammunition to attack the administration.[117] Roosevelt agreed that Hawaii was "insidious" in its impact on the
military and was especially sensitive to the political problem. "The real
point of the matter is that while Hawaii will not, in all probability, be attacked again, the eyes of the country are, and will be, on Hawaii and all
conditions there."[118] He told Biddle he supported removal of Green and
rotation of officers to break up the entrenched army elite and improve
administration. Stimson responded by telling FDR that if he wanted the
"fortress" of Hawaii defended by the army he must give them proper authority, and he added facetiously that if Roosevelt wanted to abolish martial law, Harold Ickes would have to take responsibility for defense. Roosevelt quickly agreed with Stimson.[119] While he proceeded to assure the
press that he thought martial law could be "relaxed," he made no effort to
intervene on the scope of military authority—he seemed untroubled by
the reports of civil liberties abuses.[120]

In January 1943, with Roosevelt's support, Ickes and Stimson finally
brokered a compromise providing for a gradual restoration of authority
to Hawaii's civilian government, but only "when and as the military situation permits," and subject to reversal at any time. The president issued
an official letter approving the arrangement. "I can readily appreciate the

difficulty in defining exactly the boundaries between civil and military functions. I think th[is] formula . . . meets the present needs."[121] In accordance with the deal, on February 8, 1943, Emmons issued a decree, effective March 10, returning authority over eighteen governmental functions to the territorial government. On February 17 the Hawaiian legislature was finally allowed to meet, after a fifteen-month recess. For the first time in a decade, there were no Nisei legislators—the eight prewar Japanese American representatives either had been pressured not to run or had been defeated for reelection, while Senator Sanji Abe, who remained in detention, had resigned.

Notwithstanding the partial restoration of civilian rule, the army insisted on retaining special emergency powers, including censorship powers, curfew enforcement, and control of alien populations, as well as regulation of labor in defense-related jobs and control of prostitution. The martial law regime continued to exercise broad powers over "security." The military governor also stated publicly that the "privilege" of habeas corpus remained suspended and continued the use of provost courts to try military officials and those accused of offences involving them.[122] Again, the military was not shy about playing the race card. As one friendly observer wrote:

> It is generally assumed that if the Japanese population in Hawaii were less numerous, the military authorities would be much more willing to relinquish their control over civilian affairs. Here the decision of the authorities seems to be justified by the record. Thorough policing and selective detention of the Japanese are regarded as effective means of handling this difficult problem. The facts that there have been no interracial disturbances of consequence and that the Japanese have been well behaved are seen as evidence that the Army's methods are producing satisfactory results.[123]

Despite the language of the agreement, there were no further changes in the scope of military rule in the following eighteen months, even as the United States moved closer to victory over Japan and the threat of invasion grew increasingly remote. Emmons refused to make further changes in the scope of martial law before his departure. His successor, General Robert C. Richardson, who assumed the title of military governor on June 1, 1943, would prove determined to retain power.

COURT CHALLENGES TO MARTIAL LAW

Even as Stainback and Ickes pursued their political campaign against military rule, the system of military tribunals was challenged in court. Again, none of the Issei or Nisei confined by the provost courts or military commissions bought legal challenges to military control in the territory.[124] Yet their presence cast an enormous shadow over the legal proceedings, as the army increasingly turned to a brandishing the "Japanese peril" to legitimate martial rule.

The first legal challenge was that of Dr. Hans Zimmerman, a naturalized citizen and U.S. Army veteran of German ancestry who was a naturopathic physician in Honolulu. Arrested after the Pearl Harbor attack for alleged subversive activities, Zimmerman was held incommunicado alongside Japanese American internees at Sand Island. On December 19 he was examined by a hearing board that refused to inform him of the charges against him and decided after a ten-minute proceeding to hold him indefinitely. In February 1942, learning that he was slated to be shipped to the mainland for confinement, Zimmerman's wife Clara submitted a petition on his behalf for a writ of habeas corpus to the United States District Court in Honolulu. On February 19, 1942 (ironically, the very same day that Executive Order 9066 was signed), Federal Judge Delbert E. Metzger issued a ruling that he believed the writ should be issued as a matter of law but was constrained to obey the military governor. "I feel the court is under duress and is not able to carry out the functions of the court as is its duty."[125]

Following Metzger's ruling, Zimmerman was sent for detention at Camp McCoy, Wisconsin (the same base where the Nisei soldiers of the 100th would be stationed). Clara followed him to the mainland. With the aid of the ACLU, she brought a habeas corpus petition there and obtained a writ. At the suggestion of the Provost Marshal General's Office, Emmons then ordered Zimmerman shipped swiftly back to Hawaii, where he could be confined under martial law. Zimmerman's lawyers proceeded to appeal Metzger's original denial to the Court of Appeals for the Ninth Circuit. A. L. Wirin submitted an *amicus curiae* brief in support. Meanwhile, the army accepted the offer of California Attorney General Earl Warren to submit an *amicus* in support of martial law in Hawaii.[126] Warren, a primary instigator of the removal of Japanese Americans, had praised DeWitt's removal orders in a public address as a shining example of "martial rule." He stated publicly in the brief that martial law was the best policy, and that he welcomed further martial law in California.[127]

In October 1942 the Ninth Circuit denied Zimmerman's petition on the grounds that the prisoner had been given a hearing by the military commission. Soon after, the ACLU announced that it would file an appeal to the U.S. Supreme Court. To avert a hearing of the case by the high court, in which the army would have to present its charges, Assistant Secretary of War McCloy ordered Zimmerman released.[128] It was not until March 1943, however, that he was actually freed from custody, barred from Hawaii, transported to the mainland and deposited in San Francisco.

The next challenge to the martial law regime came from two other German Americans, Edwin Seifert and Walter Glockner, who were also arrested after Pearl Harbor and thereafter held incommunicado. Although Seifert was accused of being an anti-Semite, and Glockner had allegedly given the Hitler salute to friends in 1938 and invited them onto a German boat, no specific charges were filed against the two. In July 1943, four months after the proclamation restoring partial civilian rule was issued, the two men applied for writs of habeas corpus. Judge Metzger was prepared this time to contravene the orders of the army. Announcing his judgment that Governor Stainback's proclamation reestablishing civilian rule implied the restoration of habeas corpus, the judge ordered Lieutenant General Robert C. Richardson Jr., Emmons's successor as military governor, to appear before him and to produce the two prisoners. Richardson refused to receive the summons served on him (his military guard forcibly ejected the federal marshals who the judge had ordered to serve the papers), and while he did accept service of the writs, he refused to produce the prisoners. Metzger waited three days for compliance. When the U.S. Attorney Angus Taylor informed him of Richardson's refusal to obey his orders, he cited the general for contempt and fined him five thousand dollars.[129] Richardson responded with General Orders No. 31. These sweeping decrees (put together by Colonel William Morrison, who had relieved Green as executive officer in March 1943) forbade any court in Hawaii from receiving habeas corpus petitions. Moreover, it threatened Judge Metzger, if he did not abandon all court proceedings on habeas corpus petitions, with a five thousand dollar fine and punishment of up to five years at hard labor. Metzger refused to withdraw his ruling, and a standoff ensued.

The controversy soon attracted nationwide attention. Pennsylvania Congressman Herman Eberharter (a member of the Dies Committee who would subsequently dissent from a committee report attacking the loyalty of Japanese Americans) said that Hawaii was a "testing ground" for the authority of the military and predicted that the case would govern how military trials would be regarded on the continental United States.[130] McCloy, although privately horrified by the general's actions, publicly supported him, arguing that the judge had "erroneously construed" the March 1943 declaration restoring civilian rule.[131] Conversely, newspapers nationwide, even though they admitted that martial law might well still be necessary, vehemently denounced Richardson's action as high-handed and tyrannical.[132]

Richardson, joined by Fleet Commander Admiral Chester Nimitz, justified his conduct by insisting publicly that martial law was vital to the territory's survival. If the army permitted any petitions on habeas corpus to be heard, all aspects of martial law would be opened to judicial review, and army and navy officials would be forced to justify all the general orders regulating security and other functions.[133] The Japanese presence was the main buttress for the army's case. The archly conservative *Chicago Tribune* (which scored Richardson's orders as an example of the dictatorial impulses of Roosevelt's New Deal) polled a group of legal experts on the constitutionality of military justice.[134] The experts who supported Richardson "cited the fact that there are approximately 125,000 citizens of Japanese ancestry on the islands, and 35,000 Japan aliens. They argue that even though a majority of those persons may be loyal, the military authorities, and not the courts, should have power to pass on their loyalty."[135] Another newspaper, underlining the gravity of the order, pointed out that if it was upheld on appeal by the Ninth Circuit, some 1,400 internees, mostly Japanese, would be able to apply for writs of habeas corpus to free themselves from army custody.[136] To resolve the deadlock, Assistant Attorney General Edward Ennis and Solicitor General Charles Fahy were sent to consult with Judge Metzger, and they brokered a compromise. In October the two prisoners at bar were brought to the mainland, out of the judge's jurisdiction, and freed—thus mooting their case. General Richardson withdrew his orders, while Judge Metzger, upon a showing by the War Department that Richardson had acted under orders from Army Chief of Staff General George Marshall, reduced the fine to $100.[137] Finally, in January 1944 President Roosevelt offered Richardson an unconditional pardon, erasing the fine and halting the general's appeal of Metzger's rulings.

DUNCAN V. KAHANAMOKU

Although the cases of Zimmerman, Seifert, and Glockner had focused public attention on military government in Hawaii, the military tribunals had continued operating unhindered through the months that followed. Eventually, however, a major challenge came in the person of Lloyd C. Duncan. On February 24, 1944, Duncan, a civilian working for the navy, was arrested for assaulting two marine sentries at the gate of the Pearl Harbor naval base. Brought before the provost court, he was convicted and sentenced to six months in prison. Duncan proceeded to challenge the legality of the military tribunals and denied the army's right to try civilians. Garner Anthony agreed to represent him. In March 1944 Duncan submitted a habeas corpus petition before Judge Metzger. General Richardson and Admiral Nimitz responded with sworn affidavits opposing the issuance of a writ. They insisted, without clarification, that Hawaii remained in "imminent danger" of Japanese invasion, and that martial law and suspension of the writ of habeas corpus were essential to the war effort. To rally support, they trotted out a Japanese peril, claiming that martial law was justified by the menace posed by the presence of 124,000 U.S. citizens of Japanese ancestry—67,000 of whom were dual citizens. "A number of these persons are known to be loyal to Japan and are thus dangerous to the United States. A number are interned."[138] Hoping to avoid another deadlock, Biddle sent an assistant, E. J. Jones, to ask the judge to set the matter down for trial without issuing a writ that would liberate the prisoner. Despite the pleas of the government, on April 1 Metzger nevertheless issued a writ and set the matter down for a full evidentiary hearing.

The *Duncan* habeas corpus hearing opened on April 5, 1944, eleven months after the Supreme Court's *Hirabayashi* decision was announced and barely a week after the Court agreed to hear the *Korematsu* case. As with the Japanese American cases, the Justice Department was given the task of preparing the government briefs, though its staffers had grave doubts about the constitutionality of marital law.[139] Edward Ennis, sent by Attorney General Biddle to Hawaii to argue the case on behalf of Richardson and his regime, had a difficult task showing a state of immediate peril to the war effort sufficient to justify military tribunals. Richardson and Nimitz attempted to present Hawaii as vulnerable to invasion, with its safety dependant on military judgment. Richardson, called as a witness, affirmed that a Japanese submarine had been contacted near Oahu, and that further raids might occur. Admiral Nimitz, similarly, did his best to defend the official line, adding that Tokyo could still gain precious information from submarine landings and espionage parties, and that in bad weather conditions a Japanese carrier force could approach the islands. "We are in no mood for another Pearl Harbor," he proclaimed.[140] Under close questioning by Anthony, however, both commanders were forced to admit that any sizable Japanese invasion was very improbable. Meanwhile, Anthony introduced a magazine article by Fleet Admiral Edwin (Bull) Halsey, stating that the Japanese fleet had been destroyed—clearly Tokyo could not assemble such any such force from its decimated navy.[141]

Given the weakness of the invasion threats, Ennis and the Justice Department were forced to find other grounds to sustain the provost court. To defend the continuation of martial law, which gave the military tribunals the authority to judge civilian cases, the government described the peril caused by the presence of Japanese Americans as their chief justification. The position they took, ironically, was exactly the same one that McCloy and the War Department chiefs had disavowed (and forced General DeWitt to abandon) in the *Hirabayashi* case the previous year: namely, that the loyalties of Japanese Americans could not be relied on or determined, on racial grounds—irrespective of time factors. It was ironic that Edward Ennis should be charged with putting forward such a position. Ennis had opposed mass removal of West Coast Japanese Americans in 1942 and had then struggled unsuccessfully to expose the duplicity of the War Department and the fraudulent nature of DeWitt's *Final Report* in the government brief in the *Korematsu* case. In connection with this line of argument, Ennis focused on the alleged dual nationality of the Nisei—the old nativist canard—as a factor placing Hawaii in direct peril.[142] He used the *Hirabayashi* opinion as authority: "I might say at the outset that the Supreme Court of the United States, in *Hirabayashi v. United States*, recited in some detail in the opinion the situation as to dual citizenship of American citizens of Japanese ancestry on the mainland of the United States."[143]

Ennis's presentation bears citation and analysis at some length, as a demonstration of the ways in which the government stigmatized Japanese Americans when it suited their purpose, obscuring the American citizenship of the Nisei and the constitutional rights of the entire group. He started his argument by introducing figures on the population of the territory, broken down by race, to demonstrate the preponderance of Japanese Americans:

> The appraisals of the military situation in this Territory, which is the basis for the contention of the need of the continuation of martial rule in the respect that it still exists here, is based in part upon the nature of the population, and in part upon the relationship of part of the population to the enemy which is being fought in this area of the war
>
> The Court: What is the nature of this population?
>
> Mr. Ennis: Well, your honor, the exhibit will show that the population in large part is of Japanese ancestry, a factor which the Supreme Court of the United States in the *Hirabayashi* case said was a military consideration which the Military Commanders could take into account in formulating the curfew law which was placed in effect at the beginning of the war.
>
> The Court: Well, what is that proportion?
>
> . . .
>
> Mr. Ennis: Well, that proportion of the population which is of the Japanese race is—giving you the figures relative to the last three figures I gave you for the same dates—162,690, 163,478, and 164,268 [estimated census figures, respectively, for the Japanese population of Hawaii on July 1, 1943, January 1, 1944, and July 1, 1944].
>
> The Court: That's Japanese, racially Japanese?
>
> Mr. Ennis: That's right, your Honor, yes.
>
> The Court: It doesn't show how many of them are aliens, or does it: and how many are native born?
>
> Mr. Ennis: This particular exhibit and this part of the evidence does not show, your Honor, the part that are alien and native born, but the testimony will do that, which I am about to produce.

Ennis proceeded to call a pair of witnesses to testify on the dual nationality of the Nisei. One was Lieutenant Andrew S. Wong, a Chinese American Intelligence officer who had formerly been Chief of Hawaii's Bureau of Vital Statistics. Wong reported on Japanese birthrates and called attention to the low rate of prewar requests for expatriation.[144] The other was a Nisei lawyer, Robert K. Murakami, who testified regarding expatriation and Japanese law.[145]

Ennis climaxed this line of questioning by calling General Richardson, who testified that the nature of Hawaii's population was an essential factor in "appraising the possibility" of attack and invasion—no doubt because Richardson had admitted that the possibility of any such invasion was remote, he and Ennis adroitly spoke, not of defending against any actual or imminent attack, but considering whether one could occur:

> It is absolutely necessary that the military commander in this area have some means at his disposal for controlling the movements and activities of people whom he suspects may be potentially disloyal. Of course, my remarks do not apply to the entire Japanese population. But it would be naïve to assume that in a population of 160,000 that we did not find a group of potentially disloyal Japanese. As a matter of fact, we know that some of them are not loyal to America. They have so stated when they have been brought before the internment boards. And I have been forced to put them in internment camps for the security of these islands.[146]

When asked by Ennis whether he suspected any particular subgroup of Japanese, he added:

> There are the aliens, pure and simple; there are the Japanese who were born here and are American citizens; there are other Japanese who have been expatriated; and those have been born here but registered by their parents in the Japanese consulate and upon whom the Japanese government professes to exercise a certain degree of loyalty and allegiance.[147]

Although Anthony argued repeatedly that the whole argument about the Japanese Americans was irrelevant and insisted that the concept of a dual citizen was vague at best, he felt obliged to respond. After cross-examining Murakami on the difficulties that prewar Japanese had in expatriating, he then called Dr. Shunzo Sakanishi, a University of Hawaii professor, to testify on the efforts of local Nisei to facilitate expatriation, including the petition signed by fifty thousand Nisei requesting assistance from the U.S. State Department.[148] Anthony responded to what he called Ennis's "innuendo" against the loyalty of Japanese Americans by introducing into evidence a magazine article published by General Richardson, "Hawaii: Fortress of the Pacific," in which the general stated that those Japanese who were dangerous or potentially dangerous had been interned and those who remained had on "innumerable occasions" proven their loyalty to the United States and had avoided any incidents that would cause trouble.[149]

In addition to arguing that Japanese Americans could not be trusted, the Justice Department put forward a second argument that intersected with the *Hirabayashi* and *Korematsu* cases. Ennis maintained that continued martial law in Hawaii was necessary because military tribunals were the only means by which the army could enforce military orders. When asked why he could not simply use the machinery for military areas put into place under Executive Order 9066, Richardson testified that the kind of powers he would enjoy under Executive Order 9066 were insufficient because his orders would be enforceable through civilian courts, which would be "subject to all sorts of influences, political and otherwise" that posed an intolerable interference with his orders.[150]

In rebuttal, Anthony pointed to the *Hirabayashi* decision as authority for the proposition that a modified military rule was possible and explained that P.L. 502 and P.L. 503, the laws voted by Congress to enforce General DeWitt's removal of West Coast Japanese Americans, provided clear criminal penalties for disobeying military orders. Governor Stainback testified that in January 1944 he had met with Richardson to recommend rescission of martial law, as all of the purposes of martial law could be carried out through the designation of military areas and the enforcement of military orders, as the Supreme Court had upheld in *Hirabayashi*.[151]

On April 13, 1944, Judge Metzger ruled in favor of Duncan. Restating his conviction that habeas corpus had been restored with the reinstatement of civilian government in March 1943, he declared that the military court that had tried Duncan had acted illegally. The verdict was therefore null, irrespective of the defendant's guilt or innocence. Metzger ordered the prisoner released. The day after Metzger issued the writ, Harry E. White also challenged his sentence. White, a civilian with no connection to the military, had been arrested in August 1942 and orally charged with embezzlement by a provost court. The court overruled all challenges by White's lawyer to its jurisdiction, as well as his requests for a jury trial and for time to prepare a defense. Instead, White was speedily convicted and sentenced to five years in prison. When Metzger ordered White liberated, the Army Provost Marshal General's Office immediately undertook an appeal of the *Duncan* and *White* rulings before the Ninth Circuit.

Even as the martial law government pursued its appeal, American victories in the Solomon and Mariana Islands and the push on the Philippines eliminated any conceivable Japanese threat to Hawaii. Under pressure from the civilian territorial government and the Interior Department, the army began to abandon its insistence on special powers. In mid-July 1944, when President Roosevelt visited Hawaii on an inspection tour, General Richardson met with him. The general proposed that martial law be abolished, at least in name. He nevertheless requested a presidential decree that would grant him special emergency powers, especially to control aliens and citizens of Japanese ancestry, in essence retaining the arbitrary authority he possessed.[152] (Richardson meanwhile renounced the self-created title of military governor, but took the grandiloquent title of military commander of the territory.) Roosevelt preferred a full return to civilian rule, though he assured Stimson that martial law could be restored at the least sign of trouble, and the White House asked the Interior Department to draft a proclamation restoring full civilian government. Still, despite the lack of any evident invasion threat and in the face of Ickes's pleas that he act immediately to restore habeas corpus, the president delayed all action, and it was not until October 24, 1944, the day of the Battle of Leyte Gulf and two weeks before the presidential election, that FDR signed an executive order officially ending martial law and dissolving the military tribunals.[153]

Despite the formal revocation of martial law, those already imprisoned by the military tribunals remained in confinement. The Ninth Circuit heard argument on the *Duncan* and *White* appeals during the first days of July 1944. In its appeal, especially in *Duncan*, Justice Department officials repeated the arguments they had used before Metzger, redoubling their appeal to race-based hostility against Japanese Americans. The government brief argued starkly that military tribunals were essential because Hawaii's racially mixed population, with its preponderance of Japanese Americans, hindered impartial justice. In particular, the reintroduction of civilian courts, with trial by jury, would lead to Japanese Americans, including people whose loyalty was suspect, being called for jury duty, since they could not be legally excluded from service.[154]

On November 1, 1944, in a split decision, the appellate court reversed Metzger's ruling, and reinstated the sentences of Duncan and White.[155]

The court found that martial law and military tribunals had been legally imposed, as they insisted that civil courts "had been disabled from functioning" both in 1942 and 1944 (the fact that any disability was entirely a product of military decrees closing the courts, and not their own incapacity, was left unmentioned). The appellate judges explicitly endorsed the army's contention that martial law was necessary to enforce military orders and to control Japanese Americans, who could be expected to be disloyal on racial grounds:

> Governmental and military problems alike were complicated by the presence in the Territory of tens of thousands of citizens of Japanese ancestry besides large numbers of aliens of the same race. Obviously the presence of so many inhabitants of doubtful loyalty posed a continuing threat to the public security. Among these people the personnel of clandestine landing parties might mingle freely, without detection. Thus was afforded ideal cover for the activities of the saboteur and the spy. . . . To function in criminal matters the civilian courts must assemble juries; and citizens of Japanese extraction could not lawfully be excluded from jury panels on the score of race—even in cases of offenses involving the military security of the Territory. Indeed the mere assembling of juries and the carrying on of protracted criminal trials might well constitute an invitation to disorder as well as interference with the vital business of the moment.[156]

The Ninth Circuit's ruling, which came as a surprise to all of the parties, left the status of those convicted by the military tribunals uncertain. In search of a final resolution, Anthony, joined by the ACLU, petitioned for review by the U.S. Supreme Court, which in February 1945 agreed to hear the cases (which had by then been consolidated under the caption *Duncan v. Kahanamoku*—the famous surfing champion Duke Kahanamoku, as county sheriff, serving as official respondent). Osmond Fraenkel, a distinguished ACLU lawyer, agreed to represent White, while Garner Anthony represented Duncan and Edward Ennis again appeared on behalf of the military[157]. Even though Duncan and White were not Japanese, the Court's agreement to hear their cases attracted widespread attention because of the evident similarities between the Hawaii martial law cases and the "Japanese internment" cases of *Hirabayashi* and *Korematsu*. (Indeed, in a striking coincidence, on the very same day that the Court agreed to take the Hawaiian cases, it announced that it had denied a petition for rehearing of *Korematsu*.)[158] Opponents of the preceding decisions hoped that the Hawaii cases would lead to a reversal of the earlier cases, while the army may have expected that its actions would be upheld under similar provisions.

In the event, the cases were not argued until December 7, 1945, the fourth anniversary of the Pearl Harbor attack. By that time, there had been some shifts on the Court, as two *Korematsu* dissenters were absent. Justice Robert Jackson was away on leave during the fall of 1945 as prosecutor in the Nuremberg trials, leaving the Court reduced to eight members. Meanwhile, a new justice, Harold Burton, had been appointed to replace the retiring Owen Roberts.[159] Even more important, President Roosevelt had died and World War II had ended; as a result, the case would no longer be tried in a wartime atmosphere of pressure for unity and obedience to leadership.

On February 25, 1946, the Supreme Court announced its decision, striking down the convictions of Duncan and White by a 6–2 margin. Although the majority opinion was written by Hugo Black, author of the *Korematsu* opinion, it more resembled the Court's opinion in *Endo*. As in the case of Mitsuye Endo, the Court upheld an application for a writ of habeas corpus on narrow grounds. In *Duncan*, the Court ruled that the Organic Act of Hawaii had not contemplated the supplanting of all civilian laws under martial law and the convening of Military tribunals, and that Congress had not expressly authorized such actions.[160] Justice Black concluded his opinion with a historical disquisition on liberty, in pointed opposition to the army's authoritarian rule in Hawaii: "Our system of government clearly is the antithesis of total military rule and the founders of this country are not likely to have contemplated complete military dominance within the limits of a Territory made part of this country and not recently taken from an enemy. They were opposed to governments that placed in the hands of one man the power to make, interpret and enforce the laws."[161]

Despite the ringing tones of Black's opinion, the failure of the Court to deal squarely with the unjust confinement of American citizens, and the close relation of martial law to the Japanese American presence, drew a fiery concurrence by Justice Frank Murphy. As in his dissenting opinion in *Korematsu* and his previous concurrence in *Endo*, Murphy reserved his most powerful language for the denunciation of bigotry against Japanese Americans. In particular, Murphy savaged the government's contention that military tribunals that denied procedural rights to all citizens were essential to avert the menace to security posed by the presence of ethnic Japanese jurors:

> There was thus no security reason for excluding [Japanese-Americans] from juries, even making the false assumption that it was impossible to separate the loyal from the disloyal. And if there were problems arising from the use of racially mixed juries, elimination of all jury trials was hardly a reasonable or sensible answer to those problems. Especially deplorable, however, is this use of the iniquitous doctrine of racism to justify the imposition of military trials. Racism has no place whatever in our civilization. The Constitution as well as the conscience of mankind disclaims its use for any purpose, military or otherwise. It can only result, as it does in this instance, in striking down individual rights and in aggravating rather than solving the problems toward which it is directed. It renders impotent the ideal of the dignity of the human personality, destroying something of what is noble in our way of life. We must therefore reject it completely whenever it arises in the course of a legal proceeding.[162]

Murphy also rebuffed the army's contention that a civilian court could not be relied on to try violations of military orders by noting that, beyond the fact that there was no way to prove this, inasmuch as the martial law regime had ordered courts not to assume such jurisdiction, Congress had enacted laws providing civilian enforcement and penalties for violating military orders.[163]

By the time the *Duncan* ruling was announced, there were only a handful of prisoners convicted by military courts remaining in Hawaii, and they were freed afterwards. The decision—like the history of martial law in general—attracted comparatively little attention or citation among scholars of civil liberties in succeeding decades: the creation of military tribunals by the Bush administration in the years after 2001 to classify both alien nationals and U.S. citizens (in the case of José Padilla) declared "enemy combatants," and to place them in indefinite confinement at Guantanamo Bay, does not seem to have ushered in a movement for a new look at the *Duncan* decision. It is not clear whether this is because the ruling was not issued until after the conduct it examined was finished, or because of its cautious approach to the question of military tribunals.[164] Yale University law professor Eugene Rostow, who had denounced the removal of Japanese Americans as "our worst wartime mistake" and had written an influential critique of the Court's reasoning in the *Korematsu* case, praised the decision but complained that even though the *Duncan* decision represented a full repudiation of the logic the Supreme Court had earlier accepted in *Korematsu*, the Supreme Court had not taken advantage of the opportunity to reverse itself openly.[165] Nor did the *Duncan* case lead to a re-examination of martial law, or to successful damage suits against the military officials responsible, although the Justice Department did a confidential internal investigation. In January 1946, as *Duncan* was being decided, Senator Pat McCarran introduced a resolution for a congressional investigation into the workings of martial law, but it was killed by the audit and control committee.

CONCLUSION

Japanese Americans, despite their small numbers, succeeded in altering the nation's social and political landscape during World War II. The exploits of Nisei combat units threw into sharp relief the patriotism and American faith of the Nisei. As President Harry Truman told the veterans of the 442nd Regimental Combat Team in 1946 when he received them at the White House, "You fought not only the enemy, but you fought prejudice—and you have won."[166] The wartime Japanese American experience also clearly demonstrates the moral and symbolic value of military service to claims for citizenship. The presence of Nisei in uniform, and their outstanding combat record, provided the JACL and other advocates for Japanese Americans a compelling argument for fair treatment of the entire group. Government leaders from President Roosevelt and Secretary of War Stimson down agreed that the "Japanese-Hawaiians," in particular, formed one of the most outstanding units in the army, and they readily admitted that their interest in closing the camps and in releasing Japanese Americans was actuated in large part by the efforts of the soldiers. Japanese Canadians would encounter more intensive discrimination and official restrictions than their southern neighbors in the early postwar years, in part because they did not have the same opportunity to demonstrate their patriotism.

Japanese Americans likewise contributed to shaping American law during this period. The efforts of Nisei to protest arbitrary evacuation and confinement led to a set of landmark cases testing the limits of civil liberties and the authority of the federal government in time of war. In contrast, although Japanese Canadians, as noted, joined together to contest forced property sales, they had no means of challenging their removal in the courts. At the same time, Japanese Americans in Hawaii were brought to bar symbolically, as proxies in the larger struggle for the constitutional rights of civilians of all groups against (prolonged) arbitrary government. The Justice Department, whose leaders had opposed mass incarceration, sought to prop up military rule by taking refuge in the very sort of racist falsehoods and stereotypes they had rightly deplored in the hands of the Western Defense Command.

The U.S. Supreme Court, which had the task of final determination of these cases, proved a weak reed in support of equality under law. Using tortured logic (and on the basis of tainted evidence), it justified race-based classifications in the name of national security in the *Hirabayashi* and *Korematsu* cases. Even in the *Endo* and *Duncan* cases, where the Court struck down arbitrary detention of American citizens, the majority ducked the larger constitutional issues caused by mass confinement and military rule. Nevertheless, the *Duncan* decision undercut, if only symbolically, the logic of military supremacy on which the confinement of Japanese Americans was built, while the *Endo* decision would have great consequences in opening the doors of the camps, for confined Japanese Americans to return to their homes and resume their free existence.

Yet such victories for Japanese Americans came at a disproportionately high price, first in the horrific casualty rate among Nisei soldiers forced to prove their loyalty, and then in the lasting divisions that the issue of military service marked within the community. To begin with, the enormous difference between the enthusiastic response to recruitment of volunteers by Nisei in Hawaii, where they were more accepted in mainstream society, and those from the West Coast, who had been locked up in camps, pointed up the hidden price both Japanese Americans and the rest of the nation paid for the mass incarceration policy. Later, the contradiction between the government's undemocratic treatment of Japanese Americans and its policy of military conscription heightened the aggrieved feelings of many in the camps. It inspired a brave group of activists, the draft resisters, to insist on restoration of their constitutional rights before they would risk their lives in combat, and to persevere in the face of the consequences, including prison and public obloquy.

Finally, all Americans in Hawaii suffered heavily from the exaggerated official and popular fears of Japanese Americans. In order to defend against threats of attack and subversion, the Army established a military

dictatorship after Pearl Harbor, on the assurance that it could be liquidated within weeks, but did not restore full civilian rule for nearly three
years. The military regime was marked by official censorship, stringent
labor regulations, and denial of habeas corpus. Worst of all, even though
the civilian courts were able to judge civil cases, the "Military Governor"
imposed a system of military tribunals to try criminal cases, courts that
offered a travesty of justice. The Army was able to hold on to power long
after there was any realistic invasion threat and to legitimize all these fundamentally tyrannical institutions by brandishing the Japanese American
"menace." The durability and popularity of the military dictatorship are
a frightening precedent for the survival of American institutions in time
of war and offer a discouraging message about the capacity of civilian
governors to roll back limitations on democratic rights, even when there
is no justification for them. Futhermore, although the scope of federal
authority in states differs from that in territories, the events in Hawaii
demonstrate how determined government officials were to control Japanese Americans, even without hard evidence of threats to security. In
the prevailing climate of uncertainty, if Issei and Nisei on the mainland
had not been singled out for exclusion or if they had resisted in sufficient
numbers, the White House might well have imposed some form of martial law on the entire West Coast, as California gubernatorial candidate
Earl Warren advocated during the fall of 1942 in his defense of the Army's
conduct in Hawaii (and as Franklin Roosevelt contemplated in early 1943
when his advisers feared that the Supreme Court would overturn Executive Order 9066). The sacrifice of the Issei and Nisei in accepting removal
may thus perhaps be said to have preserved the fundamental liberties of
other West Coast Americans.

[6] THE END OF CONFINEMENT AND THE POSTWAR READJUSTMENT OF ISSEI AND NISEI

ALTHOUGH THE SUPREME COURT'S *ENDO* DECISION IN DECEMBER 1944 provided the essential legal support (and political cover) for the opening of the WRA camps and unrestricted release of their inmates, it came at the end of a long process of internal conflict and negotiation within the executive branch, one that mirrored in many respects the battle over revoking martial law in Hawaii. Certainly, from the time in early 1943 that the War Department announced the recruitment of Nisei soldiers and the government established a joint board to examine the loyalty of individuals, it could no longer logically justify a blanket exclusion policy for Japanese Americans who had been approved. The army's dilemma became increasingly awkward during 1943 and 1944, as the prospect of a Japanese invasion of the Pacific Coast grew increasingly remote, and civilian authorities within the government, beginning with the WRA and eventually including the Interior Department, lobbied energetically for the reopening of the Pacific Coast to the Japanese Americans.

Yet the White House and the War Department were reluctant to take any visible steps to reopen the West Coast during these two years. First, as previously noted, by demonstrating that any danger to security was controllable, such a policy might weaken the army's position against the legal challenges to Executive Order 9066 that were then working their way through the courts. Also, General DeWitt refused to alter or withdraw his exclusion orders. DeWitt was adamant that Japanese Americans continued to pose a menace, and that it was impossible to determine their loyalty. He refused to let even token numbers of Japanese Americans, such as families of soldiers, enter the excluded zone, and only following pressure from his superiors (and under strong protest) did he even permit Nisei soldiers on furlough into the area. In April 1943 DeWitt publicly testified before a House committee that he did not agree that any Japanese Americans should be permitted on the West Coast. "I don't want any of them there. They are a dangerous element. . . . I am opposing [return] with every proper means at my disposal."[1] During a press conference afterward, DeWitt (in what he believed was an off-the-record remark) summarized his attitude: "A Jap's a Jap." The remark was immediately and widely reported, and it sent shock waves through the government and nation.[2] DeWitt's obstructionism and public defiance of War Department policy led to calls within the government for his transfer.

Meanwhile, West Coast political leaders and a solid phalanx of public opinion remained vehemently opposed to any resettlement by Japanese Americans. As California Governor Earl Warren stated at a governors' conference in mid-1943, "We don't propose to have the Japs back in California during this war if there is any legal means of preventing it."[3] In June 1943 a subcommittee of the House Un-American Activities Committee, supposedly investigating "un-American activities in the Japanese War Relocation centers," held public hearings in Los Angeles. The city was heavy with racial and ethnic tension. That same week, its neighborhoods had exploded into the so-called zoot suit riots, in which mobs of white servicemen violently attacked young Mexican Americans and African Americans wearing zoot suits. The committee hearings offered church groups and nativist organizations such as the American Legion a privileged platform to express racial hostility to Japanese Americans and campaign for their permanent exclusion from the state. The committee drew from the testimony in filing its biased report on Japanese Americans.[4]

Dillon Myer exposed the War Department's own internal dilemma on the lifting of exclusion in March 1943 when he wrote McCloy to ask whether there was any "objection" to permitting loyal Japanese Americans to return home. Myer considered the existing "leave clearance" system unjust, and he proposed immediately lifting all exclusion on those not deemed disloyal, or at least allowing gradual return to categories of inmates to the West Coast, even as the WRA allowed Japanese Americans to relocate without restriction in the rest of the country and encouraged them to disperse.[5] McCloy stated to Bendetsen his conclusion that there was in fact no longer any military necessity for continued exclusion, but he added that the War Department would not "of its own motion" take any action to lift it. McCloy stated that he was preparing a response to the WRA stating that there was such an "objection." He confessed that he did not actually believe in this position but added that "it was largely based on an extreme loss of patience with the WRA."[6] In the event, as noted, the response to Myer, issued under Secretary Stimson's signature, cleverly sidetracked debate over exclusion by focusing on the question of segregation. The question of return therefore hung in the air for several months, while the WRA established a separate segregation facility at Tule Lake and partitioned the inmates.

Once the segregation was accomplished, the next push toward lifting exclusion began, this time with the imprimatur of President Roosevelt. In July 1943 a group of pro-administration members of Congress sponsored passage of a resolution by the Senate requesting the issuance of a report on Japanese American segregation and relocation. Their goal was to forestall a critical report on the WRA from Senator Albert Chandler's Millitary Affairs Committee, which had launched an investigation of the camps, and to rebut allegations by conservative newspapers and members of the House Un-American Activities Committee of "coddling" of the inmates. The final report, issued in September 1943 in the name of James Byrnes, director of the Office of War Mobilization (himself a longtime senator), described conditions in the camps and trumpeted the success of the segregation program.[7] In a transmittal letter (drafted under McCloy's supervision), President Roosevelt put West Coast whites on notice that, with segregation of the "disloyal" accomplished, exclusion of loyal citizens could not be maintained indefinitely: "We shall restore to the loyal evacuees the right to return to the evacuated areas as soon as the military situation will make such restoration feasible. Americans of Japanese ancestry, like those of many other ancestries, have shown that they can, and want to, accept our institutions and work loyally with the rest of us, making their own valuable contribution to the national health and well-being."[8]

Even as the president's letter was issued, General DeWitt and Colonel Bendetsen were removed from the Western Defense Command via face-saving promotions. To replace them, the War Department chose General Delos Emmons, the former Hawaiian commander who had resisted pressure from the White House for mass confinement of Japanese Americans in the territory during 1942. Soon after, on November 1, 1943, the War Department announced that, because of American advances in the Pacific, the West Coast was no longer an active theater of operations. In the wake of these events, the way seemed paved for the final lifting of exclusion and the full-scale opening of the camps.

Yet the policy remained in effect for more than a year afterward. A number of causes conspired to delay it, notably the disturbances at Tule

Lake. Tabloid newspapers, relying on distorted accounts, ran lurid stories of the "Tule Lake Riot" and spread tales that WRA officials had been abducted. West Coast political leaders and nativist groups, who hoped to prevent any of the inmates from returning to their homes, quickly seized on the events as proof that no Japanese American could be trusted. In December 1943 the *Los Angeles Times* ran a "poll" called "the Jap questionnaire." Timed for release on the second anniversary of Pearl Harbor and composed of slanted questions that identified Japanese Americans with the Japanese enemy, the poll revealed that readers "voted" by a 90 percent majority to exclude all Japanese Americans from the West Coast, and by smaller majorities to deport all Issei and Nisei to Japan and thereafter to bar all Japanese immigration.[9] Ironically, even though the segregation center had been created specifically to confine those whom the government deemed "disloyal," so that the other, "loyal" inmates could be freed from their influence and resettled, the reports of the Tule Lake disturbances created a political storm against both the Nisei at large and the WRA that put the Roosevelt administration on the defensive and froze all consideration of changes in the status quo. Emmons and McCloy agreed that opening the West Coast in such a climate—irrespective of the lack of military necessity for exclusion—was unthinkable.[10] Even the imposition of the draft on Nisei in January 1944 failed to lead to any consequent step-up in release of other inmates.

Biddle grasped that the problem was essentially one of public relations and political cover. In addition to designing the citizenship renunciation bill to control disloyal inmates, he offered in late 1943 to have the Justice Department take over Tule Lake, in order to make clear to public opinion the distinction between "loyal" and "disloyal," or even to absorb the entire WRA to provide it better political protection. However, following detailed negotiations by Byrnes and Harold Smith, director of the Bureau of the Budget, Roosevelt ultimately decided to place the WRA under the jurisdiction of the Interior Department (Harold Smith persuaded Interior Secretary Harold Ickes to retain Dillon Myer, despite the criticism he had faced). Once the transfer was accomplished in February 1944, Ickes and Undersecretary Abe Fortas then took some weeks to familiarize themselves with the situation of Japanese Americans. After working with Myer to design plans for the reopening of the West Coast, they began campaigning within the government to have exclusion lifted promptly. Ickes argued that continued confinement of Japanese Americans in camps in the absence of any military necessity was immoral and unhealthy, and that the continued exclusion of the Nikkei from the West Coast stigmatized the entire group, with the result that continued resettlement of individuals elsewhere had grown increasingly difficult. Ickes and Fortas gradually won the consent of Stimson and McCloy for the rapid lifting of exclusion, since there was no longer any national security imperative for keeping the Japanese American confined. Still, the War Department chiefs (and to a lesser extent Attorney General Biddle) remained concerned about defusing violent West Coast opposition to return, particularly following reports during early 1944 of Japanese atrocities in the Philippines.

The matter of opening the camps was brought up by Ickes at the cabinet meeting of May 26, 1944. However, President Roosevelt vetoed the immediate release of the inmates. Despite his earlier pledge to Congress to expedite return, FDR, caught up with election-year politics and fearful of public disturbances, decided that presence of Japanese Americans on the West Coast would arouse too much conflict, and he refused to permit even a gradual and small-scale return policy until after the November election. Even more strongly than his advisors, he believed that dispersion of Japanese Americans outside the West Coast—a few families in each county of the nation—was both feasible and desirable, and he preferred to continue the leave clearance program to maximize "internal quiet."[11] Roosevelt's order to delay lifting exclusion thus meant that tens of thousands of people remained confined behind barbed wire for an additional six months or more, even though government officials privately agreed that they posed no danger to security. The War Department interpreted the president's orders as a request for continuation of the status quo. Thus, although small numbers of Japanese Americans from selected categories—such as families of soldiers—were permitted to move back to their West Coast homes during the following months, there was no public announcement that exclusion was being modified. As a result, Japanese Americans throughout the country remained stigmatized, and resettlement even outside the West Coast stalled.

In October 1944 the Supreme Court heard arguments in the *Korematsu* and *Endo* cases, and on November 7 President Roosevelt was elected to a record fourth term of office. A few days later he granted his advisors authorization to begin planning the lifting of exclusion, on the assumption that the justices would rule against the government and that with the election season over it was now safe to think of shutting down the camps.[12] In the end, Roosevelt allowed first the army, then the Supreme Court, to absorb the responsibility for the action. Secretary of War Stimson prepared a public announcement that the army was lifting mass exclusion of its own volition by the beginning of the new year. The proclamation ending exclusion was issued by the new Western Defense commander, General Henry Pratt, on Sunday, December 17, 1944, the day before the Supreme Court announced its *Endo* decision. (One of the justices—most likely Felix Frankfurter—presumably tipped off the War Department that a decision was about to be issued so that the army could anticipate it). The West Coast mass exclusion orders were ordered officially lifted effective January 2, 1945.

Once the decision to open the camps was made, government officials struggled to limit the number of Japanese Americans returning to the West Coast. WRA officials admitted that they had no legal right to prevent inmates from resettling in their home region, but nevertheless pushed them strongly to relocate elsewhere. Dillon Myer, in hopes of inspiring an orderly flow of migrants, continued the policy of granting an allowance of twenty-five dollars and job and housing assistance to all inmates resettling outside the excluded area. However, he required those who wished financial assistance for a return to the West Coast to submit detailed relocation plans, which the WRA deliberately took its time processing in order to slow the rate of return.[13] Harold Ickes warned that inmates would be better off remaining outside the West Coast (and was embarrassed when his remarks were cited in public as support for West Coast nativists).

Meanwhile, the Western Defense Command, still hesitant to trust Japanese Americans, proposed to undertake a new set of loyalty hearings for those seeking to re-enter the West Coast excluded zone. The WRA protested that such hearings would duplicate its own efforts and sow public doubt about the accuracy of the screening of inmates that had already taken place. The army then agreed that it would issue a series of individual exclusion orders (of doubtful constitutionality) to Japanese Americans in Tule Lake and those others whose loyalty it suspected. The Western Defense Command agreed to a maximum of ten thousand exclusion orders. The army also issued a set of confidential orders to keep some individual inmates (presumably those whose loyalty remained suspect) confined to camp.

There was an almost immediate legal challenge to the individual exclusion policy by George Ochikubo, a California-born dentist. His case was not entirely new. Ochikubo, who had been an outspoken opponent of government policy during the time he was confined at the Topaz camp in 1942 and 1943, had been granted a leave permit by the WRA in late 1943, over the opposition of joint board members who considered him a troublemaker. Ochikubo, however, declined to resettle alone outside the West Coast—instead he hoped to return home with his wife and children. Thus, in mid-July 1944 ACLU lawyer A. L. Wirin brought suit on behalf of Ochikubo and two other Nisei plaintiffs in Los Angeles Superior Court, seeking an injunction preventing the Western Defense Command from continuing to enforce the exclusion of Japanese Americans from the West Coast.

The case threw the army and the Justice Department into a dilemma. They felt unable to defend convincingly the ban on Japanese Americans on grounds of national security or invasion threats. However, in the wake of the president's orders maintaining exclusion until after the November election, and with the *Korematsu* case pending, they sought to avoid any hearing on the merits of the policy. Instead, to gain time they applied to have the case moved from state to federal court. Wirin then applied in federal court for a preliminary injunction preventing the federal government from enforcing its exclusion order on Ochikubo. Edward Ennis (freshly returned after arguing the *Duncan* appeal in San Francisco) and his deputy John Burling objected to stalling and proposed mooting the case by admitting Ochikubo back to the excluded area. The Western Defense Command declined on the grounds that Ochikubo posed a potential danger. Instead, in early September, shortly before Ochikubo's case was to be heard, the army rapidly devised new procedures for individual exclusion orders and drafted a set of standards and guidelines for judging loyalty. After convening a special hearing board, they summoned Ochikubo and his lawyers to testify, immediately ruled that he posed a danger to national security, and imposed an individual exclusion order barring him from the West Coast. A federal judge, citing the hearing, denied Wirin's request for a preliminary injunction, but the challenge to the legality of individual exclusion orders remained open.[14]

The Ochikubo case came up for a full hearing in federal court at the end of February 1945. By then the United States had retaken the Philippines and invaded Iwo Jima, Japan's naval and air forces were all but obliterated, and the threat of large-scale Japanese invasion had been largely removed. Still, as in the *Duncan* case, army officers did their best to conjure up the specter of submarine attacks and commando raids in order to justify a threat of Japanese American sabotage and assistance to the enemy—they even insisted, with rather wild logic, that the virtual destruction of Tokyo's war machine actually increased the possibility of suicide raids on California, as a face-saving maneuver by the defeated enemy. Refusing requests by both Ochikubo's lawyers and the judge that they clarify the exact basis on which they determined that a given individual composed a security risk, the army officers concluded, in essence, by describing their standards (falsely) as varied and unknowable and stressing the necessity for deference to military judgment.[15] On June 1, 1945, federal judge Pierson M. Hall disposed of the case, but without resolving the underlying issue. He found, on the one hand, that the Western Defense commander had no authority to exclude any Japanese American from the West Coast, but meawhile ruled that the army could still have a U.S. attorney arrest those who entered the excluded zone. The army then appealed the judgment to the Ninth Circuit.[16] In the end, Ochikubo and the others excluded by individual order were denied legal permission to return home until August 1945, when the surrender of Japan brought about the cancellation of all exclusion orders and mooted the case.

THE WRA PUSH TO CLOSE THE CAMPS

Meanwhile, the preparations for mass return to the West Coast started in earnest during 1945. The WRA announced in mid-January that it would close the eight remaining camps other than Tule Lake (Jerome having already closed in mid-1944) by the end of the year. The WRA's decision to speed closing of the camps left the inmates and their supporters bewildered and outraged. Although they agreed with WRA leaders that life in confinement was difficult and demoralizing, critics asserted that the federal government could not simply throw the inmates out of camp—it had a responsibility to provide sufficient funding for housing and services to aid the former inmates in reintegrating themselves into life outside. Without large-scale assistance, Japanese Americans, especially the older Issei who had lost their possessions during evacuation, could not be expected to leave camp and fend for themselves amid white hostility and threats of violence. Fair Play and religious groups that had long supported Japanese Americans (most often, ironically, by calling for the closing of the camps) now called for the WRA to reconsider its decision.

The WRA's policy caused inmates in the different centers to band together. Delegates from the different camps pooled their money to convene an All Center Conference, which met in Salt Lake City from February 18 to February 24, 1945. They drew up a petition and a list of twenty-one detailed recommendations for the WRA. The recommendations included the creation of special government agencies to provide grants or loans for those requiring funds; long-term loans to permit inmates to reestablish their prewar farms and businesses; the establishment of relocation agencies staffed by Japanese Americans; government transportation of individual inmates' property from the camps to their new homes; effort by the WRA to recover properties lost by Japanese Americans as a result of evacuation; establishment of hostels and old-age homes to house returnees; aid for students; and provisions to permit those who failed to relocate successfully to return to camp. Dillon Myer responded to all suggestions by insisting that the rapid winding up of the camps was imperative, and that the care and reestablishment of the Japanese Americans would be primarily a responsibility of local welfare agencies, although the WRA and other federal agencies might assist.[17]

With the end of exclusion and the opening up of the camps, the inmates began departing at an accelerated pace. The WRA responded by successively cutting all but essential services within the camps as the year 1945 went on. All schools were closed after the end of the spring 1945 term, and cooperatives were scaled back during the summer. Japan's surrender in August 1945 further hastened the process of exit from the camps. By the fall of 1945 few inmates were left except the older people, including Issei bachelors who had nowhere to go, plus some families with small children. WRA officials pressed these last inmates to depart and at the end of the year finally resorted to rounding up the handful of remaining inmates and transporting them forcibly back to their original points of departure. At Tule Lake, where inmates remained confined through the end of the war, a process of emptying began afterward, until the high-security camp closed its doors in March 1946.

RESETTLEMENT AND RETURN TO THE WEST COAST

As they left camp, Japanese Americans were faced with difficult decisions over where to go and how to remake their lives. A significant number of inmates, disgusted by endemic prejudice and stripped of their belongings in the process of removal, chose to relocate outside the Pacific Coast. In some cases, they settled in areas surrounding the camps—a group of chick sexors established themselves in Arkansas and other areas of the rural South. However, in most cases they moved into communities where there was already a significant Japanese American resettler colony and they had relatives or friends to provide shelter and serve as supporters and resources. Chicago, which had already become the destination of choice among wartime resettlers, swelled with the new arrivals. Its Japanese population reached an estimated twelve thousand during 1946–47, and as many as twenty-two thousand lived there at some point. Other cities, including Cleveland, Detroit, Philadelphia, and Denver, also continued to welcome new migrants. New York not only continued to welcome migrants but was a port of entry, and sometimes settlement, for returning Nisei GIs. As the WRA wound up its services in late 1945, Japanese communities organized nonprofit organizations such as the Chicago Resettlers Committee and the Greater New York Committee for Japanese Americans to fill the gap. The JACL (which remained based in Salt Lake City through 1952) organized chapters in a number of eastern and midwestern cities to provide assistance to the newcomers. The JACL organ *Pacific Citizen* continued regular publication, as did bilingual vernacular newspapers such the *Colorado Times* and the *Utah Nippo*. They were soon joined by a series of new publications outside the West Coast, including the newspapers *Chicago Shimpo*, *Hokubei Shimpo*, and *Nisei Weekender*, as well as a short-lived monthly photomagazine, *Nisei Vue* (which would be supplanted by another periodical, *Scene*).

Meanwhile, despite the efforts of the WRA and other agencies to steer the former inmates away from the West Coast, most of those who left camp chose to return to their previous home states as soon as it was possible to do so. A significant fraction of Japanese Americans still had farms or businesses on the West Coast, and they remained attached to the area they knew. Older Issei and Nisei hoped to re-establish their former family connections and community ties. Even young Nisei who lacked such assets or interests felt a responsibility to return in order to care for their elders. The returnees were soon joined by thousands of others who had resettled elsewhere during the war, but who now wished to move back to California or the other Pacific Coast states. By early 1946 approximately half of the former inmate population was residing in the areas comprising the old excluded zone.[18]

Like their counterparts further east, Japanese Americans on the West Coast mobilized to offer what help they could to aid fellow returnees. Community organizations, veterans' groups, and churches resumed operations, and the JACL set up chapters in areas with large Nisei populations. A handful of prewar Japanese newspapers, notably *Rafu Shimpo* in Los Angeles and San Francisco's *Nichi Bei* (retitled *Nichi Bei Times*), returned to print—*Kashu Mainichi* continued its Japanese edition but abandoned its English page—while a new group of Nisei journals saw the day, including the *Northwest Times* in Seattle and *Crossroads* in Los Angeles. Local Fair Play Committees mobilized to welcome back Japanese Americans and provide them aid in finding shelter and employment.[19] West Coast WRA offices, in addition to bringing together private agencies, intervened with newspapers, meditated conflicts, and publicized discrimination. In historian Kevin Leonard's words, not since the Freedman's Bureau had any government agency so powerfully and comprehensively assisted minority citizens.[20] Nevertheless, liberal groups and Japanese Americans complained, with considerable justice, that the WRA was more concerned with moving Japanese Americans out of camp and winding down its operations than with bringing real opportunity to Japanese Americans.

In any case, the returnees faced considerable difficulties. An estimated 75 percent of Japanese Americans who had been removed from the West Coast lost all their property, and almost everybody lost something. Many inmates had stored their property in churches or warehouses and returned to discover that they had been pillaged or vandalized. Others who had entrusted their farms or possessions to non-Japanese "friends" discovered that the property had been badly kept or damaged, and there were numerous cases of tax delinquency, which the returnees had to go to great trouble to resolve. In some cases, unscrupulous whites took advantage of the anti-Japanese American climate to claim property left in their custody, remain on housing and farms they had been assigned to watch, or keep to themselves the profits they had made during the war. Mary Yogawa Saito recalled:

My family had been evacuated from Tacoma, Washington. We sold our dry cleaning business for a mere $600 with the stipulation in the sales contract that we could reclaim our business for the same price after the war concluded. . . . Arriving [back] in Tacoma, I discovered that our buyers had betrayed our agreement by selling the business and leaving the city without a forwarding address. The new owners were hostile and uncommunicative. To make a long story short, with little money and very little faith in the American justice system, I tore up the sales contract in frustration.[21]

In conjunction with the loss of their goods, the returnees experienced widespread economic discrimination. Issei who had built prosperous prewar businesses were unable to secure credit to reopen their shops or were refused the necessary licenses by state authorities and forced to start from scratch as domestics, gardeners and agricultural laborers. Countless Nisei, irrespective of their training and qualifications, were relegated to low-status manual labor jobs. Many stores refused, not just to hire Nisei, but even to serve Japanese American customers.

It was also difficult for returnees to secure proper housing amid postwar shortages. The prewar Little Tokyos had been appropriated to house some of the 250,000 African American war workers who moved to the West Coast during the war. Even as black groups organized welcomes for returning Japanese Americans, returnees made efforts to find alternative housing so as not to force their tenants to relocate immediately.[22] Unable to afford down payments and hemmed in by restrictive covenants, many returnees were forced into rundown lodgings in slum areas, or were housed by the WRA in temporary trailer parks, such as one in Winona, California. (A group of some 500 returnees in Los Angeles who found shelter in a trailer park in Burbank in late 1945 were evicted in mid-1947 when the site was sold).[23] There was widespread hostility to the former inmates among locals. One central valley Nisei later recalled being visited by a group of white vigilantes: "We talked until nearly midnight. They wanted me to promise to go, and I refused. There was not one that I knew, and I knew everyone that lives for miles around. I told them I had a brother . . . fighting in Italy. I told them he fought for the right of his people to live as Americans. I told them he hadn't turned tail when the going was tough, and that I wasn't going to either. When they left, I shook hands with all of them. None of them have been back."[24]

There were sporadic outbreaks of terror—thirty-seven cases of violence against the returnees were reported, including shots fired into the homes of farmers, plus torching of housing and farm equipment.[25] In the only case to be prosecuted, that of three Auburn, California, whites who confessed to burning down Sumio Doi's barn, the defendants were acquitted after their attorney told the jury, "This is a white man's country."[26] The incidents attracted national outrage. Harold Ickes denounced the "planned terrorism by hoodlums" who were practicing "Nazi storm-trooper tactics" in an attempt to "set up an economic beachhead on the property of the evacuees."[27]

Official attitudes on the West Coast were uneven. California Governor Earl Warren, reversing his previous attitude of outspoken hostility to Japanese Americans, publicly urged Californians to welcome the returnees, and Attorney General Robert Kenny pledged to protect their civil rights. Los Angeles Mayor Fletcher Bowron, who had been one of the leading instigators of evacuation, personally met and greeted groups of returnees at Union Station.[28] Nevertheless, West Coast states used legislative means to discourage resettlement. Oregon, which had no alien land legislation on its books in the prewar era, voted a new and restrictive law. California, which in 1943 had passed for the first time a law barring "Japanese aliens" from obtaining fishing licenses, amended it in 1945 to bar "aliens ineligible to citizenship," a transparent ploy. Meanwhile, the state legislature voted to fund escheat suits to seize Nisei-owned land purchased by Issei and managed in their capacity as legal guardians, on the grounds that such purchases violated the state Alien Land Act. In all, fifty-nine escheat suits were brought by the state of California in the four years after 1943, compared to fourteen in the previous thirty years. Japanese Americans were forced to pay enormous sums (usually half the assessed value of the land) to quiet title, while the threat of seizures made property insurance and mortgages difficult and expensive to acquire. It was not until 1948, when the Supreme Court struck down enforcement of the Alien Land Act in *Oyama v. California* and overturned the discriminatory fishing license act in *Takahashi v. California Fish and Game Commission*, that this state-sponsored harassment ceased.[29]

DEPORTATION

The process of clearing the camps of the inmates adjudged "loyal" after the Supreme Court's *Endo* decision was mirrored in distorted fashion by the treatment of the "disloyal" inmates in Tule Lake. Even after the Court issued its ruling and the West Coast reopened to Japanese Americans, the "no-no boys" and those who had requested repatriation remained barred from release. On the contrary, the opening of the West Coast unleashed a wave of panic among the already beleaguered Nisei at Tule Lake. Most did not wish to be sent out of camp to start anew in a hostile nation with no resources. In particular, draft-age males—who had answered "no-no" in disproportionate numbers in order to avoid military service—now feared being conscripted, based on their American citizenship, into the army of the nation that had imprisoned them. Many Nisei also feared that their parents would be deported once the war was over, and that they would be forever separated from their families. Army representatives guaranteed that if the Nisei at Tule Lake would renounce their citizenship, using the denationalization law the Justice Department had pushed through the previous year, they could remain untouched in camp until the end of the war. These assurances, plus pressure from parents who faced deportation to keep families united, and large-scale harassment from the pro-Japanese "resegregant" faction, incited some five thousand Nisei, approximately 70 percent of the Tule Lake Nisei population, to formally renounce their American citizenship during the first months of 1945. Ironically, the government then began releasing various Issei considered nondangerous from Tule Lake, while keeping under close guard the Nisei who had renounced their citizenship to stay with their families.[30]

With the end of the Pacific War in August 1945, the Nisei at Tule Lake who had retained their American citizenship became eligible for release. Meanwhile, the "renunciants" discovered that surrendering their citizenship left them effectively stateless and vulnerable. In October 1945 the Justice Department announced that it would begin deportation. Unwilling to be sent to an exhausted Japan that was a foreign land to them, thousands of Nisei, claiming that their renunciations were obtained under duress, petitioned to withdraw their requests for deportation and get back their citizenship. However, the Justice Department refused. In the spring of 1946, as the WRA prepared to close Tule Lake, its officials shipped a last remaining group of Kibei "resegregants" to Crystal City, alongside the interned Issei and their children in the "family internment camp," as it decided their fate. With the aid of lawyer Wayne Collins, who accepted their cases, almost all the Nisei renunciants who had withdrawn their applications for repatriation succeeded in staving off deportation, and in 1947 they were released and permitted to stay in the United States. However, they were forced to sue in court and fight—sometimes as long as ten or even twenty years—to have their citizenship restored.[31]

Ultimately some 3,000 Issei and 1,327 Nisei who had requested "repatriation" agreed to be shipped to Japan. In the fall of 1945 the U.S. government began transporting these inmates to holding facilities and prisons, notably Fort Lincoln and Santa Fe. As ships returned from East Asia bringing back soldiers, the State Department began organizing facilities to deport these inmates to Japan. The so-called repatriates formed part of a mass movement of ethnic Japanese who had been forced out of the Japanese colonies of Korea and Manchuria or deported from their countries of settlement. Their plight was poignant. The Issei deportees had not generally seen their native land for decades, and they were generally unable to adjust comfortably to the changes in the country and rebuild their lives there. The Nisei, most of whom had never seen Japan, faced life in a foreign place. Cut off from their former lives and occupations and forced to start anew without U.S. government aid, they arrived soon after the Japanese surrender to find the formerly proud empire on its knees. Japan had been devastated by wartime bombing and by the expense of combat. Even the most primitive food and housing were difficult to obtain, and employment even more so. Ironically, many Nisei found jobs in Japan working (often as translators) for the American occupation authorities, or as English teachers.

Even as the U.S. government took Issei and their families who had accepted repatriation from Tule Lake and Crystal City for shipment to Japan, officials in Washington faced the question of what to do with the 2,200 Latin American Japanese (almost all of them Peruvians) whom the government had seized during the war and interned at Crystal City. Although President Truman issued a proclamation in the summer of 1945 authorizing the United States to deport any enemy aliens considered dangerous to security, once the Japanese surrender brought a close to World War II the concerns that had prompted the Americans to push for the confinement of the Latin Americans became less vital, and the State Department no longer had an interest in holding them to use in potential hostage exchanges with Japan.[32] On the contrary, it was not clear how to dispose of them, as the wartime agreements with Latin American countries did not set forth arrangements for postwar handling of internees. Government officials in Lima, wishing to avoid inflaming popular anti-Japanese sentiment, informed Washington that they would not permit Japanese Peruvians to return. State Department officials then tried to press the internees to move to Japan, on the argument that Peru would never accept them back and that they would either not be permitted to stay in the United States or would not be allowed to bring in their families. Approximately 900 people "voluntarily" accepted the American offer of transportation to their ancestral homeland, and beginning in late 1945 they were shipped to Japan along with the Japanese American repatriates. However, the remainder of the internees, who were composed of some 150 Japanese nationals and 250 wives and Nisei children (includ-

ing 25 children born in camp, who were thereby American citizens), refused deportation to Japan and announced their readiness to return to
Peru. Hoping to accommodate them, in April 1946 the State Department
declared that Latin American Japanese were no longer enemy aliens and
could thus be legally returned to Latin America. American diplomats
proceeded to schedule interviews with Peruvian officials to press them to
take back their former residents. The Peruvians refused to accept the return of any Japanese nationals, and only after considerable prodding did
they agree even to permit the entry of those who could claim special circumstances, such as having Peruvian citizenship or marriage to Peruvian
women. Seventy-nine internees were deported to Lima by air in October 1946.[33] Meanwhile, Justice Department lawyers, anxious to get rid of
the remaining internees, instituted proceedings for their involuntary removal and deportation to Japan (on the rather specious grounds that they
had entered the United States illegally). Attorney Wayne Collins, who had
defended the Japanese American renunciants against deportation, took
up their case. In June 1946 he filed suit in federal district court in San
Francisco on behalf of a pair of Japanese nationals from Peru, Iwamori
Sasegawa and Chika Yamasaki.[34] While their cases were being litigated,
Collins succeeded in persuading the Justice Department to allow them
to leave government custody and be granted temporary "parole" if they
could find sponsors. Seabrook Farms in New Jersey, a leading frozen-
food business that had been the largest single employer of resettlers from
the WRA camps, agreed to employ families of Latin American Japanese
under "relaxed internment," while others found sponsors in the western
United States. The deportation proceedings were soon suspended, as the
Justice Department preferred to await the results of State Department
discussions with Peru before recommending deportation of the Latin
Americans to Japan as a last resort. However, the Peruvians maintained
their refusal to repatriate their ethnic Japanese. Finally, in 1953, after several years of wrangling, Congress agreed to suspend all deportation proceedings and permit those Latin American Japanese who were still in the
country to remain as legal residents.

THE "REPATRIATION" OF JAPANESE CANADIANS

Compared with the United States, there was no great sense of urgency in
Ottawa about the condition of confined Japanese residents or the need

to arrange for their release, and certainly no great movement nationwide to permit them to return to their former homes. Rather, opinion leaders nationwide showed a remarkable complacency about official treatment of Japanese Canadians. At the end of 1943 the Toronto *Globe and Mail* insisted editorially that, apart from their forced migration, the Japanese Canadians had received very lenient treatment.[35] In early 1944, Norman Robertson, undersecretary of state for external affairs (and a British Columbia native), wrote in a memorandum to Prime Minister King, "On the whole, I think our treatment of the Japanese in Canada has not been unduly harsh and can be defended as reasonable in the circumstances."[36] Unlike in the United States, the approaching end of the Pacific War and the return of troops did not lead to the end of the emergency restrictions against people of Japanese ancestry in Canada, but to their renewal and reinforcement.

From the time of removal, Canadians on the West Coast and elsewhere began discussing postwar policy. At the extreme were advocates of the deportation of all ethnic Japanese to Japan after the war. This group included editors of newspapers such as the *Victoria Daily Colonist,* Vancouver Mayor J. W. Cornett, and Liberal MP A. W. Neill. Another group, which included the *Vancouver Sun,* the Vancouver City Council, and most of the province's MPs, agreed that mass deportation was an ideal solution, but they also were prepared to support a "moderate" solution whereby Japanese Canadians would be permitted to remain in the country provided they were scattered among the various provinces. A few brave figures, such as Angus MacInnis, leader of the social-democratic Cooperative Commonwealth Federation (CCF), denounced the idea of mass deportation as "Nazi tactics." However, not even the CCF's membership agreed on whether to permit Japanese Canadians to return to the West Coast after the end of the war.[37]

In the spring of 1944 Norman Robertson and his department were assigned to formulate plans for dealing with Japanese Canadians after the war. In seeking a "solution" to the "Japanese problem," they sought to counter continuing pressure in Parliament. British Columbia MPs led by Liberal Ian Mackenzie and Conservative Howard Green remained firm in their insistence that all Japanese Canadians be permanently excluded from the West Coast, if not expelled altogether from Canada.[38] Cabinet officials likewise sought to respond to members of the CCF, who had taken up the defense of equality for Asian Canadians and who ridiculed the Liberal government for stripping voting rights from the migrants who had left British Columbia. In April the External Affairs officials proposed a cautious compromise to the Cabinet War Committee: all disloyal Japanese would be deported to Japan, while those who were loyal would be permitted to settle in Canada and be restored in their citizenship rights.[39] In August 1944 King finally proclaimed the new policy in Parliament. He admitted that "It is a fact that no person of Japanese race born in Canada has been charged with any act of sabotage or disloyalty during the war." (Of course, while King did not say so, no Japanese immigrant had been charged with any disloyalty either.) He nonetheless announced his intention to put together "a quasi-judicial commission to examine the background, loyalties and attitudes of all persons of Japanese race in Canada to ascertain those who are not fit persons to be allowed to remain here."[40] Any Japanese deemed to be disloyal would be deported to Japan as soon as possible, and those among them who were Canadian citizens would be stripped of their citizenship. Others who might wish to relocate to Japan would be encouraged to do so, while all further Japanese immigration would be halted. Yet, King insisted that to punish those who were not guilty of any crime with deportation would be unjust. Thus, Issei and Nisei who were loyal to Canada would be permitted to stay, but in accordance with the legitimate opposition of British Columbia to having a concentrated return of Japanese, they would be "distributed" throughout the country and a limit would be imposed on their residence in British Columbia. King concluded that his goal remained, as always, to join in a continental policy. "The situation in the United States in a great many essentials is the same as our own. . . . There is no need for an identity of policy, but I believe there is merit in a substantial consistency of treatment in the two countries."[41]Although King clearly considered his policy more just than that of West Coast MPs who insisted that all Japanese Canadians be permanently removed, the result was both arbitrary and punitive—whereas those in the United States adjudged disloyal were simply barred from release during the war, the Canadian government clearly signaled its intention to clear out as many as possible on the basis of their "disloyalty.".

The government's policy was not put into effect for several months after King's speech—the prime minister clearly hoped that the tensions would ease as the war drew to a close. Mackenzie and his British Columbia colleagues, fortified by public opinion in the province nevertheless kept up the pressure for restriction with public statements advocating permanent exclusion of Japanese Canadians.[42] Mackenzie promised the

Canadian Legion that he would not "remain 24 hours" in a government that allowed the inmates to return.[43] At a nominating convention in Vancouver in 1945, Mackenzie took as a campaign slogan, "Not a Japanese from the Rockies to the Sea." The racist drumbeat from the West weighed heavily on the government, especially as the time for federal elections neared. Conversely, leaders of other provinces, such as Quebec Premier Maurice Duplessis, expressed their opposition to the resettlement of Japanese Canadians in their areas. The situation became critical as 1945 dawned, and in the United States the WRA began opening the camps. As Japanese Americans moved in ever-greater numbers back to the West Coast, government officials in Ottawa became panicked that Japanese Canadians would expect to do the same thing, especially since it was clear that a Japanese invasion was no longer a serious possibility. Once deprived of both the fig leaf of continental security and the pretext of coordinating policy with the United States, the Canadians adopted a policy that sacrificed the individual rights of Japanese Canadians to the need to appease racist public opinion on the Pacific Coast and nationwide, putting it into effect by means of a plan marked by dishonesty and subterfuge.[44]

In February 1945 the Labour Department announced the issuing of a "repatriation survey" that all adult Japanese Canadians would be ordered to complete, asking whether they preferred "repatriation" or "resettlement." In April RCMP officers administered the survey to the fifteen thousand inmates remaining in the settlements in British Columbia. People in the camps were forced to made their decisions rapidly, with no chance to consult with relatives and come to a family decision, and they were further motivated in their responses by their well-founded resentment over the government's arbitrary actions, which did not inspire their confidence that official claims of fair treatment would be honored. Also, while Canadian officials publicly insisted that the choice was strictly a matter for the Japanese Canadians and there was no official pressure applied, it was too obvious for words that the choice was far from free: there was an enormous and deliberate built-in bias. Ostensibly the survey simply asked whether the individual wished to "repatriate" to Japan or to stay in Canada. However, the phrase "repatriation" ignored the fact that a large majority of those in the camps were not Japanese, but Canadian citizens who had never even been to Asia. More important, Issei and Nisei and their families who accepted deportation were permitted to stay in British Columbia until after the war. They were then offered free passage to Japan and the restoration of all money that remained from the forced sales of their properties. Conversely, government proclamations required those who wished to stay in Canada to move east of the Rockies and disperse forthwith. The failure to accept employment or move east of the Rockies, noted an official press release, "may be regarded, by the proposal Loyalty Tribunal, when it is established, as evidence of lack of co-operation with the Government of Canada."[45] In other words, those in British Columbia had to agree to relocate, without notice and for an indeterminate period, to faraway communities, where they then had to accept whatever employment was found for them. Although they had been stripped of their farms and property, they were required to attend to this resettlement using their own resources, without official aid, and were warned that they would have to wait for a considerable period to receive even the proceeds of their confiscated assets. Worst of all, even if they moved, the government refused to offer any guarantee that they would not subsequently be deported as well.[46] T. B. Pickersgill, the new commissioner of Japanese placement, candidly told settlement residents during interviews that the government was offering generous terms to voluntary repatriates because of opposition to Japanese in Canada.[47] In a letter sent along with the survey, Pickersgill extolled the advantages of repatriation: "This assured assistance from the government, as outlined in this notice, will mean to many who desire repatriation, relief from unnecessary anxiety and it will allow them to plan for their future, and that of their children, along economic, social, and cultural lines which they fear may be denied them were they to remain in Canada."[48]

In such circumstances, the results were predictable: 6,844 adults (or whom 3,921 were Canadian citizens) and 3,503 children signed the form. They represented approximately 81 percent of the adults in British Columbia and some 15 percent of those who had already relocated to the East. The government also deemed refusals by Japanese Canadians to fill out the survey or to accept immediate resettlement as positive proof of mass disloyalty, and marked all such people out as candidates for deportation as well.[49] Despite the veiled threat of deportation implicit in the demands that the inmates resettle, less than a thousand took the opportunity to migrate east during 1945. Even the Labour Department's order that those who refused to accept offers of employment in the East be let go from their jobs in the settlements failed to alter the situation.

In essence, as the popular magazine *Saturday Night* pointed out, by means of an "incidental clause" in a document offering them free transportation to Japan, Ottawa had lured thousands of citizens to surrender all their rights, without being guaranteed any other citizenship.[50] However, the truth was that many of the inmates living in the settlements were simply reluctant to leave their home province and be scattered into an unfamiliar and hostile environment, with no compensation and with uncertain job and living prospects. They knew that many of those who had moved east had experienced discrimination and poor living conditions. Also, many people were occupied with caring for aged or ill family members who were unable to travel. They preferred to stay in the communities they had constructed, where they at least had some resources. Even those who genuinely wished to leave Canada for Japan were not necessarily loyal to the emperor but were forced to make the best life for themselves amid great difficulties. Certainly, the government made it difficult for people to remain in Canada. The Issei and Nisei had already been stripped of their property by the forced sales, and they remained barred from purchasing new property anywhere in Canada. In July 1945 the cabinet agreed to Justice Minister Louis St. Laurent's recommendation that the ban on land-ownership be maintained after the war so as not to detract from repatriation.[51] Nevertheless, like their counterparts at Tule Lake who had agreed to renounce their citizenship, many of the "repatriates" soon had second thoughts. The idea of return to Japan became even less attractive as Japan faced defeat and it became clear that life there would be marked by privation. Within months after the repatriation survey, some four thousand people petitioned the government to revoke their acceptance of repatriation, claiming that their agreement had been the product of intimidation. Labour Minister Mitchell disingenuously denied any official pressure on the choice. To avoid embarrassment to the government, he finally agreed to consider, on a case-by-case basis, only those petitions brought by Canadian-born citizens before September 2, thereby imposing the date of Japan's surrender as an arbitrary index of good faith. However, he explicitly refused all petitions from Japanese citizens and did not express himself in regard to those from naturalized citizens.[52]

In October 1945, one month after the Japanese surrender brought an end to World War II, the dominion government introduced Bill 15, a measure to provide it with continuing emergency powers after the termination of the War Measures Act, which was set to expire at the end of the year. The measure maintained the exclusion of Japanese Canadians from the West Coast and the bars on their purchase of land or on starting businesses without government permission. In addition, one section of the act, clause G, granted Ottawa control over exclusion, deportation, and denationalization of civilians. Although Japanese Canadians were not explicitly named, it was clear that they were the targets of such legislation. The prime minister and his cabinet assumed that the bill would pass easily and would permit them to undertake the deportation of the ten thousand "disloyals" quickly and efficiently.

However, the project was countered by a developing phalanx of pro–Japanese Canadian opinion, mobilized under the leadership of the Toronto-based Nisei group Japanese Canadian Committee for Democracy (JCCD) and by the Co-operative Committee on Japanese Canadians.[53] The CCJC, originally founded in Toronto in 1943 by progressive white Christians to assist in resettlement of migrants, responded to the move for mass deportation by transforming itself into a national federation of trade unions, religious groups, and human rights activists, and by joining forces with the Vancouver Consultative Council, itself a coalition of West Coast progressive and religious groups working for fair play for Japanese Canadians. The CCJC–VCC coalition sent representatives to meet with government officials, held public forums, and published press releases and informational material, most notably Howard Norman's pamphlet, *What about the Japanese Canadians?*, which attacked deportation as a violation of human rights and called on the government to aid resettlement efforts. Bill 15, with its provisions for arbitrary denationalization and deportation, presented a clear target around which opposition could form, especially since its timing coincided with another measure, introduced by Secretary of State Paul Martin, to codify Canadian citizenship. The CCJC organized a letter-writing campaign opposing deportation, and sent every MP copies of a new pamphlet, *From Citizens to Refugees—It's Happening Here!*[54] Representatives of the CCF nationwide joined in the chorus of dismay over deportation, while mainstream newspapers such as the *Winnipeg Free Press* and the *Toronto Daily Star* proclaimed that the policy made a mockery of Canadian claims to democracy and Canada's pretensions to oppose racial discrimination.[55]

As a result of the CCJC campaign, the government changed tactics. Clause G was stricken from the bill, which was passed without it. Instead, at the prime minister's request, Justice Minister Louis St. Laurent drew up three orders-in-council, which gave him substantially identical powers to those he had previously sought from Parliament. By tabling the orders-in-council, the government bypassed Parliament and did not face any opposition to the measures. On December 17 the prime minister issued the new orders. The principal provision was P.C. 7335, which outlined who could be deported. This included any Japanese nationals still in confinement; naturalized Canadian citizens who had made a request for repatriation and had not revoked it before Japan's surrender; and native-born Canadians who had requested "repatriation" and had not revoked their request before deportation orders were issued. Importantly, the order included an additional category, which represented by far the most numerous: wives of those men who faced deportation and all their children under sixteen could be forcibly deported as well.[56] A companion order, P.C. 7336, authorized the government to strip all citizens it deported of their Canadian citizenship.

As if this was not already sufficiently harsh, P.C. 7337 gave the government the power to create a three-person commission to look into the "loyalty" of Japanese nationals and naturalized Canadian citizens during the war, and determine their "loyalty," for purposes of deportation. However, while the commission was not assigned to look into the loyalties of native-born Canadians—as opposed to naturalized immigrants—the commissioners could nevertheless recommend the deportation of any person of Japanese ancestry which was felt to be "in the national interest." Thus, in practice, all Japanese Canadians faced involuntary expulsion and revocation of citizenship at the pleasure of the government, with no due process or specific grounds required for expulsion and no machinery for appeal. As a result, not only the 4,700 people who had revoked their "repatriation" requests, but their wives and children who had not agreed to anything, were in imminent danger of involuntary removal, while even those who had previously resettled and had never wished for repatriation faced the threat of deportation.[57] After General Douglas MacArthur, the supreme commander of Allied Powers in Japan, agreed to accept repatriated Japanese from Canada, the government scheduled the first shipment for January 6, 1946.

THE BATTLE IN THE COURTS

The promulgation of the new regulations and the commencement of shipping operations led Japanese Canadians and their allies to mount an emergency legal challenge to the deportation. The CCJC, in association with the JCCD, raised money for the court costs and arranged for the hiring of a well-regarded Toronto lawyer, Andrew Brewin, to issue writs against the attorney general on behalf of Yea Nazu, a naturalized Japanese immigrant, and Utka Shimoyama, a native-born Canadian citizen. On January 5, 1946, in accordance with an order of reference from the government, the Supreme Court of Canada agreed to hear the case. In addition to the groups that lined up in support of the CCJC suit, Tommy Douglas, CCF premier of Saskatchewan, offered his official backing through the filing of a *Factum* by the province's attorney general. The CCJC meanwhile organized mass publicity about its efforts, including a public meeting and rally in Toronto attended by some one thousand people.

The Canadian Supreme Court heard the case on January 25, 1946. Justice Minister Louis St. Laurent, who had become the chief advocate for deportation within the cabinet, selected a Québécois attorney, Maitre Aimé Geoffrion, to defend the government's position. The province of British Columbia supported the federal government with its own brief. The issue presented was deceptively simple and technical: whether the orders-in-council were *intra vires* (within the government's authority) or *ultra vires* (beyond the powers of the government) under the War Measures Act. The CCJC's principal argument was that no powers of "deportation" could be applied to Canadian citizens, whether naturalized or native-born, under the law of nations. Geoffrion argued that since a state of emergency still existed, the government had the power to extend the War Measures Act in order to take any action it deemed necessary and had properly done so. On February 20, 1946, the Supreme Court issued its ruling. The judges, in accordance with the reference, did not address the morality of the government's policy, but they unanimously agreed that the government had the power to deport Japanese nationals. They split, however, over the issue of whether others also could be forcibly removed. The extremist minority, who included Chief Justice Thibaudeau Rinfret, Associate (later Chief) Judge Robert Taschereau, and Judge Patrick Kerwin, ruled that the orders-in-council gave the government authority to strip any Canadian citizen of Japanese ancestry of their citizenship and to deport whom it chose. However, the four other judges, R. L. Kellock, A. B. Hudson, I. C. Rand, and J. W. Estey, declared that the government did not have the authority to deport women and children involuntarily, although they themselves divided on whether any Canadian citizens could be stripped of their citizenship and deported without their consent.[58]

Although the Court's decision technically opened the way for mass deportation, its mixed verdict complicated the government's plans. Newspapers and political leaders in British Columbia, predictably, praised the verdict and called for deportation proceedings to start. Vancouver MP

Howard Green (who had favored mass expulsion of Japanese Canadians and proposed establishing those who refused to go to Japan on some island in the Pacific) called for the Pacific Coast to be made a permanent "protected area" closed to Japanese and warned that if Japanese Canadians returned to the West Coast there would be bloodshed.[59] On the other side, public sentiment against deportation began to be felt nationwide. The CCJC began an immediate campaign to raise more funds for a final appeal of the orders to the Privy Council in London and organized a letter-writing campaign to the prime minister. A Civil Rights Defense Committee organized in Winnipeg. Meanwhile, in Montreal an usual alliance came together between English Canadians and French Canadians, as the Quebec nationalist St. Jean Baptiste Society, the YMCA, and the Canadian Jewish Congress joined forces to support the Montreal Committee on Canadian Citizenship/Le Comité pour la défense de la citoyenneté canadienne to save Japanese Canadians from deportation.[60] Committee members, under the leadership of Frank R. Scott, Forrest La Violette, Therese Casgrain, and Jacques Perrault, denounced the deportation policy as "dangerous and attacking the fundamental rights of minorities" and joined in fundraising for the appeal.[61] Meanwhile, individual Japanese Canadians in British Columbia who faced deportation started habeas corpus proceedings.

In response to the pressure from both sides, Prime Minister King temporized. He announced that any Japanese Canadian who still desired repatriation would be granted government assistance and free passage. As a result, in May 1946 the first of the "repatriation ships" left Vancouver, carrying what would eventually reach a total of some four thousand "voluntary repatriates" by the end of the year—approximately half of these people were Canadian-born, mostly underage children of Issei repatriates. King insisted privately that he was not impressed with the arguments against deportation of Japanese Canadian "repatriates," whom he regarded as ready to move to Japan when they still thought Tokyo would win the war.[62] However, he was willing to look into a face-saving way to withdraw the deportation policy, if it could be managed without alienating potential Liberal voters in British Columbia. When a visiting delegation from the CCJC asked King to either permit an appeal to the British Privy Council or cancel the deportation orders, he agreed to the first alternative. Observers agreed that there was little chance that the Supreme Court's judgment would be upset, since the Privy Council had a well-established tradition of not overruling courts in Great Britain's dominions. Nevertheless, the government used the excuse of the appeal to hold its involuntary deportation policy in abeyance during the months that followed. The case for the deportation orders was reargued in London in July 1946, and in December the Privy Council finally announced its ruling. The council not only sustained involuntary deportation of Japanese nationals but overruled the majority of the Canadian Supreme Court by concluding that the government had authority under the War Measures Act to undertake involuntary deportation of Canadian citizens. The government was now free to undertake involuntary deportation at will.

By this time, however, the political and demographic situation had shifted. The "voluntary repatriates," the portion of the Japanese Canadian population deemed most pro-Japanese, had departed. Meanwhile, an equivalent number, hoping to avoid eventual deportation, moved east. As a result of these twin population movements, the ethnic Japanese population in the camps in British Columbia had shrunk from twenty-one thousand before Pearl Harbor and sixteen thousand during most of the war years to less than seven thousand, who huddled together in New Denver as the other settlements were closed. The Labour Department expanded its existing network of placement offices in Canadian cities, and opened a set of hostels in former POW camps and other facilities in Saskatchewan, Manitoba, Ontario and Quebec, to which it removed those remaining in the settlements. With the end of the wartime ban on Japanese Canadian settlement in Toronto, the Queen City became the nation's largest Japanese population center, while significant communities took root in Hamilton and Montreal. The prairie provinces became acclimated to their small Japanese populations—even Alberta's leaders, who had extracted the promise from the federal government that wartime resettlers would be removed afterward, feared the negative impact on its sugar beet industry of an exodus of Japanese laborers and finally acquiesced in their staying. In 1946 the Canadian government also closed down the POW camp at Angler, where the "troublemakers" had been held. Approximately one-third of the 425 internees still confined there agreed to be deported to Japan, and another third accepted resettlement within Canada. Some 128 Issei and Nisei who refused either course were removed to a hostel in Moose Jaw, Saskatchewan. Even after authorities announced plans to close the hostel, these inmates refused to leave, and a set of them undertook a hunger strike to demand reparation for their losses. Eventually, in the spring of 1948, the Canadian government forcibly broke the strike and dispersed the inmates [63]

Despite the scattering of populations, powerful forces continued to demand deportation of Japanese Canadians. Not only was public opinion in British Columbia still heavily biased against any return of the Japanese population to the West Coast, but there was strong feeling over the matter within King's cabinet. Surprisingly, it was not Mackenzie, the West Coast native, but Louis St. Laurent, who led the forces for mass deportation. At a privy council meeting on January 22, 1947, the justice minister insisted that the Japanese Canadians would never fit into Canadian life and would be "troublesome" if they were not deported, and he warned that their continued presence would lead to pressure "to have the Japanese in Canada given the same rights as the white population."[64] However, King concurred with other ministers that civil liberties associations had turned public opinion against forcible deportation, and that the government would face attacks for a policy that was illiberal and "almost inhuman" if it proceeded with involuntary deportation. Since four thousand had already been sent, and more shipping would not be available for several months, it was better to suspend further deportations in exchange for a policy of dispersal. On January 24 he publicly pledged that a mass repatriation policy was "no longer necessary," and that there would be no involuntary deportation of Japanese Canadians. However, he approved a renewal of the measures restricting people of Japanese ancestry in their movements in British Columbia, excluding them from the West Coast, and maintaining the bar on fishing licenses for Japanese. He claimed that this was necessary to assure that those in the camps would resettle elsewhere, and that those who had found new homes would remain dispersed.

In March 1947 the Continuation of Transitional Powers Act was introduced, granting a year's extension to the orders. CCF leaders protested the renewal, noting that it was two years after the war and any security requirement was clearly absent, but in April 1947 it passed with a large majority.[65] Even after obtaining such a reprieve, British Columbia Liberals, led by Premier Byron "Boss" Johnson, put pressure on the government to make the ban on Japanese permanent. As 1948 dawned, they reminded King and his cabinet that by-elections were scheduled for that summer in Vancouver and Yale, and they warned that the Liberal Party would lose both seats unless Japanese Canadians remained excluded. King was primarily sensitive to this argument. When members of the Liberal caucus protested the injustice of such a nakedly self-serving policy, he responded that he was for the rights of minorities, but "a minority constituted by a handful of Japanese" had to be compared to "the minority constituted by the entire population of British Columbia."⁶⁶ In March 1948 the cabinet introduced a measure prolonging for an additional year the restrictions. Despite verbal opposition from the CCF, it was enacted on March 31, 1948. Ironically, the CCF won both seats in the summer by-elections.⁶⁷

Despite the renewal of exclusion, it was clear that prewar racial prejudice, discredited by its association with Nazism and by Canada's new international responsibilities, was losing its former influence. In 1947 Parliament overturned Chinese exclusion and granted Chinese Canadians suffrage rights. The victory demonstrated that exclusion of Japanese Canadians from citizenship rights could not be long maintained. On June 15, 1948, Parliament voted to grant Canadian citizens of Japanese ancestry the right to vote in federal elections. British Columbia, however, remained recalcitrant in its attitude. Provincial laws barring Japanese from mining and from commercial fishing remained on the books into the postwar years. It was not until March 1949, just before Ottawa withdrew its final wartime controls on Japanese Canadian return to the coast, that the assembly in Victoria finally voted to open suffrage for ethnic Japanese in its provincial elections. On April 1, 1949, almost four years after the end of the war, Japanese Canadians were at last permitted to resettle on the West Coast. However, by this time most former West Coast residents had established themselves and started new lives elsewhere, and they had little to return to in British Columbia as a result of the forced sale of their assets. Thus, the vast majority of Japanese Canadians, at least initially, decided not to attempt any return to their prewar communities.⁶⁸

SHIFTING OPINIONS AND EVACUATION CLAIMS

The removal and confinement of Japanese Americans were carried out in response to widespread public demand on the West Coast. As the war went on, however, support for the rights of Japanese Americans, which had been scattered and muted in the spring of 1942, grew powerful. To some degree this shift reflected the calming of fears over a Japanese invasion of the mainland, as well as public embarrassment over the nation's fighting a war for democracy while thousands of citizens remained behind barbed wire. The heroic combat record of Nisei soldiers, fighting to defend the freedom denied their families, undoubtedly played an essential role in changing public opinion as well. The resettlement of Japanese Americans helped bring home to other Americans (particularly those outside the West Coast) the injustice of their treatment. Finally, the efforts of Dillon Myer and the WRA (in conjunction with the OWI) to create a positive public image of the inmates helped shape popular reactions to official policy. Although the WRA's intent was chiefly to build support for resettlement by playing up the patriotic cooperation of Japanese Americans with a benevolent government, and not to hold official actions up to criticism, their insistence upon the loyalty and good citizenship of the inmates inevitably called into question the entire rationale for removal and confinement.

The shift in public sentiment should not be overstated—the majority of Americans no doubt remained unaware of the existence of the camps throughout the war, and many of those who did know instinctively supported the government. Still, by the time the last camp closed, the tone of public discourse, even on the West Coast, had shifted decisively. Influential critics such as Eugene Rostow, Carey McWilliams, and Milton R. Konvitz denounced the incarceration of Japanese Americans as (in Rostow's words) "our worst wartime mistake."[69] Liberals and labor leaders (apart from Teamsters chief Dave Beck) made public statements in behalf of the Nisei and organized Fair Play and resettlement committees to aid the returnees. In late 1946, with the blessing of the WRA leaders and outside supporters, artist Miné Okubo published *Citizen 13660*, a narrative of her camp experience illustrated by the artist's sketches. The book was widely and respectfully reviewed.[70] When a show of Okubo's works was sent to tour the West Coast, one anonymous (presumably white) critic commented acerbically on both the evident Americanism of the Japanese Americans she portrayed and the paradoxes inherent in Establishment backing for such a show:

It is the best imaginable commentary on the whole cockeyed situation that existed with reference to the Nisei during the war. You may be sure that no inmate of Dachau ever won a prize in a Leipzig annual during his confinement. Some of Miss Okubo's designs and stylizations are interesting, but the show is valuable mainly as a document [*sic*] record of an episode in the history of a group which was, apparently, quite as Americanized and quite as good-natured in adversity as any of the Kelly-Kaplan-Caruso combinations which traditionally symbolize the people of this country.[71]

On the political side, the camps remained a potent symbol of racism and official injustice, and they played an undoubted role in reducing white support for discriminatory legislation, even on the West Coast. When anti-Japanese activists in California sought to strengthen the state's Alien Land Act via a referendum on November 1946, the measure was defeated by an almost two-thirds majority. At the same time, the JACL undertook a program of lobbying for civil rights legislation and sponsorship of court challenges to discriminatory laws that lent it a nationwide profile, including a laudatory feature on lobbyist Mike Masaoka in *Readers Digest.*[72]

The shift in public opinion, combined with activism by Japanese Americans, made possible the beginnings of a decades-long process of official reconsideration of the wartime removal and confinement of Japanese Americans, which would culminate in the organization of a mass Redress Movement by former inmates. The origins of the process are diverse. As far back as the spring of 1942, the Tolan Committee recommended some sort of remedial legislation. During the war various supporters of Japanese Americans, notably Socialist leader Norman Thomas and African American journalist George Schuyler, publicly advocated compensation to the inmates. A. L. Wirin gave a talk at Heart Mountain on collecting "damages."[73] However, the government was slow to consider any such measure. When the Women's International League for Peace and Freedom informed Dillon Myer in September 1945 of its resolution calling for reparations for property losses, Myer responded that the WRA had no authority to implement such a measure and Congress had shown no interest.[74] Myer privately favored such a measure, however, and during the latter half of 1945, he lobbied his Interior Department superiors to press for action.

Myer's suggestions were taken up with alacrity by Interior Secretary Harold Ickes, who had silently deplored evacuation when it was first promulgated and who had become a powerful defender of Japanese Americans. Believing, with good reason, that the president's own intervention would set the tone for any executive branch efforts, Ickes attempted to attract the support of President Harry Truman. Truman paid no special attention to the question of Japanese Americans until December 1945, when he learned from Eleanor Roosevelt of the discrimination and violent resistance facing returnees in California. The president was outraged by the violence and snapped, "These disgraceful actions almost makes you believe that a lot of our Americans have a streak of nazi in them."[75] Truman asked his attorney general, Tom Clark, whether there was some way that the federal government could either compel state authorities to enforce the law or assume jurisdiction itself, stating, "It certainly makes me ashamed." When Clark responded that the federal government generally lacked authority to act, Truman directed him to investigate all incidents and take action where appropriate.[76] Truman's evolving pro-Nisei attitude was also shaped by admiration for the remarkable wartime record of the 442nd Regimental Combat Team. In February 1946 he sent special greetings to the first postwar JACL convention in order to call attention to the "high patriotism" of Nisei soldiers. "Their service is a credit not only to their race and to America, but to the finest qualities in human nature."[77]

A week after the president's JACL message, Ickes resigned from the cabinet. While his replacement, Julius Krug, was being confirmed by Congress, Undersecretary Oscar Chapman, a strong supporter of civil rights who enjoyed a close relationship with the president, took control of the Interior Department. Under Chapman's leadership, department lawyers joined WRA staffers to design a property compensation bill. The bill provided for the establishment of a three-person Evacuation Claims Commission within the Interior Department that would adjudicate claims for personal property or assets that arose as a result of the "evacuation and exclusion programs." In April 1946 the Interior Department officially submitted the bill to Congress. It was not expansive in its provisions. As Secretary Krug explained in his cover letter, "The standard excludes claims that are largely speculative and less definitely appraisable, such as claims for anticipated wages or profits that might have accrued had not the evacuation occurred, for deterioration of skills and earning capacity, and for physical hardships of mental suffering."[78] In addition to these limitations, a cap of $2,500, including payment for attorney's fees, was placed on awards and a clause was presented making the payment of such an award "final and conclusive" and forever discharging all other claims by Japanese Americans on the subject. In July 1946 (immediately after a well-publicized visit to the White House by the members of the 442nd Regimental Combat Team) Truman sent public letters to the heads of the Senate and House Judiciary Committees urging passage of the evacuation claims bill. Claiming that it would be "a tragic anomaly" to celebrate the achievements of the Nisei soldiers while ignoring the losses that they and their families had suffered due to the government's actions, Truman called passage of the bill "A task that, in all good conscience, should be done if the government is to accord justice to those of its people who, during the war, were dealt with so harshly."[79] The president's support was insufficient, however, to push through the legislation. A week after Truman sent his letter, Representative Clair Engle of California telephoned the White House to explain that the bill would be "political dynamite in California" and its passage would lead the Hearst press to "crucify every Democrat who is running for re-election in California."[80]

Although there were no significant losses by California Democrats in the November 1946 elections (apart from that by Jerry Voorhis, who was unseated in a red-baiting campaign by the young Richard Nixon, for reasons unrelated to his position on Japanese Americans), the Republicans took control of both houses of Congress. Administration liberals realized that they would require outside lobbying help to pass the bill. They soon found a partner in the JACL. Already, at its spring 1946 convention, the JACL had voted to adopt an aggressive political program, including equality in naturalization rights and "reparations" for wartime property losses.

In late 1946 the JACL sent Executive Secretary Mike Masaoka to Washington to lobby for pro-Japanese legislation. (For tax purposes, he spun off the JACL Anti Discrimination Committee as a separate body from the parent organization). In late January 1947 Masaoka met at the White House with presidential assistants David Niles and Philleo Nash, Truman's "minority group" liaisons. Masaoka proposed that the government provide a lump-sum payment of a thousand dollars to each "evacuee" and then make provision for litigation in the Court of Claims for any sums over that provided. Such liberalization, Masaoka said, would be fairer and "would save both the evacuees and the government a lot of time and money."[81] If such a lump-sum payment were not possible, Masaoka proposed that at least certain intangibles losses such as goodwill be recoverable, as well as the difference between white administrators' wages and inmate wages for work done in camp.[82] Niles and Nash quickly convinced Masaoka that such provisions would both wreck any possible chance of the existing bill's passage and arouse the enmity of the Interior Department, as they had already submitted their own bill. Instead, Niles and Nash suggested that Masaoka look to the President's Committee on Civil Rights, appointed by Truman in December 1946 to report on discrimination against African Americans, as a possible source of support for the legislation.[83] Dillon Myer also expressed opposition to an "indemnity" rather than a "claims" bill—only the requirement that the Japanese Americans show receipts, he claimed, would suffice to demonstrate the magnitude of actual losses. Leonard Broom of University of California nonetheless put together a study (subsequently published as *Removal and Return*) quantifying the various economic costs of removal and confinement to the inmates.

The evacuation claims bill was reintroduced in the spring of 1947 as H.R.3999. While it was largely identical to the previous bill, this time the attorney general was made the adjudicator of all evacuation claims. The bill's supporters organized a round of congressional hearings. The star witness was Dillon Myer, who deplored removal as unjustified and racially motivated.[84] The House committee issued a report strongly favoring the bill: "To redress these loyal Americans in some measure for the wrongs inflicted upon them . . . would be simple justice."[85] Representative Francis Walter stated that Japanese Americans were "innocent victims of an order that probably should never have been issued."[86] On July 24, 1947, the House approved H.R. 3999 without a dissenting vote. However, because Senate leaders wished to hold their own hearings, and to question the attorney general on the manner in which claims investigations would be made, the bill was held over until 1948.[87]

Meanwhile, as Niles and Nash proposed, Mike Masaoka appeared before the President's Committee on Civil Rights. While his prepared statement stressed the connections between Nisei and other minority groups, his presentation underlined the special problems of Japanese Americans, including Alien Land laws that curtailed property ownership, exclusion of Japanese from immigration and naturalization, and property claims.[88] Committee members praised Masaoka's testimony, adding that he had opened up to them a whole new field of civil rights violations, and they invited him shortly afterward to serve as an official consultant. In October 1947 the committee issued its landmark report, *To Secure These Rights*, which would stand as a blueprint for later African American civil rights legislation. Although it focused on black Americans, the report contained provisions urging the end of anti-Asian discrimination in immigration and naturalization laws and the abolition of alien land laws. In particular, it forthrightly denounced the "evacuation and exclusion of persons of Japanese descent" as "the most striking mass interference since slavery with the right to physical freedom" and called for a federal commission to inquire into the entire matter:

> We have not felt that it would be proper or feasible for this Committee to try and review all the facts of the evacuation program. . . . But

we are disturbed by the implications of this episode so far as the future of American civil rights is concerned. Fundamental to our whole system of law is the belief that guilt is personal and is not a matter of heredity or association. Yet in this instance no specific evacuees were charged with disloyalty, espionage or sedition. The evacuation, in short, was not a criminal proceeding involving individuals, but a sort of mass quarantine measure.[89]

The committee strongly recommended property claims legislation. As the report stated, "The government has acknowledged many Japanese Americans evacuees suffered considerable losses though its actions and through no fault of their own. We cannot erase all the scars of evacuation; we can reimburse those who present valid claims for material losses."[90]

The committee's report helped bring the demands of Japanese Americans to a primary place in the administration's concerns.[91] Shortly after it was issued, the JACL received a tip that Truman was planning a civil rights message to Congress. Masaoka pleaded with Niles and Nash to make sure that the president prominently included the evacuation claims and naturalization provisions. At the same time, he faced off against criticism from JACL directors (including his brother Joe Grant Masaoka) that "this bill as presently worded is of very little, if any, real value to the evacuees." Worried, Mike Masaoka solicited the opinion of several lawyers, most notably former Attorney General Francis Biddle. Biddle responded that since the Supreme Court had upheld the original removal in the *Korematsu* case, the JACL had little case against the government in legal terms. Paraphrasing Biddle, Masaoka told his colleagues that "pots and pans money" was about all that could be expected: "This bill is one of grace and generosity on the part of this government, and . . . whatever we receive from the bill is 'so much gravy,' for the government is not obligated in any way, except possibly morally, for compensating the losses sustained. In fact, since the United States Supreme Court declared in the Korematsu case that the evacuation was constitutional, even the moral obligation may be questioned."[92]

In early February 1948 President Truman sent his civil rights message to Congress. The Japanese Americans were not forgotten. The president stated:

During the last war more than 100,000 Japanese-Americans were evacuated from their homes in the Pacific states solely because of

their racial origin. Many of these people suffered property and business losses as a result of this forced evacuation and through no fault
of their own. The Congress has before it legislation establishing a
procedure by which claims based upon these losses can be promptly
considered and settled. I trust that favorable action on this legislation
will soon be taken.[93]

Truman's inclusion of the evacuation claims bill in his message on civil
rights lent it additional visibility, and presumably greater legitimacy. Soon
after, in March 1948, Senate hearings began on the bill. Chapman and
Masaoka were able to mobilize a parade of witnesses to testify in favor of
the bill, most notably former assistant secretary of war John McCloy, by
then American high commissioner in Germany. McCloy in turn told the
senators that his former boss, the retired secretary of war Henry Stimson,
had authorized him to state Stimson's opinion that passage of the bill was
a "just obligation." Chapman himself reiterated the government's own responsibility. Although the Interior Department no longer had any official
interest in Japanese Americans, he noted, it remained committed to "fair
treatment and proper discharge of the government's obligations." Chapman's arguments struck home. The *Washington Post* noted that Japanese
Americans had not sought redress for the humiliation to which they were
subjected nor for the trespass on their constitutional rights as American
citizens. It called compensation for material losses a minimal apology and
a matter of "elementary justice."[94] Even Republicans, though unwilling to
take sides on the injustice of Executive Order 9066, were willing to express
a measure of contrition. According to a Senate report, "The question of
whether the evacuation of the Japanese people from the West Coast was
justified is now moot. The government did move these people, bodily,
the resulting loss was great, and the principles of justice and responsible
government require that there should be compensation for such losses."
Ironically, the JACL chose to disassociate itself somewhat from the administration during the lobbying campaign that followed. As the other bills in
Truman's civil rights package were introduced and it became obvious that
the southern-dominated Congress would block all such legislation, Masaoka grew anxious. He told the Senate subcommittee that the evacuation
claims measure was a different case from civil rights protections. His fears,
however, soon dissipated in the face of broad support for the measure.[95]

On June 2, 1948, following its passage in the Senate, President Truman signed the evacuation claims bill into law. Interestingly, the bill was

the only part of Truman's civil rights program enacted by Congress, and thereby (despite Masaoka's disclaimer) the first civil rights–identified bill since Reconstruction to become law. It provided up to $25 million to compensate Japanese Americans for actual losses pursuant to their "evacuation." The bill constituted the federal government's first official recognition of the burdens it had perpetrated on the inmates, and its enactment revealed how far the idea of civil rights for Japanese Americans had traveled in just a few years.

Yet in spite of the act's historic nature, as Masaoka himself later put it, "The victory turned out to be only a partial one, and a costly and vital learning experience in dealing with the feds."[96] To obtain a noncontroversial piece of legislation that could command majority support, the JACL had accepted a government-drafted bill with glaring weaknesses. First, Washington did not officially admit wrongdoing or violation of civil rights. Those Japanese Americans who wished to recoup losses were forced to swear that this was their sole and final claim against the government for the wartime events. Congress refused to settle claims for lost wages, fire sales, pain and suffering, or any of the other indirect costs of removal and confinement. Even the procedure instituted for allowable claims under the act was exceedingly harsh. The former inmates were in effect required to sue the government for damages, and to produce receipts and other proof of their losses. The Justice Department strongly contested each claim, using a legalistic definition of what could be counted as a "loss." By 1950 the department had heard barely two hundred claims of the twenty-three thousand filed. Masaoka was able to speed up the process by agreeing to have claimants make a compromise settlement of the lesser of $2,500 or three-quarters of the amount sought, but even then the last claim was not settled until 1965. In all, the government paid $38 million to settle claims for damages totaling $131 million—a fraction of actual losses by Japanese Americans. Many families paid more in lawyers' fees than they received in compensation. In a sense, the Evacuation Claims Act resembled many government actions taken during the war. Although meant to atone for wrongs and aid the Japanese Americans, it ended by bringing misery to many of those affected.

Moreover, its passage did not lead to redress and may well have hindered it. In the years after 1948, neither Congress nor the Truman administration undertook further investigation or re-evaluation of Executive Order 9066 and its consequences, as the President's Committee on Civil

Rights had urged. The JACL also failed to push for an official investigation, or to discuss more comprehensive reparations. JACL activists had never considered redress for removal a priority, compared to their higher goal of amending exclusionary immigration and naturalization laws so that Issei could obtain American citizenship and new Japanese immigrants could come to the United States. This goal they ultimately achieved as part of the otherwise repressive McCarran-Walter Immigration Act of 1952, which passed over President Truman's veto.

To be fair, the JACL leaders were conscious that Japanese Americans were in a weak position to bring further claims as long as the *Korematsu* and *Hirabayashi* decisons remained good law and evacuation had the official imprimatur of legality. In 1955–56, shortly after Congress prolonged the Evacuation Claims Act to allow arbitration of continuing claims that had still not been resolved, JACL lawyers debated bringing a legal challenge to the Supreme Court decisions under a writ of *coram nobis*. However, the lawyers involved believed the risk of failure too great to justify the costs of such litigation.[97]

PROPERTY CLAIMS IN CANADA

There was also a push for reparations in Canada during the postwar years. During 1946 a group of Issei banded together to challenge the forced sales and low prices that the Issei and Nisei owners had received. The CCJC appointed a committee to look into the property question, while the JCCD did a survey of former property owners in Toronto. They discovered that property worth an estimated $1,400,395.66 had been sold for $351,334.86. Andrew Brewin, who had represented the Japanese Canadians fighting deportation, agreed to take up the issue of compensation for property. Brewin proposed the creation of a judicial commission to investigate potential fraud and negligence of the custodian of enemy property in the disposition of property. After hearings before the parliamentary Public Accounts Committee, at which numerous abuses were revealed, the government agreed to establish a royal commission, and on July 18, 1947, Order-in-Council P.C. 1810 established the commission, renamed the Bird Commission after Justice Henry Bird of the British Columbia Supreme Court was picked to lead it. The announcement that a property commission had been appointed to examine Japanese Canadian losses received largely positive coverage on both sides of the 49th parallel. There is no sign, however, that the Canadian action influenced the passage of evacuation claims legislation in the U.S. Senate over the following months.

While originally the Bird Commission was authorized to propose compensation only to those who could prove that the custodian of enemy property had failed to exercise "reasonable care" to prevent loss, theft, or vandalism, in the face of widespread criticism that this was insufficient, the cabinet resolved on June 25, 1947, that the commission could examine differentials between the sale prices obtained by the custodian and the fair market value at time of sale—though with no consideration of deterioration of the properties that had been forcibly vacated or fluctuations in market prices. For unknown reasons, this decision was not publicly announced until September, with the result that relations between the different groups of claimants and the government, and their attitude toward each other, grew strained.

Testimony before the commission began in December 1947. As in the United States, the property claims commission agreed only to look at actual property losses, and not lost wages . Moreover, its reference was limited to losses during the time the custodian held inmate property. The National Japanese Canadian Citizens Association (NJCCA) (which had replaced the JCCD at the beginning of 1947) and the CCJC took responsibility for organizing efforts to obtain valuations and proof that the proceeds from the sales were insufficient. Because Japanese Canadians had been so widely dispersed by the government, the commission scheduled hearings in Toronto, Montreal, Kamloops, and other cities, where individual claimants could testify about their losses and be examined by commission members about their proof.

After several months of testimony, it became clear that there was no single reliable basis or standard to apply in judging compensation—the commission awarded some claimants considerably more than others for losses of similar scale. Moreover, the more technical and complex property claims would require considerable time and lawyers' fees to unsnarl, and they threatened to delay indefinitely the resolution of all other claims. Given the extremely narrow terms of the commission's mandate and their feeble ability to influence its decisions, CCJC and the NJCCA activists knew that they could not expect large-scale damages. Thus, like the JACL in the United States, they reluctantly agreed to a compromise. The commissioners would authorize a fixed settlement of 5 percent of claims on those that the commission agreed to uphold, and all except very complex claims would be thereby resolved. Japanese Canadians would sign a waiver promising not to pursue further compensation.

In the spring of 1950, the Bird Commission published its report. It found that the amounts paid Japanese Canadians for their properties were substantially below the fair market value for such belongings. The biggest rip-offs, they found, had been in the Fraser Valley, where the custodian had sold off properties to the Veterans Land Act administrator for barely half their value. Despite credible evidence of underpricing in the city of Vancouver, however, the commission declined to issue a finding of underpayment. In all the report recommended a payment of $1,222,929.26 to cover losses on some 2,400 claims. Claimants were forced to pay a retainer fee of 1 percent of their total claim, plus 5.75 percent of the proceeds for valuation and other services to the CCJC (which proceeded to close its operations following the awarding of compensation). A group of Nisei objected to the small size of the compensation package and criticized the CCJC and the NJCCA for accepting the settlement. They formed the Toronto Claimants Committee to continue fighting. However, they were unable to win further compensation and ultimately disbanded.

CONCLUSION

The Allied victory in the Pacific and the end of World War II led to dramatic shifts in the lives of Japanese North Americans. Indeed, it is not too much to say that the early postwar years were almost as vital as the wartime events in determining the location of Japanese communities, and the nature and condition of their inhabitants. During this period, in both the United States and Canada, the former inmates were released from camp and worked to establish themselves outside, either in new communities outside the West Coast or (in the United States) in their former Pacific Coast locations. Impoverished by their removal and excluded from the wartime economic boom, most had to accept low-paying menial jobs and struggle to support themselves and their families. Because of lack of money for better housing, together with widespread racial discrimination, they were forced to crowd into housing in urban slum areas or in racially shifting "buffer zones" between black and white areas. Meanwhile, thousands of Issei and Nisei in the United States and Canada who had agreed to deportation under duress were forced to battle in the courts to win the right to remain, while those who accepted "voluntary" expulsion to Japan had the task of beginning life anew in a devastated country most could only dimly recall or had never known. In both countries, as a matter of elementary justice, the government agreed to accept claims for compensation for property losses, but, given the narrow range of the losses considered and the difficulty of proving amounts, the relief finally granted was more symbolic than real. All the same, the civil rights of people of Japanese ancestry were dramatically expanded in the postwar years. Nisei in British Columbia and throughout Canada, who had been long deprived of voting rights, were enfranchised. Japanese Americans won signal victories in the Supreme Court over the alien land acts and other forms of racial discrimination, and in 1952 Issei were finally allowed to become American citizens.

The end of the war brought a stark divergence between official actions in the United States and Canada with regard to people of Japanese ancestry. To be sure, this was not altogether a new development. Despite various self-justifying assertions by Prime Minister King and political leaders in Ottawa that their arbitrary wartime treatment of Japanese Canadians was designed to coordinate with Washington's, the two countries' policies were in fact quite distinct from the start.[98] The WRA provided housing and education for camp inmates, sponsored camp newspapers, and supported leisure activities and cooperatives. Japanese Canadians did not receive such assistance and had to rely on religious and nonprofit groups for aid or use their own funds. Furthermore, the large-scale official confiscation and forced sale of the properties of Japanese Canadians had no parallel south of the border, while there were no battalions of Nisei soldiers in Canada to demonstrate the loyalty of the group. Postwar policy nonetheless differed in kind as well as degree between the two nations. In the United States, exclusion was lifted as of the beginning of January 1945, and Issei and Nisei returned to the West Coast in large numbers even before the war was over. In contrast, Ottawa's policy, designed to appease the demands of racist whites in British Columbia and to win their votes, was to pressure Japanese Canadians into giving up their citizenship and leaving the country entirely, or failing that, to move east of the Rockies and disperse into small groups.

How do we explain this striking contrast? It is tempting to make invidious comparisons between enlightened American rulers and bigoted Canadian ones, or to draw facile conclusions about national character. However, the truth is that the leadership of the two nations was not so far apart in their general ideas. Even after his advisors agreed that there was no longer any military threat justifying the continued existence of the camps, U.S. President Franklin Roosevelt delayed lifting exclusion for six months out of political self-interest and fear of violent West Coast reaction. Similarly, the president and his advisors all agreed that Japanese Americans would be better off resettling in small groups outside the West Coast, and they devoted their efforts to promoting dispersion with such tools as they had. White House officials recognized, nonetheless, that they had no power to keep Japanese Americans from returning to their homes or to compel them to settle elsewhere. Mackenzie King and his cabinet, conversely, extended the authority they had been granted originally for national defense into the postwar period, despite the lack of any conceivable national security justification, in order to institute a compulsory dispersal policy.

Instead, the basic differences between the two countries were constitutional and political. Because of the liberties guaranteed in the Bill of Rights, the powers that the U.S. government held over Japanese Americans were limited, especially once the war drew to a close. While the U.S. Supreme Court was prepared, in the *Korematsu* decision, to grant the army considerable leeway to take actions in the name of national security, the justices simultaneously ruled in *Ex Parte Endo* that loyal citizens could not be kept in confinement indefinitely, and they struck down wartime military rule in *Duncan v. Kahanamoku*. The Court's ruling lent constitutional approval, and political cover, to the lifting of exclusion, even before the end of the war. Canada's Supreme Court, operating in a common-law system that enshrined parliamentary supremacy and did not include a bill of rights, did not challenge the government's ability to declare or extend its emergency powers. The cabinet thus was enabled to contemplate radical limitations on the fundamental liberties of citizens, even in peacetime.

The other consideration was the role of West Coast leaders in playing the race card. During the war years many California politicians, appealing to popular opinion, made public statements denouncing Japanese Americans as spies and opposing their postwar return to the coast. So strong was the opposition that John Bricker, Republican candidate for vice president in 1944, proposed that West Coast residents be permitted to vote on whether or not to permit Japanese Americans to return to their region. However, once the Supreme Court ruled and the army declared exclusion lifted, figures such as Governor Earl Warren and Los Angeles Mayor Fletcher Bowron called for public obedience to the orders and helped welcome the returning inmates. (By these actions, Warren may arguably have succeeded in redeeming his tarnished reputation for civil rights, thereby making possible his emergence as a national political figure and his eventual appointment to the U.S. Supreme Court.) As a result, terrorist attacks were not widespread and public tolerance began to prevail, at no apparent political cost to the public officials responsible. In contrast, British Columbian MPs and local leaders persisted in whipping up popular racism and brandishing the threat of violence to blackmail Ottawa into violating the rights of Canadian citizens of Japanese ancestry. Cabinet ministers and advisors were unwilling to call their bluff, or to look at events south of the border in order to realize their error, and the Liberal Party suffered as a result the taint of racism and the loss of a pair of seats in the 1948 election.

[7] REDRESS AND THE BITTER HERITAGE

THE PHYSICAL TRACES OF WARTIME JAPANESE AMERICAN confinement rapidly vanished once the inmates had been released, as the government's War Surplus Division sold off or disposed of the facilities on the camp sites. Native Americans reclaimed the land on their reservations in Arizona where the Poston and Gila River camps had been. Farmers in neighboring towns in Idaho, Utah, and Wyoming bought old barracks from the camps there for use as barns or for housing construction — one set of nurses' barracks from Gila River was even moved to Phoenix and transformed into a dormitory for baseball players. Yet the spiritual legacy of confinement carried over for a time, and the treatment of the Japanese Americans occupied a visible, if hardly central, place in American culture as well as politics during the early postwar years. A wide selection of novels and sociological analyses (generally by non-Asians) that recounted the wartime events began to trickle out in the years that followed.[1] In addition to Mine Okubo's *Citizen 13660*, significant works included Karen Kehoe's novel *City in the Sun* (1946); Morton Grodzins's exposé *Americans Betrayed* (1949), and the two volumes of the JERS study directed by Dorothy Swain Thomas, *The Spoilage* (1946) and *The Salvage* (1952). Although no Hollywood films were produced on the camps, the 442nd was the subject of a feature film, *Go for Broke!* (1951), and injustice against Japanese American veterans was referenced in Otto Preminger's Hollywood drama *Daisy Kenyon* (1947).

Yet, for a variety of reasons, in the two decades that followed the 1948 Evacuation Claims Act the memory of "evacuation" dimmed in the public consciousness and largely disappeared as a subject of national memory and debate. Mainland Japanese Americans were anxious to forget the wartime horrors and get on with their lives, even as Hawaiians drew the curtain on the martial law period. Once Congress repealed the exclusion of Japanese immigrants and granted citizenship to Issei in 1952, Nisei organizations scaled back their involvement in political activism and minority issues. From 1954 to 1967 no new, full-length studies of the wartime Japanese American experience emerged.[2] Similarly, John Okada's novel *No-No Boy* (published in a tiny edition in 1957 and largely ignored) was for a generation the only large-scale literary treatment of the camps. In a climax of willed concealment, Vanya Oakes (who had reported a decade earlier on violence against camp inmates returning to the West Coast) published a children's book, *Roy Sato, New Neighbor* (1954) that not only failed to mention the wartime events but portrayed uninterrupted generations of Japanese Americans in California. Similarly, a mass-market paperback on the 1960s' television series *Star Trek* obscured actor George Takei's childhood confinement at Rohwer by stating simply that he was born in Los Angeles, moved with his family to Arkansas during World War II, and returned afterwards, without further explanation.[3]

Ironically, as the nation passed through the Korean War and the anticommunist frenzy of the McCarthy period, the wartime Nisei experience resonated closely with events. The Internal Security Act of 1950 (also known as the McCarran Act), enacted over President Harry Truman's veto, gave the president and the attorney general power to confine arbitrarily all those they considered a threat to the government. Although no subversives were actually detained, the act provided a disturbing echo of the treatment of Japanese Americans, not least because the Tule Lake camp, empty since the last inmates departed in 1946, was among the centers mobilized to hold those confined in case need arose. Meanwhile, loyalty exams became a subject of national attention and frenzied discussion. The tragic experience of the loyalty questionnaires for Japanese Americans and their role in stigmatizing individuals for "thought crimes" was forgotten or suppressed.[4]

Granted, the subject of Japanese Americans was not forgotten entirely in Washington. In December 1957, at the time that the evacuation claims program (whose final expiry date had been extended by act of Congress a few years earlier) was officially terminated, the Eisenhower administration offered muted regret for Executive Order 9066. Assistant U.S. Attorney General George S. Doub stated, "This oppressive measure was not a military necessity but constituted a tragic failure of principle by the executive branch in accomplishing it and the judicial power in sustaining it."[5] In 1959 Attorney General William Rogers, celebrating the restoration of citizenship to some 5,000 of the 5,700 Tule Lake inmates who had renounced their citizenship in 1944–45, publicly referred to evacuation as a "mistake,"[6] while Doub expressed the hope that the Japanese Americans "would have the charity to forgive their government."[7] National newspapers such as the *New York Times*, *Chicago Sun-Times*, and *Denver Post* hailed the announcement, which they termed an apology and confession of wrong, as justified and positive measures. In this same period, *Newsweek* ran an article saying that Executive Order 9066 and the removal of Japanese Americans had been "a blessing in disguise" because the Nisei were clearly better off afterward. Although numerous Japanese Americans protested this notion, it did reflect a popular consensus.[8]

Beginning in the mid-1960s, the past treatment of Japanese Americans returned to public attention. In a political climate shaped by the influence of the civil rights and Black Power movements and opposition to the Vietnam War, the official injustice of the camps appeared shocking. Discussion of the wartime events was furthered by a pair of 1965 documentaries that touched on the subject, the CBS-TV broadcast "Nisei: The Pride and the Shame," hosted by Walter Cronkite, and Richard Kaplan and a biographical film, *The Eleanor Roosevelt Story*. A new set of books on the camps began to appear, notably Anne Reeploeg Fisher's *Exile of a Race* (1965); Allan Bosworth's *American Concentration Camps* (1967); Bill Hosokawa's *Nisei: The Quiet Americans* (1969); Audrie Girdner and Anne Loftis's, *The Great Betrayal* (1969) and Roger Daniels's *Concentration Camps, USA* (1971). In April 1967 the U.S. Supreme Court ruled in *Honda v. Clark* that prewar U.S. depositors with holdings in the Yokohama Species Bank, whose assets had been seized by the government during the war, should be reimbursed for their holdings, and at the dollar exchange rate prevailing at the time of seizure rather than the current rate. *Time* magazine printed an editorial that, while hailing the decision, expressed regret that the Supreme Court had not overruled its precedent upholding the legality of the government's wartime removal of Japanese Americans, and called for a reconsideration of the question.[9]

Most important, many Japanese Americans re-examined their previous emphasis on assimilation and support for the government during this period and became active in social change. Younger generations of Nisei and Sansei protested their marginalization as nonwhites in American society and fought for "yellow power." As ethnic studies and Asian American studies programs were inaugurated in colleges and universities, large numbers of Japanese Americans began learning some of their group's history. They expressed growing outrage over the official crimes that had been perpetrated on their community and encouraged their elders to break their silence about the trauma and injustice they had experienced. Japanese American community activists and organizations called for official accountability. Various oral history projects, notably at California State University, Fullerton, collected reminiscences of former inmates, and local museums featured exhibitions of works by inmate artists. Issei and Nisei authors put out a series of memoirs, monographs, and fictional works about the camps. These works, of which Jeanne Wakatsuki Houston's memoir *Farewell to Manzanar* (1974) and Michi Nishiura Weglyn's historical study *Years of Infamy* (1976) are probably the best known, highlighted the injustice and the trauma of confinement.[10]

Meanwhile, in 1969 the Manzanar Committee, a grassroots, Los Angeles-based committee led by a former inmate, Sue Kunitomi Embrey, inaugurated an annual pilgrimage to the ruins of Manzanar (which, like all the other camps, had been dismantled and deserted immediately after the war). In 1973 the Manzanar Committee erected a monument there with a plaque recalling the government's unjust actions and referring to Manzanar as a "concentration camp." All these actions drew sharp criticism from a circle of conservatives, notably a white California woman named Lillian Baker, who denied that there had been any camps for Japanese Americans with barbed wire fences during the war and insisted that the government had treated Japanese Americans with justice and humanity.[11]

In conjunction with the community reappraisal, at the dawn of the 1970s a diverse conglomeration of individuals and groups came together to support reparative justice for Japanese Americans. Part of the initial impetus for community awareness and organization arose through a public campaign to repeal Title II, the section of the Internal Security Act of 1950 that had provided for concentration camps to be held in readiness for subversives. As a group whose members had suffered arbitrary incarceration, Japanese Americans took the lead in fighting for repeal. Although the repeal movement started with the assistance of only small contingents of civil libertarians, churches, and labor unions, it soon grew to include major civil rights and political organizations (as well as a timely endorsement from retired chief justice Earl Warren), and within eighteen months repeal was enacted by a large majority in Congress.

In the wake of this success, Japanese Americans around the country began exploring the question of seeking an apology and restitution from the government for their own incarceration. In the process, the phrase "reparations" was changed to the more palatable "redress."[12] Nisei and Sansei activists in Seattle (where they were encouraged and incited by the combative Chinese American playwright/activist Frank Chin) formed the Evacuation and Redress Committee. Meanwhile, Edison Uno, who had been confined as a teenager in the camps and in Crystal City, took the lead in lobbying the JACL to take action.[13]

In response to Uno's campaign, the JACL voted resolutions in favor of compensation at its national conventions in 1972, 1974, 1976, and 1978 and formed a National Redress Committee but did not make the campaign for reparations a priority. No doubt its leaders realized that there was no community consensus behind such a step. Rather, as historian Roger Daniels pointed out, perhaps one-third of Japanese Americans favored a national campaign for reparations, one-third were opposed, and one-third felt neutral. Many former inmates, scarred by the wartime experience, felt that no amount of compensation could make up for the hardships they had suffered, and considered it better to move on with their lives and distance themselves from the past.[14] In addition, it was patent that the issue of assessing financial compensation for past wrongs would be difficult and divisive, especially given the apparent prosperity of the ethnic Japanese population—JACL leader Mike Masaoka considered the quest for individual reparations futile, and he proposed instead a collective settlement that could be placed in a larger fund for civil rights and elder care.[15] To build consensus and encourage community participation, Japanese American community leaders seized on the point that Executive Order 9066 had never been formally withdrawn (though it became inactive with the official termination of World War II in December 1946) and focused their lobbying on the legal issue. They won an initial success in 1976, when President Gerald Ford officially revoked Executive Order 9066 and declared that the wartime removal of Japanese Americans had been "wrong" and a "tragedy." "We now know what we should have known then—not only that evacuation was wrong, but Japanese-Americans were and are loyal Americans."[16]

Although Ford's action was not intended to support moves for reparations (indeed, some advisors favored it precisely in order to forestall them), it encouraged redress supporters to redouble their efforts. One dedicated activist in Washington, D.C., Aiko Herzig-Yoshinaga, undertook a massive unpaid personal project. Despite having no previous training as an archivist, she traveled daily to the National Archives for a period of nearly three years, during which time she accumulated and cataloged tens of thousands of documents relating to the confinement of Japanese Americans. In the process of reviewing official files, she uncovered a "smoking gun" in the form of the censored (and supposedly destroyed) initial version of General DeWitt's Final Report on Evacuation, which stated clearly that the West Cost Defense commander had pushed for mass removal because he considered it impossible to trust or determine the loyalty of any Japanese American on racial grounds. This report belied the army's repeated insistence in public statements and Supreme Court briefs that the principal cause of its actions was insufficient time to make individual determinations of loyalty in a wartime emergency, and it highlighted both the official racism that informed De Witt's decision and the government manipulation of evidence that had taken place in the course of the wartime court cases.

In 1979 William Hohri, a community activist in Chicago, founded an umbrella group, the National Council for Japanese American Redress, to lobby for financial reparations from the government and to raise money for court suits. Hohri and other redress leaders agreed on a two-pronged approach. Japanese Americans would lobby Congress for redress legislation. Meanwhile, Hohri would institute a class action suit for damages resulting from the mass confinement of Japanese Americans. (The class action suit, *Hohri v. U.S.*, was filed in 1983. It listed twenty-one legal injuries that the government had inflicted on Japanese Americans and sought damages of $10,000 per person on each count. It was dismissed by a District of Columbia judge on grounds of statute of limitations, was revived in part by an appellate court ruling, and rose to the U.S. Supreme Court before being remanded to another court and finally dismissed in 1988.) Soon after, in consultation with Hohri, a group of Seattle-based activists persuaded local congressman Mike Lowry to present a bill granting a $25,000 payment to all inmates or to their heirs.[17]

Mike Masaoka of the JACL took the position that Lowry's bill had no chance of passing. Instead, following consultation with Japanese American members of Congress, notably Hawaii Senator Daniel Inouye, the JACL and its allies called for the establishment of a government commission to review the history of the wartime events. Hohri and others on the more radical wing of the redress movement opposed the idea of a historical commission, insisting that the facts behind their confinement were already well known and that a commission would protract and perhaps neutralize the issue. Nevertheless, the JACL's strategy prevailed, and a bipartisan coalition of Nisei and other members of Congress sponsored a bill for such a commission. (Even Senator S. I. Hayakawa, Republican of California, who opposed redress, agreed to cosponsor the measure, arguing that a detailed historical study of the wartime events was overdue.) To further broaden the acceptability of the measure, the investigation was to include not only the case of Japanese Americans but the Aleuts and Pribilof Islanders who had been removed from islands in Alaska during the war in the face of a Japanese attack and confined for the balance of the conflict.

With the passage of the bill in the summer of 1980, the U.S. Commission on Wartime Relocation and Internment of Civilians (CWRIC) was created. Its mission was to examine the facts regarding the origins of Executive Order 9066 and the "detention in internment camps of American citizens," and to make recommendations regarding the issuing of an official apology and financial compensation. President Jimmy Carter proceeded to select the members of the CWRIC. Joan Z. Bernstein, a well-regarded attorney, was appointed as chair, and other members were selected among present and former congressmen as well as a former Supreme Court justice, Arthur Goldberg. Judge William Marutani, a teen-aged inmate at Tule Lake and former JACL attorney, was the only Japanese American commissioner selected. Aiko Herzig-Yoshinaga was appointed as a consultant, and she and a team of researchers proceeded to assemble massive documentation for the use of CWRIC members.

Despite their disagreement over the establishment of a historical commission, the different groups active in the redress movement joined together with the JACL to marshal their collective forces for the CWRIC's scheduled hearings. The hearings, which took place between July and December 1981, were held in Boston, New York, Chicago, Alaska, and on the West Coast. During these hearings, dozens of former inmates came to testify. In many, perhaps most, of the cases, their testimony represented the first time they had ever spoken publicly about their wartime experience. The breaking of the silence induced an extraordinary community-wide catharsis and on more than one occasion moved audience members to tears.

In addition, the commission scheduled a series of fact-finding hearings in Washington and invited testimony from people who had been in the government during the war and were familiar with the policy. These hearings ignited controversy. A number of prestigious figures, among them former Supreme Court justice Abe Fortas and presidential assistants Edward Ennis and James Rowe, criticized the removal of Japanese Americans and spoke in favor of an official apology. Dillon Myer, who was on his deathbed, was too ill to testify. Somewhat surprisingly, however, in view of his expressed past views about the injustice of removal, he provided a letter through Lillian Baker deploring the use of the word "concentration camp" to describe the WRA's "relocation centers" and praising the agency's treatment of the inmates. Karl Bendetsen likewise testified in defense of the army's actions, insisting that Japanese Americans had posed a threat to national security. The chief antagonist to redress was the aged John J. McCloy. The former assistant secretary of war (who had become a prestigious establishment public figure in the postwar age, in such positions as director of the World Bank) clearly believed that the Japanese American call for redress amounted to a scurrilous attack on the nation's wartime leadership as racist. He was vociferous in his defense of President Roosevelt and Secretary of War Stimson as men who were guided by the highest of motives, and who had acted on sufficient cause in a wartime emergency. McCloy remained resolute in the face of a hostile audience of Japanese Americans and their supporters, though he caused a collective gasp when he seemed to indicate in his testimony that Executive Order 9066 had been just revenge for Tokyo's attack on Pearl Harbor.[18]

Following the completion of the hearings, the committee members turned to consider the documents that Aiko Herzig-Yoshinaga and her team had provided. A Washington-based attorney, Angus MacBeth, was assigned to prepare a historical study, *Personal Justice Denied*, based on the collected documents and testimony, which was released in February 1983. Four months later, on June 16, 1983, the CWRIC issued a separate set of recommendations. The commission agreed that Japanese Americans has suffered a great historical injustice:

> In sum, Executive Order 9066 was not justified by military necessity, and the decisions that followed from it—exclusion, detention, then ending of detention and the ending of exclusion—were not founded upon military considerations. The broad historical causes that shaped these decisions were race prejudice, war hysteria and a failure of political leadership. Widespread ignorance about Americans of Japanese descent contributed to a policy conceived in haste and executed in an atmosphere of fear and anger at Japan. A grave personal injustice was done to the American citizens and resident aliens of Japanese ancestry who, without individual review or any probative evidence against them, were excluded, removed and detained by the United States during World War II.[19]

The commission unanimously recommended the passage of a joint resolution of Congress containing an official apology and the establishment of a fund for educational and humanitarian purposes. In addition the commissioners recommended that a tax-free award of twenty thousand dollars be granted to each surviving person—though not their descendants—who had been covered under Executive Order 9066. (A single member of the CWRIC, California Republican congressman Dan Lungren, dissented from the final recommendation.)

Although the CWRIC's report and recommendations provided a strong official endorsement for redress legislation, both were met with immediate challenges. John J. McCloy led the charge against redress. In April 1983 McCloy published an op-ed piece in the *New York Times* in which he denounced redress as a canard of a "Japanese-American lobby." Without mentioning his own role in the policy, McCloy not-so-subtly connected Japanese Americans with Japan, arguing that since the entire blame for the treatment of Japanese Americans lay with the Japanese attack on Pearl Harbor, any compensation should come from Tokyo. Soon after, a former National Security Agency employee, David D. Lowman, earned generous press coverage when he came forward with accusations that *Personal Justice Denied* was fundamentally flawed because it had not included an examination of the MAGIC intercepts contained in the Defense Department's document collections, which Lowman had helped organize for publication. Lowman (who had not appeared during the CWRIC hearings, clearly preferring to reserve his information) now insisted that the intercepted Japanese diplomatic code excerpts revealed large-scale spying by Japanese Americans before Pearl Harbor and concluded that the government had thus acted properly in rounding up the entire ethnic Japanese population. The CWRIC quickly produced an addendum to *Personal Justice Denied* stating that there was no evidence that the MAGIC intercepts either demonstrated actual spying by Japanese Americans or had any bearing on the government's decision to remove them, but the damage was done, especially when McCloy—who had previously disclaimed knowledge of any actual espionage in his CWRIC testimony and other public statements—took up Lowman's position and alleged that the MAGIC cables had in fact influenced the government's decision. Lowman proceeded to repeat his charges during testimony before a House of Representatives subcommittee hearing on payments to camp survivors in June 1984. Although lawyer/scholar Peter Irons and Col. John A. Herzig, a retired army counterintelligence specialist, offered a detailed rebuttal of Lowman's charges based on an examination of the information in the cables, the members of Congress on the panel expressed skepticism regarding their testimony. In part as a result, redress legislation remained stalled in Congress for three years, although it appeared to have majority support.[20]

Meanwhile, a parallel legal proceeding, fueled by the CWRIC's inquiry, came together. The Supreme Court's decisions in the "Japanese internment" cases of Gordon Hirabayashi, Minoru Yasui, and Fred Korematsu had weighed heavily on Japanese Americans. As noted, the rulings not only sanctioned the government's wartime actions but presented a major obstacle to further evacuation claims or other restitution afterward. For this reason, over several decades JACL lawyer and former president Frank Chuman had discussed at various times the idea of using the little-used writ of *coram nobis*, which is designed to remedy fundamental error or manifest injustice, to overturn the verdicts. However, Chuman had not been able to pursue such an appeal. He was daunted by the high standard of proof of misconduct required for such a case, and by the fact that no previous conviction upheld by the U.S. Supreme Court had ever been overturned. However, once Aiko Herzig-Yoshinaga uncovered powerful evidence regarding War Department manipulation of evidence in the cases, the chance of success became considerably stronger. In 1981, as part of the process of writing a book on the wartime cases, Peter Irons interviewed the three Nisei defendants in the wartime Supreme Court cases. Irons suggested bringing a *coram nobis* petition using historical material that he and Herzig-Yoshinaga had uncovered. After obtaining the consent of all the former defendants, Irons recruited a volunteer legal team, directed by Sansei attorneys Dale Minami, Peggy Nagae, and Kathryn Bannai, to handle the three petitions.

In January 1983, a few weeks before *Personal Justice Denied* was released, Irons and the legal team filed the first petition, that of Fred Korematsu. The Justice Department, after receiving an extension of time to respond in order to take account of the CWRIC's forthcoming recommendations, issued its response in October 1983. The government brief (prepared by federal attorney Victor Stone, who would be assigned to argue all three cases) agreed that the removal of Japanese Americans had been an "unfortunate episode" but moved that the *coram nobis* petition be dismissed and Korematsu's conviction instead be vacated by a kind of official grace. Following a hearing on November 10, 1983, U.S. Judge Marilyn Hall Patel summarily granted the *coram nobis* petition, reversing Korematsu's conviction. In her opinion, Patel found that there was substantial support in the evidentiary record that the government had deliberately omitted relevant information and provided misleading information in its papers.

The cases of Minoru Yasui and Gordon Hirabayashi proved more complicated and protracted in their progress through the courts. In 1984 District Judge Robert C. Belloni issued an order vacating Yasui's conviction, in accordance with the Justice Department's motion, but declined to either grant Yasui's *coram nobis* petition or to make findings of fact regarding the record of official misconduct. Yasui and his lawyers appealed the ruling, but he died before the appeal could be decided, mooting the case. Unlike in the other two cases, the Justice Department (presumably under pressure from Reagan Administration hardliners) seriously contested Gordon Hirabayashi's petition. When the case was brought for a hearing in June 1985 before Judge Donald S. Voorhees, the government called a set of witnesses—most notably David Lowman—to testify regarding the MAGIC cables and alleged spying by Japanese Americans before Pearl Harbor to justify its actions. In February 1986 Judge Voorhees issued a mixed opinion. He found that government misconduct had resulted in fundamental error and therefore granted Hirabayashi's *coram nobis* petition and vacated his conviction for refusing to obey the evacuation order. At the same time, however, he upheld Hirabayashi's conviction for violating military curfew orders, on the grounds that such orders required a lesser showing of military necessity. This ruling satisfied neither side, and both proceeded to appeal. In September 1987 a three-judge panel of the U.S. Court of Appeals for the Ninth Circuit overturned the remaining conviction and ordered Hirabayashi's *coram nobis* petition granted in its entirety, noting that the twin convictions grew out of a single series of indictments that had been tried together and decided together. The appellate court judges proclaimed that the record demonstrated that racial bias was "the cornerstone of the internment orders" and that government misconduct had materially affected the argument of the case.[21]

Even as the *coram nobis* legal effort had been fueled by the redress movement and the work of the CWRIC, the victories of the former Supreme Court defendants provided fresh impetus for congressional action on redress. After a number of attempts to bring legislation to the floor of Congress and to obtain a vote met with defeat, in the summer of 1988 the Civil Rights Restoration Act, H.R. 442 (named in honor of the 442nd Regimental Combat Team), was at last approved by Congress. It was signed by President Ronald Reagan in August 1988, in the last months of his presidency. The law established a fund of some $1.2 billion, from which each Japanese American affected by Executive Order 9066 would receive a $20,000 tax-free payment, while the remainder of the money would be awarded for educational and other programs by a new non-profit body, the Civil Liberties Public Education Fund. Congress did not provide for a speedy allotment of the funds, however, and it was not until the middle years of the administration of President George H. W. Bush that the first redress checks were sent to the former inmates.

The postwar disappearance of Japanese American confinement as a subject of public discourse in the United States was closely paralleled in Canada, where the case of the Japanese Canadians remained obscured through the postwar years. In 1961 former prime minister Louis St. Laurent defended the removal decision in a television interview, claiming that there was reason to doubt the loyalty of Japanese Canadians on racial grounds: "Blood is thicker than water." Three years later, however, Prime Minister Lester Pearson drew new attention to the historical injustice when he delivered a speech at the opening of the Japanese Canadian Cultural Centre in Toronto in which he publicly referred to removal as "a black mark" in the nation's history (although he did conclude that Japanese Canadians had benefited from resettlement and dispersion). By the beginning of the 1970s, as Canada reopened its doors to Asian immigration on an equal basis and the government instituted a policy of official multiculturalism and ethnic affirmation, Japanese Canadians began to organize remembrances and educational campaigns on the model of those taking place south of the border. The new spirit of affirmation was dramatized by the publication within a short space of time of Joy Kogawa's novel *Obasan* (1975), which soon became a classic work of Canadian literature, and Ken Adachi's historical study of Japanese Canadians, *The Enemy That Never Was* (1976). However, the efforts of the National Association of Japanese Canadians (NAJC) and other groups to lobby for redress met with official resistance. Canadian war veterans who had been captured in the fall of Hong Kong and placed in Japanese prisoner-of-war camps opposed what they considered special treatment for Japanese Canadians. Furthermore, Liberal Prime Minister Pierre Elliot Trudeau (who in 1970 had invoked the same War Measures Act under which Japanese Canadians had been confined as part of a crackdown on Quebec nationalists) remained hostile. While Trudeau admitted during a speech in Tokyo in 1976 that the wartime treatment of Japanese Canadians represented a deprivation of civil rights, he publicly rejected the principle of reparations for past injustices (which evidently extended to those still living).[22]

In 1984 Trudeau resigned, and the Conservative government of Brian Mulroney was swept into office by elections shortly afterward. Mulroney was sympathetic to claims by Japanese Canadians (and may also have hoped to use redress as incentive for Tokyo to sign a free trade treaty), but he hesitated to place a dollar amount on a settlement. The NAJC responded by commissioning a study from the esteemed accounting firm of Price Waterhouse. It estimated that the official actions had cost the Japanese community in Canada some $333 million in revenue and $110 million in property (in 1986 dollars). In addition to the impressive size of this damage claim, both Japanese Canadians and government officials focused on the progress of redress in the United States. In 1988, even as the United States Congress passed H.R. 442, a final round of negotiations was scheduled between Japanese Canadians and the Mulroney government on a redress package. When the parties became deadlocked, the prime minister named his close collaborator, Secretary of State Lucien Bouchard, to lead the government's team. Bouchard used his influence to broker an agreement on a redress package, and the plan was voted into law in September 1988, some six weeks after redress was enacted in Washington. The terms of the Canadian settlement, which included an official apology and a redress payment, largely mirrored that in the United States. However, in a small act of Canadian one-upmanship (as well as a recognition of the particular harshness with which Japanese Canadians had been treated), Ottawa provided a $21,000 redress payment as compensation for the wartime confinement of Issei and Nisei, and the Mulroney government offered expedited payments to individuals.[23]

The cause of redress for the Japanese removed from the Pacific coast of Mexico and for the Latin Americans who were rounded up during World War II did not find any similar resolution. Peru and Mexico refused to offer apologizes for their wartime conduct or to grant any compensation for lost property or arbitrary arrest of their citizens and longtime residents of Japanese ancestry. Nor did those who were brought to the United States fare much better despite the education and lobbying efforts of a California-based group, the Coalition for Justice, led by the redoubtable activist Grace Shimizu. Since these Issei and Nisei were not subject to confinement under Executive Order 9066, they were not included in the redress settlement that Japanese Americans were offered, and Japanese American advocates did not insist on their inclusion as a necessary part of legislation. A class-action lawsuit brought during the 1990s resulted in a settlement, which granted a maximum payment of $5,000 to those who had been brought to the United States and confined. Although some former internees accepted the settlement as the best deal they were likely to be offered, the members of the Coalition for Justice refused the lesser payment and continued their efforts to foster legislation that would permit equal compensation for Latin American internees.

In any case, the North American redress settlements, whatever their financial importance and public visibility, were primarily symbolic in nature. They could not and did not erase the official injustice that had been committed, though they may have helped former inmates to achieve closure and a sense of vindication. Yet, paradoxically, the redress movements brought renewed attention to the government's wartime actions in the generation that followed, and not just within Japanese communities. First, Japanese confinement remained a frequent point of reference for other groups seeking reparations, such as the Chinese Canadians seeking restitution for the head tax imposed on past Chinese immigrants and the leaders of the movement among African Americans for reparations for slavery, who pointed to the redress movement and settlements as precedent. More broadly, as a result of redress the confinement of Japanese Americans (and Canadians) became a popular subject in mainstream school curricula, newspaper editorials, and museum exhibits, and of ever-increasing numbers of scholarly and popular books. Indeed, in some sense the popular response exemplified William Dean Howells's famous aphorism that Americans love tragedies with happy endings. That is, for many ordinary Americans the granting of redress to the former inmates was a triumph, rather than a threat, because it both underlined the isolated and past nature of official injustice and exemplified the triumph of American democracy over prejudice. As FCC chairman William E. Kennard (himself an African American) stated in a patriotic address: "Founded in the spirit of indomitable independence, and guided by principles, of liberty, justice and equality, our nation has been challenged throughout its history to reconcile those lofty notions with some ugly political realities. From the abolition of slavery to women's suffrage, from the civil rights movement to reparations for Japanese-Americans interned during World War II, America has usually managed to find ways to do the right thing—although not always at the right time."[24]

In the process, the wartime confinement of Japanese Americans was gradually absorbed and assimilated into a patriotic narrative. This narrative presented official policy—however mistaken—as exceptional, a case of wartime hysteria. It thereby minimized the actions and resistance of Japanese Americans (other than perhaps the contributions of Nisei soldiers) and obscured the essential role of historic patterns of white supremacy and official discrimination in making such injustice possible. On the other hand, the "happy ending" of redress did render the confinement of Japanese Americans digestible as a rhetorical reference point for debates on civil liberties and citizenship. One indication of how accepted (or safe) the issue had become was that in November 2006 the U.S. Congress unanimously enacted H.R. 1492, a bill that authorized government funds "to provide for the preservation of the historic confinement sites where Japanese Americans were detained during World War II." The measure passed with little public attention or debate and was quickly signed into law by President George W. Bush (whose cabinet featured Norman Y. Mineta, a former inmate, as secretary of transportation).

At the same time, the "War on Terror" declared by the Bush administration in the wake of the September 11, 2001, terrorist bombings of the World Trade Center and the Pentagon, and the administration's assertions of extraordinary powers following these events, including the arbitrary confinement of American citizens deemed to be "enemy combatants," ushered in renewed public debate over the nature and meaning of the wartime Japanese American experience. In 2003 Representative Howard Coble, chair of a House committee, sparked public outcry when he defended the wartime removal of Japanese Americans in a radio interview as having been a positive step carried out to protect them from vigilante violence. The tense and embattled climate also gave rise to a bitter new school of historical revisionism, in which numerous bloggers, radio commentators, and conservative speakers expressed doubts about the loyalty of Japanese Americans and argued that Executive Order 9066 had been justified: it is revealing that there was no similar movement within Canada to offer a retrospective defense of Ottawa's wartime actions.

The new revisionism was most visibly expressed by the columnist and commentator Michelle Malkin. Malkin had become a popular media figure in the United States following 9/11, as a result of a best-selling book in which she attacked immigration as a menace to national security. In 2004 she published a second book, *In Defense of Internment*, which purported to defend the federal government's removal policy as a justified reaction to prewar espionage by Issei and Nisei. Malkin's argument, and much of her evidence about the MAGIC intercepts, were taken from David Lowman's discredited work (notably a posthumous edited volume of Lowman's thesis that appeared in 2000). Her originality lay in her attempts to justify the official treatment of the inmates in the camps as well, and to posit the removal and confinement of Issei and Nisei as a model for existing White House policy toward suspected terrorists. Despite overwhelmingly negative reviews and criticism by historians, Malkin's polemic garnered substantial sales and received extensive and supportive media coverage from conservative media circles: as lawyer/historian Eric Muller pointed out, more Americans doubtless learned of the wartime confinement of Japanese Americans from Malkin's book than from the combined work of all of the scholarly researchers who had published on the subject.[25] Yet the Bush administration and Republican leaders disassociated themselves from Malkin, and she failed to shift the public consensus regarding the injustice of official policy toward American citizens of Japanese ancestry during World War II.

Even as I inserted a personal reflection into the introduction to this book, I beg leave to offer a final one in concluding it. As a historian of Japanese Americans, I am often asked what I consider to be the chief lessons of Executive Order 9066, P.C. 1486, or the fate of Japanese Latin Americans for the current day. I do not pretend to have an absolutely objective answer, but my strong feeling is that these measures demonstrate the importance of maintaining constitutional safeguards, even—especially—in wartime. Governments and their leaders simply cannot be given arbitrary powers and trusted on faith to assure fundamental freedoms. Franklin Roosevelt, a great humanitarian and liberal, failed to notice the biased and self-interested nature of the call for removal, or considered it more prudent to remove the targets of bias than to defend them from it. Hugo Black, a civil libertarian and defender of freedom, wrote the decision justifying mass removal on racial grounds. If such great men as these cannot be trusted, it seems to me that no lesser figures should. Rather, we owe it to ourselves to be jealous of our liberties.

[NOTES]

INTRODUCTION

1. Japanese communities are conventionally divided up by generation. The Issei are the first-generation immigrants, while the Nisei are their second-generation children. A subset of the Nisei is the so-called Kibei, Nisei who were sent back to be educated in Japan.

2. The official confinement of Japanese Americans in the WRA camps overlapped with a separate set of U.S. government policies toward "alien enemies," which included the Justice Department's control and detention, and in some cases internment, of Japanese, German, and Italian nationals based on suspicion of their individual actions. Insofar as ethnic Japanese were handled, I discuss these policies briefly. I have elected not to discuss the internment experience of Italian and German nationals and their families, both for reasons of space and to avoid confusion with the quite distinct experience of Japanese Americans moved on a mass basis, without due process. Instead, with those distinctions in mind, I direct the reader to the literature on these groups. See, for example, Lawrence de Stasi, ed., *Une Storia Segreta: The Secret History of Italian American Evacuation and Internment during World War II* (Berkeley: Heyday Books, 2001); Arnold Krammer, *Undue Process: The Untold Story of America's German Alien Internees* (Lanham, Md.: Rowman and Littlefield, 1997). For the confinement of Italian Canadians, see Mario Duliani, *The City without Women: A Chronicle of Internment Life in Canada during the Second World War* (Oakville, Ont.: Mosaic Press, 1994).

3. The U.S. government's actions also mirror the mass removal and confinement of ethnic Japanese following Pearl Harbor by the governments of Australia and New Zealand and the French colony of New Caledonia, and their mass postwar deportation to Japan. In addition, camps to hold ethnic Japanese were established by American forces occupying Saipan in the last months of the war. While the events in Oceania and the Pacific Islands form a useful backdrop and context for those in the Americas, they do not

have the same relevance to evaluating White House policy, and so will be dealt with only summarily.

4. Several works on Japanese Americans have chapters that briefly discuss Canada. Examples include Roger Daniels, *Concentration Camps North America: Japanese in the United States and Canada* (Malabar, Fla.: Krieger, 1993 [1981]); and U.S. Commission on Wartime Relocation and Internment of Civilians, *Personal Justice Denied* (Seattle: University of Washington Press, 1997 [1983]). Conversely, a few books on confinement in Canada, such as Ann Gomer Sunahara, *The Politics of Racism: The Uprooting of Japanese Canadians during World War II* (Toronto: Lorimer, 1981), briefly outline the actions of Canada's southern neighbor. Louis Fiset and Gail Nomura, eds., *Nikkei in the Pacific Northwest* (Seattle: University of Washington Press, 2005), discusses the history of both national groups but gives scant treatment to the wartime era. Stephanie Bangarth, *Voices Raised in Protest: Defending North American Citizens of Japanese Ancestry, 1942–1949* (Vancouver: UBC Press, 2008), compares wartime events at length but focuses on opposition to confinement and deportation and not confinement itself.

1. BACKGROUND TO CONFINEMENT

1. Dennis M. Ogawa, *Kodomo no tame ni: For the Sake of the Children* (Honolulu: University Press of Hawaii, 1978), p. 5.

2. Harry H. L. Kitano, *Japanese Americans: The Evolution of a Subculture* (Englewood Cliffs, N.J.: Prentice-Hall, 1970), pp. 12–13.

3. Japanese Canadian Centennial Project, *A Dream of Riches—The Japanese Canadians, 1877–1977* (Vancouver and Toronto: Japanese Canadian Centennial Project, 1978), p. 12.

4. On the anti-Chinese movement and exclusion, see, for example, Alexander Saxton, *The Indispensable Enemy: Labor and the Anti-Chinese Movement in California* (Berkeley: University of California Press, 1971); Erika Lee, *At America's Gates: Chinese Immigration during the Exclusion Era, 1882–1943* (Chapel Hill: University of North Carolina Press, 2003).

5. Patricia E. Roy, *A White Man's Province: British Columbia Politicians and Chinese and Japanese Immigrants, 1858–1914* (Vancouver: University of British Columbia Press, 1989), pp. 66–70.

6. Ronald Takaki, *Strangers from a Different Shore: A History of Asian Americans* (Boston: Little, Brown, 1998), p. 26.

7. Tom Coffman, *Nation Within: The Story of America's Annexation of the Nation of Hawaii* (Honolulu: EPIcenter, 2003), pp. 183–204.

8. Sucheng Chan, *Asian Americans: An Interpretive History* (Boston: Twayne, 1991), p. 12.

9. See, for example, Akemi Kikamura-Yano, ed. *Encyclopedia of Japanese Descendants in the Americas: An Illustrated History of the Nikkei* (Lanham, Md.: AltaMira Press, 2003); C. Harvey Gardiner, *The Japanese and Peru, 1873–1973* (Albuquerque: University of New Mexico Press, 1975); Yuriko Nagata, *Unwanted Aliens: Japanese Internment in Australia* (Brisbane: University of Queensland Press, 1996).

10. Yuji Ichioka, *The Issei: The World of the First-Generation Japanese Immigrants, 1885–1924* (New York: Free Press, 1988).

11. In the interests of common-sense understanding and comparison with the United States, in this volume I use the term "Canadian citizens" rather than "British Subject domiciled in Canada" to refer to Nisei and naturalized Issei. Although Canadian citizenship did not come into being as an officially recognized status until after World War II, the phrase "Canadian citizen" was informally used and universally understood.

12. Irving S. Friedman, "Australia and Japan: Conflict in the South Pacific," *Political Science Quarterly* 52, 3 (November 1937): 392–406.

13. Freda Hawkins, *Critical Years in Immigration: Canada and Australia Compared* (Montreal: McGill-Queen's University Press, 1989), pp. 7–30.

14. W. Peter Ward, *White Canada Forever: Popular Attitudes and Public Policy Toward Orientals in British Columbia* (Montreal: McGill-Queens University Press, 1978), pp. 55–58.

15. Ken Adachi, *The Enemy That Never Was: A History of the Japanese Canadians* (Toronto: McClellan and Stewart, 1976), pp. 39–42.

16. Ibid., pp. 52–54. See also Andrea Geiger-Adams, "Writing Racial Barriers into Law: Upholding B.C.'s Denial of the Vote to Its Japanese Canadian Citizens, Homma v. Cunningham, 1902," in *Nikkei in the Pacific Northwest*, ed. Louis Fiset and Gail Nomura (Seattle: University of Washington Press, 2005), pp. 20–43.

17. Jacobus tenBroek, Edward N. Barnhart, and Floyd W. Matson, *Prejudice, War and the Constitution* (Berkeley: University of California Press, 1954), pp. 22–27.

18. See, for example, Roger Daniels, *The Politics of Prejudice* (Berkeley: University of California Press, 1962); Bill Hosokawa, *Nisei: The Quiet Americans* (New York: Morrow, 1969).

19. Adachi, *The Enemy That Never Was*, pp. 41–46; Patricia E. Roy, *A White Man's Province: British Columbia Politicians and Chinese and Japanese Immigrants, 1858–1914* (Vancouver: UBC Press, 1989), pp. 310–15.

20. Lubomyr Y. Luciuk, *A Time for Atonement: Canada's First National Internment Operations and the Ukrainian Canadians 1914–1920* (Kingston, Ont.: Limestone Press, 1988).

21. Adachi, *The Enemy That Never Was*, pp. 102–3; see also Roy Ito, *We Went to War: The Story of the Japanese Canadians Who Served during the First and*

Second World Wars (Stittsville, Ont.: Canada's Wings, 1984). The pressure for soldiers ultimately led the Canadian government to impose conscription in 1917, setting off bloody civil conflict within the country.

22. This was not the first time that ethnic Japanese had served in wartime under American colors. A reported nine Issei saw service in the Spanish-American War—Kiechei Yamauchi, who enlisted in the navy in 1896 and worked as a mess hall steward for thirty years, rose to the level of chief steward to Rear Admiral Bryan. "Faithful Japanese Steward, 30 Years in Navy, Is Honored," *Nichi Bei*, January 22, 1931.

23. Franklin Odo, *No Sword to Bury: Japanese Americans in Hawaiʻi during World War II* (Philadelphia: Temple University Press, 2004), p. 35.

24. Eileen H. Tamura, *Americanization, Acculturation, and Ethnic Identity: The Nisei Generation in Hawaii* (Urbana: University of Illinois Press, 1994), p. 115.

25. Ibid., p. 62.

26. Odo, *No Sword to Bury*, pp. 94–96. Odo reports that in Hawaii, only 31 percent of Nisei had expatriated by 1933, some ten years after the Nationality Act, but that the rate increased as Japan and the United States came into greater conflict, until by 1940 four hundred Nisei were expatriating per month.

27. Helen Geracimos Chaplin, *Shaping History: The Role of Newspapers in Hawaiʻi* (Honolulu: University of Hawaii Press, 1996), pp. 141–43.

28. See, for instance, Mae Ngai, *Impossible Subjects: Illegal Aliens and the Making of Modern America* (Princeton: Princeton University Press, 2005), chap. 1.

29. Greg Robinson, *By Order of the President: FDR and the Internment of Japanese Americans* (Cambridge: Harvard University Press, 2001), p. 38.

30. Ward, *White Canada Forever*, pp. 120–23; Patricia E. Roy, *The Oriental Question: Consolidating a White Man's Province, 1914–1941* (Vancouver: UBC Press, 2003), pp. 104–8.

31. Hilda Glynn-Ward, *The Writing on the Wall* (Toronto: University of Toronto Press, 1974 [1921]).

32. Roy, *The Oriental Question*, pp. 104–8.

33. In 1929 the Canadians opened a legation in Tokyo—it was only the Dominion's third diplomatic post, after the United States and France. John D. Meehan, *The Dominion and the Rising Sun: Canada Encounters Japan, 1929–1941* (Vancouver: UBC Press, 2004).

34. Izumi Hirobe, *Japanese Pride, American Prejudice: Modifying the Exclusion Clause of the 1924 Immigration Act* (Stanford: Stanford University Press, 2001).

35. Masato Ninomiya, "Japanese Brazilian Historical Overview," in *Encyclopedia of Japanese Descendants in the Americas*, ed. Akemi Kikumura-Yano

(Walnut Creek, Calif.: Rowman and Littlefield/AltaMira Press, 2002), pp. 116–26.

36. David K. Yoo, *Growing Up Nisei: Race, Generation, and Culture among Japanese Americans of California, 1929–49* (Urbana: University of Illinois Press, 2000); Lon Y. Kurashige, *Japanese American Celebration and Conflict: A History of Ethnic Identity and Festival, 1934–1990* (Berkeley: University of California Press, 2002).

37. Charles H. Young and Helen R. Y. Reid, *The Japanese Canadians* (Toronto: University of Toronto Press, 1938), pp. 85–115. Young and Reid noted that, unlike in the United States, Buddhism had become a minority faith among the Nisei, especially in the cities, who had embraced Christianity in equal or greater proportions.

38. Jari Osborne, *Sleeping Tigers; The Asahi Baseball Story*, documentary film (Toronto: National Film Board of Canada, 2003).

39. Eiichiro Azuma, *Between Two Empires: Race, History, and Transnationalism in Japanese America* (New York: Oxford University Press, 2005), p. 111.

40. The experience of the Kibei has given rise to a somewhat biased social science literature since World War II, in which they have been assumed to be maladjusted and socially marginalized. See, for example, Adachi, *The Enemy That Never Was*, p. 174. While they certainly suffered greater job discrimination based on their language skills and may have had a distinctive attitude, it is reductive in the extreme to call them "highly disturbed" as a group. For a discussion of Kibei, see Brian Masaru Hayashi's flawed but brilliant study, *Democratizing the Enemy: The Japanese American Internment* (Princeton: Princeton University Press, 2004), pp. 46–48.

41. Minoru Yamasaki, *A Life in Architecture* (New York: Weatherhill, 1979), p. 36.

42. Forrest E. La Violette, *Americans of Japanese Ancestry* (Toronto: Canadian Institute of International Affairs, 1945).

43. Catherine Lang, *O-Bon in Chimunesu* (Vancouver: Arsenal Pulp Press, 1996), p. 17.

44. Tamura, *Americanization, Acculturation, and Ethnic Identity*, pp. 45–46.

45. Bill Hosokawa, *JACL In Quest of Justice* (New York: Morrow, 1982), pp. 48–71; Adachi, *The Enemy That Never Was*, pp. 156–60. In 1940 the JACL succeeded in getting Florin, California, to drop its Asian school.

46. John Modell, *The Economics and Politics of Racial Accommodation: The Japanese of Los Angeles, 1900–1942* (Urbana: University Press of Illinois, 1977), pp. 170–71.

47. Karl Hama (Yoneda) ran on the Communist Party ticket the following year for the California State Assembly but attracted hardly any Nisei support or (positive) attention.

48. Following a lobbying campaign by Tokutaro (Toki) Slocum, himself a veteran, in 1935 the U.S. Congress followed suit with legislation permitting a

group of some five hundred World War I U.S. Army veterans from Asian countries to be made eligible for citizenship. Bill Hosokawa, *JACL in Quest of Justice* (New York: Morrow, 1982), pp. 42–43.

49. Brian Nolan, *King's War: Mackenzie King and the Politics of War, 1939–1945* (Toronto: University of Toronto Press, 1988), p. 67.

50. Roy, *The Oriental Question*, pp. 159–61.

51. "The History of the Vote" web site, available at http://www.civilization.ca/hist/elections/el_037_e.html.

52. Michael G. Fry, "The Development of Canada's Relations with Japan, 1919–1947," in *Canadian Perspectives on Economic Relations With Japan*, ed. Keith A. J. Hay (Montreal: Institute for Research on Public Policy, 1980), pp. 24–31.

53. Gregory A. Johnson, "Canada and the Far East during the 1930s," in *Canada and Japan in the Twentieth Century*, ed. John Schiltz and Kimitada Miwa (New York: Oxford University Press, 1991), pp. 113–25.

54. John D. Meehan, *The Dominion and the Rising Sun: Canada Encounters Japan, 1929–41* (Vancouver: UBC Press, 2004), pp. 157–68.

55. Gary Y. Okihiro, *Cane Fires: The Anti-Japanese Movement in Hawaii, 1865–1945* (Philadelphia: Temple University Press, 1991), pp. 165–67. Colonel (later General) George S. Patton, head of Army G-2 from 1935 to 1937, devised an even more striking proposal, including taking selected Japanese nationals hostage and seizing all automobiles and taxis owned by local Japanese. Ibid., pp. 175–77.

56. General Hugh Drum to Adj. Gen, September 21, 1935; in AG381, Defense Mission, comments to House Military Affairs Subcommittee, reprinted in Tom Maycock, "FDR: Pacific Warlord," ms. 2000, available at http://users.erols.com/tomtud/wwwrootn1.html.

57. Franklin D. Roosevelt, Memorandum for Chief of Naval Operations, August 10, 1936, President's Secretary File 197, FDR Library, Hyde Park, N.Y. (henceforth FDRL).

58. Odo, *No Sword to Bury*, p. 106. The regulations remained in effect through the end of the war. As a result of the navy policy, the army was forced to hire large numbers of Nisei, given the overwhelming need for local labor. Fred L. Israel, "Military Justice in Hawaii, 1941–1944," *Pacific Historical Review* 36, 2 (August 1967): 245. Nisei students at University of Hawaii also drilled in the Reserve Officers Training Corps.

59. "Hawaii Orientals Are Loyal to U.S., Roosevelt Informed." *Nichi Bei*, February 12, 1938.

60. Cited in Bob Kuramoto, "The Search For Spies: American Counter-Intelligence and the Japanese American Community, 1931–1942," *Amerasia Journal* 6, 2 (Fall 1979): 49.

61. Donald H. Estes, "'Offensive Stupidity,' and the Struggle of Abe Tokus-noke," *Journal of San Diego History* 28, 4 (Fall 1984): 50.

62. Bernarr MacFadden, unidentified article in *Liberty*, cited in *Rafu Shimpo*, May 10, 1936; H. Brett Melendy, *The Oriental Americans* (Boston: Twayne, 1972), p. 154.

63. United States Supreme Court, *Gorin v. U.S.*, pp. 22, 23.

64. "Salich Trial Reveals Nisei 'Friend' as Spy," *Japanese American Mirror*, March 3, 1939, p. 1.

65. Following their conviction, Gorin and Salich appealed, and the case reached the U.S. Supreme Court, which in 1941 unanimously upheld the verdicts. United States Supreme Court, *Gorin v. U.S.*, 312 U.S. 19 (1941), pp. 21, 22.

66. H. deB. Claiborne, report, June 17, 1938, Government's Exhibit 6(h), re-printed in *Record on Appeal, United States Supreme Court* (henceforth *Record*), p. 277.

67. H. deB. Claiborne, report, November 16, 1938, Government's Exhibit 5(k), *Record*, p. 267. The report described an interview with the woman, who confessed that she had arranged a meeting with the sailor because she was in love with him. Unaware that she was being investigated as a potential spy, she assumed that such interracial intimacy was against regulations and begged her interrogator to punish her and shield him.

68. Henri deB. Claiborne, report June 7, 1938, Government's Exhibit 6(s), *Record*, pp. 287–88.

69. Copy, Undated Report, 1938, *Record*, p. 295.

70. Testimony of Hafis Salich, *Record*, p. 379. Another agent testified that Salich had a number of "Jap informants," though Salich himself did not confirm or deny this. Testimony of G. V. Dierst, *Record*, p. 26.

71. Testimony of Hafis Salich, *Record*, pp. 345–46.

72. Henri deB Claiborne, report June 7, 1938, *Record*, pp. 287–88.

73. "Tell Nisei Activities in Court," *Japanese American Mirror*, March 10, 1939.

74. "Nisei Beauty Calls on Spy Suspect, " *Rafu Shimpo*, March 15, 1936; see also Tony Matthews, *Shadows Dancing: Japanese Espionage against the West, 1939–1945* (New York: St. Martin's, 1993).

75. "Pearl Harbor Spy Admits Key Role," *New York Times*, December 9, 1953; Gavan Daws, *Shoals of Time: A History of the Hawaiian Islands* (Honolulu: University of Hawaii Press, 1968), pp. 346–47.

76. Eric Muller, "Is That Legal?" September 12, 2004, available at http://www.isthatlegal.org/mt/archives/2004_09_01_isthatlegal_archive.html.

77. Azuma, *Between Two Empires*, p. 52.

78. Gordon Chang, *Morning Glory, Evening Shadow: Yamato Ichihashi and His Internment Writings, 1942–1945* (Stanford: Stanford University Press, 1997), p. 45.

79. "Charge Nisei Contribute to War Fund," *Rafu Shimpo*, September 8, 1937.

80. Ogawa, *Kodomo no tame ni*, p. 232.

81. Azuma, *Between Two Empires*, p. 170.

82. Ayako Ishigaki, *Restless Wave: My Life in Two Worlds* (New York: Feminist Press, 2004 [1940]), p. 237. Apart from Ishigaki, who returned to the East Coast in despair over the change in Little Tokyo and shifted her focus to non-Japanese, there were few voices challenging Japan's actions. The small circle of "aka" (reds) surrounding the weekly Japanese Communist newspaper *Doho* expressed their opposition to the invasion. Nisei journalist Eddie Shimano, a liberal internationalist, joined Chinese Americans and white liberals in dockside protests against ships sending strategic materials to Japan. Betty Kobayashi, a Nisei student at McGill University in Montreal, rose at a meeting of the Canadian Youth Congress in Toronto to support a resolution for an arms embargo against Japan and a boycott of Japanese goods. *Nichi Bei*, June 7, 1938.

83. Forrest E. La Violette, *The Canadian Japanese and World War II* (Toronto: University of Toronto Press, 1948), p. 23n.

84. Sei Fujii, "Uncle Fujii Speaks," *Kashu Mainichi*, October 14, 1937.

85. "T.T." (Togo Tanaka) "Recognition at Hand," *Rafu Shimpo*, February 2, 1937; Togo Tanaka, "Post Script," *Rafu Shimpo*, September 23, 1937; Tad Uyeno, "Lancer's Column," *Rafu Shimpo*, February 19, 1940; Yuji Ichioka, Gordon H. Chang, and Eiichiro Azuma, *Before Internment: Essays in Prewar Japanese American History* (Stanford, Calif.: Stanford University Press, 2006), p. 159. Tanaka was later quoted as telling a subversive activities committee that *Rafu* reprinted numerous pro-Tokyo articles from Japanese newspapers during these years and distributed a directory that featured a photo of the Japanese emperor and empress and a Japanese caption praising militarism and the "new order in Asia" at the front. "Subversive Acts of Japs Here Related," *Los Angeles Times*, March 25, 1942.

86. Ito was brought to trial in April 1942 and exonerated by an all-white jury. Muller, "Is That Legal?"

87. North America was not the only area where the alleged pro-Japanese attitudes of Nisei led to government actions—as will be discussed in chapter 3, in 1937 the government of Peru excluded native-born children of Japanese ancestry from Peruvian citizenship. Gary Y. Okihiro, "Turning Japanese Americans," in *Encyclopedia of Japanese Descendents in the Americas*, ed. Kikumura-Kano, p. 22.

88. Meehan, *The Dominion and the Rising Sun*, p. 173.

89. Board of Review (Immigration) Report, Ottawa 1938, cited in La Violette, *The Canadian Japanese and World War II*, p. 30. Peter Ward suggests that the chief culprit in the affair was a pro-Chinese Anglican minister, F. G. Scott, who had alleged in an interview with the *Toronto Star* that Japanese

Army officers had been smuggled into Canada and were living in disguise in Pacific Coast fishing villages. Ward, *White Canada Forever*, p. 143.

90. Mario Duliani (r. Antonio Mazza), *The City without Women: A Chronicle of Internment Life in Canada during the Second World War* (Oakville, Ont.: Mosaic Press, 1994).

91. Adachi, *The Enemy That Never Was*, pp. 189–91.

92. *Special Committee on Orientals in British Columbia, Report and Recommendations, December 1940* (Ottawa: Government Printing Office, 1940), p. 16, cited in La Violette, *The Canadian Japanese and World War II*, p. 31.

93. Ito, *We Went to War*, pp. 111–12.

94. "Canada to Register All Japanese in British Columbia," *Nichi Bei*, January 14, 1941.

95. Patricia Roy et al., *Mutual Hostages: Canadians and Japanese during the Second World War* (Toronto: University of Toronto Press, 1990), p. 45.

96. For details of one such interview, see Dr. M. Miyazaki, *My Sixty Years in Canada* (privately printed, 1970), p. 21.

97. *Report of British Columbia Security Commission, Government of Dominion of Canada, Department of Labour, March 4, 1942 to October 31, 1942* (Vancouver? British Columbia Security Commission, 1942), p. 3 (henceforth *Report*). The registration revealed 23,512 people of Japanese ancestry in Canada: 6,727 Canadian-born, 7,011 naturalized citizens, 9,758 Japanese nationals, and 16 U.S. citizens. However, this figure was misleading because children under sixteen were listed only on their parents' forms and were thereby enumerated according to their parents' status. In fact, Canadian-born represented some 61 percent of the ethnic Japanese population.

98. For Canadian-American defense relations, see, for example, Roy et al., *Mutual Hostages*, pp. 35–40.

99. Stanley W. Dziuban, *United States Army in World War II. Special Studies: Military Relations Between the United States and Canada, 1939–1945* (Washington, D.C.: U.S. Government Printing Office, 1959). One article of the period reported that, "in line with the Board's work," there was a proposal to deport all illegal immigrants and to bar further Japanese immigration from Canada. However, it was not clear from what side the proposal came, and it was not put into effect. "Japanese in U.S.," *Newsweek*, October 14, 1940, pp. 42–44.

100. Assistant Secretary of War John J. McCloy, though his name did not appear on the recipient list for MAGIC intercepts, seems to have had access to the information contained therein. McCloy did not connect Japanese Americans to MAGIC and indeed denied that there was any connection. In his last years, however, at a time when he was anxious to avert an official condemnation of mass removal, he abruptly changed his story. See Klancy Clark de Nevers, "A Critique of Michelle Malkin's Rewriting of History," available at http://www.colonelandthepacifist.com/research.htm.

101. Michelle Malkin, *In Defense of Internment* (Chicago: Henry Regnery, 2004). See also David D. Lowman, *Magic: The Untold Story of U.S. Intelligence and the Evacuation of Japanese Residents from the West Coast during WW II* (Provo, Ut.: Athena Press, 2000); Keith Robar, *Intelligence, Internment, and Relocation* (Seattle: Kikar Publications, 2000). In the final chapter of this volume I will discuss the controversy over the work of the "internment deniers."

102. For a comprehensive critique of Malkin's work, see Eric Muller and Greg Robinson, "Muller and Robinson on Malkin," available at http://www.isthatlegal.org/Muller_and_Robinson_on_Malkin.html.

103. MAGIC message no. 044, January 30, 1941. Available at http://www.athenapressinc.com/mm01.htm.

104. John A. Herzig, "Japanese Americans and MAGIC," *Amerasia Journal* 11, 2 (November–December 1984): 47–65.

105. MAGIC message no. 067, May 9, 1941.

106. "Vetterli Defense Hit in Red Case," *Los Angeles Times*, July 12, 1951. Miwa succeeded in joining the U.S. Army shortly after Pearl Harbor and later served in the U.S. occupation forces in Japan.

107. John Stephan, *Hawaii under the Rising Sun* (Honolulu: University of Hawaii Press, 1984).

108. "Japan's Pearl Harbor Spy," *Washington Post*, December 10, 1978.

109. Kuramoto, "The Search for Spies," p. 49. For ONI, see also Alan Hynd, *Betrayal From the East: Japanese Spies in America* (New York: R. M. McBride, 1943).

110. "Alien-Owned Boats Seized at Hawaii," *New York Times*, May 2, 1941.

111. Israel, "Military Justice in Hawaii, 1941–1944," p. 244.

112. Andrew W. Lind, *The Japanese in Hawaii under War Conditions* (Honolulu and New York: American Council, Institute of Pacific Relations, 1943), p. 5.

113. Jim A. Richstad, "The Press and the Courts Under Martial Law in Hawaii During World War II—From Pearl Harbor to *Duncan v. Kahanamoku*," cited in Molly J. Pietsch, "Rhoda Valentine Lewis," ms., Stanford University, 2006, available at http://womenslegalhistory.stanford.edu/papers06/LewisRhodaV-bio-pitsch06.pdf.

114. J. Garner Anthony, *Hawaii under Army Rule* (Stanford: Stanford University Press, 1955), p. 4.

115. "Power to Declare Martial Law Asked," *Kashu Mainichi*, November 5, 1941.

116. Memorandum, Secretary of the Navy to the President, October 9, 1940, President's Secretary's File (Safe File: Navy Department), reprinted in "Papers of the Commission on Wartime Relocation and Internment of Civilians, Lanham, MD, University Publications of America, 1984 (hereafter CWRIC Papers), p. 19456 (reel 17, p. 9).

117. Franklin D. Roosevelt, Memorandum for the Secretary of the Navy, October 10, 1940. PSF Safe File, Navy 1934–1942, FDRL; James Miyamoto, "What about Rumors?," letter, *Rafu Shimpo*, May 11, 1941.

118. "Concentration Camp for Aliens Is Nearing Completion at Upton," *New York Times*, October 18, 1941; see also "Concentration Camps," *Rafu Shimpo*, November 2, 1941. On October 31 the *Times* published a follow-up article with a photo of the camp.

119. Louis Fiset, "Censored! U.S. Censors and Internment Camp Mail in World War II," in *Guilt by Association: Essays in Japanese Settlement, Internment, and Relocation in the Rocky Mountain West*, ed. Mike Mackey (Powell, Wy.: Western History Publications, 2001), p. 69; Tetsuden Kashima, *Judgment without Trial: Japanese American Imprisonment during World War II* (Seattle: University of Washington Press, 2003), p. 105. Just when these camps were built is not certain, but in January 1941 it was reported that a CCC camp in Columbus, New Mexico, would be used to house the Germans. In June it was reported that INS had requested $750,000 for construction of concentration camps for alien seamen. Jerry Kluttz, "The Federal Diary," *Washington Post*, January 16, 1941; June 2, 1941.

120. "U.S. Sharply Tightens Curbs on Aliens," *Christian Science Monitor*, November 19, 1941.

121. "Place aux internés aux États-Unis," *Courrier du Pacifique—San Francisco*, November 27, 1941.

122. "F.B.I. Puts Japanese Under Inquiry Here," *Los Angeles Times*, November 13, 1941. Although the Justice Department pledged that all "law-abiding" aliens would be left alone, the plan seemed not to distinguish between such categories as "law-abiding" and not.

123. "Alien Camps Urged in Fifth Column War," *Los Angeles Times*, March 16, 1941; "House Kills Bill to Detain Aliens; More Detention Camps Planned," *New York Times*, November 19, 1941.

124. "Bill to Pen Up Aliens Is Voted Down in House,' *Chicago Tribune*, November 19, 1941.

125. "Decisions in a Crisis, "*Rafu Shimpo*, December 7, 1941; "Alien Detention Measure Killed by 167–141 Vote," *Washington Post*, November 19, 1941. Earlier that year, Eliot had also led the fight against Hobbs's bill, backed by the president, to legalize wiretapping without warrant by the executive branch.

126. Modell, *The Economics and Politics of Racial Accommodation*, pp. 176–79.

127. Kurashige, *Japanese American Celebration and Conflict*.

128. One Nisei pacifist, Kiyoshi Conrad Hamanaka, requested conscientious objector status. Placed in solitary confinement in a military stockade, he ultimately agreed to serve as a medic and was released. Conversation with author, February 2007.

129. Gongoro Nakamura, "Justice Department Concurs in Contention, Issei to Be Considered Legal Residents," *Kashu Mainichi*, March 18, 1941.

130. Tamura, *Americanization, Acculturation and Ethnic Identity*, p. 85.

131. Radford Mobley, "Hawaii Looks toward Statehood," *Christian Science Monitor*, November 2, 1940.

132. "Japanese in Hawaii Vow Allegiance," *Los Angeles Times*, April 9, 1941.

133. Tom Coffman, *The First Battle: The Battle for Equality in Wartime Hawaii*, documentary film (Tom Coffman, 2006); Okihiro, *Cane Fires*, p. 184.

134. Yoshida, cited in Daws, *Shoals of Time*, p. 339.

135. Editorial. "A Timely Advice," *Current Life*, July 1941, p. 2.

136. Forrest E. La Violette, "The American-Born Japanese and the World Crisis," *Canadian Journal of Economics and Political Science* 7, 4 (1941): 517–52. For other concentration camp rumors, see Joseph Barbar, *Hawaii: Restless Rampart* (New York: Bobbs-Merrill, 1941); Robinson, *By Order of the President*, p. 88.

137. "Exposing the Peril at Panama," *Ken* 1, 1 (April 7, 1938): 40 et seq., reprinted in *Salich Record*, pp. 485–513. See also *Ken*, April 6, 1939; July 27, 1939.

138. Sutherland Denlinger, "Japanese Espionage," *New York World-Telegram*, April 9, 1938, reprinted in *San Francisco Nichi Bei*, April 11, 1938. Popular writer Fannie Hurst, following a visit Hawaii, reported in the Hearst-owned *Cosmopolitan* magazine that Japan was exerting enormous pressure on the Nisei in Hawaii, who felt a dual allegiance, and insisted (improbably) that many had claimed to be so torn that in the event of war between Japan and the United States they would feel obliged to commit suicide rather than support one against the other. "Nisei in Hawaii May Constitute Major Problem for America in Future, Says Noted U.S. Writer," *Nichi Bei*, June 18, 1938.

139. Jerry D. Lewis, "5th Column in California," *Liberty*, August 10, 1940, pp. 13–14. Various other books and articles featured wild stories of Issei and Nisei participation in espionage activities. See, for example, John L. Spivak, *Honorable Spy: Exposing Japanese Military Intrigue in the United States* (New York: Modern Books, 1939), p. 119 (land purchases on Mexican border, stockpiling oil for Japanese submarines); Curt Reiss, *Total Espionage* (New York: Putnam, 1941), p. 47 (fishing boats in Alaska); Michael Sayers and Albert B. Kahn, *Sabotage: The Secret War against America* (New York: Harper's, 1942) (guns, ammunition and maps, signaling devices on Terminal Island); Hynd, *Betrayal from the East* (acid stored in Buddhist temples, shortwave radio reporting to Tokyo, blackmail via prostitutes, etc.).

140. "Nisei Loyalty to U.S. Told in Post Article," *San Francisco Nichi Bei*, September 28, 1939.

141. "Signs of the Times," *Rafu Shimpo*, September 29, 1940. A truck farmer is a local grower who trucks in his produce to the market. Despite their small numbers in the population, Issei dominated the production and distribution of many vegetables in California

142. Bernard F. Dick, *The Star-Spangled Screen: The American World War II Film* (Lexington: University Press of Kentucky, 1985), p. 107.

143. "False Rumors Result in Uneasiness Among the Nisei," *Rafu Shimpo*, October 6, 1941.

144. Haan would later claim that he received advance word of the Japanese attack on Pearl Harbor in March 1941 from war plans that he stole from an Issei in Los Angeles. Haan's warnings, however, apparently concerned Japanese stockpiling of arms for an insurrection, rather than sending of a carrier fleet. "Attack Long Planned, Evidence Indicates," *New York Times*, December 8, 1941; "An Invasion of U.S. Termed Tokyo Aim," *New York Times*, January 12, 1942.

145. *Kashu Mainichi*, October 26, 1940.

146. "Japan Reported Drafting Sons Born in U.S.," *Chicago Tribune*, January 5, 1941.

147. "Dies Reports Sabotage Plot," *Los Angeles Times*, July 31, 1941.

148. J. Edgar Hoover, "Memorandum for the Acting Attorney General," August 1, 1941, August 8, 1941, Japanese Subversion folder, Justice Department War Division papers, RG 60.14 National Archives and Records Administration, Washington, D.C. (hereafter NARA)

149. "Dies Committee Defers Hearing," *Los Angeles Times*, September 14, 1941.

150. "U.S. Reprisals Suggested," *New York Times*, August 18, 1941.

151. Magner White, "Between Two Flags," *The Saturday Evening Post*, September 20, 1939, pp. 24–25.

152. "California Casts an Anxious Eye on Japanese Americans in its Midst," *Life*, October 17, 1940.

153. Jim Marshall, "West Coast Japanese," *Collier's*, October 11, 1941, pp. 14–15; Ernest O. Hauser, "America's 150,000 Japanese," *American Mercury* 53 (December 1941): 689–97.

154. Federal Bureau of Investigation, Memorandum, November 15, 1940, FBI records 65-286-61, reprinted in *Documents of the Commission on Wartime Relocation and Internment of Civilians* (Frederick, Md.: University Publications of America, 1983), p. 19456 (reel 17, p. 9) (henceforth CRWIC).

155. Kashima, *Judgment without Trial*, p. 37.

156. Robinson, *By Order of the President*, pp. 66–67, 71. Curtis Munson, Warren Irwin, memoranda, November 7, 11, 1941. Office of Strategic Services reports, RG 226, Reel 55, pp. 530–44, NARA.

157. Kashima, *Judgment without Trial*, chap. 1.

2. THE DECISION TO REMOVE ETHNIC JAPANESE FROM THE WEST COAST

1. See, for example, Blake Clark, *Remember Pearl Harbor* (New York: Modern Age Books, 1942); Gavan Daws, *Shoals of Time: A History of the Hawaiian Islands* (Honolulu: University of Hawaii Press, 1968), pp. 345–46. A few

latter-day apologists for Japanese American confinement have described the Niihau incident as key in prompting President Roosevelt to sign Executive Order 9066. See, for example, Burl Burlingame, "War Stories with Oliver North," *FoxNews*, January 16, 2005. This appears to be unfounded speculation. There is no evidence that the Niihau incident influenced later policy—in none of the mountain of transcripts and memoranda of War Department and White House discussions regarding Japanese Americans on the West Coast that I have reviewed is the Niihau incident even once mentioned.

2. Edwin T. Layton et al., *"And I Was There": Pearl Harbor and Midway— Breaking the Secrets* (New York: Quill, 1985), pp. 55, 74–75.

3. Garner Anthony, *Hawaii under Army Rule* (Stanford, Calif.: Stanford University Press, 1955), pp. 6, 9.

4. While official lists of the fifty-seven recorded civilian casualties did not distinguish victims by national origin, a check reveals numerous Japanese names (which would be logical, given the significant percentage of local Japanese in Oahu). For an unofficial estimate, see Burt Takeuchi, "Pearl Harbor: Asian Americans Witness Historic Air Raid," *Nichi Bei Times*, May 25, 2001; available at http://us_asians.tripod.com/articles-nihonmachi-outreach.html.

5. Allan R. Bosworth, *America's Concentration Camps* (New York: W. W. Norton, 1967), p. 46.

6. See Tetsuden Kashima, *Judgment without Trial: Japanese American Imprisonment during World War II* (Seattle: University of Washington Press, 2003), chaps. 3–7. On the process of interrogation and internment in Hawaii, see Michael John Gold, "Suspects in Paradise: Looking for Japanese Subversives in the Territory of Hawaii, 1935-1945," M.A. thesis, University of Iowa, 1983.

7. Kashima, *Judgment without Trial*. On the experience of the internees, see, for example, Louis Fiset's poignant story of the correspondence of an interned Issei man and his wife, *Imprisoned Apart* (Seattle: University of Washington Press, 1997).

8. Richard L. Neuberger, "Reveille in the Northwest," *Nation*, December 20, 1941, p. 638.

9. David A. Neiwert, *Strawberry Days* (New York: Palgrave/Macmillan, 2005), p. 104.

10. Bill Hosokawa, *Nisei: The Quiet Americans* (New York: Morrow, 1969), p. 253.

11. Roger Daniels, *Concentration Camps USA: Japanese Americans and World War II* (New York: Holt, Rinehart and Winston, 1971), pp. 35–36.

12. Frank Knox, "Report by the Secretary of the Navy to the President," December 14, 1941, PSF Navy Department File, Hawaii, FDRL.

13. Treasury Department Interoffice Communication, Ed Foley to Secretary Morgenthau, January 28, 1942, Henry Morgenthau Diaries, FDRL.

14. Francis Biddle, Cabinet Notes, December 19, 1941, Attorney General Papers, FDRL. According to one contemporary but third-hand source, which seems at least exaggerated, President Roosevelt told Secretary of War Stimson during the meeting that he wished to intern all Japanese aliens in Hawaii, preferably on an outlying island, but that Stimson preferred to leave any such action to the discretion of the local commander. Edward A. Tanm, Memorandum to FBI Director J. Edgar Hoover, December 22, 1941, 100-2-20-44, FBI files, NARA. I am indebted to Tom Coffman for sharing this document with me.

15. Greg Robinson, *By Order of the President: FDR and the Internment of Japanese Americans* (Cambridge: Harvard University Press, 2001), pp. 77–78.

16. Patricia Roy et al., *Mutual Hostages: Canadians and Japanese during the Second World War* (Toronto: University of Toronto Press, 1990), pp. 45–46.

17. Tom Sando, *Wild Daisies in the Sand: Life in a Canadian Internment Camp* (Edmonton: NeWest Press, 2002), p. 2. Interview in Barry Broadfoot, *Years of Sorrow, Years of Shame: The Story of the Japanese Canadians in World War II* (Markham, Ont.: PaperJacks Doubleday, 1979), p. 58.

18. British Columbia Security Commission, *Report*, p. 3.

19. Japanese Canadian Centennial Project, *A Dream of Riches*, p. 77. A secretary of the Fisherman's Union later recalled that he was told by RCMP police who arrested him in Steveston that he would return home within a few hours or days, but he was separated from his family for a year and never returned to Vancouver. Tsugeo Minuoka, cited in Janice Patton, *The Exodus of the Japanese* (Toronto: McClelland and Stewart, 1973), pp. 9–10.

20. Ann Gomer Sunahara asserts that the roundup and raids implemented defense decisions developed in conjunction with the Americans. However, she offers no specific evidence for this allegation, which seems doubtful on its face. Sunahara, *The Politics of Racism: The Uprooting of Japanese Canadians during World War II* (Toronto: Lorimer, 1981), p. 28.

21. "Citizens, Be Calm," *Vancouver Sun*, December 8, 1941, cited in Ted Barris, *Days of Victory: Canadians Remember, 1939–1945* (Toronto: Thomas Altenfus, 2005), p. 160.

22. Letter, H. Bruce Hutchison to Jack Pickersgill, December 16, 1941, cited in W. Peter Ward, *White Canada Forever: Popular Attitudes and Public Policy toward Orientals in British Columbia* (Montreal: McGill-Queens University Press, 1978), p. 149.

23. Forrest E. La Violette, *The Canadian Japanese and World War II* (Toronto: University of Toronto Press, 1948), p. 36.

24. Gary Y. Okihiro, *Cane Fires: The Anti-Japanese Movement in Hawaii, 1865–1945* (Philadelphia: Temple University Press, 1991), pp. 227–37; For an

extended description of the life of one such family, see Michiko Kodama-Nishimoto, "Oral History Interview with Ruth Yamaguchi," April 1992, in *An Era of Change: Oral Histories of Civilians in World War II Hawaii* (Manoa: Center for Oral History, University of Hawaii, 1994).

25. Daws, *Shoal of Time*, p. 348.

26. C. Harvey Gardiner, "The Japanese and Central America," *Journal of Interamerican Studies and World Affairs* 14, 1 (February 1972): 22. Interview with Edward Stuntz, in Roy Hoopes, *Americans Remember the Home Front* (abridged edition) (New York: Berkley Books, 1992 [1977]), p. 11. Costa Rica's action infuriated the government of Cuba, which sought to be the first nation to join the U.S. in declaring war.

27. Yuriko Nagata, *Unwanted Aliens: Japanese Internment in Australia* (St. Lucia: University of Queensland Press, 1996). See also, generally, Kay Saunders and Roger Daniels, eds., *Alien Justice: Wartime Internment in Australia and North America* (St Lucia: Queensland University Press, 2000).

28. Tadao Kobayashi, trans. Keiko Raulet-Akaza, *Les Japonais en Nouvelle-Caledonie: Histoire des émigrés sous contrat* (Nouvelle Calédonie: Publications de la société d'études historiques de la Nouvelle-Calédonie, 1992), pp. 154–56.

29. Edward Ennis interview, September 25, 1942, pp. 2–3. Morton Grodzins research notes no. 5, reel 6, p. 211, Japanese Evacuation Research Study, Bancroft Library, University of California, Berkeley (henceforth JERS).

30. Telephone call, John DeWitt with Allen Gullion, December 26, 1941, WDC-CAD 311.3 Tel Convs, quoted in Stetson Conn, "The Decision to Evacuate the Japanese from the Pacific Coast," in *Guarding the United States and Its Outposts*, ed. Stetson Conn, Rose C. Engelman, and Byron Fairchild (Washington, D.C.: United States Government, Center for Military History, 2000 [1964]), p. 128.

31. So anxious was Bendetsen to be admitted into positions of importance that he had long concealed his Jewish origins and even changed the spelling of his name from "Bendetson" shortly after Pearl Harbor in order to pass himself off more easily as Scandanavian. See Klancy Clark de Nevers, *The Colonel and the Pacifist* (Salt Lake City: University of Utah Press, 2004).

32. "Biddle Flays Un-American Employers," *Kashu Mainichi*, January 8, 1942.

33. Conn, "The Decision to Evacuate the Japanese," p. 131.

34. Ibid., p. 132.

35. "California in World War II: The Attacks on the S.S. Montebello and the SS Idaho," available at http://www.militarymuseum.org/Montebello.html.

36. "Tokyo Claims 65 Sinkings," *New York Times*, May 17, 1942.

37. One widespread, if absurd, story alleged that Issei sugar cane farmers had planted their crops in the shape of arrows to direct Japanese planes to Pearl Harbor (a target impossible to miss in any case) and to aircraft factories in

Southern California. Film mogul Samuel Goldwyn allegedly reacted to the reports by fearing that his studio would be taken for a factory, and ordering an arrow painted on the studio roof.

38. It is impossible to measure the actual level of public feeling over the chance of a Japanese raid. Comedian Groucho Marx, living in Hollywood, commented half-seriously in February that "any day I expect a forty-pound shell to come hurtling through my roof and announce the arrival of the Mikado." Groucho Marx, letter to Arthur Sheekman, February 12, 1942, in *The Groucho Letters: Letters from and to Groucho Marx* (New York: Simon and Schuster, 1967), p. 30.

39. California Joint Immigration Committee Meeting Minutes, February 7, 1942, cited in Jacobus tenBroek, Edward N. Barnhart, and Floyd W. Matson, *Prejudice, War and the Constitution* (Berkeley: University of California Press, 1954), p.78.

40. For a full study of the involvement of these organizations, see Morton Grodzins, *Americans Betrayed* (Chicago: University of Chicago Press, 1949), chap. 2. But see ten Broek, Barnhart, and Matson, *Prejudice, War and the Constitution*, who minimize the number of groups and their importance in the decision for mass removal.

41. Frank J. Taylor, "The People Nobody Wants," *The Saturday Evening Post*, May 9, 1942, p. 66, cited in U.S. Commission on Wartime Relocation and Internment of Civilians, *Personal Justice Denied* (Seattle: University of Washington Press, 1997 [1983]), p. 66. For a similar example of anti-Japanese American organizing in other states, see the account of Miller Freeman of Bellevue, Washington, in Neiwert, *Strawberry Days*, pp. 111–17.

42. Letter, Leo Carillo to Leland Ford, January 6, 1942, cited in ten Broek, Barnhart, and Matson, *Prejudice, War and the Constitution*, p. 77.

43. Robinson, *By Order of the President*, pp. 91–92.

44. See "Memo to Mayor Bowron by Alfred Cohn," January 10, 1942; Orville Caldwell, undated six-page memo, January 1942, Japanese alien file, Fletcher Bowron Papers, Huntington Library, San Marino, Calif.

45. Letter, Fletcher Bowron to Commander Edward A. Hayes, January 22, 1942, Japanese alien files, Fletcher Bowron Papers, Huntington Library.

46. Ibid.

47. Daniels, *Concentration Camps USA*, p. 68.

48. Cited in Sunahara, *The Politics of Racism*, p. 31.

49. Letter, R. O. Alexander to Chief of Staff, December 30, 1941, cited in Ward, *White Canada Forever*, p. 149. Ironically, just weeks before, Alexander and two other officers had signed a memorandum deploring the discriminatory treatment of Canadians of Japanese ancestry. See PAC, RG 24, vol. 2730 memorandum, Joint Services Committee, September 20, 1941, cited in Roy Ito, *We Went to War: The Story of the Japanese Canadians Who Served during*

the First and Second World Wars (Stittsville, Ont.: Canada's Wings, 1984), p. 125.

50. Vancouver Daily Province, January 12, 1942, cited in La Violette, The Canadian Japanese and World War II, p. 45; "Les Japonais," La Presse, December 16, 1941; "Japanese in Canada," Globe and Mail, January 6, 1942.

51. Minutes of meetings, January 8–10, 1942, Department of Labour File RG27, vol. 655, Public Archives of Canada, reprinted in Yon Shimizu, The Exiles: An Archival History of the World War II Japanese Road Labour Camps in British Columbia and Ontario (Wallaceburg, Ont.: Shimizu Consulting, 1993), pp. 34–43.

52. Ibid. Pope stated in his memoirs that he came away from the meeting "feeling dirty all over." Maurice Pope, Soldiers and Politicians (Toronto: University of Toronto Press, 1962), cited in Sunahara, The Politics of Racism, p. 33.

53. Roy et al., Mutual Hostages, pp. 81–82.

54. Sunahara, The Politics of Racism, pp. 35–36.

55. William Lyon Mackenzie King Diary, January 13, 1942. Library and Archives of Canada (hencefore LAC), Ottawa.

56. La Violette, The Canadian Japanese and World War II, pp. 47–48. The announcement left ambiguous whether this category included adult Nisei and naturalized Issei. There was no public clarification, although during the following week Labour Minister Humphrey Mitchell affirmed that all men of Japanese ancestry would be treated identically. H.H. memorandum to Deputy Minister, "Re. Movement of Japanese from British Columbia Coast," January 21, 1942, reprinted in Shimizu, The Exiles, p. 43.

57. Muriel Kitagawa, This Is My Own: Letters to Wes and Other Writings on Japanese Canadians, 1941–1948 (Vancouver: Talonbooks, 1985), p. 82.

58. La Violette, The Canadian Japanese and World War II, p. 53.

59. Sunahara, The Politics of Racism, p. 39.

60. A. Katsuyoshi Morita, Powell Street Monogatari (Vancouver: Live Canada Publishing, 1988), p. 3; Wes Fujiwara, "A Warning to Nisei Moving East," New Canadian, February 16, 1942.

61. The Canadian government's move was reported in a single brief dispatch, without analysis, in the New York Times and was not reported at all in the Chicago Tribune, Washington Post, Los Angeles Times, or Oakland Tribune. A rare newspaper to discuss the case of the Japanese Canadians was the Christian Science Monitor, whose editorial policy favored civil rights for Japanese Americans.

62. Harry McLemore, column, San Francisco Examiner, cited in Bosworth, America's Concentration Camps, p. 52.

63. "200,000 Enemy Aliens Must Quit Pacific Coast," New York Daily News, February 2, 1942.

64. Ibid.

65. Lawrence E. Davies, "Coast Axis Aliens Face Business Ban," *New York Times*, January 31, 1942.

66. Allida M. Black, *Casting Her Own Shadow: Eleanor Roosevelt and the Shaping of Postwar Liberalism* (New York: Columbia University Press, 1995), p. 143.

67. "Brown Reassures Japanese Residents," *Kashu Mainichi*, January 29, 1942; John Modell, *The Economics and Politics of Racial Accommodation: The Japanese of Los Angeles, 1900–1942* (Urbana: University Press of Illinois, 1977), p. 185.

68. U.S. Commission on Wartime Relocation and Internment of Civilians, *Personal Justice Denied*, p. 75.

69. Karl Bendetsen, memo for the Adjutant General, January 31, 1942, cited in Daniels, *Concentration Camps, USA*, pp. 54–55.

70. Grodzins, *Americans Betrayed*, pp. 67–69.

71. J. John Lawler, "Memorandum for the Files re: Japanese Alien Situation," January 27, 1942. Morgenthau Diaries, FDRL. Such a conference had been originally proposed two weeks earlier by Secretary of Agriculture Claude Wickard, who suggested planning the partial exclusion of Japanese aliens, to be replaced by Mexican or Filipino laborers, and a system of protection so that those Japanese aliens considered trustworthy could continue to harvest their crops. Letter, Claude R. Wickard to Henry Morgenthau, January 16, 1942. Morgenthau diaries, FDRL.

72. Letter, Francis Biddle to Paul McNutt, January 31, 1942, copy in Japanese American section, files of Common Council for American Unity, Immigration and Refugee Services of America Papers, Special Collections, Immigration History Research Center, University of Minnesota.

73. "Minutes of the Meeting of the Consultative Council," February 11, 1942. Japanese American section, Papers of Common Council for American Unity, Immigration and Refugee Services of America Papers, Special Collections, Immigration History Research Center, University of Minnesota.

74. Memo to President from Harold D. Smith, Director, Bureau of the Budget. President's Secretary File, 133, FDR; Audrie Girdner and Anne Loftis, *The Great Betrayal: The Evacuation of the Japanese-Americans during World War II* (New York: Macmillan, 1969), pp. 106–7. One FSA holdover who remained was photographer Dorothea Lange, whom the agency had previously employed to document the lives of migrant farmworkers and the dispossessed. At the request of the War Relocation Authority, Lange would photograph the removal of Japanese Americans. Linda Gordon and Gary Y. Okihiro, eds., *Impounded: Dorothea Lange and the Censored Images of Japanese American Internment* (New York: W. W. Norton, 2006).

75. Culbert Olson, speech, February 4, 1942, cited in Daniels, *Concentration Camps USA*, p. 60.

76. See for example, Bill Hosokawa, *JACL in Quest of Justice* (New York: Morrow, 1982), p. 144.

77. Ibid., p. 62.

78. Page Smith, *Democracy on Trial* (New York: Simon and Schuster, 1995), p. 118.

79. U.S. Commission on Wartime Relocation and Internment of Civilians, *Personal Justice Denied*, p. 84.

80. Hosokawa, *Nisei*, pp. 280–81.

81. "Facts Demanded on Coast Danger," *New York Times*, February 15, 1942.

82. Richard H. Minear, *Dr. Seuss Goes to War: The World War II Editorial Cartons of Theodor Seuss Geisel* (New York: The New Press, 1999). The cartoon is also available at http://orpheus.ucsd.edu/speccoll/dspolitic/Frame.htm. I thank Roger Daniels for this second reference.

83. "Pacific Coast Aliens," *New York Times*, February 15, 1942; Smith, *Democracy on Trial*, p.110.

84. James Omura, "The Nisei on Trial," *Current Life*, January 1942, p.16.

85. See letter, Karl Yoneda to J. Edgar Hoover, December 17, 1941; letter, Karl Yoneda to Francis Biddle, January 3, 1942, Japanese alien files, War Problems Division, Department of Justice Files, RG 44, NARA.

86. On JACL spying efforts, see Yuji Ichioka, "A Study in Dualism: James Yoshinori Sakamoto and the Japanese American Courier 1928–1942," *Amerasia Journal* 13 (1986): 71–74

87. Togo Tanaka, "Wake up, Nisei," *Rafu Shimpo*, February 14, 1942; Setsuko Matsunaga, telegram to President Roosevelt, February 10, 1942. Letters to the president from the public, reel 6, JERS.

88. See, for example, Togo Tanaka, "How to Survive Racism in America's Free Society,'" in *Voices Long Silent: An Oral Inquiry Into Japanese American Evacuation*, ed. Arthur A. Hansen and Betty K. Mitson, Fullerton Oral History Program, Japanese American Project (Fullerton: California State University, 1974).

89. An interesting community study is S. Frank Miyamoto, "The Seattle JACL and Its Role in Evacuation," file 6.24, JERS.

90. Shizue Seigel, *In Good Conscience: Supporting Japanese Americans During Internment* (San Francisco: Kansha Project, 2006), pp. 48–65.

91. See, for example, letter, Ann Ray to Norman Thomas, January 23, 1942. Correspondence files, Norman Thomas Papers, Princeton University (henceforth Norman Thomas Papers). Thomas wrote to congratulate Biddle on standing up to the political pressure for removal but made no public statements on the subject until after Executive Order 9066 was signed. Greg Robinson, "Norman Thomas and the Struggle against Internment," *Prospects: An Annual of American Cultural Studies* 29 (2004): 419–34.

92. Daniels, *Concentration Camps USA*, p. 56.

93. Peter H. Irons, *Justice at War* (New York: Oxford University Press, 1983), p. 46.

94. Smith, *Democracy on Trial*, p. 112.

95. Bosworth, *America's Concentration Camps*, p. 90.

96. Henry L. Stimson, diary entry, February 9, 1942, Henry L. Stimson Papers, Stirling Library, Yale University.

97. See letter, Fletcher Bowron to Francis Biddle, February 3, 1942. Japanese alien file, Fletcher Bowron papers, Huntington Library, San Marino, Calif.

98. Attorney General, Memorandum for the President, "West Coast prohibited areas." February 6, 1942. Edward Ennis file, Francis Biddle Papers, FDRL.

99. The position taken by Clark at the meeting is not recorded. However, his position can be inferred from the memo he produced around the same time, which decisively opposed any "mass exodus" that would eat up resources and recommended concentrating on using a permit system to remove aliens and suspect citizens from small areas around military installations. Mark W. Clark, memo, General Headquarters, ca. February 12, 1942, reprinted in Daniels, *Concentration Camps USA*, pp. 65–67.

100. Irons, *Justice at War*, p. 57.

101. Henry L. Stimson, diary entry, February 11, 1942. Henry L. Stimson Papers.

102. For an extended treatment of the influence of Franklin Roosevelt's background and race-based attitudes toward Japanese Americans in shaping his decision to approve mass removal, see Robinson, *By Order of the President.*

103. Ibid., chap. 3.

104. Henry Stimson, diary entry, February 17, 1942. Stimson Papers.

105. Ibid., February 18, 1942.

106. Henry L. Stimson, diary entries, February 20, 1942, February 26, 1942. Stimson Papers.

107. Ibid.; Francis Biddle, Cabinet Notes, February 26, 1942, Francis Biddle Papers, FDRL.

108. "Ottawa takes Wise Course," *Toronto Globe and Mail*, January 15, 1942.

109. Patricia E. Roy, *The Oriental Question: Consolidating a White Man's Province, 1914–1941* (Vancouver: UBC Press, 2003), p. 239.

110. Forrest Emmanuel La Violette, *The Struggle for Survival: Indian Cultures and the Protestant Ethnic in British Columbia* (Toronto: University of Toronto Press, 1961), p. 145.

111. See, for example, "Clear B.C. Coast of All Japs," *Toronto Star*, January 14, 1942.

112. Kitagawa, *This Is My Own*, p. 87.

113. Shimizu, *The Exiles*, p. 17.

114. Government of Canada, *House of Commons Debates, 1942*, pp. 156, 433, cited in Ken Adachi, *The Enemy That Never Was: A History of the Japanese Canadians* (Toronto: McClellan and Stewart, 1976), p. 206.

115. Roy et al., *Mutual Hostages*, p. 93.

116. Ibid., p. 92.

117. Mary Taylor, *A Black Mark: The Japanese-Canadians in World War II* (Toronto: Oberon Press, 2004), pp. 23–24.

118. Letter, Ian Mackenzie to John Hart, January 15, 1942, in Sunahara, *The Politics of Racism*, p. 41.

119. Adachi, *The Enemy That Never Was*, p. 207.

120. Ito, *We Went to War*, pp. 144–45.

121. Mackenzie King Diary, February 19, 1942, National Library and Archives of Canada, Ottawa (henceforth LAC).

122. La Violette, *The Canadian Japanese and World War II*, p. 59.

123. Bruce Hutchison, *The Incredible Canadian: A Candid Portrait of Mackenzie King* (Don Mills, Ont: Longmans Canada, 1952), p. 302. Hutchison had a private talk with King that week about the Japanese invasion threat, so he would have been in a privileged position to assess King's attitude. See King Diary, February 27, 1942, LAC.

124. Sunahara, *The Politics of Racism*, pp. 43–44. The author suggests elsewhere, however, that when and why the policy of complete evacuation prevailed remains obscure. Ann Gomer Sunahara, "Federal Policy and Japanese Canadians," in *Visible Minorities and Multiculturalism: Asians in Canada*, ed. Gordon R. Hirabayashi and K. Victor Ujimoto (Toronto: Butterworth's, 1980), pp. 112–13.

125. Mackenzie King Diary, February 23, 1942, LAC.

126. Patricia E. Roy, *The Triumph of Citizenship: The Japanese and Chinese in Canada, 1941–1967* (Vancouver: UBC Press, 2007), chap. 1.

127. A partial exception is Stephanie Bangarth, "Mackenzie King and Japanese Canadians," in *Mackenzie King: Citizenship and Community: Essays Marking the 125th Anniversary of the Birth of William Lyon Mackenzie King*, ed. John English and Kenneth McLaughlin (Toronto: Robins Brass Studio, 2002), pp. 99–123.

128. Mackenzie King Diary, February 28, 1942, LAC.

129. Smith, *Democracy on Trial*, p. 102.

130. Memorandum, John J. McCloy, "Memorandum for Mr. Patterson," July 23, 1942, Robert Patterson Papers, Library of Congress (henceforth LOC). For a fuller discussion of the memo and its significance, see Greg Robinson, "The McCloy Memo: A New Look at Japanese American Internment," HNN, September 13, 2005, http://hnn.us/articles/15673.html.

3. REMOVAL FROM THE WEST COAST AND CONTROL OF ETHNIC JAPANESE OUTSIDE

1. U.S. Commission on Wartime Relocation and Internment of Civilians, *Personal Justice Denied* (Seattle: University of Washington Press, 1997 [1983]),

pp. 10–101. No citizens of German or Italian ancestry were included in these provisions.

2. "Hawaiian Attackers Wore School Insignia," *Christian Science Monitor,* March 21 1942.

3. Jacobus tenBroek, Edward N. Barnhart, and Floyd W. Matson, *Prejudice, War and the Constitution* (Berkeley: University of California Press, 1954), pp. 113–16.

4. Statement of Edward J. Ennis, Testimony before the Subcommittee of the Committee on Immigration on "Supervision, detention and Incarceration of deportable Aliens, S. 1232, S.2293 and S. 1720," U.S. Senate, March 23–24, 1942, pp. 45, 50–51, in Edward Ennis Files, James H. Rowe Papers, FDRL. In a further leap of logic, Ennis suggested that the government's plan was not one for "concentration camps," inasmuch as the Japanese Americans would be put to work growing food instead of merely being confined!

5. Greg Robinson, *By Order of the President: FDR and the Internment of Japanese Americans* (Cambridge: Harvard University Press, 2001), pp. 128–30.

6. Executive Order 9102, March 18, 1942, CWRIC Papers, pp. 6197–99.

7. Allan R. Bosworth, *America's Concentration Camps* (New York: W. W. Norton, 1967), pp. 77–78.

8. Richard M. Neustadt, Report on Alien Enemy Evacuation, February 18, 1942, reel 3, frame 510, JERS.

9. Robert Shaffer, "Cracks in the Consensus: Defending the Rights of Japanese Americans during World War II," *Radical History Review* 72 (1998): 84–120.

10. Ibid., pp. 89–91.

11. "La Gran Oportunidad," *La Opinion*, April 27, 1942.

12. Samuel Walker, *In Defense of American Liberties: A History of the ACLU* (New York: Oxford University Press, 1990), pp. 138–42; Peter H. Irons, *Justice at War* (New York: Oxford University Press, 1983), pp. 129–30.

13. Norman Thomas, *Democracy and the Japanese Americans*, pamphlet (Postwar World Council, 1942).

14. Norman Thomas, "A Dark Day for Liberty," *Christian Century* 59 (July 29, 1942): 359–61.

15. Fumi Endow Kawaguchi, diary entry, March 4, 1942, in Sanae Kawaguchi Moorehead, with Greg Robinson, "On the Brink of Evacuation: The Diary of an Issei Woman, by Fumi Endow Kawaguchi," *Prospects: An Annual of American Cultural Studies* 28 (2003): 177.

16. Audrie Girdner and Anne Loftis, *The Great Betrayal: The Evacuation of the Japanese-Americans during World War II* (New York: Macmillan, 1969), pp. 102–3.

17. Sue Kunitomi, quoted in Ellen Levine, *A Fence Away from Freedom* (New York: G. P. Putnam's, 1995), pp. 35–36.

18. James Omura, Testimony before House Select Committee on Defense Migration, February 23, 1942, cited in Arthur A. Hansen, "Protest-Resistance and the Heart Mountain Experience: The Revitalization of a Robust Nikkei Experience," in *A Matter of Conscience: Essays on the World War II Heart Mountain Draft Resistance Movement*, ed. Mike Mackey (Powell, Wy.: Heart Mountain Wyoming Foundation, 2002), p. 99.

19. Bill Hosokawa, *Nisei: The Quiet Americans* (New York: Morrow, 1969), p. 290.

20. *Rafu Shimpo*, February 21, 1942. There is some controversy over whether Karl Bendetsen and the Western Defense Command threatened military intervention if Japanese Americans did not cooperate. Frank Abe, review of Frank Chin, *Born in the USA*, *Amerasia Journal* 30, 2 (2004): 107–11. Whether or not such a threat was explicit, it seems virtually certain that such would have been the result. For a good discussion about the politics of "loyalty," see Scott Kurashige, *The Shifting Grounds of Race* (Princeton: Princeton University Press, 2008), pp. 129–30.

21. Letter, Larry Tajiri to Alan Cranston, April 14, 1942. Director's files, Foreign Nationalities Groups, RG 208, Office of War Information Papers, NARA; Hosokawa, *Nisei*, p. 390. Not all Nisei newspapermen collaborated. James and Fumiko Omura, editor and manager of the magazine *Current Life*, relocated to Denver, where they ran an employment bureau and filed racial discrimination cases with the War Manpower Commission.

22. Isamu Noguchi, "A Plan for Government Sponsored Farm and Craft Settlement For People of Japanese Parentage," undated [March 1942], Nisei Writers and Artists Mobilization for Democracy Files, Japanese organizations files, series 11, RG 210, War Relocation Authority Papers, NARA; Galen M. Fisher, "Japanese Colony," *Survey Graphic* 32 (February 1943): 41–43.

23. Irons, *Justice at War*, pp. 81–93.

24. Ibid., pp. 93–99, 114–16. These cases are further discussed in chapter 5.

25. Bill Hosokawa, *JACL in Quest of Justice* (New York: Morrow, 1982), pp. 157–60; Deborah K. Lim, *The Lim Report* (Kearney, Neb.: Morris Publishing, 2002 [1990]), p. 65.

26. The case was brought before the 9th Circuit Court of Appeals, which dismissed the case barely fifteen minutes after the plaintiffs had completed their argument, without the defense having to present its case. Irons, *Justice at War*, pp. 176–77.

27. "Japanese Decries Evacuation," *New York Times*, June 19, 1942.

28. For the JACD and its ambivalent attitude toward mass removal, see Greg Robinson, "Nisei in Gotham: Japanese Americans in Wartime New York," *Prospects: An Annual of American Culture Studies* 30 (2005): 581–95.

29. Greg Robinson, "Norman Thomas and the Struggle against Japanese Internment," *Prospects: An Annual of American Cultural Studies* 29 (2004):

427; William Petersen, *Japanese Americans: Oppression and Success* (New York: Random House, 1971), p. 74.

30. Gary Y. Okihiro, *Cane Fires: The Anti-Japanese Movement in Hawaii, 1865–1945* (Philadelphia: Temple University Press, 1991), pp. 219–22. In March 1943, the remaining internees were moved to a new camp built at Honouliuli, where conditions were more humane and the internees could receive weekly visits from family.

31. Beth Bailey and David Farber, *The First Strange Place: The Alchemy of Race and Sex in World War II Hawaii* (New York: Free Press, 1992), pp. 6–7.

32. Dennis M. Ogawa, *Kodomo no tame ni: For the Sake of the Children* (Honolulu: University Press of Hawaii, 1978), pp. 315–17.

33. Wallace Carroll, "Japanese Spies Showed the Way for Raid on Vital Areas in Hawaii," *New York Times*, December 31, 1941; *Time*, January 5, 1942, cited in Franklin Odo, *No Sword to Bury: Japanese Americans in Hawai'i during World War II* (Philadelphia: Temple University Press, 2004), p. 140.

34. Atherton Richards, "A Proposed Solution for the Japanese Question in Hawaii," in William J. Donovan, report to the President, February 12, 1942, OSS Reports, Confidential File, FDRL.

35. John A. Balch, "Shall the Japanese Be Allowed to Dominate Hawaii?" pamphlet, January 1943, cited in Joseph Driscoll, "The Balch Plan," *New York Herald Tribune*, February 2, 1943.

36. Linton M. Collins, "Memorandum for Mr. Rowe," April 22, 1942, Hawaii file, James Rowe Papers, FDRL.

37. Albert Horlings, "Hawaii's 150,000 Japanese," *Nation*, July 25, 1942, pp. 69–71.

38. Andrew W. Lind, *The Japanese in Hawaii under War Conditions* (Honolulu and New York: American Council, Institute of Pacific Relations, 1943), p. 8. In March 1942 Tolan asked the Justice Department for a statement as to whether there had been sabotage in Hawaii at or around the time of Pearl Harbor. Although FBI Director Hoover stated unequivocally that there had not been, Attorney General Biddle, in consultation with Assistant Secretary of War McCloy, decided against making an official statement that might contradict Knox's findings. However, once the Army and Navy departments themselves sent statements to the committee, Biddle reversed course and allowed Hoover's statement to be made public. James Rowe, memorandum for the Attorney General, April 20, 1942, James Rowe Files, Francis Biddle Papers, FDRL.

39. Robinson, *By Order of the President*, p. 95.

40. Secretary of War Stimson told the cabinet that the Nisei who had already been drafted would be moved to other parts of the United States "where their loyalty would not be tempted." Henry L. Stimson, Cabinet Notes, January 30, 1942, Stimson Papers.

41. Henry L. Stimson Diary, February 26, 1942, Stimson Papers.

42. Henry Stimson, Notes after Cabinet meeting, February 27, 1942, Stimson Papers.

43. "Hawaii 'All Set,' M'Cloy Reports," *New York Times*, March 28, 1942.

44. Memo, President to Secretary of War, March 20, 1942. PSF 197-A (Japanese) FDRL; memo, President to Secretary of War and the Secretary of the Navy, April 23, 1942, PSF Knox (Navy), FDRL.

45. Henry Stimson, Notes after Cabinet meeting, April 24, May 1, 1942, Stimson Papers.

46. "Reveal Genl. Marshall's Support of Nisei," *Pacific Citizen*, January 25, 1947; Odo, *No Sword to Bury*, p. 132.

47. Odo, *No Sword to Bury*, pp. 143–65.

48. Memorandum from the President to the Secretary of War and the U.S. Army Chief of Staff, November 2, 1942, Confidential File, Navy, FDRL.

49. Harold Ickes Diary, entry November 8, 1942, Harold Ickes Papers, Library of Congress.

50. U.S. Army, Western Defense Command, *Japanese Evacuation from the West Coast—Final Report* (Washington, D.C.: Government Printing Office, 1944), p. 249.

51. Ibid, pp. 103–4.

52. Girdner and Loftis, *The Great Betrayal*, pp. 108–9; 77th Congress, 2nd Session, House Report No. 1911, "Report of the Select Committee Investigating National Defense Migration," House of Representatives, pp. 6–8, 25.

53. Letter, Clarence Lea to Franklin Roosevelt, March 5, 1942, PPF 2851, Official File 77, FDRL.

54. Robinson, *By Order of the President*, pp. 134–42.

55. Sandra C. Taylor, "The Federal Reserve Bank and the Relocation of Japanese in 1942," *The Public Historian* 5, 1 (Winter 1983): 9–30.

56. Frank S. Arnold, Michael C. Barthm, and Gilah Langer, "Economic Losses of Ethnic Japanese as a Result of Exclusion and detention, 1942–1946," report prepared for Commission on Wartime Evacuation and Internment of Civilians, June 1983, WRA Papers, RG 210, NARA. See also U.S. Department of the Interior, War Relocation Authority. *The Wartime Handling of Evacuee Property* (Washington D.C.: Government Printing Office, 1946), pp. 28–36, 48; Leonard Broom and Ruth Riemer, *Removal and Return: The Socio-economic Effects of the War on Japanese Americans* (Berkeley: University of California Press, 1949). The total can be estimated at $13 to $22 billion in 2008 dollars.

57. U.S. Department of the Interior, War Relocation Authority, *Legal and Constitutional Phases of the Relocation Program* (New York: AMS Press, 1978 [1946]), p. 11.

58. *Personal Justice Denied*, pp. 101–2; Page Smith, *Democracy on Trial* (New York: Simon and Schuster, 1995), pp. 146–49.

59. Morton Grodzins, *Americans Betrayed* (Chicago: University of Chicago Press, 1949), pp. 306–7, 313–22; Lawrence E. Davies, "Japanese Hurry to Leave Army Zone," *New York Times*, March 29, 1942.

60. Roger Daniels, *Concentration Camps USA: Japanese Americans and World War II* (New York: Holt, Rinehart and Winston, 1971), p. 81.

61. Memorandum for the Commanding General from Col. Joel F. Watson, Office of the Judge Advocate, April 23, 1942, reprinted in CWRIC Papers, p. 5211.

62. U.S. Army, Western Defense Command, *Japanese Evacuation from the West Coast: Final Report*, p. 145.

63. Ibid.

64. Ibid.; Jennifer Ho, "Passed over for Internment: Yoshiko DeLeon and the Mixed Marriage Policy of 1942," paper presented at Association for Asian American Studies, Los Angeles, 2005.

65. *Personal Justice Denied*, pp. 104–5n. In 2007 William Seltzer and Margo Anderson discovered that the Census Bureau had again breached confidentiality to reveal information about a Japanese American who had allegedly threatened President Roosevelt's life. "In 1943, Census Bureau Released Japanese Americans' Individual Data," *Los Angeles Times*, March 31, 2007.

66. "Terminaran La Evacuation de Japoneses," *La Opinion*, April 27, 1942; *Japanese Evacuation from the West Coast*, pp. 143–44.

67. Hosokawa, *Nisei*, pp. 319–20.

68. *Japanese Evacuation from the West Coast*, p. 356.

69 Yuri Tateishi, quoted in John Tateishi, ed., *And Justice for All: An Oral History of the Japanese American Detention Camps* (New York: Random House, 1979), p. 24.

70. *Personal Justice Denied*, pp. 129–30.

71. See, for example, Carey McWilliams's comment that "The army executed the assignment with tact, good judgment, and remarkable efficiency." Carey McWilliams, *Prejudice: Japanese Americans, Symbol of Racial Intolerance* (Boston: Little, Brown, 1944), p. 187; ; Paul Okimoto, unpublished memoir, 2007, collection of author, p.21.

72. Toyo Suyemoto, "Another Spring," in *Last Witnesses: Reflections on the Wartime internment of Japanese Americans*, ed. Erica Harth (New York, Palgave/Macmillan, 2001) p. 23. A widespread joke among Japanese Americans housed at the Santa Anita racetrack was to debate who had the honor of occupying the stall of the famed racehorse Seabiscuit. Gary Y. Okihiro, "Introduction," in *Impounded: Dorothea Lange and the Censored Images of Japanese Americans*, ed. Linda Gordon and Gary Y. Ohihiro (New York: W. W. Norton, 2006), p. x.

73. Charles Kikuchi diary, May 7, 1942, in John Modell, ed., *The Kikuchi Diary: Chronicle from an American Concentration Camp* (Urbana: University of Illinois Press, 1973), pp. 60–61.

74. Miné Okubo, *Citizen 13660* (Seattle: University of Washington Press, 1983 [1946]), pp. 44–45.

75. Anonymous, "Life in a California Concentration Camp," *The Nation* 154 (June 6, 1942): p. 666. Another inmate later recalled that, so far from automatically flushing, the toilets she saw did not flush, and she found latrines often filled to overflowing. Setsuko Matsunaga Nishi, letter to author, March 16, 2008.

76. Daniels, *Concentration Camps USA*, p. 89. On food poisoning and epidemics, see also Naomi Hirahara and Gwenn M. Jensen, *Silent Scars of Healing Hands: Oral Histories of Japanese American Doctors in World War II Detention Camps* (Fullerton, Calif.: Center for Oral and Public History, California State University, 2004).

77. Sato Hashizume, "The Food," in *From Our Side of the Fence*, ed. Brian Komei Dempster (San Francisco: Japanese Cultural and Community Center of Northern California, 2001), p. 23.

78. Girdner and Loftis, *The Great Betrayal*, pp. 163–65; Michi Nishiura Weglyn, *Years of Infamy* (Seattle: University of Washington Press, 1996 [1976]), p. 81. The fear of epidemics in assembly centers was one factor leading the army to urge the WRA to complete construction of more permanent camps.

79. Smith, *Democracy on Trial*, pp. 191–93.

80. Andrew Wertheimer, "Public Libraries Behind Barbed Wire: Japanese American Readers during World War II," Ph.D. dissertation, University of Wisconsin, 2003.

81. These efforts were in vain. Throughout the war years, anti-Japanese American newspapers such as the *Denver Post* continued to repeat as fact the absurd rumors of "coddling," of camp inmates dining on rare beef and liquor, or storing food in the desert for use by Japanese invaders. These stories were picked up by members of Congress such as Wyoming Republican senator Guy Robertson. Members of the House Un-American Activities Committee, led by Representative Martin Dies, scheduled hearings where disgruntled employees of the WRA spread fantastic stories. U.S. Congress, House of Representatives, "Report and Minority Views of the Special Committee on Un-American Activities: On Japanese War Relocation Centers," report no. 717, September 30, 1943.

82. *Japanese Evacuation from the West Coast*, pp. 186, 205.

83. Anthony L. Lehman, *Birthright of Barbed Wire: The Santa Anita Assembly Center For the Japanese* (Los Angeles: Westernlore Press, 1970), p. 24.

84. Takeya Mizuno, "Journalism under Military Guards and Searchlights: Newspaper Censorship at Japanese American Assembly Camps during World War II," *Journalism History* 29 (Fall 2003): 98–106.

85. Japanese American Citizens League—So. District Council, "Report on Conditions at Manzanar Relocation Center—May 26, 1942," on file with author.

86. Robinson, "Norman Thomas and the Struggle against Japanese Internment," pp. 430–31.

87. Ibid. Following Fujii's arrest, allies in the Office of War Information arranged his liberation.

88. *Japanese Evacuation from the West Coast*, pp. 218–19. There were various rumors current that the disturbance was triggered by the beating of an inmate of mixed Japanese Korean ancestry accused of informing, but this story has not been independently confirmed and is implausible.

89. Noriko Shimada, *Nikkei Americajin no Taiheiyo Senso* (Tokyo: Liber Press, 1995); Takeya Mizuno, "Government Suppression of the Japanese Language in World War II Assembly Camps," *Journalism and Mass Communications Quarterly* 80, 4 (Winter 2003): 849–65.

90. Ann Gomer Sunahara, *The Politics of Racism: The Uprooting of Japanese Canadians during World War II* (Toronto: Lorimer, 1981), p. 53.

91. Mary Taylor, *A Black Mark: The Japanese-Canadians in World War II* (Toronto: Oberon Press, 2004), p. 41.

92. Toyo Takata, *Nikkei Legacy: The Story of Japanese Canadians from Settlement to Today* (Toronto: NC Press, 1983), p. 117.

93. Taylor, *A Black Mark*, pp. 56–57.

94. "Orders from the British Columbia Security Commission: Notice to Vancouver Japanese," reprinted in Roy Ito, *The Japanese Canadians*, Multicultural Canada series (Toronto: Van Nostrand Reinhold, 1978), p. 50.

95. Rose Murakami, *Ganbaru: The Murakami Family of Salt Spring Island*, pamphlet (Japanese Garden Society of Salt Spring Island, 2005), p. 21.

96. Barry Broadfoot, *Years of Sorrow, Years of Shame: The Story of the Japanese Canadians in World War II* (Markham, Ont.: PaperJacks Doubleday, 1979), p. 90.

97. Ibid., pp. 86–88.

98. Toyo Takata later recalled that unscrupulous white staffers profited from the situation by allowing big-stakes games, formally illegal, to continue in exchange for a rake-off. Ted Barris, *Days of Victory: Canadians Remember, 1939–1945* (Toronto: Thomas Altenfus, 2005), p. 164.

99. Taylor, *A Black Mark*, pp. 37–38.

100. *Vancouver Sun*, March 1, 1942, cited in Peter Ward, *White Canada Forever: Popular Attitudes and Public Policy toward Orientals in British Columbia* (Montreal: McGill-Queens University Press, 1978), p. 162.

101. Muriel Kitagawa, "A Record of Dignity," *New Canadian*, March 5, 1942.

102. Takeo Ujo Nakano with Leatrice Nakano, *Behind the Barbed Wire Fence* (Halifax: Goodread Biographies, 1983 [1980]), p. 10.

103. Roy Miki, *Redress: Inside the Japanese Canadian Call for Justice* (Vancouver: RainCoast Books, 2004), p. 47. Resolutions also expressed community non-confidence in Etsuji Morii as liaison and called for meetings between the Japanese community and government officials.

104. Yon Shimizu, *The Exiles: Archival History of the World War II Japanese Road Labour Camps in British Columbia and Ontario* (Wallaceburg, Ont.: Shimizu Consulting, 1993), p. 60.

105. Letter, Nisei Mass Evacuation group to Austin Taylor, April 15, 1942, reprinted in Robert K. Okazaki, *The Nisei Mass Evacuation Group and P.O.W. Camp 101: The Japanese Canadian Community's Struggle for Justice and Human Rights during World War II* (Scarborough, Ont.: R. K. Okazaki, 1996), p. A-109.

106. Ibid., pp. 12–13.

107. Sunahara, *The Politics of Racism*, p. 9. A slightly different, largely verbatim, version of Miura's remarks is in Okazaki, *The Nisei Mass Evacuation Group*, p. 11.

108. Sunahara, *The Politics of Racism*, pp. 65-71.

109. Ibid.

110. Tom Sando, *Wild Daisies in the Sand: Life in a Canadian Internment Camp* (Edmonton: NeWest Press, 2002), pp. 30–32.

111. Taylor, *A Black Mark*, pp. 58–59; "Japanese in Canada," memo, Office of the Commanding General, Western Defense Command to Chief of Staff, United States Army, May 10, 1942, in "Papers of the U.S. Commission on Wartime Relocation and Internment of Civilians," ed. Randolph Boehm (Lanham, Md.: University Publications of America, 1984), 13049-13065, reel 11, pp. 973–90.

112. Sunahara, *The Politics of Racism*, pp. 73–75.

113. For the road worker experience, see Shimizu, *The Exiles*. Shimizu claims that the Nisei Mass Evacuation Group was a marginal group and not responsible for changing government policy on family evacuation, but his evidence does not seem conclusive (p. 21).

114. Milton S. Eisenhower, *The President Is Calling* (Garden City, N.Y.: Doubleday, 1974), pp. 126–34. Governor Ralph Carr of Colorado, who was not present at the meeting, represented a partial exception to this attitude. He had previously stated that he did not like the "Japanese" but would do his patriotic duty by accepting a fair share. Despite the limited and grudging nature of his position, he later charged that his support for Japanese Americans cost him his political career. Adam Schrager, *The Principled Politician: The Ralph Carr Story* (Golden, Colo.: Fulcrum Publishing, 2008), but see Greg Robinson, "Two Wartime Governors and Their Responses to Japanese Americans," *Nichi Bei Times*, July 24, 2008, available at http://www

.nichibeitimes.com/articles/community.php?subaction=showfull&id=121 6941180&archive=&start_from=&ucat=2&.

115. Letter, Milton Eisenhower to Burton K. Wheeler, April 23, 1942, WRA subject-classified correspondence files, series 16, War Relocation Authority Papers, RG 210, NARA.

116. Karl Lechmann, memorandum for Mr. [Felix] Cohen, August 10, 1942. Office files, Assistant Secretary of the Interior Abe Fortas, record group 46, box 6, entry 772, National Archives. (Emphasis added.)

117. Philip Glick, cited in U.S. Department of the Interior, War Relocation Authority, *WRA: A Story of Human Conservation* (New York: AMS Press, 1978 [1946]), p. 16. Glick later amplified his statement: "The evacuation, however unwise in fact, however unnecessary subsequent events proved it to be, was within the constitutional power of the Federal Government when undertaken and executed. [The WRA] doubted from the beginning and never ceased to doubt the validity of the detention procedures." War Relocation Authority, *Legal and Constitutional Phases of the WRA Program*, p. 17.

118. Mackenzie King Diary, June 25, 1942, LAC.

119. Letter, Secretary of War to the President, July 7, 1944, OF-197-A, FDRL; Henry Stimson Diary, July 7, 1942, Stimson Papers.

120. Letter, Henry L. Stimson to Robert Young, May 25, 1942, Japanese American files, American Friends Service Committee Papers, AFSC archives, Philadelphia.

121. Letter, Milton Eisenhower to Franklin Roosevelt, June 18, 1942, Official File 4849, FDRL.

122. Harold Ickes Diary, June 19, 1942. Harold Ickes Papers, Library of Congress; Memo for the President, June 16, 1942, OF 4849-A, FDRL.

123. Dillon S. Myer, *Uprooted Americans: The Japanese Americans and the War Relocation Authority during World War II* (Tuscon: University of Arizona Press, 1971). A scathing portrait of Myer is in Richard Drinnon, *Keeper of Concentration Camps: Dillon S. Myer and American Racism* (Berkeley: University of California Press, 1987).

124. Motomu Akashi, *Betrayed Trust: The Story of a Deported Issei and His American-Born Family during World War II* (Bloomington, Ind.: Author-House, 2004), p. 58.

125. Robinson, *By Order of the President*, pp. 146–55.

126. Takata, *Nikkei Legacy*, p.120; Ken Adachi, *The Enemy That Never Was: A History of the Japanese Canadians* (Toronto: McClellan and Stewart, 1976), p. 283.

127. Stephanie Bangarth, "The Long Wet Summer of 1942: The Ontario Farm Service Force, Small-Town Ontario and the Nisei,' *Canadian Ethnic Studies/Études ethniques au Canada* 38, 1 (2005): 40–62. Ontario differed from the prairie provinces in the conditions under which migrants were permit-

ted. Premier Mitchell Hepburn agreed to accept only young Nisei males between 18 and 35, for the duration of the war only, and did not agree to accept families until 1944.

128. Roy Miki and Cassandra Kobayashi, *Justice in Our Time: The Japanese Canadian Redress Agreement* Vancouver: Talonbooks and the National Association of Japanese Canadians, 1991), p. 41; Takata, *Nikkei Legacy*, p. 117.

129. For Japanese in Mexico, see Daniel M. Masterson with Sayaka Funada-Classen, *The Japanese in Latin America* (Urbana: University of Illinois Press, 2004), pp. 59–63; "Hard Work Won Them a Place in a Diverse Culture," *Nikkeiwest*, March 10, 2008. The community in Mexico City attracted famed theater director Saki Sano during the 1930s. Kinta Arai, a former Japanese diplomat, held a prestigious chair in Oriental Studies at the National University of Mexico. His daughter Maria earned a degree in international law from the university, becoming the first-ever Japanese woman with a law degree, and in 1936 she was named chief prosecutor in the Mexican government's crime bureau.

130. Tosuke Yamasaki, "Yamasaki Tells about Tampico," *Japanese American Courier*, July 6–13, 1935; "Evicted Nihonjin Farmers Assured of Crops," *Rafu Shimpo*, April 29, 1937; Masterson with Funada-Classen, *The Japanese in Latin America*, pp. 116–18.

131. Cited in "El Japon Prepara un Ataque contra Mexico," *La Opinion*, February 14, 1942; "Es possible un ataque japones al territorio de Baja California," *El Informador* (Guadalajara), February 8, 1942.

132. "Frente Al Peligro," *La Opinion*, February 26, 1942.

133. The extent of American complicity in Mexican removal is uncertain but probably minor. The U.S. Embassy's Economic Division and its local consulates monitored Japanese Mexicans and advised the Mexican government regarding the presence of individuals it considered dangerous. Enclosures to despatch no. 26943 of October 23, 1945, American Embassy at Mexico City, box 49, Special War Problems Division, State Department files, RG 59, NARA. Conversely, Mexico repeatedly refused to surrender any of its Japanese residents for internment in the United States, on grounds that to do so would violate Mexican sovereignty. Tetsuden Kashima, *Judgment without Trial: Japanese American Imprisonment during World War II* (Seattle: University of Washington Press, 2003), pp. 95–96. According to Sanshiro Matsumoto, a prominent Mexican Japanese, President Manuel Avila Camacho was ready to ship Japanese nationals to the United States for internment but was dissuaded from the policy by two former presidents, Lazaro Cardenas (whose wife's sister was married to a prominent Japanese, Dr. Matsutada Noda) and Pascual Ortiz Rubio, Matsumoto's close friend. "Two Former Presidents Blocked Move For Internment of Mexico's Japanese," *New Canadian*, November 3, 1954.

134. Most sources claim that January 5 was the date of the order. Masterson with Funada-Classen, *The Japanese in Latin America*, p. 126. However, for the earlier date, see "Los Japoneses no podrán estar en la costa ni en la frontera del país," *La Prensa* (Mexico City), January 3, 1942, p. 3.

135. "México desaloja de la costa a los Japoneses,' *La Opinion*, March 2, 1942; Teresa T. Kiso, "Mexican Nisei Shares Her Special World War II Evacuation Story," *New Canadian*, January 14, 1972.

136. Jesus K. Akachi et al., "Japanese Mexican Historical Overview," in *Encyclopedia of Japanese Descendants in the Americas: An Illustrated History of the Nikkei*, ed. Akemi Kikamura-Yano (Lanham, Md.: AltaMira press, 2002), pp. 213–14; Steven R. Niblo, "Allied Policy toward Axis Interests in Mexico during World War II," *Mexican Studies / Estudios Mexicanos* 17, 2 (Summer 2001): 351–73.

137. See, for example, Max Paul Friedman, *Nazis and Good Neighbors: The United States Campaign against the Germans of Latin America in World War II* (New York: Cambridge University Press, 2003).

138. Thomas Connell, *America's Japanese Hostages: The World War II Plan for a Japanese Free Latin America* (Westport, Conn.: Praeger, 2002), p. 5.

139. "F.D.R. Speech Hailed in London as 'Close to War,'" *Chicago Tribune*, October 29, 1941.

140. "Secret Bases Found within Range of Panama Canal, Roosevelt Says," *Washington Post*, September 12, 1941.

141. "Panama Action Roils Japanese," *Los Angeles Times*, November 21, 1941. Technically the law was not new but expanded a previous measure under which the Panamanian government had unjustly confiscated and sold off businesses owned by Chinese residents but had exempted Japanese.

142. The best short accounts of the deportation of Latin American Japanese are in *Personal Justice Denied*, pp. 305–14. See also C. Harvey Gardiner, *Pawns in a Triangle of Hate: The Peruvian Japanese and the United States* (Seattle: University of Washington Press, 1981); Seiichi Higashide, *Adios to Tears: The Memoirs of a Japanese-Peruvian Internee in U.S. Concentration Camps* (Seattle: University of Washington Press, 2000).

143. *Personal Justice Denied*, p. 306.

144. Letter, Secretary of State George Marshall, February 13, 1947, cited in Alfred Steinberg, "'Blunder' Maroons Peruvian Japanese in the U.S." *Washington Post*, September 26, 1948.

145. Kashima, *Judgment without Trial*, pp. 97–98. On Latin American countries generally, see Masterson with Funada-Classen, *The Japanese in Latin America*, pp. 140–48.

146. Steinberg, "'Blunder' Maroons Peruvian Japanese in the U.S."

147. Edward Ennis, "Memorandum for Mr. James H. Rowe," January 26, 1943, Edward Ennis file, James Rowe Papers, FDRL.

148. Steinberg, "'Blunder' Maroons Peruvian Japanese in the U.S."

149. Edward N. Barnhart, "Japanese Internees from Peru," *Pacific Historical Review* 31, 1 (May 1962): 171.

150. On the wartime exchanges, see P. Scott Corbett, *Quiet Passages: The Exchange of Civilians between the United States and Japan during World War II* (Kent, Ohio: Kent State University Press, 1987).

151. Ibid.

152. J. F. Normano and Antonello Gerbi, *The Japanese in South America* (New York: Institute of Pacific Relations, 1943).

153. C. Harvey Gardiner, *The Japanese and Peru, 1873–1973* (Albuquerque: University of New Mexico Press, 1975), pp. 52–54.

154. Masterson with Funada-Classen, *The Japanese in Latin America*, p. 155.

4. THE CAMP EXPERIENCE

1. Letter, John Collier to A. L. Walker, copy to John McCloy, March 6, 1942. Assistant Secretary of War Papers, RG 107, NARA, CWRIC, pp. 79–80.

2. Richard Drinnon, *Keeper of Concentration Camps: Dillon S. Myer and American Racism* (Berkeley: University of California Press, 1987), pp. 39–41. For Poston generally, see Richard S. Nishimoto, *Inside an American Concentration Camp: Japanese American Resistance at Poston, Arizona*, ed. Lane Hirabyashi (Tucson: University of Arizona Press, 1995); Paul Bailey, *City in the Sun: The Japanese Concentration Camp at Poston* (Los Angeles: Western-Lore Press, 1971). A second center, Gila River, was also built on an Indian reservation in Arizona, but in this case the WRA bypassed the BIA and dealt directly with Native American groups.

3. Audrie Girdner and Anne Loftis, *The Great Betrayal: The Evacuation of the Japanese-Americans during World War II* (New York: Macmillan, 1969), p. 246; Alexander H. Leighton, *The Governing of Men: General Principles and Recommendations Based on Experience at a Japanese Relocation Camp* (New York: Institute for Pacific Relations, 1945).

4. Robert Maeda, "Isamu Noguchi: 5–7-A, Poston, Arizona," in *Last Witnesses: Reflections on the Wartime Internment of Japanese Americans*, ed. Erica Harth (New York: St. Martin's Press, 2001), pp. 153–66.

5. Page Smith, *Democracy on Trial* (New York: Simon and Schuster, 1995), p. 259; Bailey, *City in the Sun*, pp. 122–23.

6. Kazu Iijima, interview with Sandra Taylor, October 6, 1987. Topaz Oral Histories, Marriott Library, University of Utah.

7. Jeffrey F. Burton et al., *Confinement and Ethnicity: An Overview of World War II Japanese Americans Relocation Sites* (Washington, D.C.: National Park Service, 1999).

8. Michi Nishiura Weglyn, *Years of Infamy* (Seattle: University of Washington Press, 1996 [1976]), p. 84.

9. Midori Shimanouchi Lederer, interview with Sandra Taylor, undated (October, 1987).Topaz Oral Histories, Marriott Library, University of Utah.

10. Drinnon, *Keeper of Concentration Camps*, p. 43. The guards, like other outside employees, were required to be "Caucasians" (i.e., non-Japanese). In various cases, especially as the war proceeded, WRA employed African American teachers, construction workers, and guards. These employees were granted the status of "honorary Caucasians" for the purpose of their jobs.

11. Yoriyuki Kikuchi, "An Interview with Yoriyuki Kikuchi," in *Japanese American World War II Evacuation Oral History Project: Part I: Internees*, ed. Arthur A. Hansen (Westport, Conn.: Meckler, 1991), p. 206.

12. U.S. Department of the Interior, War Relocation Authority, *WRA: A Story of Human Conservation* (New York: AMS Press, 1978 [1946]), pp. 101–2. Ironically, under the Geneva Convention the Issei, as "interned foreign nationals," were supposed to receive the same standard of food as soldiers, but there was no similar requirement under international law covering citizens.

13. Interview with Mabel Ota, in John Tateishi, ed., *And Justice for All: An Oral History of the Japanese American Detention Camps* (New York: Random House, 1979), p.111.

14. Letter, Eleanor Roosevelt to Anna Roosevelt Boettiger, June 7, 1943, reprinted in Bernard Asbell, ed., *Mother and Daughter* (New York: Coward, MacCann and Geohagen, 1982), pp.160–61.

15. See, for example, interview with Harry Ueno in Tateishi, ed., *And Justice For All*, pp. 194–95.

16. Naomi Hirahara and Gwenn M. Jensen. *Silent Scars of Healing Hands: Oral Histories of Japanese American Doctors in World War II Detention Camps* (Fullerton, Calif.: Center for Oral and Public History, California State University, 2004).

17. Girdner and Loftis, *The Great Betrayal*, p. 229.

18. Susan L. Smith, *Japanese American Midwives: Culture, Community and Health Politics, 1880–1950* (Urbana: University of Illinois Press, 2005).

19. For camp schooling, see U.S. Commission on Wartime Relocation and Internment of Civilians, *Personal Justice Denied* (Seattle: University of Washington Press, 1997 [1983]), pp. 170–72; Thomas James, *Exile Within: The Schooling of Japanese Americans, 1942–1945* (Cambridge: Harvard University Press, 1987).

20. John Howard, *Concentration Camps on the Home Front: Japanese Americans in the House of Jim Crow* (Chicago: University of Chicago Press, 2008); Kuni Takahashi, "Voice of an Issei," *Poston Chronicle*, May 9, 1943.

21. John Howard, "The Politics of Dancing under Japanese-American Incarceration," *History Workshop Journal* 52 (Fall 2001): 123–51.

22. Ibid. During a public meeting in 1943, Layle Lane, an African American teacher and civil rights activist from New York, referred to the internment of Japanese Americans in concentration camps as "a disgraceful blot" on the country's record and underlined the racist nature of the policy by pointing out that Japanese American teachers, who were predominantly women, received a maximum salary of $19 per month, while white teachers performing the same work received $150 per month. Albert Parker, "Layle Lane's Speech," *The Militant*, April 3, 1943, reprinted in *Fighting Racism in World War II*, ed. C.L.R. James et al. (New York: Pathfinder Books, 1980), p. 87.

23. For art in the camps, see, for example, Deborah Gesensway and Mindy Roseman, *Beyond Words: Images from America's Concentration Camps* (Ithaca: Cornell University Press, 1987); Karen Higa, *The View from Within: Japanese American Art from the Internment Camps, 1942–1945* (Los Angeles: Japanese American National Museum, 1994); Greg Robinson and Elena Tajima Creef, eds., *Miné Okubo: Following Her Own Road* (Seattle: University of Washington Press, 2008). For crafts, see Allen H. Eaton, *Beauty Behind Barbed Wire: Arts of the Japanese in Our War Relocation Camps* (New York: Harper, 1952); Delphine Hirasuna, *The Art of Gaman: Arts & Crafts from the Japanese American Internment Camps 1942–1946* (Berkeley: Ten Speed Press, 2005).

24. Bailey, *City in the Sun*, p. 94.

25. Stephen Fugita and Marilyn Fernandez, *Altered Lives, Enduring Community* (Seattle: University of Washington Press, 2005), pp. 185–93.

26. Richard Koichi Tanaka, *America on Trial* (New York: Carlton, 1987), p. 85.

27. Mili Shimonishi-Lamb, *And Then a Rainbow* (Santa Barbara: Fithian Press, 1990), p. 70.

28. Amy Uno Ishii, "An Interview With Amy Uno Ishii," in *Japanese American World War II Evacuation Oral History Project: Part I: Internees*, ed. Arthur A. Hansen (Westport, Conn.: Meckler, 1991), pp. 79–80. See also Minoru Mochizuki's similar description in Roger W. Axford, *Too Long Silent: Japanese Americans Speak Out* (Lincoln, Neb.: Media Publishing, 1987), p. 63.

29. Interview, Ben Tagami, in Ellen Levine, *A Fence Away from Freedom* (New York: G. P. Putnam's, 1995), p. 63.

30. Leonard Broom and John I. Kitsuse, *The Managed Casualty: The Japanese-American Family in World War II* (Berkeley: University of California Press, 1956).

31. Howard, *Concentration Camps on the Home Front*.

32. See Broom and Kitsuse, *The Managed Casualty*. For a literary representation, see Hisaye Yamamoto, "The Legend of Miss Sasagawara," in *Seventeen Syllables and Other Stories* (New Brunswick: Rutgers University Press, 2001), pp. 20–33.

33. Lawrence E. Davies, "Far West Finishes Moving Japanese," *New York Times*, November 1, 1942.

34. Sam Hohri, letter to Norman Thomas, December 29, 1942, p. 2. Norman Thomas papers.

35. The WRA's final report noted that despite the existence of gamblers, prostitutes, and gang-organized beatings, the overall crime rate in the camps compared quite favorably with that of any average American town of the same size. War Relocation Authority, *WRA: A Story of Human Conservation*, p. 93.

36. Ibid.

37. For differing accounts of the Poston strike, see, for example, Dorothy Swaine Thomas and Richard S. Nishimoto, *The Spoilage* (Berkeley: University of California Press, 1946), pp. 46–52; Girdner and Loftis, *The Great Betrayal*, pp. 261–63; Gary Y. Okihiro, "Japanese Resistance in America's Concentration Camps: A Reappraisal," *Amerasia Journal* 2 (Fall 1973): 20–33; Brian Masaru Hayashi, *Democratizing the Enemy* (Princeton: Princeton University Press, 2004), pp. 130–36.

38. The classic account of the Manzanar riot is Arthur A. Hansen and David A. Hacker, "The Manzanar Riot: An Ethnic Perspective," *Amerasia Journal* 2 (Spring 1974): 112–57. See also, for example, Sue Kunitomi Embrey, Arthur A. Hansen, and Betty Kuhlberg Mitson, *Manzanar Martyr: An Interview with Harry Y. Ueno* (Fullerton: California State University, Oral History Program, 1986); Girdner and Loftis, *The Great Betrayal*, pp. 263–65; Jeanne Wakatsuki Houston and James D. Houston, *Farewell to Manzanar: A True Story of Japanese American Experience during and after the World War II Internment* (Boston: Houghton Mifflin, 1973), p. 72ff.

39. Sam Hohri, letter to Norman Thomas, December 29, 1942. Norman Thomas papers.

40. Hayashi, *Democratizing the Enemy*, p. 122ff.

41. Bailey, *City in the Sun*, pp. 118–33; Arthur A. Hansen and David A. Hacker, "The Manzanar 'Riot': An Ethnic Perspective," in *Voices Long Silent: An Oral Inquiry into the Japanese American Evacuation*, ed. Arthur A. Hansen and Betty E. Mitson (Fullerton: California State University, Oral History Program, 1974), pp. 41–78.

42. Houston and Houston, *Farewell to Manzanar*, p. 72.

43. Shimonishi-Lamb, *And Then a Rainbow*, p. 71. See also Louis Fiset, "Censored! U.S. Censors and Internment Camp Mail in World War II," in *Guilt by Association: Essays in Japanese Settlement, Internment, and Relocation in the Rocky Mountain West*, ed. Mike Mackey (Powell, Wy.: Western History Publications, 2001), pp. 69–100.

44. Girdner and Loftis, *The Great Betrayal*, p. 246. On JERS, see Yuji Ichioka, ed., *Views from Within: The Japanese Evacuation Research Study* (Los An-

geles: UCLA Asian American Studies Center, 1989); Lane Ryo Hirabayashi, *The Politics of Fieldwork: Research in an American Concentration Camp* (Tucson: University of Arizona Press, 1999).

45. Edward H. Spicer et al., *Impounded People* (Tucson: University of Arizona Press, 1969), pp. 108–15.

46. Sandra C. Taylor, *Jewel of the Desert: Japanese American Internment at Topaz* (Berkeley: University of California Press, 1993), p. 155.

47. The Office of War Information debated at length buying *Colorado Times* in order to run it outright as a government-sponsored paper but finally abandoned the idea. The Justice Department's Special War Policies Unit put out a series of memos that summarized the week's news coverage by the Japanese-language press. For example, in December 1942 a memorandum complained of a verse by Seijiro Matsui that appeared in *Utah Nippo* and read, "The island whence the sun rises beckons me." "Highlights in the Domestic Foreign Language Press," Justice Department War Division files, RG 60.14.1, NARA.

48. Takeya Mizuno, "The Creation of the 'Free' Press in Japanese American Internment Camps: The War Relocation Authority's Planning and Making of the Camp Newspaper Policy," *Journalism & Mass Communication Quarterly* 78, 3 (Autumn 2001): 503–18.

49. Author's interview with "Y," June 2, 2004.

50. Letter, Larry Tajiri to Carey McWilliams, June 15, 1942, p. 2. Correspondence file, Box 2, Carey McWilliams papers, Hoover Institution for War and Peace, Stanford University.

51. Bill Hosokawa, "The Sentinel Story," in *Remembering Heart Mountain: Essays on Japanese American Internment in Wyoming*, ed. Mike Mackey (Powell, Wy.: Western History Pubs. 1998), pp. 68–70.

52. Taylor, *Jewel of the Desert*, pp. 138–47, 155.

53. Bailey, *City in the Sun*, pp. 171, 174.

54. Kaz Oka, "Editorial," *Poston Chronicle*, April 23, 1943; Bob Hiratsuka, "Whither 82,000 Evacuees? Return to Coast Urged," *Poston Chronicle*, April 25, 1943; Bob Hiratsuka, editorial, *Poston Chronicle*, June 13, 1943.

55. Drinnon, *Keeper of Concentration Camps*, pp. 100–104.

56. Terry Watada, *Bukkyo Tozen: A History of Jodo Shinshu Buddhism in Canada, 1905-1995* (Toronto: Toronto Buddhist Church, 1996), p. 112.

57. British Columbia Security Commission, *Report of British Columbia Security Commission. Government of Dominion of Canada, Department of Labour, March 4, 1942 to October 31, 1942* (Vancouver: British Columbia Security Commission, 1942), pp. 12–13.

58. Rose Murakami, *Ganbaru: The Murakami Family of Salt Spring Island*, pamphlet, (Japanese Garden Society of Salt Spring Island), 2005, p. 25.

59. Rev. Gordon Nakayama, CBC oral history for "The Day Before Yesterday," cited in Brian Nolan, *King's War: Mackenzie King and the Politics of War, 1939–1945* (Toronto: University of Toronto Press, 1988), p. 71.

60. Barry Broadfoot, *Years of Sorrow, Years of Shame: The Story of the Japanese Canadians in World War II* (Markham, Ont.: PaperJacks Doubleday, 1979), p. 217.

61. Ted Barris, *Days of Victory: Canadians Remember, 1939–1945* (Toronto: Thomas Altenfus, 2005), pp. 164–66.

62. The BCSC paid a $65 per student subsidy to Alberta's school board for each of the approximately 600 Japanese Canadian schoolchildren from families of beet sugar growers attending school in the province. In contrast, with small exceptions Manitoba freely admitted to its primary schools the 250 Japanese Canadian schoolchildren resettled there, and Winnipeg opened its high schools to Nisei students. British Columbia Security Commission, *Report*, p. 14.

63. Roland M. Kawano, ed., *A History of the Japanese Congregations in the United Church of Canada* (Scarborough, Ont.: Japanese Canadian Christian Churches Historical Project, 1998), pp. 66–70.

64. Watada, *Bukkyo Tozen*, pp. 120–25.

65. One source states that men in Kaslo were put to work by the RCMP chopping wood and clearing roads. At first they earned 25 cents an hour, but an RCMP official decided that was too generous, so the pay was cut to 10 cents per hour. Barris, *Days of Victory*, p. 163.

66. Broadfoot, *Years of Sorrow*, p. 202.

67. Patricia Roy et al., *Mutual Hostages: Canadians and Japanese during the Second World War* (Toronto: University of Toronto Press, 1990), pp. 136–37.

68. Forrest E. La Violette, *The Canadian Japanese and World War II* (Toronto: University of Toronto Press, 1948), pp. 205–7. At the January 1942 conference in Ottawa on Japanese Affairs discussed in chapter 2, Assistant Commissioner F. J. Mead of the RCMP read an agent's report of a secret meeting of Issei fishermen in Vancouver, in which the fishermen said that they realized the seizure was probably inevitable under war conditions. Minutes of meetings, January 8–10, 1942, cited in Escott Reid, *Radical Mandarin: The Memoirs of Escott Reid* (Toronto: University of Toronto Press, 1989), p. 162.

69. For the process leading up to property sales, see Ann Gomer Sunahara, *The Politics of Racism: The Uprooting of Japanese Canadians during World War II* (Toronto: Lorimer, 1981), pp. 102–6.

70. Ibid., p. 206.

71. Mary Taylor, *A Black Mark: The Japanese-Canadians in World War II* (Toronto: Oberon Press, 2004), p. 131.

72. Sunahara, *The Politics of Racism*, pp. 109–10.

73. Roy Miki, *Redress: Inside the Japanese Canadian Call for Justice* (Vancouver: RainCoast Books, 2004), pp. 42–43.

74. La Violette, *The Canadian Japanese and World War II*, pp. 217–19. One source says that the confusion arose from a lawyer's error—because the commissioner of placement continued to use the stationery of the defunct British Columbia Security Commission, the BCSC was incorrectly named as respondent. Taylor, *A Black Mark*, p. 103.

75. Ken Adachi, *The Enemy That Never Was: A History of the Japanese Canadians* (Toronto: McClellan and Stewart, 1976), p. 322. Ann Gomer Sunahara points out that Justice Thorson had been a member of the 1942 cabinet that had agreed to remove the Japanese Canadians. *The Politics of Racism*, p. 109.

76. See Philip Glick to Dillon Myer, Memorandum for the Director, June 22, 1942. Confidential subject-coded correspondence file, 19.200/39.050, War Relocation Authority Papers, RG 210 NARA.

77. Roger Daniels, *Concentration Camps USA: Japanese Americans and World War II* (New York: Holt, Rinehart and Winston, 1971), p. 111.

78. Confidential memorandum on conferences in Washington, D.C., by Dr. Alexander Meiklejohn and Roger Baldwin, September 15 and 16, 1942. Japanese Evacuation files, Papers of the American Civil Liberties Union, Princeton University.

79. Allan W. Austin, *From Concentration Camp to Campus: Japanese American Students and World War II* (Urbana: University of Illinois Press, 2004), p. 24; Robert O'Brien, *The College Nisei* (Palo Alto, Calif.: Pacific Books, 1949).

80. Franklin Roosevelt, letter to Culbert Olson, May 25, 1942. Official File 197-A, FDR L.

81. Dillon Myer, Press Conference, May 14, 1943, Public Statements by Director, reel 21, p. 33, WRA Papers, JERS.

82. Austin, *From Concentration Camp to Campus*, pp. 11, 152–53.

83. U.S. Department of the Interior, War Relocation Authority, *The Relocation Program* (New York: AMS Press, 1975 [1946]), pp. 10–12.

84. War Relocation Authority, *WRA: A Story of Human Conservation*, p. 36.

85. War Relocation Authority, Administrative Instruction no. 22, July 20, 1942.

86. Eric L. Muller, *American Inquisition: The Hunt for Japanese American Disloyalty during World War II* (Chapel Hill: University of North Carolina Press, 2007), pp. 29–30.

87. War Relocation Authority, *WRA: A Story of Human Conservation*, pp. 36, 38–40.

88. Philip Glick, letter to Maurice Walk, October 1, 1942. Series 19 correspondence file, WRA papers, RG 210, NARA.

89. For a critical analysis of the evolution of the statement (drafted by OWI director Elmer Davis) and Roosevelt's attitude, see Greg Robinson, *By Order*

of the President: FDR and the Internment of Japanese Americans (Cambridge: Harvard University Press, 2001), pp. 163–73.

90. Timothy Turner, "First Lady Here to Visit Hospitals," *Los Angeles Times*, April 27, 1943. Mrs. Roosevelt repeated her views in a popular magazine piece she published in fall 1943. Eleanor Roosevelt, "A Challenge to American Sportsmanship," *Collier's* 112 (October 16, 1943): 21, 71.

91. Many Japanese Americans and allied groups, even those bitterly critical of the camps, agreed to collaborate with the WRA campaign. For one notable example, see Greg Robinson, "Birth of a Citizen: Miné Okubo and the Politics of Symbolism," in *Miné Okubo: Following Her Own Road,* ed. Greg Robinson and Elena Tajima Creef (Seattle: University of Washington Press, 2008), pp. 159–76.

92. Inspector's Training Manual [1943], Entry 480, Box 1725, Record Group 389, Records of the Office of the Provost Marshall General, National Archives; Eric Muller, "Is That Legal," May 19, 2005, available at http://www.isthatlegal .org. See also Muller, *American Inquisition*, chaps. 3–5.

93. Florence Ohmura Dobashi, "The Loyalty Questionnaire," in *From Our Side of the Fence: Growing Up in America's Concentration Camps*, ed. Brian Domei Dempster (San Francisco: Japanese Cultural & Community Center of Northern California, 2001), p. 6.

94. Miné Okubo, *Citizen 13660* (Seattle: University of Washington Press, 1983 [1946]), pp. 206–7.

95. Muller, *American Inquisition*, chaps. 7–8.

96. U.S Department of the Interior, War Relocation Authority, *The Evacuated People: A Quantitative Description* (New York, AMS Press, 1975 [1946]).

97. U.S Department of the Interior, War Liquidation Agency Unit, cited in "Coastal Japanese Number 60 Percent Pre-war Count," *Rafu Shimpo*, August 20, 1947; Greg Robinson, "Nisei in Gotham: Japanese Americans in Wartime New York," *Prospects: An Annual of American Culture Studies* 30 (2005): 581 95.

98. On the experiences of wartime resettlers generally, see U.S. Department of the Interior, War Agency Liquidation Unit, *People in Motion: The Postwar Adjustment of the Evacuated Japanese Americans* (Washington, D.C.: U.S. Government Printing Office, 1947); Dorothy Swaine Thomas, assisted by Charles Kikuchi and James Sakoda, *The Salvage: Japanese American Evacuation and Resettlement* (Berkeley: University of California Press, 1952); Allan W. Austin, "Eastward Pioneers: Japanese Americans Resettlement during World War II and the Contested Meaning of Exile and Incarceration," *Journal of American Ethnic History* 26 (Winter 2007): 58–84.

99. Interview, Sumi Seo, in Levine, *A Fence Away from Freedom*, pp. 166–67.

100. Robinson, "Nisei in Gotham," pp. 585–86.

101. War Relocation Authority, *The Relocation Program*, p. 220.

102. Fugita and Fernandez, *Altered Lives, Enduring Community*, pp. 122–25.

103. On housing discrimination and concentration, see Charlotte Brooks, "In the Twilight Zone between Black and White: Japanese American Resettlement and Community in Chicago, 1942–1945," *Journal of American History* 86, 4 (Fall 2000): 1655–87.

104. Taylor, *A Black Mark*, pp. 68–69.

105. H. T. Pammett, Memorandum for Mr. Macnamara, "Program for Reallocation of Japanese," February 8, 1943, RG 27, v. 169, Labor Department Files, LAC.

106. Letter, S. Morley Scott, Under Secretary of State for External Affairs, to Spanish Consul General, November 10, 1943, file 3464-B-40C, External Affairs, LAC.

107. La Violette, *The Canadian Japanese and World War II*, pp. 117, 170–71. La Violette asserts that the U.S. government urged that Japanese Canadians in the ghost towns be forcibly resettled, but the evidence for this claim is not apparent.

108. Adachi, *The Enemy That Never Was*, pp. 260–61.

109. Ibid., p. 258.

110. Addie Kobayashi, *Exiles in Our Own Country: Japanese Canadians in Niagara* (Richmond Hill, Ont.: Nikkei Network of Niagara, 1998).

111. La Violette, *The Canadian Japanese and World War II*, pp. 153–54.

112. "Disposing of the Japanese," *Globe and Mail*, November 22, 1943; "Our Japanese Problem," *Globe and Mail*, November 30, 1943.

113. Montreal Japanese Canadian History Committee, "Ganbari: Reclaiming Our Home/Ganbari: un chez-soi retrouvé," pamphlet, Montreal, 1998, p. 9.

114. Greg Robinson, "Two Other Solitudes? Historical Encounters between Japanese Canadians and French Canadians," in *Contradictory Impulses: Canada and Japan in the 20th Century*, ed. Greg Donaghy and Patricia Roy (Vancouver: UBC Press, 2007), pp. 140–57.

115. "Race Restrictions at University Hit," *Montreal Gazette*, November 2, 1944.

116. Cited in La Violette, *The Canadian Japanese and World War II*, p. 306.

117. Sugihara, *The Politics of Racism*, pp. 116–17.

118. U.S. Commission on Wartime Relocation and Internment of Civilians, *Personal Justice Denied*, pp. 250–52.

119. Drinnon, *Keeper of Concentration Camps*, p. 112. In summer 1944 stockade prisoners launched another hunger strike against their confinement, which lasted nearly a month but encountered little more success. Ibid., p. 130.

120. Carey McWilliams, *Prejudice: Japanese Americans: Symbol of Racial Intolerance* (Boston: Little, Brown, 1944).

121. Weglyn, *Years of Infamy*, pp. 246–58. See also generally Donald E. Collins, *Native American Aliens Disloyalty and the Renunciation of Citizenship by Japanese Americans during World War II* (Westport, Conn.: Greenwood

Press, 1985); Barbara Takei, *A Question of Loyalty: Internment at Tule Lake* (Klamath Falls, Ore: Shaw Historical Library, 2005).

122. Dillon S. Myer, *Uprooted Americans: The Japanese Americans and the War Relocation Authority during World War II* (Tucson: University of Arizona Press, 1971), p. 244.

123. On Tule Lake and the rise of the resegregant movement, see, for example, Motomu Akashi, *Betrayed Trust: The Story of a Deported Issei and His American-Born Family during World War II* (Bloomington, Ind.: AuthorHouse, 2004), pp. 129–46.

124. Tom Sando, *Wild Daisies in the Sand: Life in a Canadian Internment Camp* (Edmonton: NeWest Press, 2002), p.28.

125. Takeo Ujo Nakano with Leatrice Nakano, *Behind the Barbed Wire Fence* (Halifax: Goodread Biographies, 1983 [1980]), pp. 38–42.

126. Robert K. Okazaki, *The Nisei Mass Evacuation Group and P.O.W. Camp 101: The Japanese Canadian Community's Struggle for Justice and Human Rights during World War II* (Scarborough, Ont.: R. K. Okazaki, 1996), pp. 37, 48, 59.

127. Nakano, *Within the Barbed Wire Fence*, p. 88. According to one report, conditions were so poor in the "ghost towns" that citizens of Japan, despite their own wartime privations, sent shipments of miso via the Red Cross to ease hunger there. It is not clear whether food was distributed only to internees in the POW camp at Angler or to inmates in camps as well. Janice Patton, *The Exodus of the Japanese* (Toronto: McClelland and Stewart, 1973), p. 30.

128. Letter, Tokikazu Tanaka to Lt. Col. Geo. C. Meachum, January 16, 1944; Memorandum, Lt. Col. Geo C. Meachum, January 17, 1944, reprinted in Okazaki, *The Nisei Mass Evacuation Group*, pp. A-126, A-127.

129. Sando, *Wild Daisies in the Sand*, pp. 76–78; Okazaki, *The Nisei Mass Evacuation Group*, p. 62.

130. Tetsuden Kashima, *Judgment without Trial: Japanese American Imprisonment during World War II* (Seattle: University of Washington Press, 2003), pp. 111–13.

131. D. M. Ladd, Memorandum for the Director, "Apprehensions of Japanese Individuals," April 6, 1943, FBI papers, p. 3910, NARA. By March 1943, according to FBI records, 5,186 German aliens, 5,126 Japanese aliens, and 2,273 Italian aliens had been apprehended, of whom 1,655 Germans, 2,747 Japanese, and 227 Italians were interned. Enclosure, letter, J. Edgar Hoover to Francis Biddle, March 2, 1943, 100–2-3882, War Division, RG 44, Justice Department Records, National Archives.

132. Kashima, *Judgment without Trial*, pp. 111–13.

133. Priscilla Wegars, "Japanese and Japanese Latin Americans at Idaho's Kooskia Internment Camp," in *Guilt by Association*, ed. Mackey, pp. 145–83.

134. Max Paul Friedman, *Nazis and Good Neighbors: The United States Campaign against the Germans of Latin America in World War II* (New York: Cambridge University Press, 2003), pp. 147–48.

135. Edison Uno, "Crystal City Internment," *Pacific Citizen*, March 10, 1967.

136. Ibid.; Karen L. Riley, *Schools Behind Barbed Wire: The Untold Story of Wartime Internment and the Children of Arrested Enemy Aliens* (Lanham, Md.: Rowman & Littlefield, 2002).

137. Riley, *Schools Behind Barbed Wire*; Greg Robinson, "Review of Riley, *Schools Behind Barbed Wire*," *American Historical Review* 108, 2 (April 2003): 541.

5. MILITARY SERVICE AND LEGAL CHALLENGES

1. Figures on the total number of Nisei soldiers are vague, and there is no consensus among historians as to the total number. Shortly after the end of the war, the War Department Public Information Division stated officially that, according to War Department records, 33,330 Americans of Japanese ancestry (including 40 noncitizens) had served in the United States Army between July 1, 1940, and November 30, 1945. Letter, Kendell W. Fielder to Mike Masaoka, April 15, 1947, correspondence files, Mike Masaoka papers, University of Utah. By early 2008 Seiki Oshiro, a researcher for the Japanese American Veterans Assocation, had compiled a list of 31,341 names of soldiers.

2. "Nisei and the Draft," *Current Life*, October 1940, p. 12.

3. "Japanese American Soldiers"; *John Aiso and the M.I.S: Japanese American Soldiers in the Military Intelligence Service, World War II* (Los Angeles: Military Intelligence Service Club of Southern California, 1988), pp. 15–16.

4. Deborah K. Lim, *The Lim Report* (Kearney, Neb.: Morris Publishing, 2002 [1990]), p. 37; Michi Weglyn, *Years of Infamy* (Seattle: University of Washington Press, 1996 [1976]), p. 38.

5. Franklin Odo, *No Sword to Bury: Japanese Americans in Hawai'i during World War II* (Philadelphia: Temple University Press, 2004), pp. 107–11.

6. Ralph G. Martin, *Boy from Nebraska: The Story of Ben Kuroki* (New York: Harper's, 1946); Frank "Foo" Fujita, *Foo: A Japanese-American Prisoner of the Rising Sun* (Denton, Tex.: University of North Texas Press, 1993).

7. Lyn Crost, *Honor By Fire: Japanese Americans at War in Europe and the Pacific* (Novato, Calif.: Presidio Press, 1994), pp. 47–57.

8. Joseph D. Harrington, *Yankee Samurai: The Secret Role of Nisei in America's Pacific Victory* (Detroit: Pettigrew Enterprises, 1979), p. 112; U.S. Commission on Wartime Relocation and Internment of Civilians, *Personal Justice Denied* (Seattle: University of Washington Press, 1997 [1983]), p. 255.

9. Memorandum, General John L. DeWitt to Col. Theodore J. Koenig, GSC, Military Utilization of United States Citizens of Japanese Ancestry, July 21, 1942, Records of the Secretary of War, RG 107, NARA, reprinted in CWRIC papers, pp. 5171–94, reel 14, pp. 853–77.

10. Harrington, *Yankee Samurai*, pp. 113–16; Greg Robinson, *By Order of the President: FDR and the Internment of Japanese Americans* (Cambridge: Harvard University Press, 2001), pp. 164–65.

11. Memorandum, Elmer Davis to Franklin Roosevelt, October 2, 1942, CWRIC papers, p. 13755.

12. Donald E. Collins, *Native American Aliens: Disloyalty and the Renunciation of Citizenship by Japanese Americans during World War II* (Westport, Conn.: Greenwood Press, 1985), p. 23; Robert Asahina, *Just Americans: How Japanese Americans Won a War at Home and Abroad* (New York: Gotham Books, 2006), pp. 45–46; Robinson, *By Order of the President*, p. 167.

13. John McCloy, Memorandum for the Secretary of War, October 15, 1942, Records of the Secretary of War, RG 107, NARA, reprinted in CWRIC papers, p. 13779.

14. Henry L. Stimson, draft letter to the President, October 14, 1942, with Stimson's handwritten notes (undated), RG 407 (Adj. General 1940–1942 Classified), NARA, CWRIC papers, pp. 13761–64.

15. Marshall's assistant, S.L.A. Marshall, insisted that the project was directed by the chief of staff, and that it was Marshall who pressed McCloy to enlist Nisei. Asahina, *Just Americans*, p. 45.

16. Odo, *No Sword to Bury*, p. 188. The reason for the inequality of quotas was not apparent, since the male military-age population in the two areas was approximately equal, unless it was meant to compensate for the existing Japanse American troops from Hawaii.

17. Robinson, *By Order of the President*, pp. 167–68.

18. Eric Muller, *Free to Die for Their Country: The Story of the Japanese American Draft Resisters in World War II* (Chicago: University of Chicago Press, 2001); "War Department Re-affirms Faith in Nisei," *Poston Chronicle*, February 20, 1943.

19. U.S. Commission on Wartime Relocation and Internment of Civilians, *Personal Justice Denied*, pp. 215–19. See also memorandum, John DeWitt to Chief of Staff, January 27, 1943, cited in Muller, *Free to Die for Their Country*, p. 47.

20. "A Voice That Must Be Heard: Excerpts from Statements Regarding Americans of Japanese Ancestry," pamphlet, War Relocation Authority 1943, New York Public Library.

21. Mike Masaoka, with Bill Hosokawa, *They Call Me Moses Masaoka: An American Saga* (New York: Morrow, 1987), p. 126.

22. "Combat Team Quota to Be Filled by Draft," *Poston Chronicle,* February 21, 1943.
23. Weglyn, *Years of Infamy,* p. 136.
24. Masaoka, *They Call Me Moses Masaoka,* p. 135.
25. For an extended discussion of Finch, see John Howard, *Concentration Camps on the Home Front,* p. 2. Following a vicious speech against the recruits in the House of Representatives by race-baiting Mississippi Congressman John Rankin, First Lady Eleanor Roosevelt feared the Nisei would receive a hostile reception in the Jim Crow South. In response to her intervention, Secretary McCloy personally inspected the area to promote a welcoming attitude among locals. Crost, *Honor by Fire,* p. 65.
26. Daniel Inouye, interview for DENSHO, cited in Stephen Fugita and Marilyn Fernandez, *Altered Lives, Enduring Community* (Seattle: University of Washington Press, 2005), p. 89.
27. Crost, *Honor by Fire,* pp. 73–116.
28. Ibid., p. 136.
29. Chester Tanaka, *Go for Broke: A Pictorial History of the Japanese American 100th Infantry Battalion and the 442nd Regimental Combat Team* (Richmond, Calif: Go for Broke, 1982), p. 73, cited in CWRIC, *Personal Justice Denied,* p. 257.
30. Masayo Duus, *Unlikely Liberators: The Men of the 100th and 442nd* (Honolulu: University of Hawaii Press, 1987).
31. CWRIC, *Personal Justice Denied,* p. 256; Harrington, *Yankee Samurai,* p. 363. The definitive history of the Nisei MIS staffers is James C. McNaughton, *Nisei Linguists: Japanese Americans in the Military Intelligence Service During World War II* (Washington, D.C.: U.S. Army Center of Military History, 2007).
32. James Oda, *Heroic Struggles of Japanese Americans: Partisan Fighters from America's Concentration Camps* (Hollywood: James Oda, 1981), p. 97.
33. "Stimson Raps Critics of U.S. Nisei Policy," *Pacific Citizen,* October 30, 1943; "Secretary Stimson Describes Attack on Nisei GI as 'Outrage,'" *Pacific Citizen,* April 7, 1945.
34. Franklin Roosevelt, speech, Puget Sound, Wash., August 12, 1944, President's Speech File 1944, Office File 1820, FDR Library, Hyde Park.
35. Franklin Roosevelt, Columbus Day address to the American Republics, reprinted in *New York Times,* October 13, 1944.
36. Franklin Roosevelt, press conference no. 982, November 21, 1944, in Franklin D., Roosevelt, *Complete Press Conferences of FDR* (New York: Da Capo Press, 1973), 24:247–48.
37. Letter, Elmer Davis to President Roosevelt, October 2, 1942, CRWIC papers, p. 13755.
38. Muller, *Free to Die for Their Country,* pp. 60–63.

39. Sandra C. Taylor, *Jewel of the Desert: Japanese American Internment at To-paz* (Berkeley: University of California Press, 1993), pp. 171–72; "Nisei Must Fight for Recognition," *Topaz Times*, July 12, 1944.

40. Letter/petition, Mothers' Society of Minidoka to Eleanor Roosevelt, February 20, 1944, correspondence group 100, Eleanor Roosevelt papers, FDRL.

41. Letter, Eleanor Roosevelt to Fuyo Tanagi, March 4, 1944, correspondence group 100, Eleanor Roosevelt papers, FDRL.

42. "Nisei Democrat Lauds Roosevelt's Policies," *Kashu Mainichi*, October 25, 1936.

43. Okamoto sought aid from outside activists such as Socialist leader Norman Thomas, but his disjointed arguments and the nasty anti-Semitic tinge in his complaints over "ascendancy of Jewish influence" in the Roosevelt administration alienated them. Letters, Kiyoshi Okamoto to Norman Thomas, February 10, 1943; Kiyoshi Okamoto to Margaret Anderson, March 16, 1943; Margaret Anderson to Norman Thomas, March 23, 1942, reel 2, Norman Thomas papers.

44. Heart Mountain Fair Play Committee Circular, March 4, 1944, cited in Muller, *Free to Die for Their Country*, p. 83.

45. See A[sael]. T. Hansen, "The Reaction of Heart Mountain to the Opening of Selective Service to the Nisei," April 15, 1944, Community Service Reports, War Relocation Authority paper, RG 210, NARA (Microfilm M1342, reel 17).

46. A significant literature has grown up around the FPC draft resistance movement. Aside from Muller's *Free to Die for Their Country*, notable works include Frank Abe's film *Conscience and the Constitution*, 1999; Frank Chin, *Born in the USA: A Story of Japanese America, 1889–1947* (Lanham, Md.: Rowman and Littlefield, 2002); *A Matter of Conscience: Essays on the World War II Heart Mountain Draft Resistance Movement*, ed. Mike Mackey (Powell, Wy.: Heart Mountain Wyoming Foundation, 2002), p. 56.

47. Frank S. Emi, "Protest and Resistance: An American Tradition," in *A Matter of Conscience*, ed. Mackey.

48. See Hansen, "The Reaction of Heart Mountain."

49. Lim, *The Lim Report*, pp. 127–30; Yosh Kuromiya, "Fighting for My Country, My Constitution," in *Resistance: Challenging America's Wartime Internment of Japanese-Americans*, ed. William Minoru Hohri et al. (Lomita, Calif.: Epistolarian, 2001), pp. 64–65.

50. Letter, Roger Baldwin to Kiyoshi Okamoto, April 9, 1944, cited in Roger Daniels, *Asian America: Japanese and Chinese in the United States since 1850* (Seattle: University of Washington Press, 1990), p. 277, n. 119. In defiance of the national line, Southern California ACLU attorney A. L. Wirin took up the defense of the Fair Play Committee leaders in court.

51. Hansen, "The Reaction of Heart Mountain."

52. Muller, *Free to Die for Their Country*, pp. 125–28.

53. Ibid., pp. 131–61.

54. Ibid., p. 143.

55. Roy Ito, *We Went to War: The Story of the Japanese Canadians Who Served during the First and Second World Wars* (Stittsville, Ont.: Canada's Wings, 1984), pp. 108–9.

56. Ibid., p. 150.

57. "Turn in Uniforms, Varsity Japs Told," *Toronto Star*, January 7, 1942.

58. See, for example, *La Patrie*, December 10, 1941; *Toronto Star*, January 15, 1942.

59. Ito, *We Went to War*, pp. 157–60.

60. Cabinet Conclusions, "Enlistment of Canadian-born Japanese in the Canadian Army," RG2, Privy Council Office, series A-5-a , vol. 2636, reel T-2364, LAC.

61. Mary Taylor, *A Black Mark: The Japanese-Canadians in World War II* (Toronto: Oberon Press, 2004), p. 115.

62. Ken Adachi, *The Enemy That Never Was: A History of the Japanese Canadians* (Toronto: McClellan and Stewart, 1976), pp. 293–94.

63. "Fred Kagawa's War," *Aldernews* 11, 23 (November 2004): 1, 3.

64. Ito, *We Went to War*, pp. 200–201.

65. Adachi, *The Enemy That Never Was*, p. 292.

66. Ito, *We Went to War*, p. 201.

67. Forrest E. La Violette, *The Canadian Japanese and World War II* (Toronto: University of Toronto Press, 1948), p. 233.

68. See, for example, "Vive la démocratie!" *Montréal-Matin*, February 16, 1946.

69. Adachi, *The Enemy That Never Was*, p. 293.

70. Much of this section is taken from Peter Irons's definitive study of the "internment cases," *Justice at War* (New York: Oxford University Press, 1983).

71. On the Yasui family, see Lauren Kessler, *Stubborn Twig: Three Generations in the Life of a Japanese Family* (New York: Random House, 1993).

72. Irons, *Justice at War*, pp. 82–84.

73. Ibid, pp. 90–93

74. For Korematsu's biography, see Eric Paul Fournier, *Of Civil Rights and Wrongs: The Fred Korematsu Story*, documentary film, 2000.

75. Interview, Mitsuye Endo, in John Tateishi, *And Justice For All: An Oral History of the Japanese American Detention Camps* (New York: Random House, 1979), pp. 60–61.

76. Irons, *Justice at War*, pp. 102-3.

77. "Nab Japanese Visiting State," *Milwaukee Journal*, July 11, 1942; "Test of Jap Internment Decrees Filed in U.S. Court," *Los Angeles Times*, August 20, 1942; author correspondence with Edgar Wakayama, March 2006; Irons, *Justice at War*, p. 115.

78. *JACL Bulletin* 142, April 7, 1942, cited in Lim, *The Lim Report*, pp. 65, 72. As mentioned previously, the JACL's *amicus curiae* (friend of the court) briefs in these cases were ghostwritten by Morris Opler, a community analyst at Manzanar, during the evenings after work. Although Opler had no legal training, he was well informed as to the nature of the Japanese community and the impact of evacuation on its members.

79. Samuel Walker, *In Defense of American Liberties: A History of the ACLU* (New York: Oxford University Press, 1990), pp. 139–42.

80. Irons, *Justice at War*, pp. 155–59.

81. U.S. Supreme Court, *Minoru Yasui v. United States*, 320 U.S. 115 (1943).

82. Irons, *Justice at War*, pp. 207–14. Robinson, *By Order of the President*, pp. 190–191; As this book went to press, Eric Muller brought out an article with the compelling thesis that Edward Ennis and the other Justice Department lawyers defending the *Hirabayashi* case knew, or had reason to know, that the risk of any Japanese invasion of the West Coast during 1942 was remote. Therefore any army claims of military necessity were entirely fraudulent. Eric L. Muller, "Hirabayashi: The Biggest Lie of the Greatest Generation," UNC Legal Studies Research Paper no. 1233682, August 18, 2008. Available at http://papers.ssrn.com/sol3/papers.cfm?abstract_id=1233682.

83. Jacobus tenBroek, Edward N. Barnhart, and Floyd W. Matson, *Prejudice, War and the Constitution* (Berkeley: University of California Press, 1954), pp. 214–15.

84. U.S. Supreme Court, *Kiyoshi Hirabayashi v. United States*, 320 U.S. 81 (1943), p. 98.

85. U.S. Supreme Court, *Minoru Yasui v. United States*.

86. Irons, *Justice at War*, pp. 144–51, 162.

87. Ibid. pp. 265–68.

88. Ibid., pp. 278–92.

89. U.S. Supreme Court, *Toyosaburo Korematsu v. United States*, 323 U.S. 214 (1944). As in the *Hirabayashi* case, the caption listed only the appellant's Japanese name. The only Justice to refer to Korematsu by his generally used American first name, Fred, was Justice Frank Murphy, who did so in his concurring opinion in *Endo*.

90. Ibid., p. 223.

91. Ibid., pp. 243, 246

92. Ibid., p. 242. Black felt obliged to answer the dissenters by adding language about race being a protected category. "It should be noted, to begin with, that all legal restrictions which curtail the civil rights of a single racial group are immediately suspect. That is not to say that all such restrictions are unconstitutional. It is to say that courts must subject them to the most rigid scrutiny." See U.S. Supreme Court, *Toyosaburo Korematsu v. United States*, p. 216. Both the opinion and the implications of this passage have lent the

case central history in civil rights law. Neil Gotanda, "The Story of Korematsu: The Japanese-American Cases," in *Constitutional Law Stories*, ed. Michael Dorf (New York: Foundation Press, 2004), pp. 249–96; Greg Robinson and Toni Robinson, "*Korematsu* and Beyond: Japanese Americans and the Origins of Strict Scrutiny," *Law and Contemporary Problems* 68, 2 (Spring 2005), 29-55.

93. U.S. Supreme Court, *Ex Parte Mitsuye Endo*, 323 U.S. 283 (1944). For the significance of the case, see Patrick Gudridge, "Remember Endo?" *Harvard Law Review* 116 (2003): 1933–70.

94. My discussion of martial law and its challengers draws heavily from two indispensable works: J Garner Anthony, *Hawaii under Army Rule* (Stanford: Stanford University Press, 1955); and Harry N. Scheiber and Jane L. Scheiber, "Bayonets in Paradise: A Half-Century Retrospect on Martial Law in Hawaii, 1941–1946," University of Hawaii Law Review, 19 (Fall 1997): 477–648.

95. Scheiber and Scheiber, "Bayonets in Paradise," p. 488.

96. Garner Anthony, *Hawaii under Army Rule* pp. 8, 48. Fred Patterson, a Honolulu lawyer, later related the description of an officer wearing a tin hat and carrying a gun who had entered the courthouse after the Pearl Harbor attack, ejected the judges, and sat down at the bench. He placed his gas mask and his gun on either side, stuffed a big cigar in his mouth, and announced that his court was in session. "Charge Abuse of Civilians in Hawaii Courts," *Chicago Tribune*, July 2, 1944.

97. Attorney General of Hawaii, report to Governor to Ingram Stainback, December 1, 1942. pp. 7–8. Reprinted in Anthony, *Hawaii under Military Rule*, p. 195.

98. Fred L. Israel, "Military Justice in Hawaii, 1941–1944," *Pacific Historical Review* 36, 2 (August 1967): 247–48.

99. E. J. Botts, cited in "Charge Abuse of Civilians in Hawaii Courts."

100. "Abe Detained in Hawaii," *New York Times*, September 8, 1942.

101. Anthony, *Hawaii under Army Rule*, pp. 28–29.

102. Cited in *Nevada State Journal*, December 25, 1942, p. 7.

103. Lester Petrie, "The New Honolulu," *Collier's*, March 21, 1942, pp. 22–31; "Honolulu Mayor Defends Army Rule of Hawaii," *Chicago Tribune*, January 11, 1943.

104. Report, Thomas Green to John McCloy, June 2, 1942, cited in Odo, *No Sword to Bury*, p. 244.

105. Letter, Frank Knox to the President, August 19, 1942. OF 400 (Hawaii), FDRL.

106. Garner Anthony, "Martial Law in Hawaii," *California Law Review* 30, 4 (May 1942): 371–96.

107. William Norwood, "The Country Speaks: Honolulu," *Christian Science Monitor*, October 12, 1942; Harold Ickes diary, April 26, 1942, Harold Ickes papers, LOC.

108. Israel, "Military Justice in Hawaii," pp. 250–56.

109. Norman M. Littell, *My Roosevelt Years* (Seattle: University of Washington Press, 1987), pp. 124–25.

110. Abe Fortas, Memorandum to the President, August 28, 1942, PSF 400 (Hawaii), FDRL.

111. Charles Fairman, "The Supreme Court on Military Jurisdiction: Martial Rule in Hawaii and the Yamashita Case," *Harvard Law Review* 59, 6 (July 1946): 836. Fairman, a political science professor at Stanford University and major in the army reserve, had earlier supported both martial law and Executive Order 9066 in sweeping terms. Charles Fairman, "The Law of Martial Rule and the National Emergency," *Harvard Law Review* 55 (November 1942): 1253–1303.

112. Letter, General Delos Emmons to Assistant Secretary of War John J. McCloy, December 15, 1942, cited in Scheiber and Scheiber, "Bayonets in Paradise," pp. 553–54.

113. Harold Ickes Diary, October 18, 1942. Harold Ickes Papers, LOC; *Nevada State Journal*, December 26, 1942.

114. Scheiber and Scheiber, "Bayonets in Paradise," p. 546. Emmons himself later testified that in December 1942 he had informed Ickes that Hawaiians would vote 10 to 1 in favor of martial law if it came to a referendum. "Hawaii Doctor Rests Suit over Seizure in War," *Chicago Tribune*, December 20, 1950, p. 14.

115. "Martial Law in Hawaii Due for Partial Civil Setup," *Christian Science Monitor*, December 29, 1942. The article asserted that the chief danger was of attacks on local Japanese by Filipinos "from the back jungles of their native islands" who were quick to use knives to express "strong personal feelings."

116. Letter, James Rowe to the President, December 10, 1942, PSF (Executive Office of the President, James Rowe), FDRL.

117. Attorney General, Confidential Memorandum for the President re: Hawaii, December 17, 1942, PSF-133 (Justice), FDRL. One source states that by late October Biddle and Ickes had secured the president's agreement for Green's withdrawal—if so, nothing was done about it then. Littell, *My Roosevelt Years*, p. 124.

118. FDR, memorandum for the Attorney General, December 18, 1942, PSF-Justice Department, FDRL.

119. Henry Stimson Diary, December 27, 1942, Henry Stimson papers.

120. "Eased Army Rule Is Seen for Hawaii," *New York Times*, December 30, 1942.

121. Letter, February 1, 1943, President Roosevelt to the Secretary of War. *Duncan v. Kahanamoku*, Record on Appeal, U.S. Supreme Court, 1945.

122. "Hawaii Army Rule Relaxed," *Washington Post*, February 9, 1943.

123. William Norwood, "Easing of Martial Law in Hawaii Tests Democracy," *Christian Science Monitor*, January 21, 1943.

124. Scheiber and Scheiber, "Bayonets in Paradise," pp. 580–82, attributes the lack of contest to Nisei suspicions of the justice system, mixed with low morale and outside pressure to demonstrate loyalty.

125. "Habeas Corpus Denied," *New York Times*, February 22, 1942.

126. Message, General Emmons to Adjutant General, July 20, 1942, ASW 014.311 Hawaii, NARA, reprinted in *American Concentration Camps*, ed. Roger Daniels (New York: Garland, 1989).

127. "Future Martial Law Need Cited," *Los Angeles Times*, June 5, 1942. The attorney general's support for martial law became an important issue in the 1942 gubernatorial election, in which Warren unseated incumbent Culbert Olson.

128. Affidavit of General Thomas Green, cited in "General Admits Deal in Case of Interned Medic," *Chicago Tribune*, December 10, 1950. The affidavit arose as part of Zimmerman's unsuccessful damage suit against Emmons and the government.

129. "Dispute in Hawaii Eased," *New York Times*, October 22, 1943.

130. "Army General Defies Court in Honolulu," *Gettysburg Times*, August 26, 1943.

131. "Richardson Is Upheld in Defiance of Court," *Sheboygan Times*, August 27, 1943.

132. See, for example, the (nationally syndicated) editorial "Martial Law," *Lima News*, September 21, 1943.

133. "Call Martial Law Vital to Hawaii," *New York Times*, September 16, 1943. Because the *Times* article presented the military viewpoint so faithfully, and because General Julius Ochs Adler, a member of the family that owned the newspaper, was associated with Richardson, Ickes complained bitterly that the article was officially written, or at least inspired, by the military governor's office. Scheiber and Scheiber, "Bayonets in Paradise," p. 445, n. 602.

134. "The Military Tyrant," *Chicago Tribune*, August 27, 1943.

135. "Scan Hawaiian Law for Clew to General's Act," *Chicago Tribune*, August 28, 1943.

136. "Holds in Contempt General in Hawaii," *New York Times*, August 25, 1943. Where the figure of 1,400 came from was not clear—since the total number of Japanese who had been interned between 1941 and 1944, most of whom had been shipped to the mainland—was 1,396. Other newspapers stated that 300 internees at most were being held in Hawaii.

137. "Habeas Corpus Row in Hawaii Flares Anew," *Chicago Tribune* October 23, 1943.

138. "Hawaii Still Fears Threat of Invasion," *Troy Record*, March 31, 1944.

139. Norm Silber and Geoffrey Miller, "Toward Neutral Principles in the Law: Selections from the Oral Histories of Herbert Wechsler," *Columbia University Law Review* 93, 4 (May 1993): 883.

140. "Jap Sub Seen 20 Miles from Pearl Harbor; Enemy Plane Spies upon Pearl Harbor," *Nevada State Journal*, April 12, 1944, p. 1.

141. Garner Anthony, *Ex Parte Duncan*, argument, April 8, 1944, in *Duncan v. Kahanamoku*, record on appeal, U.S. Supreme Court, 1945, pp. 654–55.

142. The Justice Department was not the first to seize on the dual nationality question as an excuse for bias—various public and private-sector employers forced Nisei job applicants to show proof of expatriation. Odo, *No Sword to Bury*, p. 245.

143. Edward Ennis, *Ex Parte Duncan*, argument, April 8, 1944, in *Duncan v. Kahanamoku*, record on appeal, U.S. Supreme Court, 1945, p. 946–47. In fact, the court's only comment on the matter in the opinion was a brief (and vague) passage: "Congress and the Executive, including the military commander, could have attributed special significance, in its bearing on the loyalties of persons of Japanese descent, to the maintenance by Japan of its system of dual citizenship," *Kiyoshi Hirabayashi v. United States*, 320 U.S. 81 (1943), p. 97.

144. Testimony of Andrew S. Wong, *Ex Parte Duncan*, in *Duncan v. Kahanamoku*, record on appeal, U.S. Supreme Court, 1945, pp. 964–77.

145. Testimony of Robert K. Murakami, *Ex Parte Duncan*, in *Duncan v. Kahanamoku*, 979–90. Ennis stressed that the *Hirabayashi* opinion was "in the same tenure" on dual citizenship as Murakami's testimony. Ibid., p. 990.

146. Testimony of Lt. General Robert C. Richardson, Jr. *Ex Parte Duncan*, in *Duncan v. Kahanamoku*, pp. 1022–23.

147. Ibid., p. 1024.

148. Testimony of Shunzo Sakanishi, *Ex Parte Duncan*, in *Duncan v. Kahanamoku*, pp. 1082–95.

149. Lt. General Robert C. Richardson, Jr., "Hawaii: Fortress of the Pacific," *Army and Navy Journal*, December 1943, cited in *Duncan v. Kahanamoku*, pp. 659–65. Anthony likewise pointed to the number of Nisei enlistees in the army, and introduced figures showing that over 7,000 Japanese Americans were employed on military bases.

150. Testimony of Lt. General Robert C. Richardson, Jr., *Ex Parte Duncan*, in *Duncan v. Kahanamoku*, p. 1029. This response furnished a rare public demonstration of the contempt that the military governor and his associates repeatedly expressed in private toward civil authorities, and their generally authoritarian outlook. Scheiber and Scheiber, "Bayonets in Paradise," p. 553.

151. Testimony of Hon. Ingram Stainback, *Ex Parte Duncan*, in *Duncan v. Kahanamoku*, pp. 834–35.

152. General Robert Richardson to Samuel Rosenman, August 1, 1944, enclosing Richardson letter to John McCloy, June 16, 1944, OF 400-Hawaii, FDRL.

153. Scheiber and Scheiber, "Bayonets in Paradise," pp. 604–6.

154. *Ex Parte Duncan*, 9 Cir., 146 F.2d 576.

155. Ibid. Out of concern for stirring up discord in wartime, the lone dissenter, Judge Albert Lee Stevens, did not release his opinion until 1946.

156. Ibid., p. 580.

157. It is unclear why Ennis, and not the U.S. solicitor general, argued the government brief—presumably Ennis's familiarity with the case made him a preferred advocate.

158. "Supreme Court to Review Hawaii Martial Law Cases," *Christian Science Monitor*, February 12, 1945, p. 9.

159. Ironically, Roberts had investigated at length the system of military tribunals during the visits of the Roberts Commission to Hawaii in January 1942 and had noted that they presented many legal problems. Richard V. Haller, "Martial Law Stirs Debate," *Washington Post*, May 15, 1942.

160. U.S. Supreme Court, *Duncan v. Kahanamoku*.

161. Ibid., p. 322. Black's interpretation of martial law was not shared by all his brethren. In a concurrence, Chief Justice Stone used *Hirabayashi* as authority for the proposition that the executive branch had broad discretion in determining when the public emergency is such as to give rise to the necessity of martial law, and in adapting it to the need. However, he added that nothing in the record suggested that the courts could not have functioned properly or that a civil trial would have disturbed public order. Ibid., p. 336. In contrast, justices Burton and Frankfurter dissented, arguing that in the wartime emergency it was up to the executive branch and Congress, not the courts, to decide how far the needs of martial law extended. Ibid., pp. 355–68.

162. Ibid., pp. 333–34.

163. Ibid., p. 332.

164. While the court had stated in the *Ex Parte Milligan* decision in (1866) that military courts could not constitutionally operate anywhere that civil courts were in operation, Black's opinion left open the question whether Congress could have constitutionally provided for military tribunals. This led various observers to suggest that, even in overturning military tribunals, the court had actually weakened the common law standard enunciated in *Milligan*. See, for example, Robert Cardon. "Trial of Civilians by Martial Tribunals in Hawaii," *Michigan Law Review* 45, 1 (November 1946): 86–91.

165. Eugene V. Rostow, "Hawaii Case Parallel Seen," *New York Times*, April 4, 1946.

166. Crost, *Honor by Fire*, p. 306.

6. THE END OF CONFINEMENT AND THE POSTWAR READJUSTMENT OF ISSEI AND NISEI

1. General John DeWitt, testimony before House Naval Affairs Committee, April 13, 1942, CWRIC, pp. 14698–99.
2. General John DeWitt, press conference with newspapermen, April 13, 1943, cited in CWRIC, *Personal Justice Denied*, p. 223.
3. G. Edward White, *Earl Warren: A Public Life* (New York: Oxford University Press, 1982), p. 73.
4. U.S. Congress. House, Special Committee on Un-American Activities, Report no. 717, *Report and Minority Views of the Special Committee on Un-American Activities on Japanese War Relocation Centers* (Washington, D.C.: Government Printing Office, 1943). The committee centered its report on testimony by a disgruntled former WRA employees, Edwin Best and Harold Townshend, who told wild stories of luxurious conditions in the camps and Japanese army units training there. When Dillon Myer complained that Townshend's testimony contained forty-one separate errors and distortions, a committee member brazenly responded that in fact there were only thirty-seven. The bias and slipshod methods the committee demonstrated in making its report may have contributed to its temporary decline in power (which lasted until its rebirth at the dawn of the McCarthy era). James T. Sparrow, "Fighting over the American Soldier: Moral Economy and National Citizenship in World War II," Ph.D. dissertation, Brown University, 2002.
5. Dillon Myer, letter to Henry Stimson, March 11, 1943, RG 107, Box 7, NARA, reprinted in CWRIC papers, pp. 122772–82.
6. Col. Karl Bendetsen, Memorandum to Commanding General, Western Defense Command, May 3, 1943, "Notes on Conferences With Assistant Secretary of War John J. McCloy," RG 107, Records of the Assistant Secretary of War, NARA, posted on NARA Archives Research site, ARC Identifier 296056. Available at http://arcweb.archives.gov.
7. U.S. Government, Office of War Mobilization, *Report on Senate Resolution no. 166 Relating to Segregation of Loyal and Disloyal Japanese in Relocation Centers and Plans for Future Operation of Such Centers, September 14, 1943* (Washington, D.C.: GPO, 1943).
8. U.S. Senate, 78th Congress, First Session, Doc. 96, "Message from the President of the United States Transmitting Report on Senate Resolution No. 166 Relating to Segregation of Loyal and Disloyal Japanese in Relocation Centers and Plans for Future Operation of Such Centers," September 14, 1943, p. 2.
9. "Results of Our Reader Poll," *Los Angeles Times*, December 6, 1943.

10. Letter, General Delos Emmons to John McCloy, November 10, 1943, RG 107, Box 9, NARA, reprinted in CWRIC, pp. 806–7.

11. Greg Robinson, *By Order of the President: FDR and the Internment of Japanese Americans* (Cambridge: Harvard University Press, 2001), pp. 233–37.

12. Francis Biddle, diary entry, November 10, 1944, Francis Biddle papers, FDRL.

13. Dillon Myer, memorandum for the Secretary of the Interior, December 14, 1944, WRA files, Harold L. Ickes papers, LOC.

14. Eric L. Muller, *American Inquisition: The Hunt of Japanese American Disloyalty in World War II* (Chapel Hill: University of North Carolina Press, 2007), pp. 124–32.

15. Ibid.

16. Judge Hall, in an analysis that resembled that of Judge Metzger in *Duncan*, declared that Executive Order 9066 had created a limited version of martial law on the West Coast, but that the act of Congress in providing for enforcement via civilian courts limited the authority of the military. *Ochikubo v. Bonesteel*, 60 F. Supp. 916. Ironically, the army then sought in its appeal to refute the judge's reasoning by arguing that military orders were enforceable through civilian courts under Executive Order 9066—the very position that General Richardson and the Justice Department had challenged in *Duncan*.

17. Letter, [Masaru Narahara] All Center Conference to Dillon Myer, June 18, 1945, attached to letter, Masaru Narahara to Roger Baldwin, July 18, 1945, Japanese American files 1945, Reel 230, American Civil Liberties Union papers, 1917–1950, Princeton University Library (copy in Library of Congress).

18. Lawrence E. Davies, "Pacific States," *New York Times*, April 21, 1946.

19. For private efforts, see, for example, Marshall Field Conference, memorandum to the secretary of the interior, "Relocation of the Japanese to the West Coast," June 6, 1945, Japanese Americans, minority files, John Anson Ford papers, Huntington Library, San Marino.

20. For WRA efforts to aid returnees, see Kevin Allen Leonard, "Years of Hope, Days of Fear," Ph.D. dissertation, University of California, Davis, 1992, p. 232. This aspect is downplayed somewhat in Leonard's book *The Battle for Los Angeles: Racial Ideology and World War II* (Albuquerque: University of New Mexico Press, 2006).

21. Mary Yogawa Saito, "Going Home," in *Nanka Nikkei Voices: The Resettlement Years, 1945–1953* (Los Angeles: Japanese American Historical Society of Southern California, 1998), p. 17.

22. Scott Kurashige, *The Shifting Grounds of Race: Blacks and Japanese Americans in the Making of Multiethnic Los Angeles* (Princeton: Princeton University Press, 2008), while not ignoring tensions and conflicts, discusses the

Nisei–black encounter in a generally positive light. For a more pessimistic view, see Kariann Yakota, "From Little Tokyo to Bronzeville and Back," M.A. thesis, University of California, Los Angeles, 1994.

23. "87 Winona Families Ready to Move into New Locale," *Rafu Shimpo*, July 17, 1947.

24. Anonymous Nisei quoted in U.S. Department of Interior, War Agency Liquidation Unit, *People in Motion: The Postwar Adjustment of the Evacuated Japanese Americans* (Washington. D.C.: Government Printing Office, 1947), p. 10. The hostility was not confined entirely to whites—editor V. N. Ramajo of the Los Angeles-based *Philippines News-Herald* editorialized against the return of Japanese Americans to California—although more often the threat of hostility from Filipino Americans and other Asians was used as a pretext for anti-Nisei discrimination by bigots.

25. For the return experience, see, for example, Roger Daniels, ed., *American Concentration Camps* (New York: Garland, 1989), pp. 159–64.

26. "The Nisei Come Home," *The New Republic*, July 9, 1945, pp. 45–46.

27. Harold Ickes, cited in "Planned Terrorism," *Washington Post*, May 17, 1945.

28. "Plan for Japanese Return Stirs Pacific Coast Region," *Christian Science Monitor*, December 19, 1944. For official West Coast reaction to resettlement of Japanese Americans, see generally U.S. Department of Interior, *People in Motion*.

29. On the *Oyama* and *Takahashi* cases, see Greg Robinson and Toni Robinson, "*Korematsu* and Beyond: Japanese Americans and the Origins of Strict Scrutiny," *Law and Contemporary Problems* 68, 2 (Spring 2005). The same year, in *Shelley v. Kraemer* and *Hurd v. Hodge*, cases involving African Americans, the high court struck down the enforcement of restrictive covenants that had limited housing for Japanese Americans, while in *Perez v. Sharp*, a case brought by a Mexican American and an African American, California's Supreme Court threw out the state law against interracial marriage.

30. CWRIC, *Personal Justice Denied*, pp. 250–52. Total requests for renunciation and deportation reached approximately 20,000 by the end of 1945.

31. Michi Weglyn, *Years of Infamy* (Seattle: University of Washington Press, 1996 [1976]), pp. 246–58. See also generally Donald E. Collins, *Native American Aliens Disloyalty and the Renunciation of Citizenship by Japanese Americans during World War II* (Westport, Conn.: Greenwood Press, 1985); Barbara Takei, *A Question of Loyalty: Internment at Tule Lake* (Klamath Falls, Ore.: Shaw Historical Library, 2005).

32. After the end of the war, Mexico reopened its excluded areas to ethnic Japanese. A fraction of those who had been removed, mostly men whose property had been preserved by non-Japanese wives or friends, elected to return. Still, State Department representatives continued to press for repatriation

of "obnoxious" Japanese nationals in Mexico, on grounds of self-interest. While American Embassy officials confessed that there was very little direct evidence of any specific acts by any Japanese, they "will always be potential dangers politically and even, perhaps, commercial rivals to the United States." S. Walter Washington, memorandum to the Secretary of State, "Lists of Obnoxious Japanese for Possible Repatriation," October 23, 1945, Box 188, Special War Problems Division section, State Department Files RG 59, NARA.

33. "Peru Japanese Board Plane for Former Homes," *Pacific Citizen,* November 4, 1946.

34. "Peruvian Japanese Seek Court Aid to Stop Deportation," press release, July 7, 1946, American Civil Liberties Union. Minority files, 1946, ACLU papers, Princeton University.

35. "Disposing of the Japanese," *Globe & Mail,* November 22, 1943.

36. Norman Robertson, memorandum of March 27, 1944, *Documents in Canadian External Relations,* part 1, p. 1132, cited in Escott Reid, *Radical Mandarin:The Memoirs of Escott Reid* (Toronto: University of Toronto Press, 1989), p. 164. Reid portrays Norman Robertson as sincerely believing in the policy, even in later years. Conversely, Gordon Robertson praises Robertson for his understanding of "the art of the possible"—understanding that removal and deportation of Japanese Canadians was inevitable, he therefore told Mackenzie King what he wanted to hear in order to influence the policy toward moderation, whereas Hugh Keenleyside foolishly harmed his career by opposing them. Gordon Robertson, *A Very Civil Servant: Mackenzie King to Pierre Trudeau* (Toronto: University of Toronto Press, 2000).

37. Patricia E. Roy, *The Triumph of Citizenship: The Japanese and Chinese in Canada, 1941–1967* (Vancouver: UBC Press, 2007), pp. 118–22.

38. "Green Wants All Japanese Removed," *Vancouver Sun,* August 10, 1942; "Our Japanese Problem," *Globe and Mail,* November 30, 1943.

39. Mary Taylor, *A Black Mark: The Japanese-Canadians in World War II* (Toronto: Oberon Press, 2004), pp. 146–47. The plan also called permitted Japanese Canadians to buy land outside British Columbia and to be accepted for enlistment in the armed forces. These more liberal provisions, however, were vetoed by Prime Minister King.

40. Canada, *House of Commons Debates,* August 4, 1944, p. 5914, reprinted in Ken Adachi, *The Enemy That Never Was: A History of the Japanese Canadians* (Toronto: McClellan and Stewart, 1976), pp. 431–34.

41. Ibid.

42. Roy, *The Triumph of Citizenship,* pp. 130–37.

43. "Ian Mackenzie Says Japs Must Go," *Lethbridge Herald,* June 6, 1944.

44. Adachi, *The Enemy that Never Was,* pp. 278–79; Ross Lambertson, *Repression and Resistance: Canadian Human Rights Activists, 1930–1960* (Toronto: University of Toronto Press, 2005), pp. 111–13.

45. "The Japanese Canadians," *Winnipeg Free Press*, March 28, 1945.

46. Ann Gomer Sunahara, *The Politics of Racism: The Uprooting of Japanese Canadians during World War II* (Toronto: Lorimer, 1981), pp. 118–19.

47. Patricia Roy et al., *Mutual Hostages: Canadians and Japanese during the Second World War* (Toronto: University of Toronto Press, 1990), p. 162.

48. T. B. Pickersgill, "Notice Concerning Voluntary Repatriation," cited in Muriel Kitagawa, *This Is My Own: Letters to Wes and Other Writings on Japanese Canadians, 1941–1948* (Vancouver: Talonbooks, 1985), p. 204.

49. Sunahara, *Politics of Racism*, pp. 118–20.

50. Cited in "Our Own Japanese," *Winnipeg Free Press,* September 7, 1945.

51. Cabinet Notes, July 5, 1945, Privy Council Series A-5-A, vol. 2636, reel 2634, LAC.

52. Adachi, *The Enemy That Never Was*, pp. 303-4; Roy et al., *Mutual Hostages*, pp. 170–71.

53. I do not mean to suggest either that the CCJC held the monopoly on organization or that deportation was the sole issue involved. The Japanese Canadian Committee for Democracy, though it worked in conjunction with the CCJC, was a distinct organization with separate goals and its own newspaper, *Nisei Affairs*. Meanwhile, there were other campaigns to defend the rights of Canadian citizens, notably that of the progressive activists and students in Montreal who succeeded in persuading McGill University to end its ban on Nisei students in the fall of 1945.

54. Edith Fouke, *They Made Democracy Work: The Story of the Cooperative Committee on Japanese Canadians*, pamphlet, Toronto, 1951; Lambertson, *Repression and Resistance*, pp. 115–23.

55. Roy, *Triumph of Citizenship*, p. 189.

56. Order-in-Council P.C. 7335 re Deportation of the Japanese, reprinted in Adachi, *The Enemy That Never Was*, pp. 429–30. Mary Taylor notes that the preamble to the order represented a glaring example of the government's use of subterfuge. It stated that the repatriates had "manifested their sympathy for Japan by making requests for repatriation to Japan." This imputation of disloyalty, when the form made no provision for determining such sentiments, was heavily criticized. Taylor, *A Black Mark*, p. 157.

57. Forrest E. La Violette, *The Canadian Japanese and World War II* (Toronto: University of Toronto Press, 1948), pp. 253–54.

58. Ibid., pp. 258–69. For a fuller account of the legal campaigns in Canada and the United States and the court decisions, see generally Stephanie Bangarth, *Voices Raised in Protest: Defending North American Citizens of Japanese Ancestry, 1942–49* (Vancouver: UBC Press, 2008).

59. "Predicts Bloodshed if Japs Re-engage in B.C. Fishing," *Toronto Star*, April 6, 1946.

60. Roy et al., *Mutual Hostages*, p. 178.

61. "Form Committee," *Montreal Gazette*, February 28, 1946.

62. Mackenzie King Diary, February 19, 1946, p. 3, LAC.

63. On the lives of the resettlers and their struggle for equal opportunity, see Peter Takaji Nunoda, "A Community in Transition and Conflict: The Japanese Canadians, 1935–1951," Ph.D. dissertation, University of Manitoba, 1991. On the Moose Jaw incident, see Roy Miki, *Redress: Inside the Japanese Canadian Call for Justice* (Vancouver: RainCoast Books, 2004), pp. 135–38.

64. Mackenzie King Diary, January 22, 1947, p. 2, LAC.

65. "Urges Revocation Wartime Orders against Japanese," *Lethbridge Herald*, March 4, 1947, p. 9.

66. Mackenzie King Diary, February 18, 1948, p. 2, LAC

67. Sunahara, *The Politics of Racism*, pp. 148–50.

68. Adachi, *The Enemy That Never Was*, pp. 346–49.

69. Eugene Rostow, "Our Worst Wartime Mistake," *Harper's*, September 1945, pp. 193–201; Carey McWilliams, *Prejudice: Japanese Americans, Symbol of Racial Intolerance* (Boston: Little, Brown, 1944); Milton R. Konvitz, *The Alien and Asiatic in American Law* (Ithaca: Cornell University Press, 1946).

70. Greg Robinson, "Birth of a Citizen: Miné Okubo and the Politics of Symbolism," in *Miné Okubo: Following Her Own Road*, ed. Greg Robinson and Elena Tajima Creef (Seattle: University of Washington Press, 2008), pp. 172–91.

71. Anonymous exhibition review, cited in "Life of the Nisei," *Utah Nippo*, April 26, 1946.

72. Alfred Steinberg, "Washington's Most Successful Lobbyist—Mike Masaoka," *Reader's Digest* (May 1949): 125–29.

73. "Evacuation Damages," *Utah Nippo*, February 5, 1945.

74. Letter, Dillon Myer to Mrs. Henry Cadbury, September 26, 1945, subject-coded correspondence file, 21.010, group 16, War Relocation Authority papers, RG 210, NARA.

75. Letter, Harry Truman to Eleanor Roosevelt, December 21, 1945, Eleanor Roosevelt correspondence file, Harry S Truman Library, Independence, Missouri (henceforth HSTL).

76. Letter, Harry Truman to Tom Clark, December 21, 1945. Tom Clark papers, HSTL. Harry Truman, memorandum to the Attorney General, January 17, 1946, President's Secretary's File, 197, HSTL.

77. Harry Truman, "Statement to the Japanese American Citizens League," February 7, 1946, Reprinted in "Pres. Truman Sends Special Greetings to Nisei Convention," *Utah Nippo*, February 18, 1946.

78. Letter, Julius Krug to Samuel Rayburn, April 24, 1946, Dillon Myer files, HSTL.

79. Letter, Harry Truman to Sen. Pat McCarran, July 22, 1946, PSF 6-Y, HSTL.

80. Memorandum to file, W.J.H., July 29, 1946, PSF 6-Y, HSTL .

81. "Mike Masaoka Reviews Nisei Problems in Conference with White House Representative," *Pacific Citizen*, January 25, 1947.

82. "Propose $1000 a Head Straight 'Claims Bill,'" *Rafu Shimpo*, January 25, 1947.

83. "White House Attention Called to Problems of Issei and Nisei, "*Utah Nippo*, January 31, 1947.

84. "Mass Wartime Removal of Japs from West Coast Unjustified?" *Ironwood Daily Globe*, February 6, 1947.

85. "Justice Department Admits 'Mistake' of Evacuation," *Pacific Citizen*, May 22, 1959.

86. Cited in Nancy Nanami Nakasone-Huey, "In Simple Justice: The Japanese-American Evacuation Claims Act of 1948," Ph.D. dissertation, University of Southern California, 1986, p. 207.

87. "Senate Tables Claims Bill until next Session of Congress," *Utah Nippo*, August 1, 1947.

88. "President's Civil Rights Group Considers Problems of Nisei under California Restrictions," *Pacific Citizen*, April 19, 1947.

89. U.S. Government, President's Committee on Civil Rights, *To Secure These Rights: Report of the President's Committee on Civil Rights* (Washington, D.C.: Government Printing Office, 1947), pp. 30–31.

90. Ibid., pp. 158–59.

91. The JACL's partnership with the administration appeared in other areas. In January 1948 the Supreme Court struck down enforcement of the Alien Land Act in the case of *Oyama v. California*, in which the JACL was represented by Dean Acheson, Truman's former assistant secretary of state (and, soon after, his secretary of state). That same month, the Justice Department agreed to submit an amicus curiae brief supporting the JACL in the case of *Takahashi v. California Fish and Game Commission*, which involved laws barring fishing licenses to "aliens ineligible to citizenship." Following another argument by Dean Acheson, the Supreme Court ruled in favor of the JACL in June 1948. Greg Robinson and Toni Robinson, "Korematsu and Beyond."

92. Mike Masaoka, progress report to JACL, January 17, 1948, Civil Rights Files, Mike Masaoka papers, Marriott Library, University of Utah.

93. Harry Truman, Special Message to the Congress on Civil Rights, February 2, 1948, in *Public Papers of the Presidents of the United States: Harry Truman: Containing the Public Messages, Speeches and Statements of the President: Vol. 3, 1948* (Washington, D.C.: Government Printing Office, 1966), p. 121.

94. "Elementary Justice," *Washington Post*, April 12, 1948.

95. Nakasone-Huey, "In Simple Justice," pp. 215–16.

96. Mike Masaoka, with Bill Hosokawa, *They Call Me Moses Masaoka: An American Saga* (New York: Morrow, 1987), p. 207.

97. Frank Chuman, letter to author, April 7, 2006.

98. About the only detectable instance of any coordination took place in the spring of 1942, when the U.S. Army raised questions regarding the security of the Canadian Pacific Railroad, along which the "internee" camps were located at a number of points. "To minimize the threat of sabotage, Canada closed certain camps and took additional police measures elsewhere." Dziuban, *Military Relations between the United States and Canada*, p. 284.

7. REDRESS AND THE BITTER HERITAGE

1. Some of the fictional works that referenced confinement were Florence Crannell Means, *The Moved Outers* (1945); Anne Emery, *Tradition* (1946); Toshio Mori, *Yokahama, California* (1949); and Hisaye Yamamoto's short story "The Legend of Miss Sasagawara." James Edmiston's novel *Home Again*, written in the postwar years, was published in 1955. Nonfiction works included Ansel Adams's pamphlet *Born Free and Equal* (1944); Alexander Leighton, *The Governing of Men* (1945); Ralph Martin, *Boy from Nebraska* (1946); Toru Matsumoto, *Beyond Prejudice* (1946); Bradford Smith, *Americans from Japan* (1948); Leonard Broom and Ruth Reimer, *Removal and Return* (1949); and the WRA's own series of publications. Other books begun during the postwar years but published later were Monica Sone's *Nisei Daughter* (1953); Allan Eaton's *Beauty Behind Barbed Wire* (1952); Jacobus tenBroek et al.'s *Prejudice, War, and the Constitution* (1954); and Leonard Broom and John Kitsuse's *The Managed Casualty* (1956).

2. There were a few exceptions to the overall silence—Stetson Conn's 1960 study of the U.S. Army was devoted to the decision to evacuate, as was a section of Francis Biddle's 1962 memoir *In Brief Authority*. The 1955 movie *Bad Day at Black Rock* alludes to injustice against Japanese Americans, while the independently produced film *Hell to Eternity* (1960) was the first Hollywood feature to portray the camps.

3. Stephen E. Whitfield and Gene Roddenberry, *The Making of Star Trek* (New York: Ballantine, 1968), p. 245.

4. See Muller, *American Inquisition*; Masumi Izumi, "Ending 'American Concentration Camps,'" *Pacific Historical Review* 74, 2 (May 2005): 165–94.

5. Cited in Harry K. Honda, "Very Truly Yours," *Pacific Citizen*, January 2, 1958.

6. "Justice Department Admits 'Mistake' of Evacuation," *Pacific Citizen*, May 22, 1959.

7. "Editorial Samplings of Nation's Press Supports Justice Dept. View on Evacuation," *Pacific Citizen*, June 5, 1959.

8. Ibid. "A Blessing in Disguise," *Newsweek*, December 29, 1958, p. 12.

9. "Wrong Partially Righted," *Time*, April 21, 1967, p. 25. The same sentiments were amplified the following week in an editorial in *Time*'s sister publication, *Life*. "Epilogue to a Sorry Drama," *Life* 62 (April 28, 1967): 4.

10. On the role of historians and activists in challenging representations and meanings of the camp experience, see especially Alice Yang-Murray, *Historical Memories the Japanese American Internment and the Struggle for Redress* (Stanford: Stanford University Press, 2007).

11. Dana Meyers Bahr, *The Unquiet Nisei: An Oral History of the Life of Sue Kunitomi Embrey*, (New York: Palgrave Macmillan, 2007); Lillian Baker, *The Concentration Camp Conspiracy: A Second Pearl Harbor* (Lawndale, Calif.: AFHA Publications, 1981).

12. Gordon Hirabayashi, "The Career of a Painful Social Movement: Japanese American Redress Campaign," in *Asian Canadians: Regional Perspectives Proceedings of Asian Canadian Symposium V*, ed. Gordon Hirabayashi and Victor Ujimoto (Halifax: Mt. Saint Vincent University, 1981), pp. 391–98.

13. Uno also conducted a one-man crusade over several years to pressure retired chief justice Earl Warren to apologize for his wartime actions toward Japanese Americans as California attorney general and governor. Warren privately expressed contrition to Uno at a Bill of Rights Dinner in 1973 and gave assurances that he would deal more thoroughly with the question in his upcoming memoirs. In fact, in the volume, published posthumously in 1977, Warren expressed limited regret over his complicity but also added a measure of self-justification. Earl Warren, *The Memoirs of Chief Justice Earl Warren* (Garden City, N.Y.: Doubleday, 1977), p. 149.

14. Roger Daniels, *Asian Americans: Chinese and Japanese in the United States since 1850* (Seattle: University of Washington Press, 1988), p. 334.

15. Masaoka, *They Call Me Moses Masaoka*, p. 322.

16. President Gerald Ford, Proclamation 4417, "Confirming the Termination of the Executive Order Authorizing Japanese-American Internment during World War II," February 19, 1976.

17. William Hohri, *Repairing America* (Pullman: Washington State University Press, 1983).

18. Kai Bird, *The Chairman: John J. McCloy and the Making of the American Estaablishment* (New York: Simon and Schuster, 1992), p. 8; William Minoru Hohri, *Repairing America: An Account of the Movement for Japanese American Redress* (Pullman: Washington State University Press, 1988), p. 162.

19. "Recommendations," reprinted in CWRIC, *Personal Justice Denied*, p. 459.

20. U.S. Congress, *Japanese American and Aleutian Wartime Relocation Hearings Before the Subcommittee on Administrative Law and Government Relations of the Committee on the Judiciary, House of Representatives, Ninety-Eighth Congress, Second Session on H.R. 3387, H.R. 4110, and H.R. 4322, June 20, 21, 27 and September 12, 1984* (Washington, D.C.: Government Printing Of-

fice 1985); Mitchell T. Maki, Harry H. L. Kitano, and S. Megan Berthold, *Achieving the Impossible Dream: How Japanese Americans Obtained Redress* (Urbana: University of Illinois Press, 1999).

21. Peter Irons, ed., *Justice Delayed: The Record of the Japanese American Internment Cases* (Middletown, Conn.: Wesleyan University Press, 1989), p. 34.

22. "'Blood Thicker Than Water'—St. Laurent," *New Canadian*, October 21, 1961; Roy Miki and Cassandra Kobayashi, *Justice in Our Time: The Japanese Canadian Redress Settlement* (Vancouver: Talonbooks, and Winnipeg: National Association of Japanese Canadians, 1991), pp. 130–37. Trudeau had earlier deplored the Canadian government's postwar deportation policy. "Trudeau calls J.C. Evacuation 'Scandalous' as Equal Status Law Made," *New Canadian*, October 30, 1968.

23. Roy Miki, *Redress: Inside the Japanese Canadian Call for Justice* (Vançouver: RainCoast Books, 2005).

24. William E. Kinnard, "Lift Every Voice," *Pittsburgh Courier*, December 19, 1998. The same year, in his own nod to redress, President Bill Clinton awarded Fred Korematsu the Presidential Medal of Freedom.

25. Michelle Malkin, *In Defense of Internment: The Case for "Racial Profiling" in World War II and the War on Terror* (Washington, D.C.: Henry Regnery, 2004); David D. Lowman, *Magic: The Untold Story of U.S. Intelligence and the Evacuation of Japanese Residents from the West Coast during WW II* (Provo: Athena Press, 2000). The author joined in an online critique of the revisionist thesis that was widely read and cited among bloggers, and co-founded a historians' group to protest Malkin's distortions. See Eric Muller and Greg Robinson, "Muller and Robinson on Malkin." Available at http://www.isthatlegal.org/Muller_and_Robinson_on_Malkin.html.

[ACKNOWLEDGMENTS]

PERHAPS FITTINGLY, GIVEN THE VARIED AND FAR-FLUNG NATURE OF the events discussed in this book, the work itself has undergone a series of evolutions. In the process, what began as a relatively brief narrative plus collected documents morphed into a full-length monograph. Its existence is a product of the efforts of two editors at Columbia University Press: James Warren, who commissioned the book in the first place, and Peter Dimock, who inherited the project upon Jamie's departure and told me to write the book that I really wanted to write. Anne McCoy and Anita O'Brien offered sensitive copyediting.

I am ever conscious of the further debts I have incurred in pursuing this project. First, it has piggybacked to a significant extent on material uncovered in the course of research on other projects, and I am thus glad to tender bonus thanks to sponsors. The Université du Québec À Montréal's PAFARCC grant program, the Social Science and Humanities Council of Canada, and the Fonds Québécois de la Recherche sur la Société et Culture all provided me with research funds that did double duty supporting this project. I was able to work in concentrated fashion thanks to fellowships from the Huntington Library and the American Council for Learned Societies. I have found material at numerous libraries and archives (some online). Among the most heavily treaded are the DENSHO project; Doe and Bancroft Libraries, University of California, Berkeley; Franklin D. Roosevelt Library, Hyde Park, New York; New York Public Library; Harry S Truman Library, Independence, Missouri; Marriott Library, University of Utah; McLennan Library, McGill University; National Archives of Canada, Ottawa; U.S. National Archives, Washington, D.C.; UBC Library special collections and Vancouver Public Library, Vancouver; Newspaper Division and Manuscripts Division, Library of Congress; Bobst and Tamiment Libraries, New York University; Young Research Library, UCLA; and the Huntington Library. I owe special appreciation to all the librarians and staff who assisted me. Marian Yoshiki-Kovinick, librarian at the (now-defunct) Southern California branch of the Archives of American Art, was a particularly kind colleague, who provided both aid and enthusiasm.

At Université du Québec À Montréal and its sister institutions in Montreal. I have been lucky to find circles of Americanist and Canadianist colleagues who have served as guides and sounding boards for my ideas. Andrew Barros, Frank Chalk, Charles-Philippe David, Magda Fahrni, Francois Furstenberg, Frédérick Gagnon, Christopher Goscha, Denise Helly, José Igartua, Junichiro Koji, Isabelle Lehuu, Paul-André Linteau, Leonard Moore, Bruno Ramirez, and Élisabeth Vallet merit special mention. I also have been blessed with dedicated graduate assistants who have served as my eyes and ears in archives: Dominic D'Amour, Jean-Philippe Gagnon, Sylvain Hétu, Francis Langlois, Karine Laplante, Guillaume Marceau, Vicki Onufriu, Guillaume Pilon, Christian Roy, Sébastien Roy, and Maxime Wingender.

I stated in a previous book that my work would have been impossible (I might as well have said inconceivable) without the research and compilation efforts of Aiko Herzig-Yoshinaga and the CWRIC staff. I now add to this the kind generosity with which Aiko and her late husband Jack Herzig opened doors for me, shared material and gave me the benefit of their enthusiasm.

I have been pleased to know and collaborate on projects with a series of outstanding scholars and friends, notably Eric Muller, my friend and "partner in crime" in refuting Michelle Malkin's work, Elena Tajima Creef, Shirley Geok-Lin Lim, Floyd Cheung, and Yujin Yaguchi.

Like all other historians in this field, I have been marked by the influence and assistance of Roger Daniels, who is a model of generosity, intellectual rigor, and passionate attachment to the subject. I have also been fortunate to know Arthur Hansen, an esteemed historian who is also a great mentor for younger scholars. The late Lawrence W. Levine, an extraordinary historian, was an inspiring force in my life.

Among the colleagues who have given me advice, invited me to share my work before audiences, or shared research with me, Eiichiro Azuma, Taunya Banks, Jane Beckwith, Ben Carton, Greg Donaghy, Shelley Fisher Fishkin, Max Friedman, Tom Fujita Rony, Saverio Giovacchini, Neil Gotanda, Teru Graves, Jennifer Ho, Lynne Horiuchi, John Howard, Masako Iino, Tom Ikeda, Carol Izumi, Masumi Izumi, Jerry Kang, Karl Kwan, the late John M. Maki, Effie Lee Morris Jones, Takeya Mizuno, Philip Tajitsu Nash, David Neiwert, Setsuko M. Nishi, Gary Okihiro, Jacques Portes, John Price, Patricia Roy, Damon Salesa, Kay Saunders, Kenji Taguma, Quintard Taylor, Ed Wakayama, Frank H. Wu, Paul Yamada, and Stan Yogi figure prominently. I have learned a great deal from a number of former inmates and other witnesses, some now deceased, who shared papers or stories with me: Midge Ayukawa, George Brown, Frank Chuman, Michi de Sola, Frank Emi, Robert Frase, Kiku Funabiki, Motoko Ikeda-Spiegel, Donald Hata, Bill Hosokawa, Ernie and Chizu Iiyama, Nori Ishimoto, Sue Kikuchi, Michi Kobi, Yuri Kochiyama, Yosh and Irene Kuromiya, Hugh Macbeth, Arthur Miki, S. Frank Miyamoto, Kim Nagano, Gene Oishi, Paul Okimoto, Ruth Okimoto,

Miné Okubo, Toru Saito, Terry Shima, Cedrick Shimo, Guyo Tajiri, Shinkichi Tajiri, Paul Takagi, Conrad Yama, Mitsuye Yamada, Hisaye Yamamoto, Alfred Yankauer, and Terry Yoshikawa.

Tom Coffman, a great documentary filmmaker and independent historian, was responsible for arranging the speaking invitation by the Hawaii Historical Society that brought me to Hawaii. Tom and Craig Howes deserve major credit for getting me thinking about the wartime Hawaiian experience and martial law. Lois Coffman, Nathaniel Coffman, Walter Ikeda, Richard Kosaki, Kay Uno Kaneko, and Andrew Wertheimer provided stimulating discussion and input while I was in Hawaii.

Tetsuden Kashima has been unfailingly collegial and generous. He has shared lodging, resources, and meals, driven me around in cars, and opened doors for me to acquaintances. Most of all, Tetsu has contributed his own painstaking and highly original research and pushed forward the study of Japanese American wartime experience.

Several relatives and close friends provided support or put me up during trips: Judy Baker, Ken Feinour and Shin Yamamoto, David Latulippe and Ronald Seely, Deborah Malamud and Neal Plotkin, Michael Massing, Sanae Kawaguchi Moorehead, Chizu Omori, Julio Perez, Sydelle Postman, Katherine Quittner, Ed Robinson and Ellen Fine, Heng Gun Ngo, Jaime Restrepo, Ian Robinson, Jocelyn and Ariella Robinson, Tracy Robinson, Rob Rosen, Bob Sandler and Ann Dwornik, Nikki Sandler, Fidel Zavala and Mark Williams. I am also deeply indebted to those who read parts of the manuscript: Stephanie Bangarth; Matthew Briones, Thom Kulesa, Eric Muller, and Setsuko Matsunaga Nishi. My agent, Charlotte Sheedy, stepped in with helpful advice and support and helped arrange—without fee—for the making of a contract for the expanded final version of the book.

My *conjoint* is a constant source of comfort. A few beloved friends help make my life worth living: Marco Mariano, Robert Moulton, T. S. Pan, Thanapat Pawjit, and Hengfu Wang.

This book is dedicated to the memory of my mother Toni Robinson and my aunt Lillian S. Robinson, two beloved women in my life who were also treasured scholarly collaborators. Each was heavily involved in the making of this book. Toni was my lawyer, and acted as my agent in negotiating the original contract for this book, then helped me figure out some of the orientation of the volume. Lillian was a close companion throughout my first years in Montreal, and she was an indefatigable champion. I was fortunate enough to have her wide experience and contacts at my disposal in locating people and things, and clarifying ideas.

INDEX